Monographische Reihe von >Benedictina<

Biblisch-Ökumenische Abteilung

Colloquium Oecumenicum Paulinum

Vol.21

2 THESSALONIANS AND PAULINE ESCHATOLOGY

FOR PETR POKORNÝ ON HIS 80TH BIRTHDAY

Edited by
CHRISTOPHER TUCKETT

Peeters
2013

C. Breytenbach — K.P. Donfried — D. Gerber — M.D. Hooker
R. Hoppe — V. Mihoc — P. Pokorný — B. Standaert — C. Tuckett

2 THESSALONIANS AND PAULINE ESCHATOLOGY

FOR PETR POKORNÝ ON HIS 80TH BIRTHDAY

Edited by
CHRISTOPHER TUCKETT

Peeters
2013

A catalogue record for this book is available from the Library of Congress.

D/2013/0602/163
ISBN 978-90-429-3005-6
No part of this publication may be multiplied, saved in an automated data file or made public in any way whatsoever without the express prior written consent of the publisher.

Members of the Colloquium Oecumenicum Paulinum (through 2012)

†S. Agourides	E. Grässer	R. Penna
J.-N. Aletti	†J. Gribomont	C. Perrot
J. von Allmen	G. Häfner	M. Pesce
D. Attinger	F. Hahn	†R. Pesch
J. M. G. Barclay	L. Hartman	A. Pitta
†C. K. Barrett	J. Herzer	J.-M. Poffet
†M. Barth	O. Hofius	P. Porkorný
†W. M. Bédard	M. D. Hooker	†I. de la Potterie
†P. Benoit	R. Hoppe	A. Puig y Tarrech
†E. Best	D. G. Horrell	M. Quesnel
R. Bieringer	January Ivliev	Y. Redalié
†J. Blank	†J. Jeremias	Ch. Reynier
M. Bockmuehl	I. H. Jones	†B. Rigaux
M. Bouttier	Ch. Karakolis	S. Romanello
C. Breytenbach	J. Karavidopoulos	†J. Sanchez Bosch
C. Burini	†C. Kearns	J. Schlosser
S. Byrskog	†K. Kertelge	†R. Schnackenburg
†J.-M. Cambier	H.-J. Klauck	U. Schnelle
†M. Carrez	†J. Kremer	W. Schrage
†M.-A. Chevalier	†W. G. Kümmel	†E. Schweizer
S. Cipriani	J. Lambrecht	L. T. Simon
R. F. Collins	L. Legrand	†M. M. Smith
†Irenée Compagnon	†X. Léon-Dufour	Th. Söding
†B. Corani	E. Lohse	B. Standaert
J. M. Court	†L. de Lorenzi	†G. Strecker
†A. L. Descamps	†S. Lyonnet	†V. Subilia
†E. Dinkler	M. Y. MacDonald	G. Tatum
K. P. Donfried	†G. W. MacRae	†M. Thrall
†F. Dreyfus	F. Manzi	P. Tomson
J. D. G. Dunn	D. Marguerat	D. Trakatellis
†J. Dupont	†J. McHugh	C. M. Tuckett
†E. E. Ellis	†Ph. Menoud	†G. Turbessi
†C. F. Evans	†H. Merklein	†W. C. van Unnik
F. Festorazzi	V. Mihoc	A. Vanhoye
O. Flichy	M. M. Mitchell	†A. Vögtle
J. Fotopoulos	†D. Mollat	J. S. Vos
J. Galanis	F. Montagnini	†D. E. H. Whiteley
G. Galatis	†C. F. D. Moule	U. Wilckens
C. Gerber	J. Murphy O'Connor	C. Wolff
D. Gerber	†F. Neirynck	M. Wolter
M. Gielen	†N. A. Nissiotis	†C. Zedda
J. Gnilka	†B. Orchard	D. Zeller
M. Gourgues	D. Patte	†M. Zerwick

Participants du XXIInd Colloquium Oecumenicum Paulinum
September 11-15, 2012

R. Bieringer • C. Breytenbach • R. Collins • K. Donfried
O. Flichy • D. Gerber • M. Gourgues • M. Hooker • R. Hoppe
J. Ivliev • I. Jones • C. Karakolis • D. Marguerat • V. Mihoc
P. Pokorný • A. Puig y Tarrech • Y. Redalié • S. Romanello
J. Sclosser • B. Standaert • G. Tatum • C. Tuckett • M. Wolter

TABLE OF CONTENTS

Introduction
Christopher Tuckett   1

Un essai de lecture de 2 Th 1,1–2,12
Daniel Gerber   13

Thanksgiving and Prayer. Appeal to Discipline the Disorderly (2 Thess 2,13–3,18)
Vasily Mihoc   33

La deuxième lettre aux Thessaloniciens
Benoît Standaert   71

Issues of Authorship in the Pauline Corpus: Rethinking the Relationship Between 1 and 2 Thessalonians
Karl Donfried   81

1 Thess 5,1-11 im Kontext der Eschatologie des 1. Thessalonicherbriefes
Rudolf Hoppe   115

1 Kor 15,20-28: Weltgeschichte und persöhnliche Hoffnung im Lichte des paulinischen Evangeliums
Petr Pokorný   139

2 Corinthians 5,1-10 in Context
Morna Hooker 165

Liberation of Enslaved Bodies: Christian Expectancy according to Rom 8,18-30
Cilliers Breytenbach 197

Contributors 215

INTRODUCTION

Christopher Tuckett

The essays in this volume comprise the papers which were presented and discussed at the 42nd meeting of the *Colloquium Oecumenicum Paulinum*, which was held at the Abbey of St Paul's Outside the Walls in Rome from 11th – 15th September 2012. With the exception of the 40th meeting of the Colloquium, the pattern of the meetings has remained constant over the years: either one Pauline letter, or a significant section of a letter, has been taken as the focus of the meeting, with papers presented giving detailed exegetical studies of sections of the letter, or part-letter, chosen for the main theme. Ever since the inception of the Colloquium then, the pattern has been to work through the Pauline corpus systematically. By the time we had reached 2012, all the New Testament Pauline letters (including both the unquestionably authentic letters and the possibly deutero-Pauline corpus) had been treated, with the exception of 2 Thessalonians. In planning for the 2012 meeting, it was decided that it would be highly desirable to try to treat 2 Thessalonians in order to complete the coverage of the whole Pauline corpus (before perhaps starting again!); however, it was also felt that 2 Thessalonians alone was not extensive enough to provide enough material to justify the writing, and detailed discussion, of six or seven full papers. It was therefore decided that the Colloquium would seek to cover 2 Thessalonians in its entirety in some of the exegetical papers; but that other papers would be devoted to a more general topic within Pauline study. Given that 2 Thessalonians is itself very focused on the theme of eschatology, it was therefore decided to devote the remaining sessions to discussions of Pauline eschatology. Further, given the very fruitful pattern of working developed by the Colloquium over many years of having papers prepared treating particular passages, followed then by detailed discussion in small groups as well as in plenary sessions, it was decided to keep this pattern even while addressing a wider topic. Hence the papers on eschatology were given as detailed exegetical discussions of particular key passages within the Pauline corpus for any discussion of Paul's eschatology.

The papers that were given at the Colloquium were thus slightly diverse in one way, though with a clear unity at another level. Two papers treated the text of 2 Thessalonians in detail (Gerber on 1,1 – 2,12; Mihoc on 2,13 – end). Given the contested nature of the authorship issue relating to 2 Thessalonians (an issue which had provoked much discussion at the previous Colloquium where 2 Timothy and Titus were discussed), a more general paper on the authorship question (partly couched in more general terms in relation to the Pauline corpus, partly specifically in relation to the Thessalonian letters) was presented (see Donfried). A more general paper (in the form of a public lecture addressed to a more general audience) on 2 Thessalonians was given by Standaert. The remaining four papers focused on key passages for any study of Paul's eschatology in the unquestionably authentic letters: thus Hoppe treats 1 Thess 5,1-11, Pokorný analyses 1 Cor 15,23-28, Hooker discusses 2 Cor 5,1-10, and Breytenbach covers Rom 8,18-30.

The papers themselves are presented here in their entirety. All of them are very full and raise a large number of critical issues. During the Colloquium itself, each paper was discussed in detail and a number of points emerged from those discussions. In what follows, therefore, I note some of these issues, although this is done in the full realisation that many other issues are raised by the essays themselves, and also by the Pauline texts, could not be treated for reasons of time.

In relation to the papers specifically treating 2 Thessalonians, much of the discussion focused on the question of the authorship of 2 Thessalonians itself, and also the issue of the relation between 2 Thessalonians and 1 Thessalonians. Inevitably, in a colloquium with many participants, there was more than one view expressed! For some, 2 Thessalonians is clearly deutero-Pauline (and all exegesis proceeds from that assumption); for others, there is no clear-cut evidence that it is not Pauline and hence one should assume that it is genuine until it is clearly shown not to be.

A common feature emerging from those defending Pauline authorship was an appeal to the claim at the start of the letter that it has been written by three co-authors: the letter is ostensibly written by Paul, Silvanus and Timothy (2 Thess 1,1). As such this might explain some of the data we have (cf. Donfried, Mihoc). On the other hand, other arguments adduced in the defence of Pauline authorship included the claim that 2 Thessalonians is Pauline through and through, either in toto (cf. Mihoc), or at least in relation to 1 Thessalonians (Donfried: 1 Thessalonians and 2 Thessalonians agree with each other so closely that there is no need to postulate another author, given that 1 Thessalonians is accepted as unquestionably authentic.)

From the side of those disputing Pauline authorship of 2 Thessalonians, there were questions about some of these claims. The issue of joint authorship provoked the question of precisely how such co-authorship would have worked in practice. (If the letter was dictated, who did the actual dictation? How much control would one of the other co-authors have had in relation to the final version if the letter were dictated by another co-author?) Further, there were questions about why such an appeal (to co-authorship) is necessary or relevant in the discussion. Are there facets of 2 Thessalonians that seem sufficiently *un*usual within the broader Pauline corpus to need such a theory of co-authorship to explain them? Or are there such facets distinguishing 2 Thessalonians from 1 Thessalonians? (Though the same co-authors are the ostensible senders of both letters.) Further, are these differences at the level of (simply) style? Or are there more substantial differences of substance between 2 Thessalonians and 1 Thessalonians, or between 2 Thessalonians and the rest of Paul? If so, is a theory of co-authorship sufficient to explain such difficulties of integrating the letter within the wider Pauline corpus? At what point would such difficulties become so significant that they imply not simply a model of co-authorship (with perhaps Paul taking a rather less prominent role in the writing process) but one of a different author?

Potentially productive suggestions about the nature of the relationship between 2 Thessalonians and 1 Thessalonians were raised by the papers of Gerber and Standaert. Taking up the suggestions of others (especially Redalié), Gerber suggests that 2 Thessalonians can be usefully seen as a "relecture" of 1 Thessalonians. The notion of "relecture" is well known from other areas (notably in relation to Johannine studies). For Gerber, the idea is developed on the presumption that 2 Thessalonians is pseudepigraphical: the letter is then a "relecture" of 1 Thessalonians by a later writer, not by Paul. But the notion of "relecture" (as developed here) does not necessarily imply any outright contradiction with the earlier text which is "relu". It is rather an attempt to fill in gaps, to develop some hints suggested briefly in the earlier text, and to respond to a new situation. (On the other hand, it could be that the same basic model could still be retained by defenders of Pauline authorship: as Donfried argues here (though without using the category of "relecture" explicitly), 2 Thessalonians may be a letter by Paul (and Silvanus and Timothy!) responding to a new situation of intense persecution facing the Thessalonian community.) Standaert adopts a not dissimilar stance in referring to the ancient category of *mimesis* as the model with which to explain 2 Thessalonians alongside 1 Thessalonians. ("Relecture" is of course a modern term; *mimesis* is a term, and a category, at home in ancient rhetoric.)

It may be that categories such as "relecture", or *mimesis*, may help us to avoid some of the possible dangers raised by other language which can be used in modern discussions, e.g. putting the issue in terms of whether 2 Thessalonians is a "forgery" or not. The word "forgery" in English is perhaps quite a loaded term, with some significant negative value judgements associated with it. These may of course be justified in one way: if indeed 2 Thessalonians was pseudonymous was a "forgery", both in the sense of not being by Paul and also deliberately intending to deceive others into thinking that it was by Paul, it might well have been rejected in the early church if it had been discovered not to be genuine. But that is perhaps a matter for the possible reception history of the text in the early church. Such an attitude need not necessarily be ours. Whether pseudonymity as such is ethically (or theologically) "good" or "bad" in relation to contemporary viewpoints is perhaps another matter. In any case, we should perhaps bear in mind the point made by Standaert (at the end of his essay) that, if one wishes to seek to make Paul speak to new situations and new times, one cannot simply repeat the words of the past unchanged: some novelty and change is demanded if a voice from the past is to have contemporary relevance in changed circumstances and situations.

In relation to the broader theme of the Colloquium, the question inevitably arose of how far, in relation to the specific issue of eschatology, the outlook of 2 Thessalonians fits with, and agrees with, that of 1 Thessalonians in particular, or with that of Paul more generally.

Even in relation to the narrower comparison of 2 Thessalonians with 1 Thessalonians, differing answers were given. For Mihoc and Donfried, there is no real difference discernible: 2 Thessalonians agrees without difficulty with 1 Thessalonians, and both are thoroughly Pauline. For Gerber, the nature of "relecture" implies perhaps no real contradiction between the two, even though there is some shift in emphasis, e.g. to fill in some of the "gaps" in the earlier text that is being "relu". In the paper of Hoppe, however, rather more of a difference was claimed. Hoppe suggests that 2 Thessalonians shifts the emphasis (perhaps quite considerably) from 1 Thessalonians in that the theme of judgement for outsiders, which is not necessarily a very major topic in the first letter, becomes the dominant theme in 2 Thessalonians: 1 Thessalonians develops its eschatology and its eschatological language and ideas to establish and enhance the identity of the Christian community as the elect of God who will thereby be saved at the End, whereas in 2 Thessalonians the accent shifts to a process of stabilising the community by developing especially the language of the destruction of outsiders. The latter theme is mentioned briefly in 1 Thessalonians, but not to anything like the same extent as in the second letter. Is this then a sign of common authorship, perhaps addressing a changed situation? Or of a different author, picking up and developing language of another person?

When one broadens the scope of the question about the eschatology of 2 Thessalonians, to consider it not only in relation to 1 Thessalonians but also to Paul more generally, other questions are also implicitly raised (and indeed are raised explicitly in some of the papers here). In particular, there is the issue of how consistent Paul might have been in his eschatological beliefs. Does such a thing as a (single) Pauline eschatology actually exist? Could it be, for example, that the eschatology of 2 Thessalonians is relatively easy to reconcile with that of 1 Thessalonians, but not so easy to reconcile with that of 1 Corinthians or Romans? One reason might be not necessarily because 2 Thessalonians is pseudonymous but because *1* Thessalonians and 1 Corinthians/Romans are not of a piece (and/or that, say, 1 Corinthians and Romans are not so easy to reconcile with each other).

The question of whether a single Pauline eschatology exists is of course part of a yet wider question: does a (single) Pauline "theology" in general exist? Is there one single, identifiable Pauline theology, in the sense of a Pauline theological "system" which Paul has worked out and developed and which displays clear coherence and inner self-consistency? Or is the process of reaching a "theology" in this sense something which Paul never attained during his lifetime? (Hence the argument of some that what we see in Paul is perhaps something like "religion" but not "theology": Paul reflects his first order religious experiences, but the process of second order reflection and systemisation of these experiences into a coherent theological schema is one in which Paul himself is still actively engaged in his letters but which perhaps never attains completion, at least during the time of his letter writing.) Certainly in the discussions at the Colloquium, these broader issues surfaced sometimes: are there some absolute fundamentals for Paul, some non-negotiable elements? Is the death of Jesus as being "for us" (in some sense) one such foundational "theological" element? Are the constants in Paul to be located more at the level of *theo*logy than of *Christ*ology, so that what is fundamental for Paul is that *God* is God, that God is consistent, the Creator, all-loving, and that God will ultimately achieve his purposes by taking responsibility for the whole of his creation? Or are Paul's "theological" outpourings still somewhat occasional, context driven, and in the form of responses to specific situations and problems – and it is up to us to try (if we can) to make a "theology" (in the sense of an ordered coherent system) out of them?

To return to the specific question of eschatology: the issue of Paul's consistency, or possible development, has in the history of scholarship classically focused on question of eschatology. Within English speaking scholarship, reference is always made to the two essays of C. H. Dodd, written in the 1930s, on this topic (see Hooker's essay here). Dodd's own proposals, arguing for an identifiable development in Paul's eschatological thinking, are not widely held today (partly because they presuppose a belief in Colossians and Ephesians as genuine Pauline letters, a view which many would be reluctant to hold today). But some aspects of Dodd's theories still exert influence. Do Paul's views shift as one moves from 1 Corinthians to 2 Corinthians? (So Dodd: on this see Hooker's essay here.) Do Paul's views shift even between the writing of 1 Thessalonians and the writing of 1 Corinthians? (See e.g. Pokorný's essay here.)

This issue was addressed directly in the paper of Hooker, focusing primarily on the passage in 2 Cor 5,1-10, a passage which has often been cited as a key piece of evidence for the theory that Paul might have changed his views from 1 Corinthians (e.g. moving away from a belief in a cosmic resurrection at the End to a more "individualised" belief that the final hoped-for state would be achieved at the moment of an individual's death). For Hooker, Paul does remain consistent in that he has not given up the idea of a cosmic final parousia at the End, even if he may also have had held (perhaps developed in light of his own circumstances of threatening death) a view that individuals pass to a (possibly intermediate) state at death, something which is to be looked forward to as being "with the Lord". But even in his latest letter (Philippians), Paul can hold the two ideas together quite happily within the same letter (cf. Phil 1,23 alongside 3,21: see the discussion in Hooker's paper here). The twin claims simply reflect different aspects of the same broad hope and confidence in God, focusing on different parts of the whole, and perhaps addressing different situations in his different letters.

That Paul does adapt his language to his context and the situation he is addressing would probably be accepted by all. The precise extent to which this happens may be more debatable. The issue was raised in the

Colloquium specifically in relation to Donfried's paper, and perhaps too by Hoppe's discussion. Donfried refers to the language of 1 Thessalonians and to many striking parallels between Paul's vocabulary as used in that letter and language associated with imperial propaganda. (Cf. the common use in both contexts of terms such as "gospel" [εὐαγγέλιον], "Lord", "peace and security", παρουσία). Is then Paul's language seeking to address, and speak to, possible "competitors" of the Christian gospel, using similar language but claiming that the Christian gospel "outdoes" any possible rival claims in the contemporary political sphere? Or can/should we explain Paul's language from his Jewish matrix (cf. Hoppe)?

There are here important questions, though it may be worth asking why such "competitor language" (in relation to imperial propaganda) seems to be more prominent in 1 Thessalonians (and 2 Thessalonians) than in other Pauline letters. (Terms such as "gospel", and "Lord", occur widely throughout Paul's letters, but the other examples cited here do not.) Was there something specific about the Thessalonian situation which led to Paul using such language in his letter(s) to this community in particular? Equally, strong appeal to Paul's Jewish matrix may also carry some problems (at a different level): claims that Paul picks up and uses the language of Jewish scriptural texts, but does so in a way that is not explicit (cf. the reference to "peace and security" in 1 Thess 5 and the parallel in Jer 6), might well explain why Paul uses such language; but would it resonate so much, or indeed be recognised at all, by Paul's readers (who in Thessalonians seem clearly to come from a non-Jewish background: cf. 1 Thess 1,9)? It must of course also be said that the contrast – imperial language or Jewish scriptural language – is no doubt not an exclusive either/or: it could well be that Paul uses language that comes from, and addresses, more than one context.

One further question that arose in some of the discussions following the papers was that of universalism. How universalistic is Paul in his eschatology? How far does Paul envisage the "salvation" (or whatever language is used) of all Christians (only), or of all human beings? The issue is of course implicitly raised by Paul's talk, especially in Rom 8, of the "groaning" and the longing of the whole "creation" (κτίσις). The issue was raised explicitly of course in Breytenbach's paper which dealt explicitly with this passage from Romans, and also in Pokorný's paper, focusing on the passage in 1 Cor 15,20-28.

The point was made forcefully by some in the discussion that the issue may be a very modern question, and that any idea of "universalism" would have been somewhat alien, if not meaningless, for someone such as Paul. Perhaps this is the case in relation to the terms and ideas of modern scholars; but at another level, it seems certain that the problem of the fate of at least one part of the (presently) non-"believing" (i.e. non-Christian) world was of deep concern to Paul, viz. the Jewish people who have not responded positively to the Christian gospel (although Rom 11 as such was not on the agenda for the Colloquium). Similarly, the issue of the destiny, and the overall welfare, of (potentially) all non-Jews is clearly at the heart of Paul's discussions in Galatians and elsewhere. Hence potentially it would seem, the issue of the fate of all human beings is implicit in much of Paul's writings.

The issue was raised especially in relation to the paper as presented by Pokorný and much of the ensuing discussion of the paper focused on this point: is Paul talking in 1 Cor 15 (esp. in vv. 22 "all in Christ shall be made alive") about the resurrection of Christians only (all those who are in Christ), or does he imply a wider purview (perhaps with an instrumental ἐν, so that "*all* shall, through Christ, be made alive)? Pokorný himself (in responding to questions) stated that he was not necessarily advocating a pan-universalistic interpretation of texts such as this, though Paul's language here may contain within it the potential for such a universalistic viewpoint. The same might be implied by the issues raised in Breytenbach's paper and the treatment of Rom 8 with the reference there to the κτίσις. Breytenbach himself argues strongly that the reference here is *not* to the totality of the human race, but only to the non-human part of the creation. For other human beings who have not responded to the Christian gospel, there is no hope. Nevertheless, it could also be argued that Paul's language here does at least leave open the possibility, and contain within itself the potential, for a wider perspective. Certainly too other passages in Paul could imply that such "potential" could be developed further. Thus Paul's language of God finally being "all in all" (1 Cor 15,28), of the last enemy to be destroyed being death (1 Cor 15,26: perhaps not just death for Christians only), or of God imprisoning *all* in disobedience so that he might have mercy on *all* (Rom 11,32) are open to similar interpretations suggesting that hope for the future is not just confined to Christian believers. If that is the case, might Paul himself have been somewhat more open, and optimistic, about the fate of non-believers than at least what may have been one of his "followers", viz. the author of 2 Thessalonians, for whom there seems to be no hope at all for outsiders and only the threat and promise of eternal punishment and damnation?

These were some of the issues which were raised by the papers presented at the Colloquium and in the ensuing discussions. Clearly there are many other issues which could be discussed usefully, and no doubt should be discussed in any full appraisal of Paul's eschatology. One such issue might be the question of how far Paul's language fits with the language of his time, especially within Jewish eschatological and/or "apocalyptic" expectations about resurrection, the afterlife etc? Where does Paul's language fit within a religionsgeschichtlich perspective? So too, as one has become accustomed more recently to pay more attention to the "Wirkungsgeschichte" of NT texts, how far does Paul fit within the broader and developing *Christian* claims about resurrection? (Cf. Mihoc's insistent reminder in his paper about the value and importance of the interpretation of NT texts by the church fathers: how far would/ was Paul welcomed by later church fathers? How far was he (quietly) modified and modulated to make him a supporter of a rather different overall eschatological viewpoint?)

It would seem that Paul remains constant and consistent in that he talks about the "resurrection" of Christ – and in this he remains rooted in, and part of, his Jewish heritage. (Talk about "resurrection" really only makes sense within a Jewish framework, as many recent writers have emphasised.) In part too he stays within that framework in talking about the hope for Christians (and/or others: cf. above). But equally, he may draw on other ideas too. Hence, for example, ideas of an intermediate state of the righteous (as e.g. in *1 Enoch*) might help to clarify Paul's language of e.g. 2 Cor 5,6-9, and Phil 1,23. Insofar then as other Jewish writers seem able to hold together similar views about the future which might at first sight appear to be in some slight tension with each other, Paul may not be as idiosyncratic as some have perhaps suggested in the past. Hence Paul can hold together his fundamental belief in the "resurrection" of Christ, and also his equally fundamental belief that Christians will share in the experience of Christ (and hence share in "resurrection" in the future), while at the same time asserting his belief in the goodness and care of God for his creatures with reference to the intermediate state of Christians who have died.

Where exactly 1 Cor 15,35ff. might fit within Jewish eschatological ideas, and indeed within later Christian beliefs, is perhaps harder to determine. The massive *dis*continuity which Paul asserts here in relation to the "body" for human beings which the resurrection will entail is somewhat unlike e.g. Jewish ideas and language of resurrection (e.g. in 2 Maccabees), which seems generally to envisage the restoration of the present physical body; it is equally unlike later Christian talk which speaks almost uniformly of the resurrection of the "flesh", i.e. the same material body as in the present (in a way then similar to that of Jewish texts such as 2 Maccabees), seeking to affirm the value and the worth of the present body in all its materiality and which rejects "gnostic" ideas which see the body as simply a prison from which the soul can escape and return to its true home. In some ways Paul thus fits well within his social, religious and cultural milieu; in other ways, he is perhaps slightly *un*usual and *a*typical. As such, he may have presented as much of a challenge to his contemporaries as he still does for us today.

The nature of the Colloquium as explicitly an "ecumenical" gathering means that those who attend come from a wide range of backgrounds, inhabiting a number of different "worlds", both academic and religious. All who attend the Colloquium are united in the view that Paul is a supremely important figure within early Christianity, that the struggle to determine his ideas and beliefs is both valuable and rewarding, and indeed that Paul may well have something vitally important to say to the present: he is not just a figure of the past who belongs to the past. For some, Paul's ideas can/should be taken over in toto and adopted in the present without change. For others, some of Paul's ideas can indeed be taken over and adopted enthusiastically, but other ideas are less easy to adopt in the present. For some, aspects of Paul's eschatology might fit into the latter category. Nevertheless, the struggle to grapple with Paul's writings, and to think through how one responds to the challenges they pose for us, remains a uniquely rewarding and enriching experience.

The particular circumstances in which the *Colloquium Oecumenicum Paulinum* takes place enhances that process of engagement and grappling in a unique way. The opportunity to meet within the context of the ongoing worshipping and prayerful life of the Benedictine community serving the Basilica dedicated to preserving the memory of Paul himself, and situated on the site of the traditional tomb of Paul, gives immense added significance and meaning to the academic discussions of Paul's writings within the colloquium itself. The very warm welcome provided by the Abbot, Fr Edmund Power, and the other members of the order, and the unwavering support for the work of the colloquium both in all the preparations as well as during the meeting itself, provided a unique setting in which to engage in our discussions. All the participants would therefore wish to place on record our very deep gratitude to Fr Power and the other members of the community for their hospitality and generosity in agreeing to host the meeting again and for all their support for the colloquium.

On 21 April 2013, Professor Petr Pokorný celebrated his 80th birthday. Petr Pokorný has been a regular participant in the Colloquium since 2002. The other members of the Colloquium would wish to dedicate this volume in his honour and with grateful thanks for all his many contributions to the work of the Colloquium and to New Testament studies.

UN ESSAI DE LECTURE DE 2 TH 1,1–2,12

Daniel Gerber

Accepter le principe d'une «Théologie polyphonique et œcuménique du Nouveau Testament»[1] suppose que l'on porte une attention soutenue à chacun des écrits de ce corpus. Aussi est-ce avec raison que la recherche néotestamentaire accorde aujourd'hui sa juste place à l'étude de la deuxième lettre aux Thessaloniciens qui, cela est indéniable, apporte une touche originale à la mosaïque formée par les vingt-sept textes réunis dans le canon et à la tradition paulinienne en particulier[2]. Son interprétation, comme on le sait, pose toutefois d'épineux problèmes qui débordent la seule question, toujours débattue, de son auteur.

Préliminaires

Témoin d'un «conflit des interprétations»[3] au sujet des temps derniers – du moins si l'on en croit 2 Th 2,1-3a –, l'auteur de 2 Th a tenté de recadrer la question du Jour du Seigneur. À cette fin, il ne s'est pas seulement contenté d'apporter quelques précisions au calendrier eschatologique. Il s'est encore employé à revaloriser le temps présent, à donner sens aux persécutions subies par ceux qui construisaient leur identité en Christ et à lever le voile sur le châtiment des réprouvés. Mais pourquoi, dans cette intention, s'être appuyé sur 1 Th, en allant jusqu'à calquer son adresse?

Les relations littéraires entre les deux épîtres, manifestes mais non explicitées en 2 Th[4], ont fait l'objet de nombreuses interprétations.

---

1. Pour cette proposition, voir D. Gerber, *Comment envisager aujourd'hui une "Théologie du Nouveau Testament"? Entre légitimité et réserves*, in E. Cuvillier et B. Escaffre (éds), *Entre exégètes et théologiens: la Bible... Actes du congrès de l'ACFEB, Toulouse 29 août – 01 septembre 2011*, Paris, Cerf, à paraître.

2. C'est ce que relève S. Schreiber, *Früher Paulus mit Spätfolgen. Eine Bilanz zur neuesten Thessalonicherbrief-Forschung*, in TRev 103 (2007) 267-284, col. 267.

3. E. Cuvillier, *Les apocalypses du Nouveau Testament*, in CEv 110 (1999), p. 17.

4. P. Metzger, *Katechon. II Thess 2,1-12 im Horizont apokalyptischen Denkens* (BZNW, 135), Berlin-New York, Walter de Gruyter, 2005, p. 73, note fort à propos: «Der II Thess gibt dem Leser oder Hörer keine Informationen an die Hand, wie er als *zweiter* Brief an die Thessaloniker verstanden werden kann».

Depuis l'enquête approfondie menée par William Wrede[5], elles constituent «l'argument déterminant [...], en combinaison avec les écarts théologiques»[6] et christologiques[7], en faveur du caractère pseudépigraphique de 2 Th – ce que suggèrent d'autres indices encore[8]: un ton relativement distant, un style lourd[9], des glissements de sens[10], un rôle singulier attribué à Paul vis-à-vis de la tradition, une «surenchère» dans la salutation autographe[11]. Mais opter pour l'hypothèse de la pseudépigraphie – position qui sera la nôtre[12] – ne fait qu'infléchir la question, qui, sur le fond, reste entière: comment aborder 2 Th, en tenant compte à la fois de ses ressemblances et de ses divergences avec 1 Th[13]? D'ailleurs, interrogera-t-on encore, «la question de l'auteur [...] commande-t-elle [seulement] tout le sens du texte?»[14]

---

5. W. WREDE, *Die Echtheit des zweiten Thessalonicherbriefs untersucht*, Leipzig, Henrichs, 1903.
6. A. DETTWILER, *La deuxième épître aux Thessaloniciens*, in D. MARGUERAT (éd.), *Introduction au Nouveau Testament. Son histoire, son écriture, sa théologie* (MdB, 41), Genève, Labor et Fides, ⁴2008, 315-326, p. 320.
7. P. MÜLLER, *Anfänge der Paulusschule. Dargestellt am zweiten Thessalonicherbrief und am Kolosserbrief* (AThANT, 74), Zürich, Theologischer Verlag, 1988, p. 66, remarque: «Die Vorstellung von Christus als dem Richter ist zentral. Eine Verbindung des Gerichtsgedanken mit einem ihm vorangehenden Heilsgeschehen ist [...] nicht festzustellen. [...] Die Christologie ist reduziert auf ein apokalyptisches Ereignis».
8. Cf. E. KRENTZ, *A Stone that Will Not Fit. The Non-Pauline Authorship of Second Thessalonians*, in J. FREY, J. HERZER, M. JANSSEN et C. K. ROTHSCHILD (éds), *Pseudepigraphie und Verfasserfiktion in frühchristlichen Briefen. Pseudepigraphy and Author Fiction in Early Christian Letters* (WUNT, 1.246), Tübingen, Mohr Siebeck, 2009, 439-470.
9. Cf. Y. REDALIÉ, *La deuxième épître aux Thessaloniciens* (CNT, 9c), Genève, Labor et Fides, 2011, p. 20.
10. W. TRILLING, *Der Zweite Brief an die Thessalonicher* (EKK, 14), Neukirchen-Vluyn, Benzinger-Neukirchener Verlag, 1980, p. 22, observe: «Positiv kann man sagen, dass sich weithin paulinische Gedanken und typische Ausdrucksformen [...] finden, dass sie aber durchweg merkwürdig "versetzt" erscheinen».
11. S. LÉGASSE, *Les épîtres de Paul aux Thessaloniciens* (LeDivCom, 7), Paris, Cerf, 1999, pp. 351.353.
12. Tenir 2 Th pour un écrit deutéro-paulinien sous-entend que la première lettre aux Thessaloniciens a été rédigée avant la seconde. Pour une remise en question de l'ordre canonique, cf. F. W. RÖCKER, *Belial und Katechon. Eine Untersuchung zu 2 Thess 2,1-12 und 1 Thess 4,13–5,1* (WUNT, 2.262), Tübingen, Mohr Siebeck, 2009, pp. 230-233.
13. Telle qu'elle est formulée, la recommandation de T. THOMPSON, *As If Genuine. Interpreting the Pseudepigraphic Second Thessalonians*, in FREY, HERZER, JANSSEN et ROTHSCHILD (éds), *Pseudepigraphie* (n. 8), 471-488, p. 488, est trop courte: «Second Thessalonians research needs to develop a rigorous hermeneutical model which adequately takes into consideration the interpretive complexities of working with a pseudepigraphon».
14. Y. REDALIÉ, *Relecture et droits d'auteur: à propos de l'interprétation de la deuxième épître aux Thessaloniciens*, in D. H. WARREN, A. G. BROCK et D. W. PAO (éds), *Early Christian Voices in Texts, Traditions and Symbols. Essays in Honor of François Bovon* (BInS 66), Leiden, Brill, 2003, 239-250, p. 239.

Parmi les principales solutions avancées, il nous semble que l'on ne peut se contenter d'alléguer que 2 Th cherche seulement à commenter ou à compléter 1 Th, voire à apporter un correctif à une interprétation fautive de certains enseignements de cette épître[15]; la relation entre les deux lettres est manifestement plus complexe. De même, il nous paraît excessif de tenir 2 Th pour une «réfutation»[16] d'1 Th; cette conclusion radicale ne tient pas suffisamment compte des accords volontairement entretenus entre les deux lettres. Nous opterons, en conséquence, pour une voie moyenne, en prenant pour guide Yann Redalié, dont les travaux s'inscrivent «dans [la] recherche d'une interprétation [de 2 Th] moins marquée unilatéralement par la question de l'auteur»[17]. Son hypothèse est celle d'une «relecture»[18] d'1 Th par l'auteur de 2 Th. Un tel processus repose sur trois axiomes, ainsi résumés par Daniel Marguerat: «1) le texte relisant se distingue du texte relu par un jeu dialectique d'amplification explicitante et de déplacement d'accent; 2) la relecture n'abroge pas la validité du texte relu, mais la présuppose au contraire; 3) la motivation à relire tient à l'évolution interne de la tradition et aux changements de situation historique»[19].

Appliquée à 2 Th 1,3-12; 2,1-12, une telle approche implique un repérage des points de contacts explicites (littéraires, verbaux ou thématiques) et implicites (l'exploitation de silences) avec 1 Th. Il conviendra donc de prêter attention à la manière dont les emprunts

---

15. Dans ce sens, TRILLING, *Der Zweite Brief* (n. 10), p. 25: «Die [...] Meinung, 2 Thess solle die Eschatologie bzw. die Naherwartung des 1 Thess "korrigieren", dürfte nicht das Richtige treffen. Besser geht man davon aus, dass der zweite Brief eine bestimmte Auffassung zurückweist, für die sich deren Vertreter auf 1 Thess berufen *konnten* und dies wohl auch taten, dass sich darin aber die Intention des Autors nicht erschöpft. Er möchte sein Schreiben als eine als notwending empfundene *weiterführende Unterweisung* verstanden wissen».

16. C'est le point de vue d'A. LINDEMANN, *Zum Abfassungszweck des Zweiten Thessalonicherbriefes*, in *ZNW* 68 (1977) 35-47, p. 39: «2 Thess ist [...] entgegen der üblichen Deutung kein "Kommentar" zum 1 Thess, sondern er ist geradezu als dessen Widerlegung bzw. "Rücknahme" konzipiert worden»; p. 47: «Der Vf des 2 Thess [sah sich] gezwungen, seine Schrift als Ersatz für den 1 Thess zu konzipieren». Il est suivi, entre autres, par W. MARXSEN, *Der zweite Thessalonicherbrief* (ZBKNT, 11/2), Zürich, TVZ, 1982.

17. REDALIÉ, *Relecture* (n. 14), p. 241.

18. Cf. REDALIÉ, *Relecture* (n. 14); ID., *La deuxième épître* (n. 9), pp. 27-29. Aussi Y. REDALIÉ, *Dualisme et contrastes apocalyptiques: les "relectures" de Mt 24 et de 2 Th*, in A. DETTWILER et U. POPLUTZ (éds), *Studien zu Matthäus und Johannes / Études sur Matthieu et Jean. Festschrift für Jean Zumstein zu seinem 65. Geburtstag / Mélanges offerts à Jean Zumstein pour son 65ᵉ anniversaire* (AThANT), Zürich, Theologischer Verlag, 2009, 79-90.

19. D. MARGUERAT, *La première histoire du christianisme (Les Actes des Apôtres)* (LeDiv, 180), Paris-Genève, Cerf-Labor et Fides, 1999, pp. 377-378.

sont «approfondis et réorientés»[20] ou les vides comblés, ainsi qu'à la façon dont le «neuf», appelé par l'émergence d'une trajectoire théologique jugée déviante et de bouleversements historiques, est articulé sur l'«ancien».

Concernant «l'évolution interne de la tradition» qui a motivé l'écriture de 2 Th, nous retiendrons la thèse de Gerhard Sellin: après une «phase de spiritualisation» – dont témoignent, en milieu paulinien, Col et Ep ainsi que 2 Tm 2,18 et 2 Th 2,2 –, un retour s'est opéré vers la dimension originellement apocalyptique de la théologie paulinienne dû au besoin d'expliquer les souffrances endurées à cause de la foi en Dieu par l'idée d'une justice rétributive lors du jugement dernier[21]. On notera que cette manière de situer 2 Th dans la dynamique de la réception de l'Évangile paulinien invite de fait à interpréter 2 Th 1,5-10 en lien étroit avec 2 Th 2,1-12. Ces deux passages – précisément les deux pièces originales majeures de 2 Th! – répondent en effet à une seule et même logique. Car, à l'évidence, soutenir l'idée que le juste jugement de Dieu s'exercera lors de la révélation du Seigneur Jésus venant du ciel ne peut que conduire à réfuter l'affirmation selon laquelle le Jour du Seigneur est déjà là!

Cependant, force est de constater que l'auteur de 2 Th ne fournit que très peu de renseignements sur les circonstances supposées qui l'ont amené à prendre la plume – ce qui est habituel pour un écrit

---

20. REDALIÉ, *La deuxième épître* (n. 9), p. 29.

21. G. SELLIN, *«Die Auferstehung ist schon geschehen». Zur Spiritualisierung apokalyptischer Terminologie*, in D. SÄNGER (éd.), *Studien zu Paulus und zum Epheserbrief* (FRLANT, 229), Göttingen, Vandenhoek & Ruprecht, 2009, 37-52, pp. 48.50, s'exprime ainsi: «In nachpaulinischer Zeit hat es […] in der Frage der Eschatologie zwei einander ablösende Phasen gegeben: (1) Eine Phase der Spiritualisierung […] und (2) – daran anschliessend – eine Phase der Reapokalyptisierung. […] Dies ist die Merkmal der dritten Generation. Vielleicht hängt das auch […] mit dem Aufkommen von Verfolgung zusammen»; voir aussi E. POPKES, *Die Bedeutung des zweiten Thessalonicherbriefs für das Verständnis paulinischer und deuteropaulinischer Eschatologie*, in *BZ* 48 (2004) 39-64, pp. 45-51. Renvoyant à M. M. MITCHELL, *A Tale of Two Apocalypses*, in *CTM* 25 (1998) 200-209, REDALIÉ, *Dualisme* (n. 18), p. 79, écrit: «Margaret Mitchell relevait que lorsque le discours de Jésus en Mt 24–25 relit celui de Mc 13 et que 2 Th 1 et 2 reprennent des thèmes eschatologiques de 1 Th 1, 4 et 5, les deux relectures ont en commun une forte préoccupation face à des persécutions devenues plus pressantes et une réflexion sur le temps qui reste, rendue plus urgente. […] Par rapport à leur texte source, […] les deux relectures opèrent un glissement d'intérêt et un développement analogue. Du seul bien salvifique promis aux élus (Mc 13,27; 1 Th 1,10; 4,17-18; 5,5.8.9), l'attention se porte davantage […] au sort qui attend les réprouvés (Mt 23,37-40; 24,42-44.45-52; 25,1-13.14-30.31-46; 2 Th 1,6.8-9; 2,10-12). Serait-ce l'aggravation des persécutions qui oriente les "relectures" de textes apocalyptiques à être plus précis […] sur le sort des réprouvés?»

pseudépigraphe. Les deux seuls «changements de situation historique» évoqués en 2 Th 1,1–2,12 sont une aggravation des persécutions ou des tourments infligés par un extérieur indéfini aux destinataires (2 Th 1,4-6) et le trouble jeté en interne par l'affirmation ἐνέστηκεν ἡ ἡμέρα τοῦ κυρίου (2 Th 2,1-3a). Qui plus est, l'incertitude au sujet de la date de rédaction de 2 Th et de ses véritables destinataires n'invite guère à chercher davantage de précisions historiques concernant le *Sitz im Leben* de cette lettre.

Relevons toutefois qu'aborder 2 Th 1,1–2,12 en termes de «relecture» se heurte à une difficulté particulière. L'auteur de 2 Th brouille, en effet, quelque peu les pistes en laissant entendre en 2 Th 2,5 que sa «relecture» s'appuie aussi sur un enseignement oral, supposé être celui de Paul, mais dont nous ne savons rien! Dans l'hypothèse de la pseudépigraphie, il se pourrait qu'il s'agisse là d'une stratégie rhétorique, calculée pour présenter les vues particulières de l'auteur sous la forme d'un enseignement paulinien antérieur, c'est-à-dire d'un savoir supposé[22]. En ce cas, cela relativiserait singulièrement l'énigme posée par l'identification de «l'homme de l'impiété» (2 Th 2,3c-4) et, surtout, de celle du fameux «retenant» (2 Th 2,6a.7b). Car il n'est pas à exclure que ces deux désignations soient uniquement des noms de fonction.

Analyse

Nous distinguerons en 2 Th 1,1–2,12 l'entrée en communication, composée d'une adresse (2 Th 1,1-2) suivie de l'exposition des motifs justifiant une action de grâce et une prière constantes (2 Th 1,3-12), et l'instruction au sujet d'événements censés se produire avant l'avènement du Jour du Seigneur (2 Th 2,1-12).

1. *2 Th 1,1-2*

En soi, l'adresse est convenue. Aucune qualification n'est ajoutée aux noms des trois expéditeurs[23], en particulier à celui de Paul. La désignation des destinataires est, elle aussi, très sobre. La salutation est habituelle. La

---

22. Cf. E. Cuvillier, *De la crise de l'espérance à la crise enthousiaste: une lecture de 1 Th 4,13-18 et de 2 Th 2,1-12*, in *BLE* 112 (2011) 41-54, p. 50.
23. Redalié, *La deuxième épître* (n. 9), p. 45, remarque: «Comme en 1 Th, la pluralité des auteurs donne sa cohérence au "nous" de l'énonciation».

répétition de la formule «Dieu [notre] père et Seigneur Jésus Christ» aux v.1b.2 ne dérange pas l'auteur. Elle annonce un style lourd.

La comparaison avec 1 Th 1,1 fait apparaître l'ajout du pronom ἡμῶν au v. 1b et celui de la formule stéréotypée ἀπὸ θεοῦ πατρὸς [ἡμῶν] καὶ κυρίου Ἰησοῦ Χριστοῦ au v. 2. Pour le reste, le calque est total. Cette reprise, presque à l'identique, ne manque pas d'étonner, étant inaccoutumée dans le corpus paulinien. La question se pose donc d'emblée: pourquoi l'auteur de 2 Th a-t-il délibérément choisi de situer sa lettre dans le champ d'une communication antérieure? Pourquoi avoir poussé la reprise de 1 Th 1,1 jusqu'à mentionner également les noms de Silvain et de Timothée, alors qu'aucun rôle spécifique ne leur est dévolu dans la lettre[24]? À n'en pas douter, l'auteur de 2 Th entendait bien que son écrit soit lu comme une lettre de «Paul» aux «Thessaloniciens». Cet appui flagrant de 2 Th 1,1-2 sur 1 Th 1,1 n'est malheureusement pas explicité dans la suite de l'écrit, ne serait-ce que par l'artifice d'une phrase comme celle qui a été employée en 2 P 3,1: «C'est déjà la seconde lettre que [nous] vous écri[vons]».

2. *2 Th 1,3-12*

La suite de l'entrée en communication se subdivise à première vue en deux parties, introduites respectivement par les expressions εὐχαριστεῖν ὀφείλομεν τῷ θεῷ πάντοτε περὶ ὑμῶν (v. 3a) et προσευχόμεθα πάντοτε περὶ ὑμῶν (v. 11a)[25]. Les mots εἰς ὃ καί, employés au début du v. 11a, établissent un lien logique entre elles[26]. La relative longueur de cette section résulte, toutefois, de ce qui apparaît être à l'analyse un développement intercalaire. Celui-ci a pour fonction d'établir un lien entre les détresses présentes et la rétribution future (v. 6-10)[27].

Les v. 3 à 10 se présentent sous la forme d'une longue phrase dans laquelle on repère trois principaux articulateurs: ὅτι (v. 3b), ὥστε (v. 4a), εἴπερ (v. 6a). Comparée à 1 Th 1,2a, la formule introductive (v. 3a)

---

24. C'est ce qu'observe TRILLING, *Der zweite Brief* (n. 10), p. 37.
25. À noter la conjonction des thèmes de l'action de grâce et de la prière en 1 Th 1,2.
26. B. RIGAUX, *Saint Paul. Les épîtres aux Thessaloniciens* (EtB), Paris-Gembloux, Gabalda-Duculot, 1956, p. 637, commente: «Dans la mesure même où cette liaison est lâche, elle reprend toute l'idée du développement précédent, et lui rattache en gros tout ce qui va suivre».
27. REDALIÉ, *La deuxième épître* (n. 9), p. 51, analyse: «L'action de grâce [...] est [...] relayée par un enseignement de style différent sur le jugement de Dieu [...]. Cette description de l'accomplissement final [...] offre à l'action de grâce sa résolution et relance la prière d'intercession conclusive des v. 11-12».

appelle quatre remarques. La construction εὐχαριστεῖν ὀφείλομεν est préférée à un simple εὐχαριστοῦμεν. Cette idée inhabituelle d'obligation[28] est explicitée par l'ajout des mots καθὼς ἄξιόν ἐστιν[29]. La précision περὶ πάντων ὑμῶν est ramenée à περὶ ὑμῶν: peut-être est-ce pour ne pas inclure ceux qui seront tancés par la suite, à savoir ceux qui disent que «le Jour du Seigneur est déjà là» (2,2) et ceux qui mènent une vie désordonnée (3,6-12). L'apostrophe ἀδελφοί est utilisée d'entrée, sans autre caractérisation des frères[30].

Annoncée par ὅτι, la raison donnée à une action de grâce répétée[31] est exprimée à l'aide de deux propositions construites de façon symétrique (v. 3b.c), insistant l'une et l'autre sur la croissance continue et débordante de la foi et de l'amour, deux qualités évoquées conjointement en 1 Th 1,3a.b; 3,6; 5,8. On notera, en particulier, la précision apportée au v. 3c par l'expression ἑνὸς ἑκάστου πάντων ὑμῶν[32]; c'est une façon d'insister sur le fait que l'amour des uns pour les autres est entier, sans failles. Une telle manière de parler de la foi et de l'amour des destinataires veut sans doute laisser fictivement entendre que, sur ces deux points particuliers, ils ne cessent d'accomplir collectivement des progrès depuis la rédaction d'1 Th.

La conséquence directe pour le «nous» qui s'exprime ici, en référence à d'autres, non identifiés, comme le suggère l'ajout de αὐτούς avant ἡμᾶς[33], est énoncée au v. 4a, où la grandeur de la fierté actuelle[34] au sujet du «vous» des destinataires est soulignée par l'emploi du verbe intensif ἐγκαυχάομαι. Ce «vous» est à nouveau caractérisé aux v. 4b.c par la «foi / fidélité»[35] et la «persévérance». Ici apparaît non pas, comme attendu, le dernier des trois termes associés en 1 Th 1,3, à savoir l'espérance, mais sa caractérisation qui «va donner au texte de 2 Th 1 son

---

28. Cf. *Barn* 5,3; 7,1; *1 Cl* 38,4.
29. Cf. Ph 1,7: καθώς ἐστιν δίκαιον.
30. Cp. 1 Th 1,4: ἀδελφοὶ ἠγαπημένοι ὑπὸ [τοῦ] θεοῦ, formule reprise plus loin en 2 Th 2,13.
31. En 2 Th 1,3-4, il n'est pas question de «souvenir» comme en 1 Th 1,2-3.
32. Cp. 1 Th 3,12: ὑμᾶς δὲ ὁ κύριος πλεονάσαι καὶ περισσεύσαι τῇ ἀγάπῃ εἰς ἀλλήλους καὶ εἰς πάντας.
33. À ce propos, REDALIÉ, *La deuxième épître* (n. 9), p. 59, estime que «le contraste se réfère à 1 Th 1,7-8, où d'autres rendaient témoignage et vantaient la foi des Thessaloniciens».
34. En 1 Th 2,19, l'orgueil de Paul au sujet des Thessaloniciens est rattaché à la venue du Seigneur Jésus.
35. Pour TRILLING, *Der zweite Brief* (n. 10), p. 47, «die Beiordnung des zweiten Substantivs […] und die Doppelung zu "Glaube" V. 3 lassen mit grosser Wahrscheinlichkeit an "Treue" statt an "Glaube" […] denken».

orientation propre»³⁶. Le lieu où se manifestent ces deux qualités est indiqué aux v. 4d.e par deux termes: διωγμός et θλῖψις³⁷. «La généralisation [et la pérennité] des épreuves en 2 Th 1,4, [qui] tranche sur [leur] caractère concret [...] en 1 Th 3,3 (ἐν ταῖς θλίψεσιν ταύταις)»³⁸, résulte-t-elle d'une relecture d'1 Th 1,6; 2,14; 3,3-4³⁹? Il n'est pas interdit de le penser. Toujours est-il que la reprise du terme θλῖψις au v. 6b, le double emploi du verbe correspondant θλίβω aux v. 6b.7a comme encore l'usage des verbes ἀνέχομαι et πάσχω aux v. 4e.5c donnent tout son poids à la notion de «persévérance», spécialement mise en avant en 2 Th.

«Mais qu'est-ce qui est "signe (ou preuve) du juste jugement" de Dieu? L'ensemble de la situation décrite aux v. 3-4 [...] ou [uniquement] les persécutions et les tribulations [...]?»⁴⁰ L'auteur de 2 Th affirme-t-il au v. 5 que ce «juste jugement»⁴¹ se manifeste déjà maintenant ou qu'il s'exercera seulement au temps de la fin? À quoi faut-il rattacher εἰς τό et quelle est la valeur, finalité ou résultat, de ces mots? L'explication de ce verset difficile, simplement apposé à ce qui précède, doit être trouvée aux v. 6-10. Introduits par εἴπερ⁴², ceux-ci se présentent en effet comme une digression interprétative, l'écho créé entre δίκαιον (v. 6a) et δικαίας (v. 5a) établissant un lien explicite entre le v. 5 et les v. 6-10.

En cette partie sans correspondances franches avec 1 Th, la logique avancée est celle d'une situation inversée (v. 6b.7a), au goût de vengeance⁴³: «détresse» pour ceux qui aujourd'hui persécutent *vs* «repos»⁴⁴ pour les «vous». C'est là une manière d'encourager ces derniers à interpréter la complexité de leur présent à partir du futur de Dieu⁴⁵. Le moment ou s'exercera ce qui est nommé au v. 5 le «juste jugement» de

---

36. REDALIÉ, *La deuxième épître* (n. 9), p. 55.
37. Cp. 1 Th 1,6: ἐν θλίψει πολλῇ.
38. LÉGASSE, *Les épîtres de Paul* (n. 11), p. 349.
39. C'est ce que se demande REDALIÉ, *La deuxième épître* (n. 9), p. 67.
40. REDALIÉ, *La deuxième épître* (n. 9), p. 61.
41. Dans le corpus paulinien, κρίσις n'est employé qu'en 2 Th 1,5 et 1 Tm 5,24. Paul emploie l'expression ἐν ἡμέρᾳ ὀργῆς καὶ ἀποκαλύψεως δικαιοκρισίας τοῦ θεοῦ en Rm 2,5.
42. RIGAUX, *Saint Paul* (n. 26), p. 622, estime: «Ici [εἴπερ] ne marque une condition que sous une forme oratoire et solennelle d'une affirmation sans conteste possible».
43. Emploi de ἐκδίκησις au v. 8b.
44. Cf. 4 *Esd* 7,36; 10,24. TRILLING, *Der zweite Brief* (n. 10), p. 52, observe: «Der Verfasser wählt kein theologisches hochbefrachtetes Wort, sondern eines das in irdischen Situationen wurzelt».
45. Cf. G. L. GREEN, *The Letters to the Thessalonians* (PNTC), Eerdmans, Grand Rapids, 2002, p. 287.

Dieu est fixé, d'après le v. 7b, au retour de Jésus[46], dépeint aux couleurs apocalyptiques[47]: ἀπ' οὐρανοῦ (v. 7b) indique que cette manifestation sera orchestrée par Dieu; μετ' ἀγγέλων δυνάμεως αὐτοῦ (v. 7c) remplace l'expression μετὰ πάντων τῶν ἁγίων αὐτοῦ employée en 1 Th 3,13; ἐν πυρὶ φλογός (v. 8a) ajoute une note dramatique à l'ensemble[48]. La sanction négative – ὄλεθρος αἰώνιος (v. 9a) – sera édictée par le Seigneur Jésus[49]. Consistera-t-elle en un éloignement loin de sa présence de gloire – sens spatial d'ἀπό aux v. 9b.c – ou résultera-t-elle de sa présence glorieuse – sens causal d'ἀπό? Il est difficile de trancher. D'après le v. 8, cette «perdition éternelle» concernera non plus seulement les persécuteurs, mais plus largement ceux qui sont présentés à l'aide de deux expressions: τοῖς μὴ εἰδόσιν θεόν (v. 8c); τοῖς μὴ ὑπακούουσιν τῷ εὐαγγελίῳ τοῦ κυρίου ἡμῶν Ἰησοῦ (v. 8d). S'agit-il des mêmes personnes[50]? Toujours est-il qu'elles sont opposées aux «saints» (v. 10b) et à «tous les croyants» (v. 10c), ceux parmi lesquels ou par lesquels le Christ sera glorifié (le sens de ἐν aux v.10b.c est équivoque)[51]. L'insertion maladroite du v. 10d permet à l'auteur de revenir au cas particulier des destinataires. Si leur «obéissance à l'Évangile» au cœur des persécutions et des détresses leur garantit le «repos» (v. 7a), cela ne signifie-t-il pas alors qu'ils seront «jugés dignes du Royaume» (v. 5b) au motif de leur persévérance et de leur fidélité dans la souffrance? Cette attitude ne répond-elle pas à l'exhortation pressante de Paul, rappelée en 1 Th 2,12, à se «conduire d'une manière digne de Dieu qui appelle à son Royaume et à sa gloire»?

Pourquoi l'auteur de 2 Th a-t-il enchâssé cette importante incise entre les v. 3-5 en amont, et les v. 11-12 en aval? Ne serait-ce pas pour expliciter l'allusion à «la colère qui vient», thème sur lequel s'arrête précisément 1 Th 1,2-10 et que ne développe pas non plus 1 Th 5,9? Dans

---

46. Cette échéance est rappelée aux v. 10a.e.
47. Cp. 1 Th 4,16-17. REDALIÉ, *La deuxième épître* (n. 9), p. 54, note: «Le langage des v. 7-10 emprunte aux représentations apocalyptiques juives de la tradition biblique et extrabiblique».
48. De l'avis de P. DE VILLIERS, *The Glorious Presence of the Lord. The Eschatology of 2 Thessalonians*, in J. G. VAN DER WATT (éd.), *Eschatology of the New Testament and Some Related Documents* (WUNT, 2.315), Tübingen, Mohr Siebeck, 2011, 333-361, p. 339, «these motifs emphasise the special role of Jesus as Lord in the execution of judgment».
49. TRILLING, *Der zweite Brief* (n. 10), p. 53, constate: «Die theo-zentrische Ausrichtung […] wird abrupt von einer christo-zentrischen abgelöst».
50. REDALIÉ, *La deuxième épître* (n. 9), p. 69, interroge: «De qui s'agit-il? Des païens ignorants de Dieu et des juifs qui n'ont pas accueilli l'Évangile […]?»
51. LÉGASSE, *Les épîtres de Paul* (n. 11), p. 371, relève: «La partie centrale de notre péricope, quittant la perspective du châtiment s'achève sur une note positive».

cette hypothèse⁵², la fonction de 2 Th 1,6-10 est de dépasser le silence observé par Paul en 1 Th, l'auteur de 2 Th n'hésitant pas à risquer un scénario apocalyptique à deux faces, concernant les croyants et les réprouvés, là où le fondateur de la communauté de Thessalonique s'est montré plus réservé.

La finalité de la prière récurrente est énoncée en deux temps, introduits l'un par ἵνα (v. 11b.c.d) et l'autre par ὅπως (v. 12). Il est tout d'abord attendu de Dieu qu'il travaille à l'accomplissement de l'appel adressé jadis aux «vous» (v. 11b) et qu'il mène à terme la «volonté bonne à faire le bien» et «l'effort de foi» (v. 11c.d) qui les caractérisent en ces temps difficiles pour eux. Ceci est nécessaire pour qu'ait lieu une glorification réciproque – à l'heure actuelle ou au jour de la parousie seulement⁵³? – du Seigneur Jésus tout d'abord (v. 12a), des «vous» ensuite (v. 12b), en vertu d'une «grâce» (v. 12c).

Le temps présent, si douloureusement marqué par l'hostilité extérieure et les souffrances qu'elle engendre, est donc présenté en 2 Th 1,3-12 comme un temps qui a du sens: il permet aux destinataires de la lettre de progresser dans la foi et dans l'amour et de manifester leur persévérance dans la durée (v. 3-4); il permet à Dieu de mener à terme, avec puissance, ce qu'a généré sont appel (v. 11-12). Conjointement, le temps présent reçoit son sens véritable de ce qui sera manifesté dans le futur lors du «juste jugement de Dieu» (v. 5). Il apparaît ainsi que l'opération qui consistait à dissocier les v. 3-5 et les v. 11-12 pour insérer le développement propre des v. 6-10 avait pour finalité d'inviter les destinataires de 2 Th à interpréter le temps présent comme une durée théologique nécessaire. Tout en les encourageant à persévérer face à l'adversité et à fixer, au-delà de leurs souffrances, l'horizon de Dieu, l'auteur de 2 Th entendait les dissuader d'accorder un quelconque crédit à ceux qui raisonnaient en termes de raccourcissement du temps présent, allant jusqu'à prétendre: ἐνέστηκεν ἡ ἡμέρα τοῦ κυρίου (2 Th 2,2).

Finement réfléchie, cette «relecture» d'1 Th 1,2-10 que propose 2 Th 1,3-12 prépare certes la deuxième pièce originale de la lettre qu'est 2 Th 2,1-12. Elle a, cependant, sa propre importance dans le projet d'écriture de l'auteur car elle y inscrit cette affirmation, fondamentale à ses yeux, que le temps présent a une valeur théologique. Surtout, on remarquera qu'en ces lignes, l'auteur de 2 Th se garde d'offrir la moindre prise à

---

52. Elle est avancée par REDALIÉ, *La deuxième épître* (n. 9), p. 74.
53. Pour TRILLING, *Der zweite Brief* (n. 10), p. 64, n. 219, «völlige Sicherheit ist [...] nicht zu erlangen».

une interprétation des souffrances endurées par les croyants dans le sens de signes annonciateurs d'une fin imminente. N'est-ce pas une telle lecture de la situation évoquée qui a conduit certains à penser que le Jour du Seigneur était là[54]? Aussi tiendrons-nous la conjonction δέ en 2 Th 2,1 – point de suture entre 2 Th 1,3-12 et 2 Th 2,1-12 – pour «un δέ de transition»[55]. Mais sans considérer, toutefois, que l'auteur passe à un autre sujet, plus important[56].

3. *2 Th 2,1-12*

Cette section débute par une requête – ἐρωτῶμεν δὲ ὑμᾶς, ἀδελφοί (v. 1a)[57] – doublée d'une injonction: μή τις ὑμᾶς ἐξαπατήσῃ κατὰ μηδένα τρόπον (v. 3a)[58]. L'argumentation produite aux v. 3b-12, qui s'appuie tout d'abord sur la mémoire supposée d'un message oral antérieur (v. 3b-5) puis sur le savoir prétendu des destinataires (v. 6-12), est sans doute «plus pastorale que spéculative»[59].

Introduit par ὑπέρ, le thème de la directive liminaire – «la parousie du Seigneur»[60] et le fait d'«être réunis en sa présence»[61] – est clairement énoncé à l'aide de deux propositions définies par un article commun et reliées entre elles par un καί consécutif (v. 1b.c). L'objet de la requête – «ne pas trop vite (ou trop facilement?) perdre la tête» et «ne pas s'alarmer» – est ensuite exprimé par deux infinitifs[62] précédés de εἰς τό (v. 2a.b). Trois canaux, par lesquels l'affirmation qui jette le trouble est susceptible d'être passée, sont alors énumérés dans cet ordre (v. 2c.d.e): un «esprit» – au sens d'une «communication prophétique inspirée»[63] –,

---

54. Cf. H. KOESTER, *From Paul's Eschatology to the Apocalyptic Schemata of 2 Thessalonians*, in R. F. COLLINS, *The Thessalonians Correspondance* (BEThL, 87), Leuven, University Press, 1990, 441-458, p. 456.
55. Ainsi RIGAUX, *Saint Paul* (n. 26), p. 647.
56. C'est ce que fait valoir TRILLING, *Der zweite Brief* (n. 10), p. 66: «Kap. 1 ist [...] nicht als Einleitung und Hinführung zum "eschatologischen Hauptstück" Kap. 2 zu sehen. Es hat eigenen Bedeutung im Gesamt der eschatologischen Thematik. Ja, es stellt sogar eine Art notwendige Voraussetzung für Kap. 2 dar».
57. Cp. 1 Th 5,12. En 1 Th 4,1, Paul emploie l'expression ἐρωτῶμεν ὑμᾶς καὶ παρακαλοῦμεν.
58. Cp. Mt 24,4b: βλέπετε μή τις ὑμᾶς πλανήσῃ.
59. REDALIÉ, *La deuxième épître* (n. 9), p. 88.
60. Cf. 1 Th 2,19; 3,13; 4,15; 5,23.
61. Cf. 1 Th 14,17: καὶ οὕτως πάντοτε σὺν κυρίῳ ἐσόμεθα.
62. RIGAUX, *Saint Paul* (n. 26), pp. 648-649, commente: «L'un est à l'aoriste [...]. C'est un fait et le verbe suivant au présent montre que ses effets durent encore [...]. Le choc reçu [...] est cause d'un état».
63. LÉGASSE, *Les épîtres de Paul* (n. 11), p. 382.

une «parole» – au sens d'un discours ou d'une prédication – et une «lettre»[64]. L'interprétation des mots ὡς δι' ἡμῶν est discutée. On ne sait au juste au(x)quel(s) des trois moyens de communication les rattacher[65]. Surtout, sont-ils à rendre par «comme *prétendument* de nous» ou par «comme *réellement* de nous»? Autrement dit, l'auteur de 2 Th suggère-t-il que la position qu'il va réfuter a été faussement attribuée à Paul ou qu'elle s'appuie sur un propos qu'il a effectivement tenu? La double option que nous avons prise, à savoir que l'auteur de 2 Th n'est pas Paul mais qu'il s'inscrit dans une démarche de «relecture» positive de 1 Th, s'accommode de la première hypothèse, sans toutefois exclure celle d'une «ambiguïté intentionnelle»[66]. L'impératif qui suit (v. 3a), exprimé avec force pour annoncer une mise au point, ne fait que souligner le caractère erroné de l'affirmation accréditée par certains: ἐνέστηκεν ἡ ἡμέρα τοῦ κυρίου. Cette phrase reprend-elle une assertion ainsi exprimée où synthétise-t-elle la façon dont l'auteur de 2 Th comprend la

---

64. TRILLING, *Der zweite Brief* (n. 10), p. 77, remarque: «Die drei Quellen nebeneinander nannte [der Verfasser] um jede Möglichkeit auszuschliessen, die überhaupt als Stütze [...] in Betracht kam».

65. Autre est l'avis de K. LILJESTRÖM, *The False Teaching and its Source According to 2 Thess 2,2: A Proposal for a "Fresh" Reading of the Old Crux*, in L. AEJMELAEUS et A. MUSTAKALLIO (éds), *The Nordic Paul. Finnish Approaches to Pauline Theology* (LNTS, 374), London, T&T Clark, 2008, 172-192, pp. 188.190 ou de G. D. FEE, *The First and Second Letters to the Thessalonians* (NICNT), Eerdmans, Grand Rapid, 2009, p. 275, pour lesquels les mots ὡς δι' ἡμῶν sont à rattacher au slogan qui suit.

66. La grammaire et le dictionnaire ne permettent pas de résoudre l'ambiguïté de 2 Th 2,2. Ce verset ne peut donc qu'être interprété en fonction de l'hypothèse générale retenue concernant 2 Th. Cela est confirmé par trois témoins parmi d'autres de ce débat. Pour LINDEMANN, *Abfassungszweck* (n. 16), p. 37, selon qui 2 Th doit remplacer 1 Th, «die nächstliegende Lösung des Problems scheint zu sein, ὡς δι' ἡμῶν unmittelbar auf ἐπιστολή zu beziehen und dann zu übersetzen: (Lasst euch nicht verwirren) durch einen Brief, der angeblich von uns kommt». Autre est l'avis de H. ROOSE, *"A letter as by Us". Intentional Ambiguity in 2 Th 2,2*, in *JSNT* 29 (2006) 107-124, pp. 111.117: «In my view, the irritating wording in 2 Thess 2,2 is best explained in terms of this kind of intentional ambiguity [in inauthentic epistles]. In 2 Thess 2,2, there is a clash of interest between, on the one hand, the author's struggle for relevance and, on the other hand, his struggle for (alleged) authenticity. He deals with this clash by deliberately employing an ambiguous wording that allows two different readings, one of which serves the purpose of relevance [...], the other one serving the purpose of (alleged) authenticity». La position d'E.-M. BECKER, *Ὡς δι' ἡμῶν in 2 Thess 2,2 als Hinweis auf einen verlorenen Brief*, in *NTS* 55 (2009) 55-72, pp. 55.64.67, est la suivante: «Die These des Beitrags ist, dass die Wendung ὡς δι' ἡμῶν in 2 Thess 2,2 nicht als direkter Hinweis an den 1 Thess zu verstehen sei, sondern dass sich hier vielmehr des pseudonyme Verfasser mit einer nicht mehr erhaltenen brieflichen Fehlinterpretation des 1 Thess auseinandersetzt und sich so indirekt um eine "richtige" Deutung des 1 Thess bemüht. [...] 2 Th 2,2 ist *nicht* auf den 1 Thess, sondern auf einen uns nicht bekannten, d.h. verloren gegangenen paulinischen oder pseudo-paulinischen Brief zu beziehen. [...] Der Verfasser des 2 Thess nimmt erst in 2,15 [...] auf den 1 Thess und die darin formulierte paulische Unterweisung explizit Bezug».

position réfutée⁶⁷? On ne peut répondre. Toujours est-il que le contexte demande de l'interpréter comme l'annonce de la venue, sinon réalisée, du moins imminente, du Jour du Seigneur⁶⁸. En effet, c'est bien d'un calendrier eschatologique, et, de ce fait, du temps dans sa durée, qu'il va être question aux v 3b-12.

Deux préalables au Jour du Seigneur sont alors rappelés: «l'apostasie» (v. 3b)⁶⁹ et la révélation de «l'homme de l'impiété» (v. 3c)⁷⁰. Nommée en premier sans autres précisions que l'article défini, l'apostasie désigne en ce contexte le succès de grande ampleur que rencontrera l'Impie, véritable anti-Dieu dont le mode opératoire sera précisé aux v. 9-10. Pour l'instant, celui-ci est présenté plus en détail aux v. 3d-4 en tant que «fils de la perdition»⁷¹, «l'adversaire», «celui qui s'élève contre»⁷², «celui qui s'assied dans le temple de Dieu»⁷³, «celui qui proclame luimême être Dieu»⁷⁴. C'est une impressionnante carte de visite qui puise de manière allusive aux pages sombres de la mémoire juive. Ce qui doit encore arriver – preuve que le Jour du Seigneur, à savoir le jour du jugement, n'est ni arrivé, ni imminent – est récapitulé par ταῦτα dans la question rhétorique du v. 5⁷⁵. L'auteur y fait usage de la première personne du singulier⁷⁶ et a recours au thème du souvenir, non de ce qui a été écrit, mais de ce qui a été dit et répété⁷⁷! «La référence à l'enseignement originaire oral de Paul [n'est-elle pas] une manière de couper court

---

67. Cf. POPKES, *Die Bedeutung* (n. 21), p. 45.

68. TRILLING, *Der zweite Brief* (n. 10), p. 78, commente: «Das Perfekt lässt keinen Zweifel daran, dass vom "da sein", nicht vom "nahe sein", "bevorstehen" u.ä die Rede ist. Darüber besteht weitgehende Einigkeit. Die Auffasungen gehen aber in der Sache auseinander, d.h. in der Präzisierung dessen, *was* damit genau gemeint sei, und in den Versuchen, eine solche These geschichtlich zu verifizieren».

69. Selon POPKES, *Die Bedeutung* (n. 21), p. 57, l'apostasie toucherait également les croyants.

70. L'expression sémitisante ὁ ἄνθρωπος τῆς ἀνομίας est à lire en parallèle avec ὁ ἄνομος au v. 8a. Pour son interprétation et son arrière-plan, voir RÖCKER, *Belial und Katechon* (n. 12), pp. 1-20.21-222.

71. Cf. v. 10: τοῖς ἀπολλυμένοις.

72. Cf. Dn 11,36-37.

73. Pour les revendications d'Antiochus IV Épiphane, de Pompée et de Caligula, cf. RÖCKER, *Belial und Katechon* (n. 12), pp. 390-399.

74. Cf. Ez 28,2.

75. L'apodose de la protase introduite par ὅτι ἐὰν μή au v. 3b manque.

76. N. BROX, *Falsche Verfasserangaben. Zur Erklärung der frühchristlichen Pseudepigraphie* (SBS, 79), Stuttgart, KWB, 1975, p. 57, range le «Ich-bzw. der Wir-Stil» parmi les «Beglaubigunsmittel».

77. L'imparfait laisse entendre que ces choses ont été plusieurs fois abordées.

et de corriger une erreur dont la source n'est pas claire [...], d'accréditer la relecture de 1 Th comme seule valable»[78]?

Pourquoi l'homme de l'impiété ne s'est-il pas encore révélé? Une réponse à cette question – mais en est-ce seulement une, tant elle est vague et énigmatique[79]! – est amorcée au v. 6, sous la forme d'un savoir supposé: quelque chose retient[80] – emploi du neutre τὸ κατέχον – cette manifestation / parousie de l'Impie qui doit s'effectuer en un temps fixé. Que «le retenant» – le masculin ὁ κατέχων renvoie-t-il à une figure positive ou négative? – s'écarte ou soit écarté (v. 7b)[81], alors seulement, poursuit l'auteur, se manifestera pleinement «l'Impie» (v. 8a), celui qui incarnera, en la portant au grand jour, l'impiété qui, pour l'heure, œuvre de manière encore voilée (v. 7a). Mais cette manifestation tournera assurément en défaite[82] lors de «l'épiphanie de la parousie» du Seigneur[83]. C'est ce qu'annonce d'emblée une première proposition relative (v. 8b.c) qui se présente comme «un bulletin de victoire anticipé»[84]. Cette venue de l'Impie, caractérisée par des signes mensongers et la tromperie séductrice (v. 9b.10a), est ensuite mise au compte d'une «énergie» satanique (v. 9a), ce qu'affirme une seconde proposition relative (v. 9-10). Ceux qui se sont laissés abuser[85] sont déclarés «perdus» (v. 10a), au motif

---

78. REDALIÉ, *La deuxième épître* (n. 9), p. 109.

79. À ce propos, on cite volontiers Saint Augustin, *La cité de Dieu* 20,19: «En disant qu'ils le savent, il n'a pas voulu le dire lui-même ouvertement. Nous donc qui ne savons pas ce qu'ils savaient, nous désirons parvenir, même en peinant, à pénétrer la pensée de l'Apôtre et sans le pouvoir; d'autant que ce qu'il ajoute ne fait qu'en rendre le sens plus obscur. Que signifie, de fait: *Dès maintenant, en effet, le mystère d'iniquité est à l'œuvre. Seulement que celui qui tient à présent, tienne jusqu'à ce qu'il soit écarté et alors se révélera l'Impie?* J'avoue que j'ignore totalement ce qu'il a pu dire» (traduction G. Combès, DDB, 1960).

80. On compte 18 occurrences du verbe κατέχω dans le NT. C. SPICQ, *Lexique théologique du Nouveau Testament*, Paris, Cerf, 1991, p. 799, relève: «Les acceptions de ce verbe sont multiples [...]: saisir, tenir fortement, retenir, détenir, contenir, prendre possession, occuper»; METZGER, *Katechon* (n. 4), p. 9, conclut de sa brève enquête: «Ein traditionell geprägter Begriff konnte nicht festgestellt werden».

81. Le v. 7b est une ellipse. GREEN, *The Letters* (n. 45), p. 318, note: «Since no agent is indicated [...] it may be just as possible that we should understand the expression as active and not passive»; RIGAUX, *Saint Paul*, p. 671, observe: «Le fait seul est indiqué mais non pas le mode».

82. RÖCKER, *Belial und Katechon* (n. 12), p. 490, remarque: «Ein hinweis auf die Dauer der Wirksamkeit des "Gesetzlosen" ist für den Verf. des 2 Thess unnötig».

83. À propos de cette expression singulière, REDALIÉ, *La deuxième épître* (n. 9), p. 114, commente avec raison: «Souligner que la Parousie est une manifestation visible à tous est déterminant pour corriger l'erreur de croire que le Jour du Seigneur est déjà là».

84. RIGAUX, *Saint Paul* (n. 26), p. 671. Cf. Es 11,4b.

85. REDALIÉ, *La deuxième épître* (n. 9), p. 116, rappelle: «C'est un lieu commun de l'eschatologie apocalyptique que, peu avant la fin, l'adversaire de Dieu et ses agents réussissent à tromper un grand nombre de personnes».

qu'ils «n'ont pas accueilli l'amour de la vérité» (v. 10b). C'est sur eux que se concentre enfin la dernière partie de ce passage (v. 11-12) – «καί marque la correspondance entre la faute et la punition»[86] – qui rapporte assez paradoxalement que Dieu déploie lui aussi une «énergie d'égarement» contre ceux qui ont pris plaisir à l'injustice et qui seront condamnés[87]. On observera qu'aux v. 9-12, l'auteur oppose à deux reprises la notion d'ἀλήθεια (v. 10b.12a) à celles de ψεῦδος / ψευδής (v. 9b.11b) et d'ἀδικία (v. 10a.12b). La finale sombre de cette section ne met que davantage en lumière, aux v. 13-14, la caractérisation positive des destinataires, de ces «vous» qui ont précisément accordé foi, non au mensonge, mais à la vérité.

Comme on le sait, les commentateurs ont rivalisé d'imagination au fil des siècles pour décoder le cryptogramme τὸ κατέχον / ὁ κατέχων. Parmi les principales propositions avancées, relevons: l'empire romain et l'empereur, Sénèque et Néron, la grâce de l'Esprit saint et l'Esprit, le dessein de salut et Dieu, la mission universelle et Paul, l'armée céleste et une ange particulier (Michaël), une puissance démoniaque et Satan, une création *ad hoc*, etc.[88]. Cette étonnante palette de solutions s'explique par la combinaison de choix différents. Selon que l'on perçoit τὸ κατέχον / ὁ κατέχων comme une chose et une entité positives ou négatives[89], selon que l'on opte pour l'authenticité ou non de 2 Th, pour telle ou telle acception de κατέχω, et selon que l'on juge nécessaire ou inutile, possible ou impossible de résoudre cette énigme etc., la conclusion tirée ne pourra être que fort différente.

Faut-il trancher? Il nous semble que tenir 2 Th pour une lettre pseudépigraphe et une relecture externe d'1 Th n'oblige pas à identifier précisément les deux figures désignées respectivement par ὁ ἄνομος et ὁ κατέχων ou encore la chose signifiée par τὸ κατέχον. Y parviendrait-on malgré tout que cela n'infléchirait pas fondamentalement la logique

---

86. RIGAUX, *Saint Paul* (n. 26), p. 679.
87. REDALIÉ, *La deuxième épître* (n. 9), p. 118, précise que «le verbe "juger" n'exprime pas seulement le jugement mais aussi la condamnation».
88. Cf. L. PEERBOLTE, *The κατέχον / κατέχων of 2 Thess 2,6-7*, in *NT* 39 (1997) 138-150, pp. 141-144; METZGER, *Katechon* (n. 4), pp. 15-47; RÖCKER, *Belial und Katechon* (n. 12), pp. 422-473. Pour une enquête approfondie sur ce qui retarde dans l'apocalyptique, on consultera METZGER, *Katechon* (n. 4), pp. 133-269.
89. Relevons les avis opposés de TRILLING, *Der zweite Brief* (n. 10), p. 90: «Das *Katechon* hat die Funktion, das Hervorbrechen des Wider-Gottes zu hemmen […]. Es muss daher eine positiv gesehene Macht sein» *vs* METZGER, *Katechon* (n. 4), p. 124: «[Die] Erprobung der Gemeinde dauert durch das *Katechon* an, weshalb die aufhaltende Kraft nicht als ein positiver Faktor verstanden werden kann».

déployée en 2 Th 2,3b-12, laquelle s'accommode tout à fait de l'hypothèse de simples noms de fonction. D'ailleurs, l'auteur de 2 Th n'a-t-il pas délibérément joué avec l'ambiguïté des termes retenus pour justement empêcher tout véritable calcul, et, par là, toute spéculation au sujet de l'avènement du Jour du Seigneur[90]? Ce qui lui importait avant tout, c'était de persuader les destinataires de sa lettre que le temps actuel a une certaine épaisseur et que l'impiété ne peut encore œuvrer que de façon retenue... parce que le «retenant» retient! Il n'est pas question en 2 Th 2,1-12 de persécutions ou d'épreuves infligées par un milieu extérieur hostile, mais d'une entreprise de séduction à très grande échelle. Différée jusqu'au «temps fixé», celle-ci doit précéder l'arrivée du Jour du Seigneur qui correspond, d'après 2 Th, à la parousie de Jésus. Jouant avec une soi-disant mémoire d'un enseignement oral antérieur au sujet du «retenant» et cachant au final une non-identification de l'Impie sous une accumulation d'informations le concernant, l'auteur de 2 Th veut donner l'impression en ces lignes qu'il est parfaitement averti de ce qui doit advenir avant le jour du juste jugement de Dieu. L'était-il réellement? Plus qu'aux révélations elles-mêmes, c'est sans doute à leur fonction de recadrage qu'il faut regarder[91], un recadrage qui a pour objectif de calmer le trouble jeté parmi les destinataires de la lettre suite à l'affirmation, soutenue par certains: ἐνέστηκεν ἡ ἡμέρα τοῦ κυρίου.

On ne manquera cependant pas de relever que le scénario eschatologique prévu s'appuie en son démarrage sur 1 Th 4,13–5,11. Il y reprend, dans l'ordre dans lequel ils apparaissent, ces trois motifs: la parousie du Seigneur (1 Th 4,15; 2 Th 2,1b); l'«être avec» le Seigneur ou le

---

90. Rappelons ici l'avis de MARXSEN, *Der zweite Thessalonicherbrief* (n. 16), pp. 84-85: «Mit Absicht redet [der Verfasser] in Rätseln. Diese Rätsel soll man gar nicht auflösen können; und darum darf man das auch nicht versuchen wollen». Autre est la position de T. ROH, *Der zweite Thessalonicherbrief als Erneuerung apokalyptischer Zeitdeutung* (NTOA/StUNT, 62), Göttingen-Fribourg, Vandenhoeck & Ruprecht-Academic Press, 2007, p. 9: «Es ist [...] ein dringendes Anliegen zu überprüfen, ob diese wissenschaftliche Resignation wirklich gerechtfertigt ist oder ob der Brief nicht doch einen konkreten geschichtlichen Kontext und Hintergrund erkennen lässt». METZGER, *Katechon* (n. 4), et RÖCKER, *Belial und Katechon* (n. 12), ont eux aussi jugé utile et possible de pousser l'enquête.

91. Cf. J. FREY, *New Testament Eschatology – an Introduction. Classical Issues, Disputed Themes, and Current Perspectives*, in VAN DER WATT (éd.), *Eschatology* (n. 48), 3-32, p. 29: «More recent developments in exegesis [...] have created a better awareness for the *function* of texts, of particular expressions and of imaginative worlds. They do not always simply convey information, knowledge or teaching but quite often other functions of eschatological language are predominant [...]: they express confidence in the fulfilment of God's promises, the call for alertness and sobriety, the call for a decision and encouragement in view of suffering and martyrdom. All these "expressive" and "pragmatic" functions of eschatological language go beyond the mere dimension of "information" or "reality"».

«rassemblement en sa présence» (1 Th 4,17; 2 Th 2,1c); le Jour du Seigneur (1 Th 5,2.4; 2 Th 2,2e)[92]. L'auteur de 2 Th ne prolonge cependant que le troisième des thèmes repris, dans une optique différente que celle envisagée par Paul en 1 Th 5,1-11. Tout en évoquant comme lui un savoir qui repose sur un enseignement oral délivré antérieurement – l'emploi de οἴδατε en 2 Th 2,6a fait écho à 1 Th 5,2 –, il ne traite plus de la ruine qui doit fondre sur ceux qui diront: «Quelle paix, quelle sécurité!» – ce sujet a déjà été abordé en 2 Th 1,6-10 où il est fait usage du terme ὄλεθρος employé par Paul en 1 Th 5,3 – ni, surtout, de la soudaineté de la venue du Jour du Seigneur, mais de ce qui doit encore arriver avant que celui-ci n'advienne. On peut donc assurément parler de «relecture» de 1 Th 4,13–5,11 en 2 Th 2,1-12. En effet, le déplacement d'accent dans le texte relisant ne conteste pas le texte relu: affirmer que la parousie de l'Impie précédera celle du Seigneur ne contredit pas en soi l'idée d'une manifestation soudaine de ce dernier; cela revient uniquement à dire qu'elle se réalisera bien de cette manière, mais seulement après le feu vert donné à l'Impie. De la même façon que 2 Th 1,6-10 meuble un silence de l'apôtre en 1 Th, ainsi en est-il, également, pour 2 Th 2,3b-12.

Relevons encore que si Paul évoque en 1 Co 15,23-28 la destruction, lors de la parousie du Christ, de «toute domination, toute autorité et puissance» et celle du «dernier ennemi», à savoir «la mort», l'auteur de 2 Th envisage ici l'anéantissement de l'«Impie». Dans les deux passages, il est fait usage du même verbe καταργέω (1 Co 15,24.26; 2 Th 2,8c). Est-ce seulement une coïncidence? Toujours est-il que le Tarsiote ne donne aucun renseignement sur le jugement dernier en 1 Co 15.

REMARQUES CONCLUSIVES

Au terme de ce bref essai de lecture de 2 Th 1,1–2,12, il apparaît que l'auteur pseudépigraphe de 2 Th est intervenu de façon décidée pour réécrire, en leur donnant un profil inédit, les passages trouvés en 1 Th 1,2-10 et en 1 Th 4,13–5,11. Pour ce faire, il a sélectionné dans le texte source ce qui l'intéressait au premier chef et l'a adapté à son projet, mais sans véritablement déconstruire le discours paulinien. C'est surtout à un travail d'écriture entre les lignes qu'il s'est employé, pour glisser dans l'écrit relu ce qu'un contexte changeant – tant au niveau des relations

---

92. Bien entendu, cela n'a pas échappé à REDALIÉ, *La deuxième épître* (n. 9), p. 29.

avec l'extérieur que sur le plan des évolutions théologiques – demandait comme explicitations. Dans cette perspective, il a surtout cherché à valoriser le temps présent en soulignant le sens théologique des souffrances endurées par les croyants, il a parlé du sort des réprouvés et a ajouté les précisions jugées nécessaires au calendrier eschatologique en y inscrivant quelques étapes obligées. Le scénario de la fin qu'il prévoit est donc le suivant: un temps de persécutions et d'épreuves, l'impiété étant encore bridée par le «retenant» qui est en place; la mise à l'écart du «retenant», au temps fixé, pour permettre à l'Impie d'accomplir son œuvre d'égarement; la venue du Jour du Seigneur, correspondant à la parousie de Jésus, moment où l'Impie sera anéanti et où s'exercera le juste jugement de Dieu qui aboutira à la perte des réprouvés et au repos de ceux qui ont accueilli la vérité et cru en elle jusqu'au bout.

Le calque presque intégral de 2 Th 1,1-2 sur 1 Th 1,1 indique peut-être la manière dont l'auteur de 2 Th entend que soit lue sa lettre, à savoir en la superposant à 1 Th, afin de repérer par transparence les accentuations nouvelles et les ajouts aux silences. C'est en tout cas ainsi que nous comprenons qu'il convient de lire 2 Th 1, 3-12 et 2 Th 2,1-12, non pas comme une action de grâce suivie du premier élément du corps de la lettre – ce que ces deux textes sont assurément –, mais comme deux volets explicatifs qui, superposés l'un sur l'autre, fournissent les informations, jugées manquantes en 1 Th, pour interpréter le temps actuel dans son lien étroit avec ce qui doit advenir.

De notre point de vue, il n'y a donc pas d'objection majeure à compter l'auteur de 2 Th au nombre de ceux qui ont fait l'effort d'actualiser le message de Paul pour répondre aux questions que soulevaient inévitablement les mutations internes et externes vécues par les communautés fondées par l'apôtre[93]. Nous l'imaginons sans trop de difficultés sur un des bancs de l'école paulinienne[94], pas forcément dans une «classe» à

---

93. À ce propos, LILJESTRÖM, *The False Teaching* (n. 65), p. 191, estime: «The author of 2 Thessalonians no doubt saw himself as a defender of correct Pauline tradition [...]. To him, Paul seemingly was not a "dogmatic" authority whose theology and thought could only be found from his surviving letters. He, instead, saw it as possible to create Pauline theology, when the material was lacking, or too ambiguous».

94. Autre est l'opinion, par exemple, de TRILLING, *Der Zweite Brief* (n. 10), p. 27: «Der [...] Verfasser stammt wohl nicht aus einer "paulinischen Schule"»; ou encore METZGER, *Katechon* (n. 4), pp. 85-86: «Der Autor [...] erkennt Paulus als formale Autorität an, der er sich bedient, um seine Position zu kräftigen. Damit ist allerdings nicht irgendein Schulzusammenhang vorausgesetzt. Die Beobachtung, dass der II Thess der paulinischen Eschatologie eher entgegensteht, scheint eher in die Richtung zu deuten, dass hier kein Paulusschüler die Autorität seines Meisters untermauert und paulinisches Erbe neu auslegt, sondern ein der

part⁹⁵, même s'il est vrai que ses vues s'ajoutent plus à celles de Paul qu'elles ne les développent. Sa hardiesse à s'aventurer là où Paul n'est pas allé⁹⁶ l'aura en tout cas conduit à prendre part à un débat important sur les choses de la fin et à apporter une réponse originale – autre que celle proposée par les auteurs de Colossiens, Éphésiens et des épîtres pastorales – à la délicate question posée par le retard de la parousie⁹⁷. Son invitation à tenir ferme dans l'adversité en regardant vers l'avenir du juste jugement de Dieu lui aurait-elle réellement attiré le regard désapprobateur de l'apôtre des nations, sous le nom duquel il a signé sa lettre?

---

paulinischen Theologie eher fern stehender Autor Paulus zu korrigieren sucht». Pour cette question, voir POPKES, *Die Bedeutung* (n. 21), pp. 41-43.

95. Relevant que «l'appartenance de 2 Th à une école paulinienne est discutée», DETTWILER, *La deuxième épître aux Thessaloniciens* (n. 6), pp. 324-325, avance: «Si l'on veut maintenir le concept d'école paulinienne pour interpréter 2 Th, il faudrait parler de différentes "classes" au sein de l'école». Il constate cependant: «Plusieurs contributions récentes accentuent la diversité et la flexibilité dans le développement de la tradition paulinienne».

96. Ainsi POPKES, *Die Bedeutung* (n. 21), p. 52: «Der Verf. des 2 Thess […] zieht […] jene Konsequenzen paulinischer Argumentationen, die Paulus selbst nicht gezogen hat».

97. PEERBOLTE, *The κατέχον / κατέχων* (n. 88), p. 149, juge que «the author of 2 Thessalonians […] would simply transform the question as to why the *parousia* has not yet come, into a new version of the same question, viz.: why has the eschatological opponent not yet come».

THANKSGIVING AND PRAYER.
APPEAL TO DISCIPLINE THE DISORDERLY
(2 THESS 2,13–3,18)

VASILE MIHOC

The Thessalonian correspondence belongs to an early date in St Paul's missionary work. But while 1 Thessalonians is undisputedly Pauline, many commentators deny the authenticity of 2 Thessalonians.

For us Orthodox the problem of the authorship of biblical writings is far from having the same weight as in Western Christianity. It was only after the Reformation that the Bible collection was officially constituted in the West as a revelatory authority by itself. In the patristic tradition, the authority of Scripture was intrinsically related to its being part of the revealed word of God as witnessed by the Church. The triad Scripture–Tradition–Church was not and cannot be divided. Patristic theology always understood the Holy Scriptures as testimonies of personal encounters of holy men and women with God, which were consensually accepted as having divine authority for God's community. Certainly the Holy Scriptures were and are the most important guiding sources for the Christian faith and life. But these sources reveal their true meaning only when interpreted in the Holy Spirit (divine-human synergy), i. e. in the Church considered in its theo-anthropic reality, and in the living context of the Holy Tradition.

The New Testament writings are accepted as authoritative by the Orthodox mainly because they are apostolic. The apostles were the living authority in the first century Church, and their words carried weight because of this personal authority. Thus both what they said while present and what they wrote while absent were equally to be obeyed. This is exactly what we read in 2 Thess 2,15: "Hold fast to the traditions that you were taught by us, either by word of mouth or by our letter."

The apostolic authors are not separated from their writings, for both these authors and what they wrote carry the same authority. Also, these authors are not separated from their communities, for the apostolic writings witness to the one Tradition overarching the entire Church. The apostolic message in one epistle is part of the fabric of the whole apostolic Tradition found in every Church.

The apostolic writings were accepted as Scriptures within a community that lays claim to the correct interpretation of these writings. The Holy Tradition is, as George Florovsky puts it, "Scripture rightly understood".[1]

Concerning 2 Thessalonians, in my view there are not enough – and not enough convincing – arguments against the authenticity of this epistle. We also need to keep in mind, when speaking about the authenticity of this letter, that St Paul did not write it alone, but together with his two beloved collaborators mentioned in the address: Sylvanus and Timothy. The first person plural is used almost always in the section of the letter which constitutes the subject of this paper. Most of the peculiarities of 2 Thessalonians can be easily explained – and actually must be explained – by this common authorship, and certainly also by the specific historical situation of the apostolic group and of the Church in Thessalonica at the time of its redaction.

The second Epistle to the Thessalonians deals with three main topics: persecution, a misunderstanding about the second coming of Christ, and continued disorderly behaviour on the part of certain believers. The epistle also continues the encouragement so evident in 1 Thessalonians. After its introductory part (1,1-12), 2 Thessalonians contains two main sections: first, the section with a doctrinal character, regarding the day of the Lord and the man of lawlessness (2,1-12), and second, the exhortatory section (2,13–3,15).

In this paper, I divide the section which was assigned to me by the president into two main parts: I. *Thanksgiving and Prayers* (2,13-17), and II. *Prayer and Work* (3,1-15); followed by the *Conclusion* (3,16-18).

I. THANKSGIVING AND PRAYERS (2,13-17)

In the view of Charles Wanamaker, the text in 2 Thess 2,1-2 functions as a *partitio*: it "lists the propositions or headings to be discussed in the main body of the communication".[2] V. 1 specifies the theme of the *probatio* or proof section of the argument, which is found in vv. 3-17: the *parousia* of Christ and the gathering of his followers at that time. V. 2 enumerates two interrelated issues to be argued in the *probatio*: first, that

---

1. G. FLOROVSKY, *The Function of Tradition in the Ancient Church*, in his *Bible, Church, Tradition: An Eastern Orthodox View*, Vaduz, Buchervertriebsanstalt, 1987, p. 75.
2. Charles A. WANAMAKER, *The Epistles to the Thessalonians. A Commentary on the Greek Text* (NIGTC), Grand Rapids MI, Eerdmans, 1990, p. 237.

the day of the Lord has not in fact occurred; and second, the concern for their stability in the faith.

In vv. 3-12 the first issue, i. e. that concerning the *parousia* of the Lord, is addressed.

Vv. 13-15 address the second issue, that the readers should not be "quickly shaken in mind" (v. 2a) and concerns their election by God and perseverance in the faith.

An exhortation, in v. 15, to "the traditions" they received both by the "word of mouth" and by "our letter" is followed, in vv. 16-17, by the "wish-prayer"[3] that concludes this section.

1. *Thanksgiving (2,13-14)*

There is a new thanksgiving in vv. 13-14 (cf. 1,3-12). Many scholars separate this prayer from its context and see it as imitating the second "prayer report" in 1 Thess 3,11-13. But could the letter's first recipients see it in that way? "In a document composed in uncials ('capital letters') and without breaks between either words or sentences – not to mention lacking paragraphs – the Thessalonians would have seen it for what it was almost certainly intended to be: a thanksgiving to God for them, standing in stark contrast to the immediately preceding gruesome litany of judgment and condemnation on those who are persecuting them."[4]

[13] Ἡμεῖς δὲ ὀφείλομεν εὐχαριστεῖν τῷ θεῷ πάντοτε περὶ ὑμῶν, ἀδελφοὶ ἠγαπημένοι ὑπὸ κυρίου, ὅτι εἵλατο ὑμᾶς ὁ θεὸς ἀπαρχὴν εἰς σωτηρίαν ἐν ἁγιασμῷ πνεύματος καὶ πίστει ἀληθείας,
[14] εἰς ὃ [καὶ] ἐκάλεσεν ὑμᾶς διὰ τοῦ εὐαγγελίου ἡμῶν εἰς περιποίησιν δόξης τοῦ κυρίου ἡμῶν Ἰησοῦ Χριστοῦ.

[13] But we must always give thanks to God for you, brothers and sisters beloved by the Lord, because God chose you as the first fruits for salvation through sanctification by the Spirit and through belief in the truth.
[14] For this purpose he called you through our proclamation of the good news, so that you may obtain the glory of our Lord Jesus Christ. (NRSV)[5]

---

3. Gordon P. WILES, *The Significance of the Intercessory Prayer Passages in the Letters of St Paul* (SNTSMS, 24), Cambridge, Cambridge University Press, 1974, pp. 22-107. Cf. WANAMAKER *The Epistles to the Thessalonians* (n. 2), p. 270.

4. Gordon D. FEE, *The First and Second Letters to the Thessalonians* (NICNT), Grand Rapids MI, Eerdmans, 2009, p. 298.

5. For the English translation of the biblical texts I use in general in this paper the *New Revised Standard Version* (NRSV). For the texts from 2 Thess analyzed in this paper, many times I propose more literal renderings.

V. 13. The opening words of this thanksgiving, "But we must always give thanks to God for you, brothers" (v. 13a), call to mind the prayer in 1,3, though the word order is slightly different. The authors continue to have a sense of divine compulsion to thank God for the believers in Thessalonica. The singular difference between the way this prayer begins and the earlier one is that to the vocative "brothers" (ἀδελφοί) the letter has here added "beloved by the Lord" (ἠγαπημένοι ὑπὸ κυρίου). In many ways this is a most remarkable addition, which is also – because of the language here used – thoroughly Pauline. Indeed, if in the opening thanksgiving of the first letter (1,4), St Paul's language echoes Deut 7,7-8 regarding Israel's constitution as Yahweh's people ("loved by God/chosen"), here the same reality is expressed in terms of ἠγαπημένοι ὑπὸ κυρίου, which is precisely the language of the Septuagint found in the blessing of Benjamin in Deut 33,12. "This [writes G. Fee] can hardly have been accidental, since we know from other places in Paul's letters that he himself was a Benjaminite (Rom 11,1; Phil 3,5), something concerning which he takes a measure of pride. What he has done, therefore, whether they would have caught it or not, is to bestow on these 'beloved' friends his own ancestral blessing: they 'are loved by the Lord'."[6]

The grounds (there is a ὅτι clause here) for thanksgiving are now different as compared with those in 1,3-12. In opposition (δέ, v. 13a)[7] to those not believing the truth from the preceding verse, the situation of the "brothers beloved by the Lord" offers the apostle and his collaborators (ἡμεῖς) good reason for giving thanks to God. "Lord", somewhat unexpected here, refers to Jesus.[8] It is true that in 1 Thess 1,4 we read

---

6. FEE, *1 and 2 Thess* (n. 4), p. 299.
7. There is clearly a contrast here, as generally is understood by the exegetes. The particle δέ is neither resumptive, referring back to 1,3 (so Martin DIBELIUS, *Die Briefe des Apostels Paulus. II. Die Neuen Kleinen Briefe* (HNT), Tübingen, Mohr, 1913, p. 34), nor simply transitional (cf. Ernest BEST, *A Commentary on the First and Second Epistles to the Thessalonians* (BNTC), London, A&C Black, ²1977, p. 311). It indicates the opposition between the destinataries of the epistle and those mentioned in v. 12.
8. That this refers to Christ and not to God (contra Béda RIGAUX, *Saint Paul: Les Épîtres aux Thessaloniciens* (ÉtB), Paris, Gabalda, 1956, p. 371; Abraham J. MALHERBE, *The Letters to the Thessalonians* (AB, 32B), New York, Doubleday, 2000, p. 436; Gene L. GREEN, *The Letters to the Thessalonians* (Pillar New Testament Commentary), Grand Rapids/Leicester, Eerdmans, 2002, p. 325; G. K. BEALE, *1-2 Thessalonians* (IVP New Testament Commentary Series), Downers Grove IL/Leicester: InterVarsity Press, 2003, p. 225) seems certain both from Pauline usage (cf. Rom 8,35; 2 Cor 5,14; Gal 2,20), and on the basis of the grammar in the present sentence. "Had Paul intended ὑπὸ κυρίου to equal the preceding τῷ θεῷ, then the simple, ordinary composition of such a sentence would have been: τῷ θεῷ ...

ἀδελφοὶ ἠγαπημένοι ὑπὸ θεοῦ ("brothers beloved by God") and in 2 Thess 2,16 God the Father is said to be ὁ ἀγαπήσας ἡμᾶς ("the one who loved us"). But the idea of the love of Christ for his disciples is also known to St Paul,[9] and is regularly associated with certainty regarding salvation. And St Paul almost always uses "Lord" in relation to Jesus rather than God, and in fact he does so in the following verse.

The addressees can be called "beloved of the Lord", because God "chose" (or "elected") them "from the beginning". The theme of God's election of his Church from eternity is also found elsewhere in St Paul (see esp. Rom 8,28-30; Eph 1,4-5). It has Old Testament roots in God's election of Israel (see Deut 7,6-8, a. o.), that is called "beloved of Him [God]" (*Bar* 3,37). The goal of God's election is "salvation" (σωτηρία), "a comprehensive indication of the bliss of the coming age, which is, in Paul's view, already a reality in the present condition of faith (see, e.g., 2 Cor 6,2)."[10] But it is evident in this letter that its main interest is in future salvation (2,10).

This new thanksgiving has in fact the function "to reassure the readers of their salvation in the face of the eschatological dangers discussed in vv. 3-12",[11] based on the fact that God has chosen or elected them (ὅτι εἵλατο[12] ὑμᾶς ὁ θεός). Understanding the precise purpose of God's election depends on the textual tradition we follow: some texts (B F G^{gr} P 33 81 syr^h cop^{bo}, etc.) read ἀπαρχὴν εἰς σωτηρίαν ("as firstfruits for salvation"); others (ℵ D K L Ψ 104 181 syr^p cop^{sa}, etc.) have ἀπ' ἀρχῆς εἰς σωτηρίαν ("from the beginning for salvation"). The textual evidence seems to be against ἀπ' ἀρχῆς ("from the beginning") and to favor the reading ἀπαρχήν (cf. *Novum Testamentum Graece* of

---

ἠγαπημένοι ὑπὸ αὐτοῦ, ὅτι εἵλατο ὑμᾶς ἀπαρχήν ('to God, ...loved by him, because he chose you as firstfruits'). Thus the awkward repetition of 'God' as the subject of Paul's sentence occurs precisely because in the meantime he has mentioned a second subject ('the Lord'), thus necessitating his return to the first noun" (FEE, *1 and 2 Thess* [n. 4], p. 300, note 98; cf. J. B. LIGHTFOOT, *Notes on the Epistles of St Paul*, London, Macmillan, 1895, p. 119; BEST, *1 and 2 Thess.* [n. 7], p. 311; I. Howard MARSHALL, *I and II Thessalonians* (NCB), Grand Rapids, Eerdmans, 1983, p. 206).

9. As Jesus did not distinguish his activity from that of God, so St Paul regards the love of God as basically one with that of his Christ (Rom 8,37; 2 Thess 2,16). See also the preceding footnote, and note 18.

10. M. J. J. MENKEN, *2 Thessalonians*, London, Routledge, 1994, p. 120.

11. WANAMAKER, *The Epistles to the Thessalonians* (n. 2), p. 265.

12. The verb αἱρέομαι (εἵλατο is indicative aorist middle 3rd person singular from αἱρέομαι), "to choose", "to elect", is not very common in St Paul's letters, occurring only in Phil 1,22, where it is used of a personal choice confronting the apostle. The verb is used of God's election of Israel in one text in the LXX, Deut 26,18.

Nestle-Aland, 27th ed.). But the reading ἀπ' ἀρχῆς makes good sense in the context, because of the strong emphasis in this passage on God's prior activity (where he is contrasting the Thessalonians' "salvation" – and thus their security – with the "judgment" of the deceived in vv. 10-12). In this understanding, St Paul would be assuring them that God's choice of them is "from the beginning [of time]" (cf. 1 Cor 2,7; Col 1,26; Eph 1,4). This is good encouragement indeed. With the majority of commentators we accept the reading ἀπ' ἀρχῆς, meaning the fact that "from the beginning God's purpose was to save the elect".[13]

There is no specification of the nature of the divine salvation (δόξα, as one dimension of this salvation, is mentioned in the next verse). The two phrases governed by the preposition ἐν, i. e. ἁγιασμῷ πνεύματος ("sanctification of the Spirit") and πίστει ἀληθείας ("faith of the truth"), describe the means by which this salvation is acquired by the believers. There is first the divine dimension of the salvation: πνεύματος is a subjective genitive referring to the work of the Holy Spirit in the sanctification of the people of God. A (theologically) more precise translation would be therefore "sanctification *by* the Spirit", because God's Spirit is here the subject of the sanctification.[14] But there is also a human response to this divine work of salvation: this response consists in the "faith in the truth" (literally "of the truth").[15] God's sanctifying work by the Spirit has precedence over the human activity of belief in

---

13. WANAMAKER, *The Epistles to the Thessalonians* (n. 2), p. 266. Also "firstfruits" (ἀπαρχήν) is an encouraging word, but in a different way. This reading would mean that the addressees are to see themselves as God's "firstfruits" *in Thessalonica*. "This imagery [writes G. Fee, whose option is for ἀπαρχήν] would function in two directions. First, it is intended to encourage them right in the midst of those who are responsible for their present grief, who are described in our verses 10–12 as to their wickedness and eventual ruin... Second, and at the same time, it would therefore also function to encourage them that God has chosen still others from among their Thessalonian compatriots, who also shall escape the deception and resultant judgment and be 'sanctified by the Spirit, as they believe the truth.' If the believing community is relatively small and currently heavily persecuted, they need to hear from the divine perspective – that is, from the perspective of 'God's having chosen them for salvation' – that there are still more, even from among their own townspeople, who will join them for obtaining the glory of our Lord Jesus Christ'." (FEE, *1 and 2 Thess* [n. 4], p. 302).

14. "Spirit" is here the Holy Spirit, and not the human spirit (cf. 1 Thess 5,23). The sanctification comes from God (cf. 1 Thess 4,3-8; 5,23) and it is elsewhere attributed by St Paul to the work of the Holy Spirit (Rom 15,16; cf. 1 Cor 6,11).

15. The word "truth" was also used in the previous section, in relation to those who refused to believe in the truth (vv. 10, 12); ἀληθείας ("truth") "is probably an objective genitive indicating that to which faith is directed" (WANAMAKER, *The Epistles to the Thessalonians* [n. 2], p. 267).

(or, of) the gospel.[16] The idea of the divine-human synergy for our salvation – fundamental in Orthodox soteriology – seems to be alluded to in this last part of v. 13.

In v. 13, St Paul joins in one sentence the divine activities of God (the Father), Christ (the Son), and the Spirit: the Thessalonians have been *chosen and called by God...*; have been evidenced by the fact that they are *loved by the Lord*; and are thus *saved through the sanctifying work of the Spirit*. We have here what G. Fee identifies as a "proto-Trinitarian formula".[17] But this author continues: "what is striking here is not what is said about God, since throughout the Pauline corpus both 'election' and 'calling' are regularly attributed to God the Father. What is striking, rather, is that language usually reserved for God the Father is here freely attributed to 'the Lord', and that language usually attributed to Christ is the special province of the Holy Spirit[18]... Thus in its second appearance in the corpus, God's love for his elect people is expressed in terms of their being loved by Christ the Lord, an attribute that in Paul's thinking is thus equally shared by Father and Son – by presupposition and without argumentation."[19]

---

16. Cf. BEST, *1 and 2 Thessalonians* (n. 7), p. 315). The sanctifying work of the Spirit and the Christians belief in the truth are the two dimensions of the salvation. As G. Fee righly notes, "Paul's word order in this case is both explicable and significant. Their becoming believers is first of all the result of God's 'sanctifying work'...; their role has been to 'believe the truth'... Thus this unique moment [that is, the moment of their coming to faith] is neither 'un-Pauline', as many assert, nor unlike the Paul of Romans and Galatians, as others seem to be anxious about. This is simply typical Paul, whose way of speaking about the saving work of Christ is regularly in response to the current situation into which he is writing" (FEE, *1 and 2 Thess* [n. 4], p. 303).

17. This formula "is borrowed from Stanley Porter (in I. H. MARSHALL, *Beyond the Bible: Moving from Scripture to Theology*, Grand Rapids, Baker, 2004, p. 122 n. 59) as a way of designating those texts where Paul himself, rigorous monotheist though he was, joins Father, Son, and Spirit in ways that indicate the full identity of the Son and Spirit with the Father, while not losing that monotheism" (FEE, *1 and 2 Thess* [n. 4], p. 300, note 96).

18. In the other five instances where St Paul speaks of Christ's love (Gal 2,20; 2 Cor 5,14; Rom 8,35; Eph 3,19; 5,2), it is regularly tied explicitly to the love expressed in his redemptive death (e.g., Gal 2,20, "the Son of God, ... who loved me and gave himself for me"). More commonly the apostle speaks of the love *of God*, as the subject of salvation. In 2 Thess 2,13, "even though the phrase 'loved by the Lord' is probably an allusion to Christ's saving work on the cross, rather than the subject of their salvation as when it is said of the Father, it is nonetheless remarkable that this particular attribution takes place in one of Paul's triadic ways of speaking about salvation. It has been suggested with considerable insight that the reason for the shift of language in this case is for it to stand in deliberate contrast to what the same Lord Jesus will do to those whom he 'will ... destroy by the splendor of his coming' (v. 8)" (FEE, *1 and 2 Thess* [n. 4], p. 301).

19. FEE, *1 and 2 Thess* (n. 4), pp. 300-301.

V. 14. The subject of the relative clause εἰς ὃ [καὶ] ἐκάλεσεν ὑμᾶς διὰ τοῦ εὐαγγελίου ἡμῶν ("for this purpose [also] he called you through our gospel") is God. Once more is stated the truth of the divine initiative in the salvation of the believers. And if the aorist εἵλατο in v. 13b was used for an action of God "from the beginning", a new aorist, ἐκάλεσεν ("called") does not refer to some remote act on God's part, but to the precise moment of their calling by God to share in Christ's salvation through St Paul's and his colleagues' preaching of the gospel in Thessalonica (cf. 1 Thess 2,12; 4,7; 5,23). Their calling was expressed διὰ τοῦ εὐαγγελίου ἡμῶν ("through our gospel"), says the apostle, because there is no hearing of the gospel and faith in it without the apostolic preaching: "But how are they to call on one in whom they have not believed? And how are they to believe in one of whom they have never heard? And how are they to hear without someone to proclaim him?" (Rom 10,14).[20]

If the "salvation" in v. 13 is referring also to the present situation of the believers, now (in v. 14b) the aim of this calling is the eschatological glory. By the phrase εἰς περιποίησιν δόξης τοῦ κυρίου ἡμῶν Ἰησοῦ Χριστοῦ ("for obtaining the glory of our Lord Jesus Christ"), the authors speak about the eschatological salvation, including Christ's return in glory and the participation of the saved people in his eternal glory. What is said here is a common and fundamental idea of St Paul's doctrine (cf. Rom 8,17.29f.; 1 Cor 15,42; 2 Cor 3,18; Phil 3,21; 1 Thess 2,12).

On three other occasions St Paul speaks of Christ in terms of "glory",[21] but when this word is used as the eschatological goal of Christian redemption, it ordinarily refers to "the glory of God the Father", as in 1 Thess 2,12 ("...God, who calls you into his own kingdom and glory"; cf. Phil 1,11; 2,11).

"Glory" is a common Old Testament word that gives expression to the sheer majesty of the eternal God, unshared by any other, and to the wonder evoked by that majesty. It is Yahweh's "glory" that Moses desired to see (Exod 33,18), and which then filled the tabernacle (40,35)

---

20. Trilling's assertion that the real Paul could not have written v. 14a because he reserved the call to salvation exclusively to God cannot be sustained. In Gal 1,6f., for example, clearly appears the connection between the call of God and the preaching of the gospel; see also Rom 10,14-17 (W. TRILLING, *Untersuchungen zum 2. Thessalonicherbrief*, Leipzig, 1972, p. 122).

21. In 1 Cor 2,8: "None of the rulers of this age understood this; for if they had, they would not have crucified the Lord of glory"; 2 Cor 3,18: "And all of us, with unveiled faces, seeing the glory of the Lord as though reflected in a mirror, are being transformed into the same image from one degree of glory to another; for this comes from the Lord, the Spirit"; and 2 Cor 4,4: "...to keep them from seeing the light of the gospel of the glory of Christ, who is the image of God".

and the temple (1 Ki 8,11). Indeed, Yahweh expressly says that he will *not* share his glory with another (Isa 42,8; 48,11, referring in this case to other "gods"). "But precisely because the divine Son already shares that glory, Paul can easily speak in such terms. In this instance, to be sure, the phrase most likely has to do with Christ's own present exaltation to glory, following his humiliation in death, an exaltation in which the Thessalonians will have a share. But even so, this attribution to Christ of language usually reserved for God is a remarkable way of speaking of the final goal of the Thessalonians' redemption".[22]

Two summary remarks on vv. 13-14:

(a) First, it is remarkable what this passage says about Christ and his work. The prominence of Jesus in this prayer indicates the high Christology characteristic of the letter. The already mentioned proto-Triadology of the passage is closely related to this high Christology.

(b) It clearly appears that the "brothers" who were to be the first readers of this letter were, according to vv. 13-14, a clearly differentiated and privileged group, "with a particular history and a glorious destiny (which links the thanks to the previous material about the End)".[23] They are "brothers beloved by the Lord", whom God (as in OT traditions of divine election) chose "from the beginning for salvation through sanctification by the Spirit and [through] belief in the truth" (v. 13). God called them to this through Paul's gospel, in order to obtain "the glory of our Lord Jesus Christ" (v. 14). The fundamental purpose of these descriptions is to provide clear answer to the always vital question "Who are we?" The word "sanctification" in particular helps to distinguish them and their present experience from the welter of idolatry and immorality implied as characteristic of the world outside the group.

2. *εἴτε διὰ λόγου εἴτε δι' ἐπιστολῆς ἡμῶν. The "word of mouth" and "our letter", equally authoritative (2,15)*

> [15] ἄρα οὖν, ἀδελφοί, στήκετε, καὶ κρατεῖτε τὰς παραδόσεις ἃς ἐδιδάχθητε εἴτε διὰ λόγου εἴτε δι' ἐπιστολῆς ἡμῶν.
>
> [15] So then, brothers and sisters, stand firm and hold fast to the traditions that you were taught by us, either by word of mouth or by our letter. (NRSV)

---

22. FEE, *1 and 2 Thess* (n. 4), p. 304.
23. Philip F. ESLER, *2 Thessalonians*, in John MUDDIMAN and John BARTON (eds), *The Pauline Epistles*, Oxford, Oxford University Press, 2010, p. 241.

V. 15 is an exhortation for the readers to live according to the apostolic tradition they have received. Again the believers are addressed as "brothers" (ἀδελφοί). The ἄρα οὖν at the beginning of this exhortation indicates it as an inference from what precedes. The content of v. 15 points to the inference being the real point of the argument in ch. 2: the believers in Thessalonica must keep the apostolic teaching regarding the second coming of Christ – what James Dunn calls a "kerygmatic tradition"[24] – and live accordingly. "The fact that the command to keep these traditions represents an inference drawn from the discussion of salvation in vv. 13f. implies that nothing less than the salvation of the Thessalonians depended on their holding of these traditions".[25]

There are two imperatives in this verse: (1) στήκετε ("stand firm"), probably an allusion back to v. 2, where the authors express their worry that the Thessalonians might be "quickly shaken in mind or alarmed" through some false teaching or prophecy regarding the day of the Lord; and (2) κρατεῖτε ("hold fast"), with the explicit object τὰς παραδόσεις ἃς ἐδιδάχθητε εἴτε διὰ λόγου εἴτε δι' ἐπιστολῆς ἡμῶν ("the traditions that you were taught by us, either by word of mouth or by our letter").

The technical terminology for the tradition (παράδοσις), for the passing on of the tradition (παραδίδωμι, "to transmit", "to hand down"), and the reception of tradition (παραλαμβάνω, "to receive") is used on several occasions in St Paul's letters (e. g., 1 Cor 11,2; 11,23-25; 15,1-3; 1 Thess 4,1; 2 Thess 3,6; cf. Phil 4,9). This "demonstrates that the communication of tradition was a regular feature in Paul's missionary activity".[26]

The concept of "tradition" (παράδοσις) has, in St Paul's letters, a Jewish background, as is evident from Gal 1,14 (cf. Mark 7,1-13 and parallel). In the tractate *Aboth* from the *Mishnah*, we find the following characteristic passage: "Moses received the Torah from Sinai and transmitted it to Joshua, and Joshua to the Elders, and the Elders to the

---

24. According to James DUNN, *Unity and Diversity in the New Testament: An Inquiry into the Character of Earliest Christianity*, London, SCM, 1977, pp. 66-69, three types of tradition may be isolated in Paul: 1) kerygmatic tradition, that is, tradition concerning the central gospel message (e. g., 1 Cor 15,1-3); 2) church tradition, that is, tradition passed on to govern the practice of the church (e. g., 1 Cor 11,23-25); and 3) ethical tradition, that is, tradition dealing with proper behaviour for Christians (e. g., 1 Cor 7,10; 11,2; 1 Thess 4,1). But are there not actually, all of these, in a way or another, "kerygmatic" traditions?
25. WANAMAKER, *The Epistles to the Thessalonians* (n. 2), p. 268.
26. WANAMAKER, *The Epistles to the Thessalonians* (n. 2), p. 268.

Prophets, and the Prophets transmitted it to the men of the Great Synagogue" (*Aboth* 1,1).[27] In the sequel to this passage, the chain of tradition appears to go on also after "the men of the Great Synagogue".[28]

The faith traditions, including (in this specific case) those regarding the coming of Christ, had been taught to them by the apostle and his collaborators[29] in two ways. But all these traditions that they received by word (διὰ λόγου), or by letter (δι' ἐπιστολῆς ἡμῶν) are equally authoritative and binding on them, as εἴτε...εἴτε ("whether... or") indicates. In δι' ἐπιστολῆς ἡμῶν most exegetes see a reference to 1 Thessalonians.[30] Some think that the reference to the present letter cannot be excluded, taking 2 Thessalonians as, chronologically, the first letter of St Paul to the Church in Thessalonica.[31] There are, however, good reasons for seeing 2 Thessalonians as coming *after* 1 Thessalonians and for understanding δι' ἐπιστολῆς ἡμῶν in 2 Thess 2,15 as a reference to a letter previously written to the Thessalonians. The most natural assumption is that this letter was 1 Thessalonians. It is likely that the original recipients of 2 Thessalonians would have interpreted the letter mentioned here as 1 Thessalonians. And the oral proclamation referred to was presumably the teaching they had already received from St Paul and his disciples.

---

27. In Hebrew, the general name for tradition is *masoret*. It is found in Ezek 20,37 and means originally "bond" "fetter". "Tradition is the discipline which establishes the correct practice and interpretation of the Torah and was therefore regarded as a hedge or fetter about the Law (*Abot* 3,14). Since this knowledge was handed down by successive generations, it was also associated with the Hebrew word *masor*, denoting 'to give over'." (Leon J. YAGOD, Tradition, in *Encyclopaedia Judaica*, second edition, vol. 20, Keter Publishing House, 2007, p. 88). In the Talmudic literature, the term *masoret* is used to include all forms of tradition, both those which relate to the Bible and those which concern custom, law, historical events, folkways, and other subjects.

28. "According to rabbinic Judaism, the teaching of the great sages in every generation in keeping with the *halakhah* is binding (Deut 17,88). Thus, the transmitters of tradition included the successors to the Men of the Great Synagogue down to modern times..." (Leon J. YAGOD, Tradition [n. 27], p. 89).

29. ἡμῶν is most probably referring as much to λόγου as to ἐπιστολῆς.

30. So, for example, Ernst von DOBSCHÜTZ, *Die Thessalonicher-Briefe* (KEK, 10), Göttingen, Vandenhoeck & Ruprecht, 1909, neu herausgegeben mit einem Literaturverzeichnis von Otto Merk, 1974, p. 301; James E. FRAME, *A Critical and Exegetical Commentary on the Epistles of St Paul to the Thessalonians*, Edinburgh: T&T Clark, 1912, p. 285; BEST, *1 and 2 Thessalonians* (n. 7), p. 318, and others.

31. So, for example, WANAMAKER, *The Epistles to the Thessalonians* (n. 2), who largely discusses the issue in his Introduction ("The Sequence of the Thessalonisan Correspondence", pp. 37-45), with this definite conclusion: "In light of this discussion, we can say that the available evidence actually supports the priority of 2 Thessalonians" (p. 45).

3. *Prayer (3,16-17)*

¹⁶ Αὐτὸς δὲ ὁ κύριος ἡμῶν Ἰησοῦς Χριστὸς καὶ [ὁ] θεὸς ὁ πατὴρ ἡμῶν ὁ ἀγαπήσας ἡμᾶς καὶ δοὺς παράκλησιν αἰωνίαν καὶ ἐλπίδα ἀγαθὴν ἐν χάριτι,
¹⁷ παρακαλέσαι ὑμῶν τὰς καρδίας καὶ στηρίξαι ἐν παντὶ ἔργῳ καὶ λόγῳ ἀγαθῷ.

¹⁶ Now may our Lord Jesus Christ himself and God our Father, who loved us and through grace gave us eternal comfort and good hope,
¹⁷ comfort your hearts and strengthen them in every good work and word. (NRSV)

After the exhortation in v. 15, the "wish prayer"[32] in vv. 16-17 comes as a conclusion of all of 2,1-17. Clear Pauline theology is also at home here.[33] This prayer's perspective is both past and present: first the authors look back to what "our Lord Jesus Christ himself and God the Father" did for the believers ("who loved us and through grace gave us eternal comfort and good hope"); then they pray for the readers' encouragement and strengthening "in every good work and word".

This prayer looks very much similar to the prayer in 1 Thess 3,11-13: in both the prayer is addressed to God the Father and the Lord Jesus Christ; in both we have a compound subject ("God the Father" and "Lord Jesus Christ") with a singular verb – which is of high theological (Christological) significance, the apostle praying together to God the Father and Christ, and to one or the other separately;[34] both prayers begin with the intensive αὐτός ("himself"), which seems to go grammatically with the first subject, although, given the singular verb, it may be taken as a collective singular; in both cases the elaboration is directed toward the second addressee of the prayer (but grammatical subject of the sentence): "the Lord" in 1 Thess 3,11, "God the Father" in the 2 Thess 2,16; both prayers share as a basic concern that the Thessalonians will be "strengthened".[35]

---

32. WILES, *The Significance of the Intercessory Prayer* (n. 3), pp. 22-107; cf. WANAMAKER, *The Epistles to the Thessalonians* (n. 2), p. 270.
33. This prayer, says G. FEE, *1 and 2 Thess* (n. 4), p. 306, "is full of striking moments regarding Pauline theology, and especially his Christology".
34. The suggestion of Frederick F. BRUCE, *1 & 2 Thessalonians* (WBC, 45), Waco, Word, 1982, p. 71, that "with two subjects the verb commonly agrees with the nearer of the two", is not convincing.
35. Cf. FEE, *1 and 2 Thess* (n. 4), pp. 307-308.

But there are also striking differences between the two. The most significant difference, of course, is that the two grammatical subjects are reversed in the present passage, so that the emphasis seems to lie with the first member, especially since in both cases this member is accompanied by the intensive pronoun αὐτός ("may our God and Father *himself* and our Lord" / "may our Lord Jesus Christ *himself* and God our Father"). If we had only one of these prayers, we could understand that the emphasis in prayer is on the first one being addressed. "But having both prayers, with their *reversal of order* and with the continuation of prayer addressed only to the *second* member, would seem to prevent that".[36]

Maybe Beda Rigaux is right when he proposes that Christ's name precedes that of God here because the context is Christological in its orientation.[37] "Our Lord Jesus Christ", put at first, the αὐτός accompanying this first subject, makes the prayer in 2 Thess 2,16-17 significantly different from that in 1 Thess 3,11-13. True, God our Father is said to be the one who "loved us and through grace gave us eternal comfort and good hope". "But then the two verbs that make up the actual prayer are (grammatically) assumed to be the joint action of the Lord Jesus and God the Father".[38] In the most natural way, the equality of Christ with God is put forward. It appears that the only theological significance to be attached to the variations in order is that there is complete equality in apostle's mind between the Father and the Son.

The apostle's petition for the Thessalonians in this prayer is twofold. First, he prays for them that God παρακαλέσαι ὑμῶν τὰς καρδίας ("comfort your hearts"). παρακαλέσαι is an aorist singular optative (as also στηρίξαι of the second petition). As has already been noted, the singular of the two verbs here raises a problem since they have two subjects ("our Lord Jesus Christ and God our Father"). The verb παρακαλέσαι is a cognate of the noun παράκλησις from the previous phrase (v. 16b) and has the sense of "to encourage", "to comfort". "Comforting the hearts" describes a specific action of God in (on) the inner being of the believers. The particular situation of persecution the Thessalonians are facing now (cf. 1,4) makes them in special need of such an encouragement from God.

But the apostle's prayer concerns both the inward state of his converts and their outward behaviour. The second request of this prayer is that

---

36. FEE, *1 and 2 Thess* (n. 4), p. 308.
37. RIGAUX, *Les Épîtres aux Thessaloniciens* (n. 8), p. 690.
38. FEE, *1 and 2 Thess* (n. 4), p. 308.

God στηρίξαι ἐν παντὶ ἔργῳ καὶ λόγῳ ἀγαθῷ ("strengthen [them] in every good work and word"). The implied object of στηρίξαι may be either "you" or a repetition of "your hearts". This second petition is bringing them back to everyday life: the authors pray God to strengthen the readers (or their hearts) both in every good work (ἐν παντὶ ἔργῳ), and in every good[39] word (καὶ λόγῳ ἀγαθῷ). Good works and good doctrine (evidently the meaning of "good word" here) are inseparable in the life of Christians. At the same time the text is now almost certainly also pointing toward 3,6-15. The prayer functions therefore "both as a form of encouragement under present duress and as (a subtle form of) exhortation regarding their perseverance under that duress".[40]

II. Prayer and Work (3,1-15)

What we propose, with other exegetes, as concerning the partition of the letter, is that with 3,1 the *exhortation* begins.[41]

To some scholars the materials in 2,13-17 and 3,1-5 seem to be unconnected with the two major concerns of the letter, viz. the timing of the day of the Lord (2,1-12), and the continued misbehavior of the disorderly/idle (3,6-15). But looking closer, it appears that the thanksgiving in 2,13-14, the exhortation that follows in 2,15, and the prayer in 2,16-17 "serve nicely to bring the issue about the timing of the day of the Lord to a fitting conclusion".[42] And 3,1-5 is a good introduction to the second theme.

The final chapter of this letter closes the Thessalonian correspondence on a balanced note of "spiritual pragmatism". The first focus is on prayer. The author asks his readers to pray for him (3,1-4). In addition, the author prays for those readers (3,5). The second focus is on work, so important for subsistence itself and for the health of the artisan Church community in Thessalonica (3,6-12). The life of faith has always rested

---

39. The adjectifs παντί ("every") and ἀγαθῷ ("good") are intended to go with both nouns, as the NIV rightly has it.
40. Fee, *1 and 2 Thess* (n. 4), p. 309.
41. Some include 3,1-5 in the *probatio* (so R. Jewett, *The Thesalonian Correspondence: Pauline Rhetoric and Millenarian Piety*, Philadelphia, Fortress, 1986, pp. 81-87), based on the supposition that τὸ λοιπόν should be understood inferentially ("therefore").
42. Fee, *1 and 2 Thess* (n. 4), p. 310. Best, *1 and 2 Thessalonians* (n. 7), p. 322, sees this pericope as "somewhat loosely attached to the preceding context and the following". "Perhaps he was interrupted in his composition of the letter after 2,17, and in returning to the letter did not give enough care to continuing his train of thought smoothly, or perhaps he originally intended to end the letter at v. 5 but then for some reason continued it": Wanamaker, *The Epistles to the Thessalonians* (n. 2), pp. 273-274

between these two poles, prayer and work. The famous principle of *ora et labora* finds in this section of the letter one of its clearest expressions. Injunctions regarding an appropriate work ethic are given. The closing words of this section provide additional instructions for the community (3,13-15).

1. *Introduction (3,1-5)*

The exhortation in 3,1-5 has a general character. If "roughly composed",[43] this pericope is no less important and rich in content. It seems intended to be a *captatio benevolentiae*, its role being to gain a good hearing from all the readers, and their obedience to the command that follows.[44] Having already dealt with the doctrinal issue regarding the day of the Lord, the writers now turn to the second major issue, that of the disorders some people were creating in the Church of Thessalonica. In any case, these verses constitute the transition to the next section. The letter's writers start this section by asking the readers' prayer on their behalf (vv. 1-2a), and offering the reason why they need this prayer (v. 2b), then make the affirmation of Christ's own faithfulness (v. 3) and the believers' readiness to do what is right (v. 4), ending with a prayer on their behalf (v. 5). "What is striking [notes Fee] especially after the preceding prayer (in 2,16–17), is the absolute Christocentricity of this passage."[45]

(a) *"Pray for us" (3,1-2)*

¹ Τὸ λοιπὸν προσεύχεσθε, ἀδελφοί, περὶ ἡμῶν, ἵνα ὁ λόγος τοῦ κυρίου τρέχῃ καὶ δοξάζηται καθὼς καὶ πρὸς ὑμᾶς,
² καὶ ἵνα ῥυσθῶμεν ἀπὸ τῶν ἀτόπων καὶ πονηρῶν ἀνθρώπων· οὐ γὰρ πάντων ἡ πίστις.

¹ Finally, brothers and sisters pray for us, so that the word of the Lord may spread rapidly and be glorified everywhere, just as it is among you,
² and that we may be rescued from wicked and evil people; for not all have faith. (NRSV)

---

43. WANAMAKER, *The Epistles to the Thessalonians* (n. 2), p. 273. TRILLING, *Untersuchungen zum 2. Thessalonicherbrief* (n. 20), p. 134, sees this roughness as a result of the inability of a later writer imitating 1 Thess 4,1-2 to provide a convincing specific occasion for the request for prayer in 2 Thess 3,1.
44. Cf. FRAME, *Epistles of St Paul to the Thessalonians* (n. 30), p. 288; FEE, *1 and 2 Thess* (n. 4), p. 311.
45. FEE, *1 and 2 Thess* (n. 4), p. 312.

V. 1. The word "finally" (τὸ λοιπόν) marks the transition to a new section[46] that is to the instruction (exhortatory) section of the letter.[47] As in most of St Paul's writings, the last part of 2 Thess is devoted to ethical instruction, called *paraenesis*. Some commentators see this section as the concluding paragraph to the prayer mode begun at 2,13. In my view, the word "finally" rather directs the reader to the concluding thoughts of the writer, which are shaped into a combined language of prayer and instruction.

In vv. 1-2 the readers are asked to pray for the progress of the gospel, so that the word of the Lord might run as a runner speeds on to the finish line. They are also asked to pray specifically for the messengers of the gospel, that they might be delivered from wicked and evil people (2a), "for not all have faith", i. e. not all respond to the message of the gospel (οὐ γὰρ πάντων ἡ πίστις, lit. "the faith is not of all", 2b). The words προσεύχεσθε, ἀδελφοί, περὶ ἡμῶν are identical to the demand in 1 Thess 5,25, where, however, the content of the prayer is not specified. The plural περὶ ἡμῶν ("for us"), often used as a polite literary plural, in this text is almost certainly intended to refer to all three of the authors of this letter, Paul, Silvanus, and Timothy,[48] but probably also for all those who are now with them in Corinth. The demand is that the readers pray not actually only for them, but for the progress of the gospel, ἵνα ὁ λόγος τοῦ κυρίου τρέχῃ καὶ δοξάζηται καθὼς καὶ πρὸς ὑμᾶς ("that the word of the Lord may spread rapidly and be glorified everywhere, just as it is among you").

The expression ὁ λόγος τοῦ κυρίου ("the word of the Lord") appears only in 1 and 2 Thessalonians among the Pauline letters (cf. 1 Thess 1,8; 4,15). "The Lord" is used here for Christ,[49] so that the expression here

---

46. Many critics arguing for a rhetorical structure to the letter regard v. 1 as beginning its *exhortatio* (WANAMAKER, *The Epistles to the Thessalonians* [n. 2], *ad loc.*, and others). Epistolary theorists tend to see here the beginning of a series of moral admonitions (JEWETT, *The Thesalonian Correspondence* [n. 41], pp. 224–5).

47. For some exegetes, vv. 1-5 seem to lie unconnected between the two major concerns of the letter: the timing of the day of the Lord (2,1-12) and the continued misbehavior of the disruptive/idle (3,6-15). But the τὸ λοιπόν at the beginning of ch. 3 clearly indicates the transition to the concluding section of the letter. And, as G. FEE, writes, "the preceding thanksgiving (2,13-14), final exhortation (2,15), and prayer (2,16-17) serve nicely to bring the issue about the timing of the day of the Lord to a fitting conclusion" (*1 and 2 Thess* [n. 4], p 310).

48. Cf. FEE, *1 and 2 Thess* (n. 4), p. 313.

49. A few mss (G P 33 489 927 vgmss) read θεοῦ here instead of κυρίου. "This could have been the result either of careless copying as such (we are dealing with a single letter [ΘΥ/ΚΥ]) or of expectation, at a time when the *nomina sacra* were consistently abbreviated

used is synonymous with "the gospel of Christ", a formula recurring quite frequently in Paul (cf. Rom 15,19; 1 Cor 9,12; 2 Cor 2,12; 9,13; 10,14; Gal 2,7; Phil 1,27; 1 Thess 3,2; 2 Thess 1,8).

The unusual use of τρέχειν with a non-human subject, for the rapid progress of the Christian mission, may be influenced by Ps 147,4 (LXX), ἕως τάχους δραμεῖται ὁ λόγος αὐτοῦ, a text speaking of God's word running swiftly. They are also asked to pray that the word of the Lord might be honoured or glorified (δοξάζηται) everywhere as it is in the Church in Thessalonica (cf. Acts 13,48). This second object of prayer means, together with the rapid spread of the word of the Lord, its acceptance in faith. The end of this verse, which is verbless in Greek, has, most probably, a present reference: "just as *it is* among you".

In v. 2, closely related with the two previously mentioned objects of the prayer of the Thessalonians, there is a third one: the authors of the letter ask for prayer ἵνα ῥυσθῶμεν ἀπὸ τῶν ἀτόπων καὶ πονηρῶν ἀνθρώπων ("that we may be rescued from wicked and evil people"). This clause clearly echoises the language of Isa 25,4, where the Septuagint differs considerably from the traditional Hebrew text, reading (in part), ἀπὸ ἀνθρώπων πονηρῶν ῥύσῃ αὐτούς ("from wicked people you will deliver them"). The verb ῥύεσθαι, used in 1 Thess 1,10 of divine eschatological deliverance or salvation, here means the deliverance or preservation from human forces who oppose the preaching of the word. There is a close parallel of this second use of the verb ῥύεσθαι in 2 Cor 1,8-11, with a similar request for prayer to expedite St Paul's deliverance from his adversaries. The passive voice of ῥυσθῶμεν in our verse means that the authors of this letter see God as the actor of this deliverance from their opponents.

The adversaries are described as τῶν ἀτόπων καὶ πονηρῶν ἀνθρώπων ("wicked and evil people"). The two adjectives are virtually synonymous. Together they present those adversaries as morally depraved and malicious. It is impossible from this description alone to say if the authors are referring specifically to the Jewish opposition, or to another category of opponents. What is clear is that there is here a case of vilification of those who oppose the preaching of the gospel.[50]

The final clause in v. 2 is not easy to translate as the genitive πάντων lacks a governing noun. The words οὐ γὰρ πάντων ἡ πίστις express a

---

and ‚the word of God' was the more common term." (FEE, *1 and 2 Thess* [n. 4], p. 313, note 9).

50. Cf. WANAMAKER, *The Epistles to the Thessalonians* (n. 2), p. 275.

truism that at first sight seems hardly necessary. But the negative way is used deliberately in this text with reference to those outside of the believing community. The faith (ἡ πίστις is here precisely the act of believing) is not the response of all to the word of God, γάρ indicating that this is the reason for which the "wicked and evil people" persecute the Christian missionaries and, as the next verse suggests, also the believers in Thessalonica. In contrast with this negative way of speaking about the opponents, the letter uses positive language in the following verses (3-4), to confess the faithfulness of the Lord and to express the confidence in the readers' obedience.

(b) *Encouragement and prayer (3,3-5)*

Vv. 3-4 follow the thought pattern of 2,13-15: an affirmation of divine care for the community (3,3, that parallels 2,13-14) is followed by an exhortation to obedience (3,4, that parallels 2,15). The indirect call to obedience in v. 4 is supported by the wish prayer in v. 5.

> ³ πιστὸς δέ ἐστιν ὁ κύριος, ὃς στηρίξει ὑμᾶς καὶ φυλάξει ἀπὸ τοῦ πονηροῦ.
> ⁴ πεποίθαμεν δὲ ἐν κυρίῳ ἐφ' ὑμᾶς, ὅτι ἃ παραγγέλλομεν [καὶ] ποιεῖτε καὶ ποιήσετε.
> ⁵ Ὁ δὲ κύριος κατευθύναι ὑμῶν τὰς καρδίας εἰς τὴν ἀγάπην τοῦ θεοῦ καὶ εἰς τὴν ὑπομονὴν τοῦ Χριστοῦ.
>
> ³ But the Lord is faithful; he will strengthen you and guard you from the evil one.
> ⁴ And we have confidence in the Lord concerning you, that you are doing and will go on doing the things that we command.
> ⁵ May the Lord direct your hearts to the love of God and to the steadfastness of Christ. (NRS)

V. 3. The abrupt transition from v. 2 to v. 3 – the authors moving from their own situation to that of the readers, and from the human faith to the faithfulness of God – is in a way assured by the use of πίστις/πιστός. Indeed, if the concluding word in the request for prayer in verses 1-2 is the noun πίστις ("faith"), the first word in this sentence is the adjective πιστός ("faithful"). These two words sit side by side, so that the Greek readers could not miss the wordplay.[51] The adversaries of St Paul and of his companions are people without faith, but the Lord is faithful. The

---

51. Cf. FEE, *1 and 2 Thess* (n. 4), p. 317.

clearly adversative δέ marks the contrast between the faithlessness of the adversaries (v. 2) and the abiding faithfulness of the Lord. The wordplay puts in opposition "the wicked and evil people", those people without faith, and the faithfulness of Christ toward those who have "faith".

Both the authors of the letter and the Christians in Thessalonica can and must rely on the faithfulness of the Lord. The Lord, in his faithfulness, will strengthen and guard them from the evil one, and this quality stands in stark contrast with the lack of faith (and the evil associated with it) mentioned in the previous verse. It is noteworthy that although this statement is probably based on 1 Thess 5,24, here the faithful one is the Lord (that is, Jesus Christ), which, again, indicates the move to a higher Christology in 2 Thessalonians.

Usually, indeed, St Paul says, in accordance with the Scriptures,[52] that "God is faithful" (1 Cor 1,9; 10,13; 2 Cor 1,18; 1 Thess 5,24). The affirmation in this verse that "the Lord is faithful" means, first, that the Lord Jesus Christ is truly God,[53] and secondly, that he would, with his divine power, "strengthen" and "guard"[54] the believers in Thessalonica ἀπὸ τοῦ πονηροῦ, "from evil", or, rather, "from the evil one" (KJV, and many other versions), which means "from Satan". The divine work of the Lord in v. 3b has also an eschatological connotation: at the time of his *parousia* the Lord Jesus Christ will render judgment against the enemies of the people of God (cf. 1,7f).

---

52. In the Torah, Yahweh is revealed as faithful at the key moment in Deut 7,9: "Know therefore that Yahweh (κύριος in the LXX) your God is God; Yahweh is a faithful God, keeping his covenant of love to a thousand generations of those who love Yahweh and keep Yahweh's commandments". Because of his faithfulness, Yahweh can do no wrong (Deut 32,4); and it is to Yahweh's faithfulness that often the people of faith in the Old Testament appeal (e.g., Ps 145,13; Is 49,7).

53. Some scholars (e.g., GREEN, *The Letters to the Thessalonians* [n. 8], pp. 337-338; MALHERBE, *The Letters to the Thessalonians* [n. 8], p. 461) argue, on the basis of this Old Testament usage, that Paul had God the Father in mind here as well. "But that seems to miss Paul's own Christology by too much" (FEE, *1 and 2 Thess* [n. 4], p. 318). For, indeed, St Paul, in all his extant letters, uses the word κύριος exclusively to refer to Christ. And in this specific context, first, "the Lord" is identified with Jesus Christ (2,16), and it is done so with the intensive pronoun "himself"; second, if in all other instances St Paul says that "God is faithful", here it is said "the Lord is faithful", an intentional change of subject; and third, in the immediate next sentence is expressed the confidence in the Lord concerning the readers' response to the appeal of the apostle and his collaborators (cf. FEE, *1 and 2 Thess* [n. 4], pp. 318-319).

54. στηρίξει and φυλάξει "are probably to be understood as progressive futures; that is, the Lord 'will continue strengthening and guarding them'" (WANAMAKER, *The Epistles to the Thessalonians* [n. 2], p. 276). This is the only text in St Paul where φυλάσσειν is used of divine protection, but this verb is commonly used in this sense in the Septuagint, especially in Psalms (cf. Ps 11,7; 15,1; 40,2; and esp. 120,7).

Who is "the evil one" at the end of this verse? τοῦ πονηροῦ can be either neuter or masculine, i.e. referring to the general phenomenon of evil or to Satan. The last demand in the "Lord's Prayer" in Matt 6,13 presents the same ambiguity. For "the evil one", the word is used in different New Testament writings (Matt 13,19; John 17,15; Eph 6,16; 1 John 2,13f). Although in other Pauline texts the neuter is used, referring to evil in general (cf. Rom 12,9; 1 Thess 5,22), here (as in Eph 6,16), most probably, the authors' thought is of Satan and of the eschatological deliverance of the believers.

V. 4 is related to the previous one: if v. 3 assures the readers that the Lord is working in strengthening and guarding them, in v. 4 the apostle and his collaborators express their confidence (πεποίθαμεν)[55] "in the Lord" that the readers are following and will continue to follow the commands addressed to them, indirectly requiring their obedience in response to this work of the Lord. Specific details of the instruction will be provided in 3,6-12.

As in other Pauline texts (cf. Gal 5,10; 2 Cor 2,3; Phm 21) where the apostle expresses confidence in his readers in situations where he most probably had reservations about how his readers would respond, this text also may reflect some reservation about the obedience of the readers.[56] That this is the case is shown by the ἐν κυρίῳ formula in v. 4a – in which, again, "the Lord" is Christ[57] –, but most of all by the commands in vv. 6 and 12, with the explicit indication that not all in the community were doing or will freely do what the letter commands them to do (cf. vv. 11f), and by the procedure instituted for dealing with refractory members of the community, in v. 14.

The verb παραγγέλλομεν ("we command", or "we instruct") clearly refers to ethical direction, as is demonstrated by its use in the subsequent verses (vv. 6 and 12). The command refers to the instructions contained in the present letter, and especially prepares the way for what will be said in vv. 6-15. The present verb ποιεῖτε ("you are doing", "you practice") implies that most of the believers were already carrying these instructions. But, as the use of the future καὶ ποιήσετε ("and will go

---

55. πεποίθαμεν, the perfect tense of the verb that means "persuade", is rendered by "confident", or "confidence" in most contemporary English versions.

56. WANAMAKER, *The Epistles to the Thessalonians* (n. 2), p. 277.

57. The expression ἐν κυρίῳ is "uniquely Pauline in the NT... This is one of the subtle phrases in this letter that directs considerable force against the theory of pseudonymity, since it is so uniquely Pauline but does not occur in 1 Thessalonians, the only Pauline letter that the writer of the present letter knows anything about" (FEE, *1 and 2 Thess* [n. 4], p. 320, note 37).

on doing", "and you will continue practicing"), also the firm instructions in vv. 6-15, and, most of all, the disciplinary procedure in vv. 14f, show that the authors of the letter were anything but confident that all the readers are or will be obedient.

V. 5. The indirect call to obedience in v. 4 is supported by the wish prayer in v. 5. It is a prayer that reflects the friendship,[58] the brotherly love of the apostle and his collaborators for the readers, a prayer of friends for friends. This prayer has to do with their relationship with God and Christ. The demand is that the Lord may "direct your hearts to the love of God and to the steadfastness of Christ". This prayer takes the audience to the source of their ability to carry out the instructions. It is probable that the authors appeal to Christ's steadfastness to provide them with the highest model during the current difficulties they are experiencing.

Again, the letter attributes to Christ the Septuagint's translation of the Tetragrammaton (YHWH) as κύριος (v. 5a). It is noteworthy that in this passage, and also in 1 Thess 3,11, St Paul and his collaborators *pray* toward Christ as Lord. The very high Christology that is assumed throughout this section of the letter is indeed noteworthy.[59]

The opening phrase, ὁ δὲ κύριος κατευθύναι ὑμῶν τὰς καρδίας ("may the Lord direct your hearts") is reminiscent of some texts in the Septuagint employing the verb κατευθύναι ("to direct") in a metaphorical sense (1 Chron 29,18; Prov 21,2 and Sir 49,3, for example, speak precisely of the Lord directing the heart). For most commentators, based on normal Pauline usage (cf. Rom 5,5; 8,39; 2 Cor 13,13), τοῦ θεοῦ is a subjective genitive after ἀγάπη, denoting God's love for the followers of Christ.[60]

---

58. FEE, *1 and 2 Thess* (n. 4), p. 321.
59. Cf. FEE, *1 and 2 Thess* (n. 4), p. 322, who also sees in this high Christology a strong argument against those who consider 2 Thessalonians as a forgery: "Here especially the theory of forgery falls on hard times; it is difficult to imagine anyone being able to enter into Paul's skin so thoroughly in this regard as this passage displays, both intentionally and otherwise. And in this regard, one should not miss that the appeal to Christ's own faithfulness lies at the heart of everything, including his confidence in prayer at the end (v. 5)" (p. 323).
60. Cf. FRAME, *Epistles of St Paul to the Thessalonians* (n. 30), p. 296; RIGAUX, *Les Épîtres aux Thessaloniciens* (n. 8), p. 699; BEST, *1 and 2 Thessalonians* (n. 7), p. 330; W. MARXSEN, *Der zweite Thesalonicherbrief*, Zurich, Theologischer Verlag, 1982, p. 98. But TRILLING, *Untersuchungen zum 2. Thessalonicherbrief* (n. 20), p. 139, who rejects the Pauline authorship of 2 Thessalonians, argues that Paul's customary usage cannot serve as a criterion for determining the meaning of the "love of God" here, and thinks that in the phrase ἀγάπη τοῦ θεοῦ the genitive is objective, the pseudonymous author of the letter wishing to direct

A similar difficulty arises in the second prepositional phrase εἰς τὴν ὑπομονὴν τοῦ Χριστοῦ ("to the steadfastness of Christ", "to the perseverance of Christ"), in which the genitive τοῦ Χριστοῦ may be either objective or subjective. Different interpretations are based on an objective meaning of this genitive: the need for the Thessalonians to have a patient expectation for the coming of Christ,[61] or then steadfastness directed to Christ in the face of "distress and disturbance".[62] But as the previous genitive τοῦ θεοῦ is subjective, most probably this τοῦ Χριστοῦ should also be rendered as subjective genitive,[63] meaning either to take Christ's perseverance as an example (cf. Jas 5,11), or to accept the perseverance that comes from Christ (cf. Rom 15,4f) – the former seeming to be the more likely possibility.[64]

Most commentators[65] see in this prayer a deliberate intertextual use of 1 Chron 29,18, where David, with reference to the gifts brought for the building of the temple, prays with the words: "The Lord, the God of our fathers, …direct their hearts to you". Using this same language, the writers of this letter pray that the Lord will "direct your hearts to the love of God".[66]

In this wish prayer, Paul asks the Lord to direct the readers' hearts to God's love for them and to the perseverance which Christ demonstrated as a basis for a proper Christian behaviour.

2. *Exhortation regarding the disorderly-idle (3,6-15)*

The exhortative section of the letter is mainly concerned with only one issue in the life of the community. "This perhaps suggests that the letter was hastily written".[67]

---

the readers' heart to love for God. See serious objections against this interpretation in WANAMAKER, *The Epistles to the Thessalonians* (n. 2), pp. 278-279.
61. Von DOBSCHÜTZ, *Die Thessalonicher-Briefe* (n. 30), p. 309.
62. TRILLING, *Untersuchungen zum 2. Thessalonicherbrief* (n. 20), pp. 330f.
63. BEST, *1 and 2 Thessalonians* (n. 7), p. 330; WANAMAKER, *The Epistles to the Thessalonians* (n. 2), p. 279.
64. Cf. WANAMAKER, *The Epistles to the Thessalonians* (n. 2), p. 279.
65. Cf. FEE, *1 and 2 Thess* (n. 4), p. 322.
66. FEE identifies three items indicating that this is deliberate intertextuality: (1) "the locution is both striking and unusual" (the verb κατευθῦναι is found elsewhere in Paul only in the prayer in 1 Thess 3,11); (2) "the phrase 'the Lord direct their/your hearts' toward God is *unique to these two passages* in the Bible"; and (3) "the phrase is found in the mouth of the great king of Israel, David himself – and in prayer! – so that it is not a merely passing phrase used by a more obscure figure" (*1 and 2 Thess* [n. 4], p. 322).
67. WANAMAKER, *The Epistles to the Thessalonians* (n. 2), p. 279.

In vv. 6-15, the letter warns the believers against the idle, or more exactly, the disorderly (v. 6), and commands them to avoid every member of the congregation who is living "in a disorderly way" (ἀτάκτως) and not in accordance with the tradition (παράδοσις) they received from the apostle. The word ἀτάκτως appears again in v. 11, where the authors describe how certain of the addressees are behaving, and the authors of the epistle themselves deny that they behaved in such a way in v. 7. It is reasonably clear from the associations of the word in vv. 6-15 that by "disorderly" the authors mean "not in accordance with the discipline of working and supporting oneself", thus behaving like the idle people (hence "living in idleness" in the NRSV).

Most commentators who accept the Pauline authenticity of 2 Thessalonians link this section with 1 Thess 4,11f and 5,14, assuming that the situation became more serious from the sending of the first letter.[68] Scholars have long explained this idleness as rooted in "eschatological" excitement produced by a belief in the imminence of the *parousia* of Christ. Believing that "the day of the Lord is at hand", being therefore imbued with feverish eschatological expectation, those people left the work and made themselves zealot propagators of their eschatological error. But there are serious reasons that question this view. G. Fee offers a list of those reasons: "First, there is not a word in the exhortation that follows that even remotely hints that this was their motive; thus the suggestion is guesswork on the part of some scholars and nothing more. Second, in verse 9 Paul reminds them that he had dealt with this concern, 'even when we were with you', and there is nothing in either of these letters indicating that eschatological fervor was there from the beginning. Third, in speaking to eschatological issues in the first letter (4,13-18 and 5,1-11), there is no hint in either case that Paul was speaking to a heightened, or intense, eschatological expectation".[69] From which Fee concludes that "we simply do not know why some of them chose not to work and thus to live off the largesse of others".[70]

R. Russell also argues that this idleness has nothing to do with end-time excitement, and proposes that it is a result of the urban poor finding support within the social networks of Christ-fearers and then giving up

---

68. Cf. von DOBSCHÜTZ, *Die Thessalonicher-Briefe* (n. 30), p. 309; FRAME, *Epistles of St Paul to the Thessalonians* (n. 30), p. 297; RIGAUX, *Les Épîtres aux Thessaloniciens* (n. 8), p. 701; BEST, *1 and 2 Thessalonians* (n. 7), p. 331.
69. FEE, *1 and 2 Thess* (n. 4), p. 324.
70. FEE, *1 and 2 Thess* (n. 4), p. 324.

work⁷¹. This view has been challenged by K. Romaniuk.⁷² A similar view to that of Russell has been proposed by R. Jewett, who says that the early Christ-movement was not likely to have been located in house-churches, but in the tenement houses of the non-élite, which would have lacked an upper- or middle-class patron, and where the system of internal support would have been jeopardized by the refusal of some members to contribute.⁷³

The authors make reference here to a "tradition that they received from us" (v. 6b). As there is no allusion in this text to a previous counsel or command on this kind of disorder, some think that 2 Thessalonians actually preceeded the first letter, and that the reference in 1 Thess 4,11 is precisely to 2 Thess 3,6-15. For other, vv. 6-12 represent a "later stratum" or a post-Pauline addition to the letter.⁷⁴ But all commentators agree that a potentially serious problem emerged in the Thessalonian Church, which this letter is intended to solve.

(a) *The issue of the dissorderly-idle people (3,6)*

⁶ Παραγγέλλομεν δὲ ὑμῖν, ἀδελφοί, ἐν ὀνόματι τοῦ κυρίου [ἡμῶν] Ἰησοῦ Χριστοῦ στέλλεσθαι ὑμᾶς ἀπὸ παντὸς ἀδελφοῦ ἀτάκτως περιπατοῦντος καὶ μὴ κατὰ τὴν παράδοσιν ἣν παρελάβοσαν παρ' ἡμῶν.

⁶ Now we command you, beloved, in the name of our Lord Jesus Christ, to keep away from believers who are living in idleness and not according to the tradition that they received from us. (NRSV)

As in other places in 1 and 2 Thess, δὲ... ἀδελφοί ("now... brothers") marks that what follows in vv. 6-15 represents a new theme. The introduction to this new theme is particularly solemn: Παραγγέλλομεν⁷⁵ δὲ ὑμῖν, ἀδελφοί, ἐν ὀνόματι τοῦ κυρίου [ἡμῶν] Ἰησοῦ Χριστοῦ ("Now we command you, beloved, in the name of our Lord

---

71. R. RUSSELL, *The Idle in 2 Thes. 3:6–12: An Eschatological or a Social Problem?*, in *NTS* 34 (1988) 105-119.

72. K. ROMANIUK, *Les Thessaloniciens étaient-ils des paresseux?*, in *ETL* 69 (1993) 142-145.

73. R. JEWETT, *Tenement Churches and Communal Meals in the Early Church: The Implications of a Form-Critical Analysis of 2 Thessalonians 3:10*, in *BR* 38 (1993) 23-42.

74. Winsome MUNRO, *Authority in Paul and Peter: The Identification of a Pastoral Stratum in the Pauline Corpus and in 1 Peter* (SNTSMS, 45), Cambridge: Cambridge University Press, 1983, pp. 82-85.

75. The verb παραγγέλλομεν occurs five times in the two letters (1 Thes 4,11; 2 Thess 3,4.6.10 and 12), in each case in relation to the present issue.

Jesus Christ"), which shows the importance of the issue addressed and the intensity of the writers disquiet. The formula "in the name of our Lord Jesus Christ", is similar to formulae used elsewhere by St Paul when he emphatically commands something regarding the behaviour of the community (1 Cor 1,10: "by the name of our Lord Jesus Christ"; 5,4: "in the name of the Lord Jesus"). The use here of this formula – "one of the most powerful forms of theological coercion available to Paul"[76] – means that the command that follows is not only of the senders of the letter, but mainly of Jesus Christ himself.

The second part of this verse shows that to this "theological coercion" is added the coercive power of the community. For, indeed, the command is firstly an instruction directed to the obedient members of the community, who are asked "to keep away from believers who are living in idleness and not according to the tradition that they received from us" (στέλλεσθαι ὑμᾶς ἀπὸ παντὸς ἀδελφοῦ ἀτάκτως περιπατοῦντος καὶ μὴ κατὰ τὴν παράδοσιν ἣν παρελάβοσαν παρ' ἡμῶν). The verb στέλλεσθαι is a middle in Greek, meaning "keep yourselves away from" (cf. Rom 16,17, where the same thing is said with quite different language regarding those who cause divisions).

The adverb ἀτάκτως (here and in v. 11), is also used in 1 Thess 5,14 ("admonish the ἀτάκτους"). And in v. 7 is found the verbal form ἀτακτεῖν. The understanding of the whole instruction here depends on the meaning which is accepted for ἀτάκτως. Originally, the word concerned undisciplined or disorderly actions or persons; but in papyri from the Hellenistic period it is used for idle or lazy individuals as well. While both meanings might fit for 2 Thess 3,6, in 3,7 and 11 the concern is clearly idle behaviour, and it can be assumed that the same is true of 3,6 as well.[77] In 1 Thess 4,11 the people are called to work with their own hands, a strong case for understanding ἀτάκτως as referring to living in idleness or laziness. But, at the same time, there is a close connection between laziness and disorderly behaviour. In 1 Thess 4,11 the writers not only call people to work with their hands, but they also exhort them to aspire to live quietly and mind their own business. The same point applies in 2 Thess 3,11, where the letter says: "For we hear that some of you are living in idleness, mere busybodies, not doing any work" (ἀκούομεν γάρ τινας περιπατοῦντας ἐν ὑμῖν ἀτάκτως μηδὲν ἐργαζομένους ἀλλὰ περιεργαζομένους). The authors go on to order such

---

76. WANAMAKER, *The Epistles to the Thessalonians* (n. 2), p. 281.
77. WANAMAKER, *The Epistles to the Thessalonians* (n. 2), p. 196.

people to work quietly (μετὰ ἡσυχίας), an obvious verbal link with the exhortation in 1 Thess 4,11, "to aspire to live quietly".

This verse says that those living ἀτάκτως are, in fact, not living "according to the tradition that they received from us" (κατὰ τὴν παράδοσιν ἣν παρελάβοσαν παρ' ἡμῶν). This means that the issue in discussion is more than simple idleness. The disorderly life of those living ἀτάκτως comes from their resistance against the teaching they received (note the use here again of the technical verb παραλαμβάνω for describing the reception of the tradition) from the apostle and his collaborators, which means that they, in fact, are resisting St Paul's authority,[78] either intentionally or, rather, unintentionally, given their evasion of responsibility (cf. vv. 7f and 11f).

As is generally known, the urban poor in the Roman world lived mostly from the generosity of some benefactors, either the emperor himself or other wealthy people. The new Christian teaching implied a radical change in this respect. It is possible that for the disorderly people in Thessalonica, joining the Christian community meant simply access to the largesse of the Church, or more particularly its wealthier members.

Significantly, the letter uses here the verb at the third person plural.[79] In this way, it isolates the disorderly people from the mainstream of the community.

The tradition (παράδοσις) to which is made reference here has a twofold character, as vv. 7-12 indicate: in vv. 7-9 the apostle and his colleagues' example is presented as normative and as a guide for responsible behaviour of the believers; and in v. 10 is cited the specific tradition concerning the duty to work.

(b) *Imitate St Paul and his collaborators (3,7-10)*

⁷ αὐτοὶ γὰρ οἴδατε πῶς δεῖ μιμεῖσθαι ἡμᾶς, ὅτι οὐκ ἠτακτήσαμεν ἐν ὑμῖν
⁸ οὐδὲ δωρεὰν ἄρτον ἐφάγομεν παρά τινος, ἀλλ' ἐν κόπῳ καὶ μόχθῳ νυκτὸς καὶ ἡμέρας ἐργαζόμενοι πρὸς τὸ μὴ ἐπιβαρῆσαί τινα ὑμῶν·

---

78. Cf. Ceslaus SPICQ, *Les Thesaloniciens ,inquiets' étaient-ils des paresseux?*, in *ST* 10 (1956) 1-13; JEWETT, *The Thesalonian Correspondence* (n. 41), pp. 104-105.

79. A later scribe introduced the second person plural ending of the verb. But the third person plural, since it is a slightly unexpected in the context, should be taken as the original reading, either in its unusual dialectical form παρελάβοσαν (ℵ* A 33 88 Basil) or in its more common form παρέλαβον (ℵᶜ K L ᶜD Ψ 81 10, etc.).

⁹ οὐχ ὅτι οὐκ ἔχομεν ἐξουσίαν, ἀλλ' ἵνα ἑαυτοὺς τύπον δῶμεν ὑμῖν εἰς τὸ μιμεῖσθαι ἡμᾶς.
¹⁰ καὶ γὰρ ὅτε ἦμεν πρὸς ὑμᾶς, τοῦτο παρηγγέλλομεν ὑμῖν, ὅτι εἴ τις οὐ θέλει ἐργάζεσθαι μηδὲ ἐσθιέτω.

⁷ For you yourselves know how you ought to imitate us; we were not idle when we were with you,
⁸ and we did not eat anyone's bread without paying for it; but with toil and labor we worked night and day, so that we might not burden any of you.
⁹ This was not because we do not have that right, but in order to give you an example to imitate.
¹⁰ For even when we were with you, we gave you this command: Anyone unwilling to work should not eat. (NRSV).

V. 7. The letter provides a motivation (γάρ) for the preceding instruction to avoid the disorderly members of the community. "You yourselves know" (cf. 1 Thess 2,1; 3,3; 4,2; 5,2) means that what follows is already known by the readers, as part of the ethical tradition received in the apostolic instruction. They know πῶς δεῖ[80] μιμεῖσθαι ἡμᾶς ("how you ought to imitate us"). In 1 Thess 1,6f and 2,14 St Paul says that the Thessalonians became imitators of the apostle and of his collaborators (ἡμῶν, 1,6), of Christians in other places and of Christ himself through their experience of suffering for their faith. This text calls for ethical conformity to his own and his colleagues' (ἡμᾶς) pattern of behaviour. This call to imitate the apostolic missionaries is not at all an indication of a new attitude by St Paul, which emerged sometimes after the death of the apostle, as Trilling maintains.[81] In undoubtedly Pauline texts the apostle also calls his readers to imitate him (cf. 1 Cor 4,16; 11,1; Phil 3,17).

The ὅτι clause introduces what the letter has to say about the example of St Paul and his fellow missionaries in this respect. First, in **v. 8a**, the letter expresses this negatively: they (St Paul and his colleagues) "were not idle" or "disorderly" (οὐκ ἠτακτήσαμεν, aorist of ἀτακτεῖν, a verb related to the adverb employed in v. 6); they were not eating "anyone's bread without paying for it" (δωρεάν).[82] St Paul's refusal to accept material support from his converts formed a part of his missionary strategy (cf. 1 Cor 9,1-18; 2 Cor 11,7). Second, in **v. 8b**, speaking positively, the writers of the letter explain that, on the contrary (ἀλλα) they gained

---

80. For the use of πῶς δεῖ in the sense of an ethical imperative, cf. 1 Thess 4,1.
81. TRILLING, *Untersuchungen zum 2. Thessalonicherbrief* (n. 20), pp. 145f.
82. The expression "to eat bread" from someone could have this sense of receiving maintenance from someone (cf. 2 Sam 9,7; 2 Ki 4,8; Ezek 12,18f).

what they needed for their life ἐν κόπῳ καὶ μόχθῳ νυκτὸς καὶ ἡμέρας ἐργαζόμενοι ("with toil and labor we worked night and day"). Both κόπος ("toil") and μόχθος ("exertion") are also found in 1 Thess 2,9 and 2 Cor 11,27. Here, as in 1 Thess 2,9, using the verbs mentioned,[83] the letter shows that St Paul's policy of self-support required considerable effort on his part (and on the part of his collaborators). This aspect is stressed once more by the statement that they worked "night and day" (νυκτὸς καὶ ἡμέρας). With what serves as an indirect word to the disorderly-idle, the end of this verse reminds them that the apostle and those with him did this πρὸς τὸ μὴ ἐπιβαρῆσαί τινα ὑμῶν ("so that we might not burden any of you").

In **v. 9** the letter reminds one of what St Paul largely taught in 1 Cor 9,4-18 about the right of the apostle to be supported by those who benefit from his apostolic work. The plural in the phrase, οὐχ ὅτι οὐκ ἔχομεν ἐξουσίαν ("not because we do not have that right"), show both that this right belongs also to the collaborators of the apostle and that they all chose not to exercise their right, "in order to give you an example to imitate" (ἵνα ἑαυτοὺς τύπον δῶμεν ὑμῖν εἰς τὸ μιμεῖσθαι ἡμᾶς). The example of St Paul and of his collaborators must be followed by the converts in Thessalonica. With this final clause, the letter "encloses" the argument that began with the same language at the beginning of verse 7, as to what they "know".

V. 10. To the example they offered, the writers of the letter added an explicit command while in Thessalonica (ὅτε ἦμεν πρὸς ὑμᾶς, "when we were with you"). There is no reference in this text to 1 Thess 4,11f, which deals with the same issue. It seems that the problem with some from the community in Thessalonica existed already at the beginnings of this Church, while St Paul and his collaborators were still with them. Which, again, means that this problem was not the result of some people's error concerning the *parousia*. By mentioning that the apostle had previously told (commanded) them in their presence that anyone unwilling to work should not be fed, the letter makes explicit the precise nature

---

83. The reading νυκτὸς καὶ ἡμέρας, a genitive of time supported by ℵ B F G 33 81 104 255 256 263 442 1611 1845 1908 2005, was also adopted by the UBS⁴; the variant νυκτὰ καὶ ἡμέραν (A D K L P MajT) emphasizes the duration of their labors: "all day and all night long" (cf. FEE, *1 and 2 Thess* [n. 4], p. 329, note 61). The whole expression νυκτὸς καὶ ἡμέρας ἐργαζόμενοι πρὸς τὸ μὴ ἐπιβαρῆσαί τινα ὑμῶν ("we worked night and day, so that we might not burden any of you") is found word for word in 1 Thess 2,9. Writing a few months later on the same issue, it is only natural that the writers should repeat this expression in their second letter.

of the disorder which has been implied hitherto – the fact that some members of the congregation are living off the others.

The imperfect form of παρηγγέλλομεν (= "we used to command", "we used to give you this command") makes us understand that they were repeatedly instructed about the necessity of working to provide for their own requirements (cf. v. 6). The ὅτι can indicate a *verbatim* quotation of what St Paul used to say to his converts, namely, εἴ τις οὐ θέλει ἐργάζεσθαι μηδὲ ἐσθιέτω ("if anyone does not wish to work, neither let that person eat"). The command seems to be a maxim, but it is not known in the form it has here from any other source. There are parallels to this saying (which has been frequently cited out of its context ever since), in Prov 10,4; 12,11; 19,15.[84] But if it was not a maxim before, it certainly became a maxim after being written down in 2 Thess 3,10. From there on, we find it quoted in innumerable texts and in a large variety of contexts.

We should take note of the precise formulation of this command. The use of the verb θέλει ("wish") clearly shows that the command was not directed to those who were unable to work or could not find work, but to those who refused to work. These last should not be allowed to eat. The expression μηδὲ ἐσθιέτω seems to indicate that there was the community's responsibility to carry out this imperative in the case of anyone unwilling to work.[85] By the repetition – now in written form – of this command, the letter provides to those responsible for the community in Thessalonica a formal support for dealing with those who preferred to rely on the largesse of the Church.

(c) *The command repeated. The disorderly to "eat their own bread"*
    (3,11-12)

The letter now both repeats and summarizes what it has said up to this point (from v. 6). But what began as an imperative to the whole

---

84. Cf. *Gen. Rab.* 2,2; Pseudo-Phocylides, *Sentences*, 153-4 (cf. WANAMAKER, *The Epistles to the Thessalonians* [n. 2], p. 285).

85. Cf. *Didache* (12,3-5), where this rule is established on how are to be received by the church community those people coming from elsewhere: a traveller visitor is to be accomodated and helped by the community no more than two or three days. "But [adds the *Didache*] if he wishes to settle among you and is a craftsman, let him work and eat. But if he has no trade, provide according to your conscience, so that no Christian shall live among you idle. But if he does not agree to do this, he is trading on the name of Christ; beware of such men" (in *Scrierile Părinților Apostolici*, Romanian transl. by Fr. D. Fecioru, coll. "Părinți și scriitori bisericești", Bucharest, EIBMBOR, 1979, p. 31).

community (to dissociate from "every brother" who is walking in a disorderly manner, and thus not in keeping with the "traditions" they had received from St Paul and his colleagues) is now directed explicitly toward the disorderly/idle themselves (though still by way of speaking to the community as a whole). The opening sentence in v. 6 is repeated in v. 11, this time with what seems to be a wordplay on the word "work". Then follows a direct command to the idle to work with their own hand and to "eat their own bread" (v. 12).

¹¹ ἀκούομεν γάρ τινας περιπατοῦντας ἐν ὑμῖν ἀτάκτως μηδὲν ἐργαζομένους ἀλλὰ περιεργαζομένους·
¹² τοῖς δὲ τοιούτοις παραγγέλλομεν καὶ παρακαλοῦμεν ἐν κυρίῳ Ἰησοῦ Χριστῷ, ἵνα μετὰ ἡσυχίας ἐργαζόμενοι τὸν ἑαυτῶν ἄρτον ἐσθίωσιν.

¹¹ For we hear that some of you are living in idleness, mere busybodies, not doing any work.
¹² Now such persons we command and exhort in the Lord Jesus Christ to do their work quietly and to earn their own living. (NRSV)

V. 11. The introductory words ἀκούομεν γάρ ("for we hear") suggest that the apostle and his collaborators have just received new information on the situation. Possibly someone from the Thessalonian community brought this information to St Paul (cf. 1 Cor 1,11; 16,17). The information concerned those of the Thessalonians who were living in a disorderly way. The phrase περιπατοῦντας ἐν ὑμῖν ἀτάκτως ("living disorderly", or "in idleness") has been picked up from v. 6 and has the same meaning here.

By the wordplay in the second part of this verse, μηδὲν ἐργαζομένους ἀλλὰ περιεργαζομένους ("not working but meddling", or, as NIV renders it in idiomatic English: "they are not busy; they are busybodies"), the letter gives some specificity to the disorder in Thessalonica.[86] The verb περιεργαζομένους (only here in Paul) means "meddling" or "interfering" with the sense of people who involve themselves in affairs that are none of their business (cf. 1 Thess 4,11, where we read the admonistion to live quietly and mind their own affairs). This specification says to us something about the nature of the disorder: it is indolence rather than rebelliousness, but as the apostle needs to repeat again

---

86. For other wordplays in St Paul see Rom 12,3; 1 Cor 11,29-34; 2 Cor 1,13; 3,2; 6,10; Phil 3,2f.

his command, it is an indication that those people who still refused to work were actually showing their lack of obedience.[87]

After instructing the responsible members of the community how to deal with the disorderly, the authors of the letter turn (in **v. 12**) to those who are guilty of this irresponsible way of living. "Such people"(τοιούτοις) are imperatively exhorted "to do their work quietly and to eat their own bread".

The letter uses here strong and coercive language, very similar to that in v. 6, the introduction to what it have to say to those living disorderly sounding here again extremely solemn and authoritative: τοῖς δὲ τοιούτοις παραγγέλλομεν καὶ παρακαλοῦμεν ἐν κυρίῳ Ἰησοῦ Χριστῷ ("now such persons we command and exhort in the Lord Jesus Christ"). The verb παρακαλοῦμεν, which means "we demand", "we require", "we exhort", or even "we beg", seems to indicate a softening of the more forceful expression παραγγέλλομεν ("we command").[88] "In the Lord Jesus Christ" (ἐν κυρίῳ Ἰησοῦ Χριστῷ) is parallel to "in the name of the Lord Jesus Christ" (ἐν ὀνόματι τοῦ κυρίου [ἡμῶν] Ἰησοῦ Χριστοῦ) in v. 6. It means that the divine authority of the Lord Jesus Christ himself stands behind this apostolic command, which, as a consequence, has full coercive power.

The ἵνα ("that") introduces the command itself: ἵνα μετὰ ἡσυχίας ἐργαζόμενοι τὸν ἑαυτῶν ἄρτον ἐσθίωσιν ("to do their work quietly and to earn their own living", lit. "that working with quietness they eat their own bread"). In 1 Thess 4,11, with reference to the same theme, the verb ἡσυχάζειν is used, a cognate of the noun ἡσυχία ("quietness") used here. "Working with quietness" is here an alternative to the tendency of these people to meddle in other people's business (v. 11). Best[89] and other argue that the reference to quietness here suggests that disorderly (or idle) people's current state is one of loud activity or excitement, associated with the millennial belief that "the day of the Lord is already here" (2,2), and that this apostolic command is meant to calm them of this "excitement" caused by the expectation of the *parousia*. But, as other commentators rightly point, there is no connection between the

---

87. See also our commentary on v. 6.
88. Cf. FRAME, *Epistles of St Paul to the Thessalonians* (n. 30), p. 306; Leon MORRIS, *The First and Second Epistles to the Thessalonians*, Grand Rapids, Eerdmans, rev. ed., 1991, p. 256; BEST, *1 and 2 Thessalonians* (n. 7), p. 340.
89. BEST *and 2 Thessalonians* (n. 7), p. 341.

command about living quietly and the issue of the *parousia*, neither in 1 Thessalonians nor in 2 Thessalonians.[90]

As the ultimate goal of following this way of life, i. e. the Church members "working quieltly", is that they should provide for themselves (this is the sense of ἑαυτῶν ἄρτον ἐσθίωσιν, "that they eat their own bread"), and to be no more a burden for the community or for some of its members.[91]

This text shows us that St Paul and his disciples had a well developed notion of contributive justice. In the Church history this teaching on the duty to work is repeated again and again.

(d) *Exhortation to the obedient believers (3,13-15)*

This section of the letter ends with an exhortation addressed to the obedient members of the Church, who are to carry out the command expressed in the precedent verses, and to make the disorderly "ashamed" (v. 14) of their conduct, and so to help them to change and to adopt the proper way of Christian life.

[13] Ὑμεῖς δέ, ἀδελφοί, μὴ ἐγκακήσητε καλοποιοῦντες.
[14] εἰ δέ τις οὐχ ὑπακούει τῷ λόγῳ ἡμῶν διὰ τῆς ἐπιστολῆς, τοῦτον σημειοῦσθε μὴ συναναμίγνυσθαι αὐτῷ, ἵνα ἐντραπῇ·
[15] καὶ μὴ ὡς ἐχθρὸν ἡγεῖσθε, ἀλλὰ νουθετεῖτε ὡς ἀδελφόν.

[13] Brothers and sisters, do not be weary in doing what is right.
[14] Take note of those who do not obey what we say in this letter; have nothing to do with them, so that they may be ashamed.
[15] Do not regard them as enemies, but warn them as believers. (NRSV)

The initial words of **v. 13**, ὑμεῖς δέ, ἀδελφοί ("but you, brothers") are not introducing a new section, as some think.[92] The more general character of the exhortation in v. 13 can easily be explained by the fact

---

90. See MARSHALL, *I and II Thessalonians* (n. 8), p. 225; WANAMAKER, *The Epistles to the Thessalonians* (n. 2), p. 287; FEE, *1 and 2 Thess* (n. 4), p. 335; etc. The claim of TRILLING, *Untersuchungen zum 2. Thessalonicherbrief* (n. 20), p. 151, that the instruction to work quietly reflects later middle-class form of Christianity not typical of St Paul's day is untenable.

91. WANAMAKER, *The Epistles to the Thessalonians* (n. 2), p. 287, writes: "Ironically, Paul's emphasis upon familial love and commitment among the members of the community may have given rise to the situation. The order that the idle must work was not only in their interest, but also in the interest of the wealthier members of the community who would have increasingly found themselves burdened by the indolent if Paul had not intervened."

92. E.g. TRILLING, *Untersuchungen zum 2. Thessalonicherbrief* (n. 20), pp. 153-154, who, however, sees only a very loose connection between v. 13 and vv. 14f., and thinks that vv. 14f.

that, if the command in vv. 11f was directed mostly to the "disorderly", now here the instruction is addressed to the responsible members of the community. They are addressed with the instruction μὴ ἐγκακήσητε καλοποιοῦντες ("do not be weary in doing what is right"). A similar exhortation, in almost the same words, is found in Gal 6,9: τὸ δὲ καλὸν ποιοῦντες μὴ ἐγκακῶμεν ("let us not grow tired of doing good"). But here "the aorist subjunctive ἐγκακήσητε appear to allude to a specific situation in which the readers are not to grow weary"[93], i.e. to the situation with the disorderly members as presented in vv. 6-12 and 14f.

The rarely used compound word καλοποιοῦντες may mean "to do the right" [94] or "to confer benefits"[95], many commentators understanding by this expression, indifferent of the translation they accept, an admonition to charitable behaviour toward the needy in the community. But, in the context, it is much more probable that the readers are exhorted "to do right" in their way of living, working for their own bread, and not to behave like the irresponsible members of the community.

After this admonition more general in character, the letter turns in **v. 14** to the question about how to discipline those who live in a "disorderly" way, a problem first addressed in v. 6. The conditional εἰ ("if") at the beginning of v. 14 suggests that apostle and his collaborators hope that the disorderly will change voluntarily as a result of the letter itself: εἰ δέ τις οὐχ ὑπακούει τῷ λόγῳ ἡμῶν διὰ τῆς ἐπιστολῆς ("but if anyone does not obey our instruction through this letter"). The "instruction" or the "rule" (λόγος, which means here a rule of conduct, "an usage rooted both in classical Greek and in Paul's understanding of the Torah, as Rom 13,9 and Gal 5,14 indicate"[96]) given διὰ τῆς ἐπιστολῆς ("through this letter") concerns precisely the theme found in vv. 6-12, and in particular the regulation given in v. 12. The "our" in the expression τῷ λόγῳ ἡμῶν, a new indication of the multiplicity of the authors of the letter, can also be understood as a note of apostolic authority.[97]

---

refer to the whole of the epistle rather than to vv. 6-12, a position which is not at all convincing; and MARXSEN, *Der zweite Thesalonicherbrief* (n. 60), p. 102.

93. WANAMAKER, *The Epistles to the Thessalonians* (n. 2), p. 288.

94. Cf. FRAME, *Epistles of St Paul to the Thessalonians* (n. 30), p. 308; Leon MORRIS, *The First and Second Epistles to the Thessalonians*, Grand Rapids, Eerdmans, rev. ed., 1991, p. 257.

95. Cf. von DOBSCHÜTZ, *Die Thessalonicher-Briefe* (n. 30), p. 315; BEST, *1 and 2 Thessalonians* (n. 7), p. 342.

96. WANAMAKER, *The Epistles to the Thessalonians* (n. 2), pp. 288-289.

97. Cf. BRUCE, *1 & 2 Thessalonians* (n. 34), p. 209.

The responsible and all the obedient members receive this direction (in v. 14b) for disciplining anyone who does not obey the injunction regarding work: τοῦτον σημειοῦσθε μὴ συναναμίγνυσθαι αὐτῷ ("take special notice of this one so that not to associate with him"). The verb σημειοῦσθε, a NT *hapax legomenon*, ordinarily means "to note down" something; in this case it means to "mark" such a person, by taking special notice of him.[98] The verb συναναμίγνυσθαι occurs elsewhere in the Pauline letters (and with the same sense in the NT) only in 1 Cor 5,9-11, where it is used twice, St Paul commanding the Church in Corinth to dissociate itself from any Christian person living in immorality. The words "not even to eat with such person" in 1 Cor 5,11 involves especially the exclusion from participation in the common meals of the community, where also the Lord's Supper took place. This precise indication is missing here, but the apostolic direction "not to associate" with the person concerned means nothing less than the excommunication of this person.[99] This discipline is not simply meant to purge the community of corrupting elements, but is meant to have a pedagogical role, as the final words of the phrase show: ἵνα ἐντραπῇ ("in order than the person may be ashamed"). The exclusion can be salutary, so that the guilty one would finally be reintegrated into the community (cf. v. 15).

This salutary purpose of dissociating from the disorderly is stressed once more in **v. 15**. The excluded one is not an "enemy", but a "brother": καὶ μὴ ὡς ἐχθρὸν ἡγεῖσθε, ἀλλὰ νουθετεῖτε ὡς ἀδελφόν ("and do not regard him as an enemy, but admonish him as a brother"). The authors of the letter are aware that the Church members can be tempted to consider the excluded ones as enemies. However, the intention expressed in the pericope may be different: St Paul and his colleagues hope that the people concerned, being put apart by the community, would come to repent. So, their exclusion from the community should not be considered as irrevocable.

The second part of this instruction, ἀλλὰ νουθετεῖτε ὡς ἀδελφόν ("but admonish him as a brother"), is not self-evident in meaning. How should this admonition be done by the community? Best[100] thinks that it refers to action to be taken while the community was assembled, which involves the exclusion being only from the Lord's Supper and the

---

98. FEE, *1 and 2 Thess* (n. 4), p. 338, note 78.
99. See H. GREEVEN, *TDNT* VII, p. 855.
100. BEST, *1 and 2 Thessalonians* (n. 7), pp. 343-344.

common meal associated with it. But nothing in the context suggests such a limited significance for the command in vv. 6 and 14. What clearly appears in this verse is that the epistle tries to moderate the believers' attitudes toward those not obeying to the rule regarding the work and to "give the community a positive action to carry out in an effort to restore the individual to fellowship".[101]

CONCLUSION (3,16-18)

Some link v. 16 to the previous section of the letter. The main reason for such a position is the consideration that after the disturbing problem regarding the disorderly members of the Church, a prayer for peace might well be appropriate.[102] But other commentaries rightly stress that, in fact, the prayer for peace in Thessalonica covered also other aspects (e. g., the external persecution). It seems rather that v. 16 was the original final benediction, followed by St Paul's remark about his signature and another benediction written also this time with his own hand (vv. 17-18). Vv. 16-18 constitute together the closing of this letter.

1. *Benediction (3,16)*

> [16] Αὐτὸς δὲ ὁ κύριος τῆς εἰρήνης δῴη ὑμῖν τὴν εἰρήνην διὰ παντὸς ἐν παντὶ τρόπῳ. ὁ κύριος μετὰ πάντων ὑμῶν.

> [16] Now may the Lord of peace himself give you peace at all times in all ways. The Lord be with all of you. (NRSV)

V. 16. The expression αὐτὸς δὲ ὁ κύριος τῆς εἰρήνης ("now may the Lord of peace himself") is peculiar, as it is the only instance in the NT writings where Christ is designated as "the Lord of peace". In various places St Paul says "the God of peace" (cf. 1 Thess 5,23; Rom 15,33; 16,20; 2 Cor 13,11; Phil 4,7.9). In the salutations of many of his letters, St Paul connects peace both with "God our Father" and "our Lord Jesus Christ" (cf. 2 Thess 1,1; Rom 1,7; 1 Cor 1,3; 2 Cor 1,2; Gal 1,3; Phil 1,2). It is true that in Col 3,15 appears the expression "the peace of Christ".

---

101. WANAMAKER, *The Epistles to the Thessalonians* (n. 2), p. 290.
102. Cf. MARSHALL, *I and II Thessalonians* (n. 8), p. 230.

The prayer to the "Lord of peace" is that he gives peace (εἰρήνη) to the readers διὰ παντὸς ἐν παντὶ τρόπῳ[103] ("at all times in all ways"). Which means a peace that is much more than the absence of conflicts. The two Thessalonian letters give us a hint about the different problems and troubles, both internal and external, to which the members of this community were exposed. The readers really needed the peace from Christ in an extensive sense.

The second benediction (v. 16b) ὁ κύριος μετὰ πάντων ὑμῶν ("the Lord be with all of you") is also unique in St Paul's letters. In Rom 15,33 and Phil 4,9, the wish is that "the God of peace" be with the readers. This wish prayer is a new case of intertextuality in this letter.[104] In Ruth 2,4, Boaz greets his workers with: "The Lord be with you"; to which they respond: "The Lord bless you". It seems that the wish in this verse, with no verb, alludes to this text of the Septuagint.

2. St Paul's personal greeting (3,17)

[17] Ὁ ἀσπασμὸς τῇ ἐμῇ χειρὶ Παύλου, ὅ ἐστιν σημεῖον ἐν πάσῃ ἐπιστολῇ· οὕτως γράφω.

[17] I, Paul, write this greeting with my own hand. This is the mark in every letter of mine; it is the way I write. (NRSV)

V. 17. After the prayer in v. 16, the apostle took up the pen himself, adding the two last verses of this letter. The change is also from plural to singular: it is now Paul himself and he alone who is writing this final word. It clearly appears as an authentication of the letter: ὁ ἀσπασμὸς τῇ ἐμῇ χειρὶ Παύλου, ὅ ἐστιν σημεῖον ἐν πάσῃ ἐπιστολῇ· οὕτως γράφω ("this greeting is [written] with my own hand, of Paul. This is the mark [or: a sign] in every letter [of mine]; this is the way I write"). The apostle generally resorted to the services of a secretary or of an amanuensis in the writing of the letter.[105] At this point in the letter's

---

103. The variant τόπῳ is found primarily in the witnesses of the Western tradition (cf. A* D* F G it[ar, c, dem, etc.] vg Ambroziaster).

104. Cf. MARSHALL, *I and II Thessalonians* (n. 8), p. 230; Richard, 385; FEE, *1 and 2 Thess* (n. 4), p. 341.

105. For the use and the role of the secretary in writing the letters in antiquity and in the case of St Paul, see G. J. BAHR, *Paul and Letter Writing in the First Century*, in *CBQ* 28 (1966) 467-469; idem, *The Subscriptions in the Pauline Letters*, in *JBL* 87 (1968) 28-33; Richard N. LONGENECKER, *Ancient Amanuensis and the Pauline Epistles*, in Richard N. LONGENECKER and Merrill C. TENNEY (eds), *New Dimensions in New Testament Study*, Grand Rapids, Zondervan, 1974, pp. 281-297.

original manuscript there certainly occurred a visible change of handwriting.[106]

The way St Paul authenticates 2 Thessalonians is very peculiar. "The mark" (or "the sign") of which Paul speaks here does not mean a signature, because in antiquity there were not signatures put at the end of letters,[107] but simply the fact that the greeting itself was written in St Paul's hand. What the apostle means by saying that he puts this "mark" or "sign" in every letter he writes? It is true that later, in other of his letters, St Paul will add himself, in his own hand, the final greeting and a few closing words (cf. 1 Cor 16,21; Col 4,18), and in Gal 6,11 and Phm 19, he identifies himself as writing the conclusion of the letter. But in none of these other places does he say specifically that this is his "mark". And why does he speak of every letter of his now, when he is still at the beginning of his epistolary activity? And, again, how could the Thessalonians themselves experience this as a usual way of their apostle authenticating his letters? Was there something similar in 1 Thessalonians, without a specific explanation? The answer to this last question is that very probably the first letter itself contained such a "mark" of the apostle. For, indeed, in 1 Thess 5,27 there is a sudden change to the first person singular, which implies the possibility – more, the probability – that the original of this letter also had the final greeting and benediction (1 Thess 5,27-28) written in St Paul's hand.

The explanation οὕτως γράφω ("this is the way I write") help the readers to identify the handwriting in the autograph as Paul's own. This authentication was necessary as letters falsely attributed to the apostle could circulate (cf. 2,2).[108]

3. *The final blessing (3,18)*

¹⁸ ἡ χάρις τοῦ κυρίου ἡμῶν Ἰησοῦ Χριστοῦ μετὰ πάντων ὑμῶν.

¹⁸ The grace of our Lord Jesus Christ be with all of you. (NRSV)

---

106. See Adolf von DEISSMANN, *Licht From Ancient East*, London, Hodder and Stoughton, ²1927, page facing 170, for an example of the change in handwriting in the greeting based on a photograph of an original letter (cf. WANAMAKER, *The Epistles to the Thessalonians* [n. 2], p. 293).
107. Ceslaus SPICQ, *Les épîtres pastorales* (ÉtB), Paris, Gabalda, 1947, p. 17.
108. JEWETT, *The Thessalonian Correspondence* (n. 41), p. 6, rightly concludes that the note in v. 17 indicates authenticity since otherwise the author would be casting doubt on other Pauline letters not bearing the addition.

The final benediction (**v. 18**), surely also written by the apostle's hand, is typically Pauline, but not identical with any found in other letters of St Paul (cf. 1 Cor 16,23; Gal 6,18; Phil 4,23; 1 Thess 5,28; Phm 25). The wording of this benediction, ἡ χάρις τοῦ κυρίου ἡμῶν Ἰησοῦ Χριστοῦ μετὰ πάντων ὑμῶν ("the grace of our Lord Jesus Christ be with all of you"), is closest to 1 Thess 5,28 and 1 Cor 16,23, though both of those texts lack the πάντων ("all of you"). The addition of "all of you" at the end of this salutation "seems to be quite in keeping with the content of the letter itself".[109]

*

My short conclusion to this analysis of this second part of 2 Thessalonians is mainly that St Paul is very much himself in every phrase and word. But we have to keep in mind that actually this letter (as also 1 Thessalonians) has not only one, but three authors, St Paul and his close companions Silvanus and Timothy. This collaborative work can easily explain most of the letter's peculiarities.

Those who think this letter to be a forgery are faced with enormous difficulties, historical, theological and literary. Why and how would a forger taken the trouble to imagine scores of incidental matters and to try to enter so thouroughly into St Paul's skin? And why, if the forgery belongs to a later time, does it keep to the grammar and stylistic matters that are related only to 1 Thessalonians in the Pauline corpus?

In our analysis we repeatedly evidenced the high Christology of this letter, and that this Christology is eloquently expressing one of the basics of Pauline theology. This aspect needs also our most serious consideration.

---

109. FEE, *1 and 2 Thess* (n. 4), p. 342.

LA DEUXIÈME LETTRE AUX THESSALONICIENS[1]

Benoît Standaert osb

Ce vingt-deuxième colloque œcuménique paulinien a, comme d'habitude, étudié de près une des lettres de Paul, à savoir la Deuxième aux Thessaloniciens. Mais il a en outre examiné aussi deux thèmes particuliers: la question de la pseudépigraphie dans le corpus des lettres de Paul et la question de l'eschatologie chez l'apôtre.

Tout se tient. La lettre elle-même parle de l'eschatologie et introduit une perspective originale sur la fin avec, par rapport à la première aux Thessaloniciens, une correction de poids. En outre, on peut observer que la lettre thématise elle-même la question de son authenticité. Ne peut-on pas dire qu'elle trahit sa pseudépigraphie en insistant justement un peu trop sur le fait qu'elle est authentique et que d'autres lettres ne le sont pas? Le mot «lettre» (4×) ne revient-il pas un peu trop souvent dans cette courte lettre pour être totalement innocent? *Excusatio non petita accusatio manifesta*.

Mon propos sera d'exposer d'abord une hypothèse de travail, puis de montrer comment s'est mise en place l'imitation. On suivra le cours de la pensée de l'auteur en exposant sa vue sur l'eschatologie et la question particulière qu'il traite avant de prendre congé. En finale, on découvrira sans doute mieux la place que cette lettre prend par rapport à d'autres lettres pseudépigraphiques. Par ailleurs, je veillerai à signaler en passant certains apports originaux de notre auteur qui rendent son écrit encore toujours intéressant à lire, en raison même du caractère pseudépigraphique de la lettre.

Une hypothèse de travail

Je partirai d'une hypothèse de travail qui m'est venue au fil des mois de lecture et relecture de la lettre. Je ne l'ai trouvée comme telle nulle part ailleurs. Elle devrait rendre compte de tout ce qu'on voit: σῴζειν

---

[1]. Cette conférence a été prononcée en italien dans la Basilique de Saint Paul-hors-les-murs, au terme des Vêpres de la communauté monastique, en la fête de la sainte Croix (14 septembre 2012).

τὰ φαινόμενα, disait-on en milieu platonicien, en rapport avec l'étude des astres et planètes. On traduit le plus souvent ces trois mots comme «sauver les apparences», mais en réalité il s'agit de «respecter tout ce qui se donne à voir» et à lire! Cela reste la règle de conduite quand on se trouve en face d'évidences difficiles à expliquer.

1. Paul est mort, à Rome. Et ce lieu-ci, avec la tombe de l'apôtre au centre, l'évoque comme aucun autre au monde. Aussitôt après sa mort certains amis se soucient de réunir quelques-unes de ses lettres. À Rome on a encore sa longue épître aux Romains. Elle est si essentielle qu'elle peut sans peine servir à d'autres communautés que celle de Rome. On a retrouvé une de ses lettres les plus anciennes, envoyée depuis Corinthe aux Thessaloniciens. Cette lettre est belle, chaleureuse, concise et riche. Il y a tout de même un problème: son eschatologie justement. Elle est contredite par les faits mêmes. Paul s'attendait alors à connaître de son vivant la venue du Seigneur, mais voilà qu'il est mort encore *avant* que n'arrive la Fin des temps. Lui-même avait évolué dans sa pensée sur cette question. Ses amis qui lui survivent, le savent bien. Que faire?

   Renoncer à publier le texte? Changer le texte? Ou encore éliminer un ou deux paragraphes qui font difficulté et publier un exemplaire tronqué? On a choisi une quatrième voie: publier le texte tel quel mais lui adjoindre une deuxième lettre. Comme on le voit avec les lettres Corinthiennes, Paul a pu écrire à plusieurs reprises à une même communauté, précisant sa pensée au fil des années. On a donc demandé à un ami de Paul qui avait le don d'écrire, de rédiger une deuxième lettre qui rejoue la question de l'attente eschatologique selon un point de vue évolué, adapté aux temps nouveaux.

2. Les plus curieux d'entre nous chercheront à identifier cet ami. Comme la lettre est écrite au nom de «Paul, Sylvain et Timothée», pourquoi ne pas chercher parmi les deux autres que Paul l'auteur ou le rédacteur présumé? Et Sylvain qui est à Rome et a eu la main dans l'édition de la Première de Pierre, n'est-il pas un candidat plausible? Cela a été proposé tant par ceux qui tiennent à l'authenticité que par les autres. On ne peut l'exclure. On verra que ce rédacteur soumis qui exécute un programme qui lui est confié, a du talent et des idées et expressions bien à lui.

3. Ajoutons une dernière remarque: l'apôtre est mort autour de l'année 67. Le terminus a quo de cette deuxième lettre serait la date de sa mort. Le terminus ad quem se trouve dans la lettre même,

croyons-nous. Au chapitre 2, l'auteur esquisse les différents épisodes qui se succéderont selon un schéma apocalyptique connu, avant que ne vienne la Fin ultime. Parmi ces épisodes il y a la profanation du Temple de Jérusalem, quand l'Adversaire viendra occuper le Lieu, «s'asseoir en personne dans le temple de Dieu» et «se produisant lui-même comme Dieu» (2,5). Disons tout de suite et comme entre parenthèses que l'apôtre dans ses lettres authentiques ne parle jamais du Temple de Jérusalem. Pour lui il n'y a plus que le temple que nous sommes, qui compte. Mais surtout, n'avons-nous pas dans ce détail une référence chronologique précieuse? Comment l'auteur aurait-il pu insérer tranquillement cet épisode dans son schéma apocalyptique avec l'intention de nous faire comprendre que le temps de la Fin n'est toujours *pas encore* advenu, si de fait les troupes de Titus avaient *déjà* occupé la ville, mis à feu le Temple, volé le candélabre d'or et emporté le grand rideau? La pointe de tout le paragraphe 2, 3 à 12 est d'affirmer que l'on ne doit pas se laisser induire en erreur quant à l'heure de la Fin. Celle-ci doit être précédée par toute une série d'événements qui n'ont toujours *pas encore* eu lieu.

Ainsi la rédaction de la lettre peut être située peu après la mort de Paul et encore avant la destruction et profanation du Temple. La fourchette se précise entre 67 et 70, et donc un peu moins de vingt ans après la première Lettre aux Thessaloniciens, datée habituellement en 51 environ. Nous sommes sans doute à Rome, et la rédaction a tout à voir avec une édition d'un premier corpus de lettres authentiques de Paul.

La stratégie de notre auteur va consister à imiter Paul, autant que possible, mais aussi à redresser ce que l'on a estimé intenable comme tel, vingt ans après la rédaction de la première lettre.

Imiter

Notre auteur imite son modèle de plusieurs manières. Il lui arrive de reprendre des mots, des bouts de phrases, des tournures stylistiques, voire des phrases entières de la Première épître. Mais il fait plus: il imite même la structure de l'ensemble. Ainsi, dans la Première Lettre on voit Paul revenir sur son point de départ et reformuler une action de grâce alors que nous sommes presque au milieu de l'épître (cf. 1 Th 2,13 et 3,9), chose qui n'arrivera plus jamais par la suite mais qui s'explique par l'intensité de ses sentiments exposés par une digression surabondante, tant il est heureux des nouvelles reçues de Timothée qui est revenu auprès de lui. Or cette action de grâce dupliquée, nous la trouvons justement en 2 Thessaloniciens (voir 1,3 et 2,13), mais si l'on regarde de près la seconde formule et ce qui suit (2,13-17), on doit reconnaître que le mouvement d'action de grâces arrive de façon sèche, tout sauf organique par rapport au contexte précédent. L'imitation est ici quelque peu servile.

En même temps on trouve jusqu'à deux fois dans ce mouvement de prière et d'action de grâce un verbe auxiliaire dont jamais l'apôtre ne se sert en un tel contexte. On y lit deux fois: «Nous *devons* rendre grâces» (εὐχαριστεῖν ὀφείλομεν, 1,3; 2,13). Ici, le rédacteur se trahit, et avoue sans doute qu'il exécute un *devoir* qui lui a été recommandé, voire imposé. Or ce sont justement ces contrastes aigus entre une imitation servile d'une part et des écarts flagrants d'autre part, qui éclairent bien la qualité originale de cette lettre: elle se veut autant que possible fidèle et se montre malgré tout différente.

Prenons le chapitre 1, dans lequel l'auteur essaie d'établir le contact avec ses destinataires, *ad captandam benevolentiam*, sur les traces de la première aux Thessaloniciens. Normalement, les écarts devraient être minimes. Et de fait, l'ouverture est strictement identique: qui pourrait trancher sur l'authenticité en lisant 1 Th 1, 1 et 2 Th 1,1-2? Sauf peut-être que la salutation en 1 Th 1,1 («Grâce et paix»), est plus sobre, alors que l'ajoute en 2 Th 1,2 («Grâce et paix *de la part de Dieu notre Père et du Seigneur Jésus*») devient redondante après le premier verset et finalement peu élégante. Et cela ne trahit-il pas une volonté de vouloir trop bien faire? Et si l'auteur fait partie d'une équipe qui édite d'autres lettres de l'apôtre, n'a-t-il pas introduit ici la formule plus riche qui est courante dans le reste des épîtres (voir Rom 1,7; 1 Co 1,3; 2 Co 1,2, etc.)?

Puis vient la première phrase qui doit rendre grâce et annoncer une première fois le sujet qui sera traité. Le tout est glissé dans une proposition longue et alambiquée (1,3-10), une anacoluthe comme Paul en a dictée des dizaines. Mais au cœur de cette imitation on est doublement surpris de trouver pas moins de dix à douze éléments inconnus de Paul, inhabituels sous sa plume, voire contraire à sa pensée (comme le ὀφείλομεν déjà signalé)[2]. C'est précisément cette conjonction d'éléments imités

---

2. Parmi les expressions inhabituelles sous la plume de Paul, notons encore: «comme il est digne/juste» (3); ἐγκαυχᾶσθαι (4), ἔνδειγμα (5), ἀνταποδοῦναι (6), ἐνδοξασθῆναι (10.12), πληρώσῃ πᾶσαν εὐδοκίαν ἀγαθωσύνης καὶ ἔργον πίστεως (11).

presque servilement et d'autres tout à fait originaux qui trahit la plume d'un rédacteur autre que l'apôtre en personne. Signalons que l'action de grâces se mue en finale en supplication (v.11), ce qui n'est pas trop cohérent ni surtout habituel chez l'apôtre.

Notons encore ce que notre collègue Raymond J. Collins a signalé comme «néologisme» significatif: «l'évangile de notre Seigneur Jésus» (v.8)[3]. Chez Paul «l'évangile» renvoie à Jésus, à sa vie, sa mort, sa pâque. Ici, c'est à la seigneurie future de Jésus que l'expression inhabituelle renvoie.

Signalons enfin la très belle tournure de réciprocité au sujet du Nom qui est «glorifié en vous et vous en lui» (1,12). Paul dans ses lettres ne manque pas d'expressions de réciprocité qui s'enracinent dans son sens de l'amitié, plus particulièrement selon la conception de la philosophie grecque. Mais nulle part il ne les emploie dans une perspective qui concerne notre relation à Dieu, comme c'est le cas ici. Ceci permet d'apprécier notre auteur qui a une capacité de penser et de s'exprimer bien personnelle et vraiment profonde.

Dans cette ouverture il importe de noter aussi tout ce qui manque par rapport aux habitudes épistolaires de l'apôtre. Nous n'apprenons rien sur la situation de Paul, aucune nouvelle circonstanciée sur les Thessaloniciens, pas de message ni de messager entre l'apôtre et sa communauté, aucune occasion précise qui oblige l'apôtre à rédiger une nouvelle lettre, pas même un renvoi à la lettre précédente... C'est peu, oui bien trop peu, quand on compare cette ouverture avec celles des lettres authentiques.

Par contre: il est question des «églises de Dieu» au pluriel, et l'horizon s'ouvre, comme il est également question de «persécutions» (διωγμοί), terme technique. Avant 70, seule la communauté à Rome a connu une persécution en règle (ainsi l'étude pertinente de Bas van Iersel en rapport avec le même terme en Mc 4,17 et 10,30)[4]. Rien ne nous permet de savoir si en Grèce ou en Macédoine il y ait eu autre chose que des vexations occasionnelles ou un mépris social plus ou moins général à l'égard du mouvement chrétien. Une «persécution» officielle de la part

---

3. Voir R. F. COLLINS, *The Letters that Paul Did Not Write. The Epistle to the Hebrews and the Pauline Pseudepigrapha*, Michael Glazier, Wilmington, Delaware, 1988, 226-232; et IDEM, " "The Gospel of our Lord Jesus" (1 Thes 1,8): A Symbolic Shift of Paradigm", in R. F. COLLINS (éd.), *The Thessalonian Correspondence* (BETL, 87), Leuven, Peeters, 1990, 426-440.

4. Bas VAN IERSEL, *Mark. A Reader-Response Commentary*, Bloomsbury Publishing PLC, 1998, *ad loc.*, et dans l'introduction, 42-44.

d'un pouvoir local romain n'est pas attestée pour cette époque en Macédoine.

On peut donc supposer que la deuxième lettre est écrite pro forma aux Thessaloniciens mais est appelée à atteindre *toutes* les communautés, quelles que soient leurs épreuves. Les «persécutions» mentionnées en 1,5 incluent plus particulièrement la communauté de Rome, éprouvée ces toutes dernières années sous Néron (64-65). Tout ceci fait sens et renforce l'hypothèse de travail avec sa cohérence.

Imiter est un des thèmes de la lettre. L'auteur imite Paul qui dit combien ses destinataires savent qu'ils doivent l'imiter (voir 3,7: οἴδατε πῶς δεῖ μιμεῖσθαι ἡμᾶς). Certains se sont interrogés: jusqu'où cette pseudépigraphie est-elle compatible, moralement, avec une vie dévouée à l'évangile et à la vérité (voir l'expression originale de «l'amour de la vérité» en 2,10)? On a parlé de «créer un faux» ou encore de «*forgery*». Aux yeux de notre auteur, sa pratique relève plutôt de la *mimèsis*, qui est un exercice littéraire reconnu et enseigné dans les écoles de rhétorique.

De fait, que peut-il y avoir de répréhensible à imiter le maître? Le thème de l'imitation dans la lettre n'offre-t-il pas une autorisation indirecte du procédé littéraire de la mimèsis? Qu'a-t-il fait d'autre que de s'exécuter, imitant tournures, anacoluthes, double action de grâce répétée comme en 1 Th (et nulle part ailleurs), doxologie finale, etc.? Il insère plus d'une fois un rappel au premier enseignement oral, ce qui lui donne beau jeu pour reformuler autrement la doctrine eschatologique de l'apôtre. Il ira même jusqu'à imiter, en finale, la signature autographe de Paul – effet rhétorique appuyé, même si invérifiable par qui que ce soit, car Paul est mort et les communautés qui recevront ce texte, n'ont pas ou plus d'autographe pour comparer! Le corpus des lettres pauliniennes qu'on est en train de composer et qu'on transmettra aux différentes églises se présentera de toute manière comme une copie de lettres conservées. L'autographe de la signature est nulle part…

L'ESCHATOLOGIE

Venons-en à l'argument essentiel de la lettre: l'eschatologie. Le thème a été abordé une première fois au ch. 1 (v. 5-10). Les six versets évoquent le moment où le Seigneur Jésus viendra, et alors «le jugement de Dieu» rendra à chacun selon ce qu'il mérite. Le thème est introduit à nouveau et de façon expresse dans les deux premiers versets du ch. 2. On y trouve la véritable *propositio* de toute l'épître. Il s'agit de mettre en garde les destinataires contre toute idée que «le Jour du Seigneur serait déjà là».

Dans les dix versets suivants l'auteur esquisse avec force le scénario auquel on doit s'attendre quand les événements de la fin et la parousie du Seigneur s'accompliront. Il se sert d'un schéma apocalyptique conventionnel et n'a d'autre préoccupation que celle de rappeler aux destinataires que la succession connue des épisodes fait que pour le moment nous ne sommes pas encore arrivés à la Fin des temps. Ce qu'il y a d'apocalyptique dans la Première Lettre n'est pas bien différent de ce que l'on trouve ici, mais l'attente eschatologique est radicalement autre: pour Paul en 1Th, la fin est imminente et la communauté est une communauté eschatologique; pour notre auteur, la fin n'est pas du tout imminente, seulement il importe de l'attendre avec tout le sérieux requis car même si la venue n'est pas pour tout de suite, elle sera un terrible jugement pour les uns et apportera le salut pour les autres. Déjà Helmut Koester avait signalé qu'on assiste à une autre eschatologie dans 1 Th et 2 Th mais que les traditions apocalyptiques étaient foncièrement les mêmes[5].

C'est dans ce paragraphe qu'on trouve une expression originale que la grande tradition méditera sans fin: «Le mystère de l'impiété – *mysterium iniquitatis*, en latin – est déjà à l'œuvre (ἤδη ἐνεργεῖται, v. 7)». L'auteur perçoit au sein de l'histoire vécue des forces destructrices à l'œuvre. Il les nomme, tantôt de façon impersonnelle, parlant par exemple de l'Apostasie, tantôt de façon personnelle, désignant l'antagoniste comme l'Homme impie, l'Adversaire, etc. Il évoque la tension qui habite le temps vécu sans chercher pour autant à l'expliquer entièrement. Au lecteur de tenir compte de ce qui est à l'œuvre, de ne pas en être dupe mais de poser les bons choix en «accueillant l'amour de la vérité, afin d'être sauvé» plutôt que de «se complaire dans l'injustice» (2,11-12; εὐδοκήσαντες τῇ ἀδικίᾳ, notons en passant l'emploi tout à fait inhabituel pour Paul du verbe εὐδοκεῖν avec ἀδικία, comme objet).

Au beau milieu de toute cette évocation apocalyptique l'auteur rappelle combien son enseignement se rattache à ce qui a été enseigné oralement autrefois (2,5). L'écrit s'appuie donc sur l'oral et l'oral doit comme authentifier l'écrit aux yeux des lecteurs, faisant comprendre que ce qui est écrit ne diffère en rien de ce qui a été dit autrefois. Belle stratégie rhétorique qui, ici encore, imite une tournure de la première lettre (1 Th 3,4), mais s'en écarte entièrement quant au contenu. Ce phénomène reçoit tout son sens dans l'hypothèse adoptée de la pseudépigraphie de la seconde lettre.

---

5. Voir Helmut KOESTER, *From Paul's Eschatology to the Apocalyptic Schemata of 2 Thessalonians*, in: R.F. COLLINS (éd.), *The Thessalonians Correspondance* (n. 3), 441-458 (458).

Un mot encore sur les indisciplinés

Après quoi on revient à l'action de grâce et, à bien des égards, on a l'impression que notre auteur va conclure et prendre définitivement congé de ses destinataires. Mais il n'en est rien. Il lui faut encore développer un dernier point. Il s'agit d'une prescription ou d'un commandement (παραγγέλλειν) supplémentaire au sujet des indisciplinés, des gens qui «vivent dans l'oisiveté» ou «mènent une vie désordonnée, ἀτάκτως».

Le thème n'est pas strictement nouveau. Il s'agit d'un autre point de la première lettre, pas trop clairement exposé dans celle-ci (voir 1 Th 5,14: νουθετεῖτε τοὺς ἀτάκτους). Notons le verbe «prescrire» ou «commander» qui reviendra jusqu'à quatre fois en huit versets et qui ne fait pas vraiment partie du vocabulaire ni de l'attitude foncière de Paul quand celui-ci exhorte (comparer Phil 2,1-4), même si on le trouve une fois dans la Première Lettre (4,11, en lien avec le travail des mains justement). La reprise est copiée du modèle, l'insistante répétition est propre à notre auteur. La pointe est sans doute de combattre la tendance à une forme de clientélisme qui constituait à l'époque une plaie assez courante.

L'auteur est plutôt vague dans sa description, alors que pour une fois il fait allusion à ce qu'il a appris: «Or *nous entendons dire* qu'il en est parmi vous qui vivent dans l'oisiveté, ne travaillant pas du tout mais se mêlant de tout». Notons le jeu de mots (μηδὲν ἐργαζομένους ἀλλὰ περιεργαζομένους, ce dernier verbe est un hapax du NT). L'auteur se sert d'une figure de style et d'une circonlocution où la réalité évoquée est supposée connue et se voit comme esquivée bien plus que désignée. Comment ne pas voir ici une trace de plus de la pseudépigraphie? Alors qu'il devrait évoquer un désordre précis ou une tare, une plaie, une déviance, l'auteur se sert d'un jeu de mots qui cache plus qu'il ne révèle ce dont il pourrait s'agir!

«Qui ne veut pas travailler, qu'il ne mange pas non plus».

Au v. 10 du même chapitre 3, il rappelle un enseignement oral de l'apôtre. Il le formule comme une règle de conduite: «Qui ne veut pas travailler, qu'il ne mange pas non plus». Voilà un enseignement original qui aura du succès au fil des siècles à venir, notamment dans le monde monastique.

Jean Cassien, dans ses *Institutions*, au livre X, quand il parle de l'acédie et de la nécessité du travail manuel, fera une relecture tout à fait remarquable des deux lettres aux Thessaloniciens, montrant avec pertinence le crescendo qui traverse les passages concernés[6]. Le moine s'en trouve exhorté à mener une vie occupée plutôt que oisive.

Augustin, de son côté, consacrera tout un petit traité sur le travail manuel des moines[7], montrant indirectement que de son temps la tendance contraire était assez répandue.

Benoît, dans sa règle, reprend le thème et insiste: «L'oisiveté est ennemie de l'âme», et «Alors ils sont vraiment moines, s'ils vivent du travail de leurs mains, comme nos Pères et les apôtres»[8].

La parfaite antithèse de cette tradition se rencontre en Syrie où des moines itinérants vivent sur le compte de leurs hôtes, ne travaillant pas et n'étant pas obligés à l'aumône. Ceux-ci s'appuient non pas sur Paul mais sur l'autorité de Jésus et ses paroles sur la conduite des envoyés deux par deux ou encore sur les oiseaux et les lys des champs...

Signalons encore une particularité originale dans la Règle du Maître, la source de la Règle de Benoît. Le Maître inverse le logion et en conclut: «Qui ne mange pas, ne doit pas non plus travailler»[9], et donc tout frère qui jeûne, pourra faire la lecture aux autres qui travaillent de leurs mains!

Aujourd'hui nous parlons du droit au travail: en face de la plaie causée par le chômage, toute société est invitée à prendre au sérieux l'offre au plus grand nombre d'un travail digne et humanisant. Créativité et inventivité viennent rejoindre un des beaux principes que nous a transmis la tradition paulinienne, s'appuyant sur son exemple de vie (Piero Rossano)[10].

---

6. Voir Jean Cassien, *Institutions cénobitiques*, livre X, 8-16, (éd. Jean-Claude Guy; SC, 109), Cerf, Paris 1965, 400-411, et B. STANDAERT, *La prima lettera ai Tessalonicesi, sorgente di vita spirituale*, dans Morna D. HOOKER (éd.), *The First Epistle to the Thessalonians* (Monographic Series of 'Benedictina', Biblical-Ecumenical Section, n°15), Rome 2003, 175-180.

7. Augustin, *De opere monachorum*, PL 40, 547.

8. Voir Benoît de Nursie, *Règle des moines*, ch. 48,8 (SC, 182), Cerf, Paris, 1972. Une même pensée sur le travail aux champs se trouve chez Cassiodore, *Institutiones*, 38, PL 70, 1105.

9. Voir *La Règle du Maître*, ch. 50,6 et surtout 53,40, (SC, 106), Cerf, Paris, 1964.

10. Piero ROSSANO, *Lettere ai Tessalonicesi* (La Sacra Bibbia), Marietti, Rome 1965, *ad loc.* Yann REDALIÉ rappelle à ce propos la constitution de l'URSS de 1936, «seul verset biblique à être présent dans la constitution d'un Etat moderne. On le retrouve en effet à l'article 12 en conclusion du chapitre 1 de la Constitution: 'Le travail est dans l'URSS un devoir et un honneur pour tout citoyen en mesure de travailler, selon le principe «que celui qui ne travaille pas ne mange pas non plus»'. Dans l'URSS se réalise le principe du socialisme. De

Conclusion

Notre auteur a exécuté avec fidélité ce qui lui a été demandé: écrire une seconde lettre, adressée pro forma aux Thessaloniciens dans laquelle il n'aborde aucun thème nouveau mais affine la pensée de l'apôtre en premier lieu sur l'eschatologie, mais également sur la conduite désordonnée de certains membres de la communauté. L'auteur imite Paul, autant qu'il le peut. Il prend toutefois ses distances quand on touche à la grande question de l'imminence de la Fin. Indirectement, il témoigne d'un regard original sur l'Église et les églises de Dieu: vivre en chrétien, c'est avoir le regard tourné vers la Fin et son sérieux.

Dans le temps qui nous reste, il s'agit de réaliser que l'évangile proclamé destine le croyant à la gloire, et que déjà le Nom du Seigneur Jésus est glorifié en nous et nous en lui par une conduite bonne. Déjà l'Esprit sanctifie, déjà la Parole accomplit sa course et est glorifiée dans le temps, mais aussi dès maintenant il y a un «mystère de l'Impiété» qui est à l'œuvre. N'en soyons pas dupe. Viendra le jour où ce qui secrètement agit dans l'histoire comme force satanique, sera démasqué et détruit à jamais. Gardons l'esprit de prière et intercédons les uns pour les autres, d'église à église. Gardons la confiance sur l'issue finale qui sera glorieuse pour qui accueille avec amour la vérité. Soyons en paix, d'une paix qui rayonne de «l'amour de Dieu» et de «la constance du Christ».

Toute cette lettre témoigne d'une liberté que d'autres n'hésiteront pas à adopter à leur tour: prolonger la pensée de l'apôtre et l'actualiser alors que les temps ont changé et que devant de nouvelles questions il ne sert à rien de répéter d'anciennes réponses (Edward Schillebeeckx). Il reste que personne n'a autant imité Paul que notre auteur, sans doute parce que personne n'était aussi lié à une tâche précise qui lui était confiée. Son travail ne ressemble à celui d'aucun autre écrit pseudépigraphique du Nouveau Testament. Malgré cette dépendance obligée, il a réussi à dire des choses neuves et inspirantes pour sa génération à lui et finalement même pour la nôtre, ici réunie, près de la tombe de l'Apôtre. «Que le Seigneur dirige nos cœurs vers l'amour de Dieu et la constance du Christ» et «que le Nom du Seigneur soit glorifié en vous et vous en lui». «Que la grâce de notre Seigneur soit avec vous tous!»

---

chacun selon ses capacités, à chacun selon son travail'». Voir *La deuxième épître aux Thessaloniciens* (CNT, 9c), Labor et Fides, Genève, 2011, 154.

ISSUES OF AUTHORSHIP IN THE PAULINE CORPUS: RETHINKING THE RELATIONSHIP BETWEEN 1 AND 2 THESSALONIANS

KARL P. DONFRIED

I. RETHINKING INHERITED PARADIGMS

1. *Theological Intention and Imperial Context*

In a *Studiorum Novi Testamenti Societas* lecture entitled "The Cults of Thessalonica and the Thessalonian Correpondence",[1] I urged that 1 Thessalonians could best be understood in light of the cultic, political and historical context of first century Thessalonica. Abstract generalizations about Pauline theology in this earliest extant Pauline letter are insufficient, it was argued, to comprehend its purpose with precision. Subsequently this essay has been commented on frequently. Having learned significantly from the ensuing discussion, my interpretation of several passages in 1 Thessalonians has sharpened and become more explicit. Indeed, a historically and culturally informed approach to this earliest known letter of Paul must ask at the outset how first-century believers in Thessalonica might have received this gospel of salvation in its imperial context. Further, it must be queried, is it possible to examine more precisely the relational milieu within Roman Thessalonica as an appropriate way of hearing the imbedded social pattern of Roman norms that Paul,[2] the Jewish believer in Christ, together with his associates, are challenging and confronting? If so, such an approach would allow the theology of this letter to be anchored more specifically within a clearly defined social and historical context. In the analysis that follows I will attempt to outline my understanding of 1 Thessalonians in a more historically distinct and unambiguous manner than in my previous publications

---

1. Karl Paul DONFRIED, *The Cults of Thessalonica and the Thessalonian Correpondence*, in *Paul, Thessalonica and Early Christianity*, London, T&T Clark, 2002, 21-48.
2. As this analysis will indicate, I maintain that both 1 and 2 Thessalonians are written by Paul, Silvanus and Timothy, with Paul as the leader of the group. Sometimes I will refer to all three writers and on several occasions simply to Paul as the leader of this group.

with the anticipation that such an attempt, together with the queries already raised, might provide new insights with regard to the exegesis of 2 Thessalonians as well. It is for this reason that the analysis of each letter is, for the most part, presented separately, for it was in following such a sequence of analysis that the proposals that follow emerged. Also, I should add that I am fully aware that in contemporary New Testament scholarship there is little unanimity and much contentiousness with regard to the intention and purpose of 2 Thessalonians; this also holds true with regard to questions of authorship as well as its relationship to 1 Thessalonians. How does one proceed through these troubled and turbulent waters? At the outset let me state unequivocally that this can only happen with your help, cooperation and insight. The complexity of the issues is daunting and they will, therefore, require collaboration, contributions and corrections from you my colleagues in this distinguished *Colloquium Paulinum*.

2. *Paul, Silvanus and Timothy: the Issue of Co-Authorship*

Before probing some of the exegetical issues involving 1 Thessalonians and 2 Thessalonians, I wanted to share some observations that involve both letters; in each the opening salutations announce Paul, Silvanus and Timothy as authors. How, one must ask, are we to understand this reference to co-authorship and how does it function? This is one of those areas where inherited theological, ideological and literary assumptions may cloud our perceptions especially with regard to the role of Paul, Silvanus and Timothy in the process of letter composition. How does Paul, for example, perceive his role in this process: what is his function and why does he need co-authors? Paul is a missionary founding new congregations whose "faith in God has become known" (1 Thess 1,8) as a result of the Apostle's proclamation that Jesus is Lord (1 Thess 2,13) and the positive reception of this gospel of God (1 Thess 2,9) by the believers in Thessalonica (1 Thess 1,6) and others in the Roman Empire. To speak of Paul as a theologian is accurate only in such a missionary context as he attempts to draw out the implications of the gospel in specific situations and as he remains in dialog with the congregations that he has helped to establish. Such sustained pastoral encouragement and nurturing is carried out through personal visits by Paul and/or his missionary associates as well as through written correspondence, the contents of which may have been discussed and composed jointly with his co-workers. In reflecting on these matters one needs to remember the significant geographical range of the Pauline missionary centers[3] throughout the Roman Empire, the large number of associates, the vast distances between churches and the extensive periods in which he is immobilized, not least as a result of lengthy imprisonments.

The names of associates and co-workers of Paul are specifically referred to in the address of the following letters:

- Paul, Silvanus and Timothy (1 Thessalonians)
- Paul, Silvanus and Timothy (2 Thessalonians)
- Paul and Sosthenes (1 Corinthians)
- Paul and Timothy (2 Corinthians)
- Paul and Timothy (Philemon)
- Paul and Timothy (Colossians)
- Paul and Timothy (Philippians)
- Paul and all the brethren with me (Galatians)

It is noteworthy that Timothy is listed as the co-author in six of these eight letters attributed to Paul. The obvious question arises whether the associates of Paul, and particularly Timothy, participated in the discussion and writing of these letters,[4] especially given the Apostle's high praise of Timothy in Phil 2,22ff: "But Timothy's worth you know, how like a son with a father he has served with me in the work of the gospel [ἐδούλευσεν εἰς τὸ εὐαγγέλιον]. I hope therefore to send him as soon as I see how things go with me; and I trust in the Lord that I will also come soon."[5] In writing to Atticus Cicero intimates the possibility of a cooperative letter: "For my part I have gathered from your letters – both those which you wrote in conjunction with others (*quas communiter cum aliis*) and those you wrote in your own name (*quas tuo nomine*)" (*Att.* 11.5.1).[6] Among the important studies of letter-writing in the Pauline

---

3. The key Pauline missionary centers would certainly include Ephesus, Corinth and Rome.

4. E. Randolph RICHARDS, *Paul and First Century: Secretaries, Composition and Collection*, Downer's Grove IL, Inter-Varsity Press, 2004, 108, writes: "Some of Paul's letters included material inserted by a coauthor into the letter during composition. This material was not part of Paul's original plan; the material sometimes interrupted his particular train of thought. Even though this material was non-Pauline, it was not un-Pauline or post-Pauline. The material was inserted during the letter's composition and thus has Paul's ultimate authorization. Some material was inserted into the letter during the early drafting of the letter. This material was usually woven rather seamlessly into the letter. Some material was added during the final editing of the letter and was not as neatly integrated."

5. Unless note otherwise, all biblical translations are from the New Revised Standard Version (NRSV).

6. Jerome MURPHY-O'CONNOR, *Keys to First Corinthians: Revisiting the Major Issues*, Oxford, Oxford University Press, 2009; cited on page 2.

period are those of Prior[7] and Richards.[8] Prior discovered only fifteen papyrus letters that fell into the category of the "cooperative letter," i.e., involving epistolary co-authorship, and Richards found only six out of 645 papyrus letters from Oxyrynchus, Tebtunis, and Zenon that had a plurality of senders. As a result Jerome Murphy-O'Connor observes that such "a tiny proportion indicates that the naming of another person in the address was anything but a meaningless convention. In fact it was especially significant and, as one might have expected, multiple sender letters are formulated exclusively in the first person plural."[9] For Murphy-O'Connor, then, those associated with Paul in the address were selected to play a role in the creation of the letter precisely as co-authors.[10] The 'I' passages in the Pauline letters (i.e., 1/2Thess; 1/2 Cor) "strengthens the communal character of the letter as a whole"[11] and the regular use of "we" throughout 1 and 2 Thessalonians[12] does recommend that they be understood as co-authors.[13] Is it not reasonable, therefore, to assume that Paul consulted with his associates as *synergoi theou* before and during the actual dictation and that he would interject items of importance to him as needed, recognizing, indeed, that each letter presented unique situations and challenges?[14] This still leaves open the extent of Timothy and Silvanus's contribution in 1 Thessalonians a well as in 2 Thessalonians, if it is indeed judged that they made genuine contributions to that letter. If one is unwilling to admit the possibility of co-authorship in 1 and 2 Thessalonians, as well as elsewhere among the Pauline letters, then a reasonable explanation will have to be developed as to why indeed Paul makes specific reference to such co-senders.

---

7. Michael PRIOR, *Paul the Letter-Writer and the Second Letter to Timothy* (JSNTSup, 23), Sheffield, JSOT Press, 1989.

8. E. Randolph RICHARDS, *The Secretary in the Letters of Paul* (WUNT, 2/42), Tübingen, Mohr Siebeck, 1991.

9. MURPHY-O'CONNOR, *Keys to First Corinthians* (n. 6), 2 and 3.

10. MURPHY-O'CONNOR, *Keys to First Corinthians* (n. 6), 3.

11. This position is argued by E. H. ASKWITH, *"I" and "We" in the Thessalonian Epistles*, in *Expositor*, 8th series 1 (1911) 149-159 and also by PRIOR, *Paul the Letter-Writer*, 40.

12. 1 Thess 2,18; 3,5; 5,27 and 2 Thess 2,5; 3,17.

13. See further, MURPHY-O'CONNOR, *Keys to First Corinthians* (n. 6), 11.

14. Markus MÜLLER, *Der sogenannte Schriftstellerische Plural*, in *BZ* 42 (1998) 183: "Das 'Wir' wird dort gebraucht, wo es um den Apostolat des Paulus und damit um 'sein' Missionswerk ingesamt geht – was mit der Nennung eines Kollecktivs in der Absenderangabe einhergeht. Wenn es freilich um Paulus ganz persönlich geht, tritt er aus der Gruppe der Mitarbeiter heraus und spricht dann für sich selbst – im Ich-Stil."

II. 1 Thessalonians: Exegetical Probings

When discussing Paul's objective in writing 1 Thessalonians, I also have 2 Thessalonians very much in mind both in terms of its intention and the question of authorship. In what follows, selected prior emphases with regard to 1 Thessalonians will be briefly summarized in order to serve as a foundation for other, related issues that today deserve concentrated consideration, among them the theme of patronage in Roman Thessalonica. Although brief reference will be made to my previous work on ways in which the Thessalonians honored their Roman benefactors,[15] the broader theme of patronage in its Roman context requires more extensive analysis and discussion given the current stage of scholarly research and interest in this area. This concern is complementary with and interdependent with our previous emphasis that 1 Thessalonians must first be understood as directly involved with the political and religious situation in the Roman dominated city of Thessalonica. Although writing to believers enveloped in a political situation saturated with persecution, the Apostle's criticism and concern encompassed as well far broader aspects of local and religious values of a pagan culture that does "not know God" (1 Thess 4,4).

1. *Religious Diversity and Political Conflict in Roman Thessalonica*

Most scholars date this first extant Pauline letter between 43 and 50 A.D.; I continue to urge the earlier dating.[16] It is written by Paul, Silvanus and Timothy to "the church of the Thessalonians in God the Father and the Lord Jesus Christ" (τῇ ἐκκλησίᾳ Θεσσαλονικέων ἐν θεῷ πατρὶ καὶ κυρίῳ Ἰησοῦ Χριστῷ; 1 Thess 1,1). This opening verse, rich in significance, raises a number of issues, among them, why here in Thessalonica, the capital of the Roman province of Macedonia and dedicated to the imperial cult of Rome, Paul employs the *nomen gentilicium*, "of the Thessalonians," instead of referring to the name of the church in the particular city as in his other letters, for example, 1 Cor 1,2: "To the church of God that is in Corinth"?

Although for purposes of illustration and clarity it will be useful to distinguish civic from religious cults, it must be remembered that this is an artificial separation since religious and political life and activity are

---

15. Donfried, *The Cults of Thessalonica* (n. 1), 36.
16. Donfried, *Chronology: The Apostolic and Pauline Period*, in *Paul, Thessalonica and Early Christianity* (n. 1), 99-117.

thoroughly intertwined in this city. During the first half of the twentieth century archaeologists discovered two temples in Thessaloniki quite close to the agora and specifically referred to the Acts 17 account of Paul in this city. One is a temple of Serapis (*serapeum*) and the other a small temple of the Roman period located under the narthex of the first where fourteen "priests of the gods" diligently performed their rites. The mysteries of the god Dionysus with their sensual provocativeness were widely practiced as well. Then, too, there are references to Zeus, Asclepius, Aphrodite, Demeter and to the cult of Cabirus, whose god promoted fertility and protected sailors.

In the midst of such a wide-ranging and diverse religious situation, Paul, Silvanus and Timothy not only give thanks in 1 Thessalonians that the believers "turned to God from idols, to serve a living and true God" (1,9), but they also redefine God as "God the Father" and twice blame the theological and ethical ignorance of the pagans on their not knowing *this* God. Thus, in 1 Thess 4,5 they makes reference to "the Gentiles who do not know God" and then in 4,13 they urge that the believers do "not grieve as others do who have no hope" precisely because through their God-given *election*[17] they believe "that Jesus died and rose again." Knowing God through faith in Jesus Christ also determines the new moral life, the life of holiness/sanctification (ἁγιωσύνη/ἁγιασμός; 1 Thess 3,13; 4.4,7); such faith indicates that God's intention for the believer is indeed salvation. Believing in, having faith in "God the Father and the Lord Jesus Christ" as well as the proper functioning of that faith is of crucial concern for the authors as they write this letter to the church of the Thessalonians. In order to answer the question before us, why Paul writes to "the church of the Thessalonians in God the Father and the Lord Jesus Christ" (1 Thess 1,1) and not to the church *in* Thessalonica, we need to examine more completely the political situation in Thessalonica at the time of Paul and how his associates interacted with it.

It is Paul the Jew, who is now "in Christ," and who interacts with the pagan culture in partnership with his co-workers.[18] Here it must be emphasized that Paul understood himself first and foremost as a Jew, in the broadest sense of that term, although a Jew distinctly different from the majority of his contemporaries: he believes that the Messiah has

---

17. *Princeps a diis electus:* the divine election of the emperor as a political concept at Rome may influence the choice of this term.

18. See further my essay *Paul's Jewish Matrix: The Scope and Nature of the Contributions*, in Thomas G. CASEY and Justin TAYLOR (eds), *Paul's Jewish Matrix*, Rome, G&BP, 2011, 11-49.

come. Not unimportant for the broader influences on especially Paul's theology, yet to be considered more fully, are passages where Paul defines himself with considerable fluency: Phil 3,5: "circumcised on the eighth day, a member of the people of Israel, of the tribe of Benjamin, a Hebrew born of Hebrews"; 2 Cor 11,22: "Are they Hebrews? So am I. Are they Israelites? So am I. Are they descendants of Abraham? So am I"; Rom 11,1: "I ask, then, has God rejected his people? By no means! I myself *am* an Israelite, a descendant of Abraham, a member of the tribe of Benjamin." Here, even at this late point in his missionary work as he writes Romans, he uses the present tense to define his identity.

Paul and those associated with him in Thessalonica proclaim a theology that is in fundamental conflict with the political theology of the Empire. A. Deissmann insightfully and cogently argued that there is a "'polemical parallelism' between the language of the cult of the ruler and the cult of Christ."[19] Among the signs pointing in this direction is the repeated use of political-religious language in Paul's earliest extant letter. Was this, including the term "gospel" (εὐαγγέλιον), simply ambiguous language that might have been misunderstood or is it intended to be intentionally provocative? My continuing study of this letter increasingly leads me to assert the latter alternative. In 2,12 God, according to the Apostle, calls the Thessalonian Christians "into his own βασιλεία"; in 5,3 ["When they say, 'There is peace and security,' then sudden destruction will come upon them, as labor pains come upon a pregnant woman, and there will be no escape!"] there is a frontal attack on the *pax et securitas* program of the early Roman empire and, in the verses just preceding this criticism, one finds three terms heavily laden with political allusions: παρουσία (2,19; 3,13; 4,5: 5,23), ἀπάντησις (meeting: 4:17), and κύριος (22 references). παρουσία is related to the ***visitation*** of a king or some other dignitary; when used as court language παρουσία refers to the ***arrival*** of Caesar, a king or an official; ἀπάντησις refers to the citizens ***meeting*** a dignitary who is about to visit the city. The term κύριος, especially when used in the same context as the two preceding terms, also has undeniable political connotations to which we will return momentarily once we have shared some preliminary thoughts on the *pax et securitas* theme in 1 Thess 5,1-11.[20]

---

19. A. DEISSMANN, *Light from the Ancient East: The New Testament Illustrated by Recently Discovered Texts from the Graeco-Roman World*, London, Hodder & Stoughton, ²1927, 342.

20. For additional comments on the *Pax et Securitas*, DONFRIED, *The Cults of Thessalonica* (n. 1), 43 and Dieter GEORGI, *God Turned Upside Down*, in Richard A. HORSLEY (ed.), *Paul*

The eschatological perspective of these verses wishes to make evident what will, in fact, bring permanent "peace and security" to Paul's ἐκκλησία, and, as a result, our authors intentionally unmask "the supposed 'peace and security' offered by Roman power..." so that the ecclesia in Christ might be able "to maintain its corporate solidarity in resistance to the dominant imperial order."[21] Harrison writes that only "those who are protected by the armor of the crucified Warrior-Lord (1 Thess 5,8.10a: cf. Isa. 59,16-18, esp. v. 17) will escape His wrath (5,3b.9a.10b). Instead of trusting in the false security of the Roman Empire, the apostle summons his converts to be alert and sober (1 Thess 5,6-8a)."[22] Harrison raises other relevant questions for us to consider as we give further detailed attention to these issues, among them whether Paul's eschatology "*intentionally* drove home the ideological collision..."?[23] and "whether some of Paul's Thessalonian auditors may have misinterpreted Paul's prophecy about the eschatological demise of the imperial clients (1 Thess 5,2-3) as a prophecy about the Roman ruler's *imminent* demise."[24] If the response to this query is positive then we will also want to ask as we proceed whether such a prophecy about the imminent demise of the Roman ruler is related to issues that emerge in 2 Thessalonians, particularly in 2 Thess 2,2-3 where the exhortation is given "not to be quickly shaken in mind or alarmed, either by spirit or by word or by letter, as though from us, to the effect that the day of the Lord is already here. Let no one deceive you in any way; for that day will not come unless the rebellion comes first and the lawless one is revealed, the one destined for destruction."

Our discussion will now turn to the use of political-religious language and its relationship to the coins that were minted in Thessalonica. The people in the eastern Mediterranean used the term κύριος to refer to the Roman emperors from Augustus on. Although the first verifiable inscription of the *Kyrios*-title in Greece dates to the time of Nero (A.D. 54-68), the numismatic evidence from an earlier period is very compelling and

---

and Empire: Religion and Power in Roman Imperial Society, Harrisburg PA, Trinity, 1997, 148-157, especially n. 17 on p. 154.

21. Abraham SMITH, *"Unmasking the Powers": Toward a Postcolonial Analysis of 1 Thessalonians*, in Richard A. Horsley (ed.), *Paul and the Roman Imperial Order*, Harrisburg PA, Trinity, 2004, 47-66.

22. James R. HARRISON, *Paul and the Imperial Authorities at Thessalonica and Rome* (WUNT, 273), Tübingen, Mohr Siebeck, 2011, 61-62.

23. HARRISON, *Paul and the Imperial Authorities at Thessalonica and Rome* (n. 22), 40.

24. HARRISON, *Paul and the Imperial Authorities at Thessalonica and Rome* (n. 22), 45.

it underscores how seriously we must take the political contexts referenced on the various coins. On the obverse of one coin from Thessalonica prior to Paul's ministry there is a head of Julius Caesar with the legend θεός that makes evident that Julius was acclaimed a god of the city; on another Octavian is designated as *divi filius*, with the divine Julius on the reverse. All of this, coupled with the use of εὐαγγέλιον (a term current in the Empire[25]) six times in 1 Thessalonians, could easily be understood as violating the "decrees of the emperor" in the most blatant manner as Acts 17,7 reports quite accurately: "They are all acting contrary to the decrees of the emperor, saying that there is another king named Jesus."[26] Paul's gospel of Jesus Christ as Lord is in fundamental opposition to the gospel of Caesar Augustus as Lord. We need to take note of one other item featured on this coin from Thessalonica: Caesar, and by implication Octavian/Augustus, is "the god of the Thessalonians." Paul's Thessalonica is marked by a clear interpenetration of the religious with the political so that they become virtually indistinguishable. The juxtaposition of the divine Julius with his son[27] Octavian/Augustus may reflect Thessalonican awareness of the emperor's status as a "son of God." We see here a clear development of a royal theology in which focused attention is given to legitimating the rule of Emperor Augustus and that of his successors. "Paul and his community," insists Crossan, "would have been hard pressed to avoid Roman imperial theology in Thessalonica during the reign of Claudius. Thessalonica's mints produced coinage for the entire province and that city accepted dynastic divinity for the emperors Augustus through Claudius."[28] This takes us right back to our starting point: we began with a query concerning the uniqueness of the opening address to "the church of the Thessalonians" and why this unique formulation was created for 1 Thessalonians. Now we can respond: this salutation is in direct response to the Roman numismatic propaganda that we have just analyzed. Paul, Silvanus and Timothy

---

25. For examples of the use of εὐαγγέλιον in the Roman Empire see Ceslas SPICQ, *Theological Lexicon of the New Testament*, Peabody, MA., Hendrickson, 1994, II.85-86. One compelling example cited by Spicq: "The birthday of the god (Augustus) began for the world the good news that he brought" (p. 86).

26. HARRISON, *Paul and the Imperial Authorities at Thessalonica and Rome*, (n. 22), 52-53, adds: "Perhaps the apostle's assertion that there was an alternative Kingdom and glory for Thessalonian believers (βασιλεία καὶ δόξα: 1 Thess 2:12) further provoked Roman sensibilities."

27. Note 1 Thess 1,10.

28. John Dominic CROSSAN and Jonathan L. REED, *In Search of Paul*, San Francisco, Harper, 2004, p. 158.

counter such propaganda by proclaiming both an alternative ἐκκλησία to those present in the city as well as an alternative κύριος to the one dominant in the Roman imperial cult. By so doing Paul and his cosenders vigorously refute and reject the major political ideology of their day and unquestionably similar conflict leads to Paul's eventual execution in Rome around A.D. 64-67 (Nero's persecution).

2. *Persecution and Martyrdom as a Result of Political Conflict*

In light of this political situation I have advocated the thesis that the deaths referred to in 1 Thess 4,13-18 probably result from an *ad hoc* persecution due to political-religious conflict generated by Paul's preaching in the city.[29] A critical verse for this discussion is 4,14: εἰ γὰρ πιστεύομεν ὅτι Ἰησοῦς ἀπέθανεν καὶ ἀνέστη, οὕτως καὶ ὁ θεὸς τοὺς κοιμηθέντας διὰ τοῦ Ἰησοῦ ἄξει σὺν αὐτῷ.

With regard to κοιμάω, the same verb used at the stoning of Stephen in Acts 7,60, John Pobee in a publication subsequent to my original discussion of the subject, agrees that κοιμάω should here be translated as a present rather than a perfect participle; he also raises an important question concerning the interpretation of the controversial phrase καὶ ὁ θεὸς τοὺς κοιμηθέντας διὰ τοῦ Ἰησοῦ ἄξει σὺν αὐτῷ in 4,14.[30] The complete text (1 Thess 4,14) reads: εἰ γὰρ πιστεύομεν ὅτι Ἰησοῦς ἀπέθανεν καὶ ἀνέστη, οὕτως καὶ ὁ θεὸς τοὺς κοιμηθέντας διὰ τοῦ Ἰησοῦ ἄξει σὺν αὐτῷ. The issue is whether διὰ τοῦ Ἰησοῦ goes with κοιμηθέντας which precedes or with ἄξει which follows. If the διὰ τοῦ Ἰησοῦ is to be taken with those words that follow then there is an element of redundancy in the σὺν αὐτῷ phrase. Pobee is to be followed in reading τοὺς κοιμηθέντας διὰ τοῦ Ἰησοῦ[31] and in understanding the preposition (διά) with the genitive (διὰ τοῦ Ἰησοῦ) as expressing attendant circumstance[32], i.e. as a result of their faith, persecution and death

---

29. Karl Paul DONFRIED, *The Theology of 1 Thessalonians as a Reflection of Its Purpose*, in *Paul, Thessalonica and Early Christianity* (n. 1), 119-138.
30. John POBEE, *Persecution and Martyrdom in the Theology of Paul* (JSNTSup, 6), Sheffield, JSOT Press, 1985.
31. Other scholars joining διὰ τοῦ Ἰησοῦ with τοὺς κοιμηθεντας include Ephraim, Chrysostom, Calvin, Lightfoot, von Dobschütz, Dibelius, and Frame; although their understanding of διὰ τοῦ Ἰησοῦ is certainly not identical.
32. POBEE, *Persecution and Martyrdom in the Theology of Paul* (n. 30), 113-114. See also the detailed discussion of this issue in James E. FRAME, *Epistles of St. Paul to the Thessalonians* (ICC), Edinburgh, T&T Clark, 1912, 169-170, and especially his citation of Musculus: "The faithful die through Christ, when on his account they are slain by the impious tyrants of the world."

they are in union with Jesus prior to His parousia.³³ Also helpful for the correct interpretation of 1 Thess 4,14 as a whole is the observation by Ellicott that the "two contrasted subjects Ἰησοῦς [ἀπέθανεν καὶ ἀνέστη] and κοιμηθέντας διὰ τοῦ Ἰησοῦ thus stand in clear and illustrative antithesis, and the fundamental declaration of the sentence ἄξει σὺν αὐτῷ remains distinct and prominent, undiluted by any addititious clause."³⁴ One possible translation of 1 Thess 4,14 might be: "For since we believe that Jesus died and rose again, God will bring with him those who have died in union with Jesus."

Harrison is to be followed that despite the advances in understanding the context for which 1 Thessalonians was written, further sustained attention needs to be given to "the epistle's context of persecution (1 Thess 1,6; 2,2.14-16.18; 3,2.4-5.7-8; cf. 2 Thess 1,4-7) and its relation to 1 Thess 4:13-5:11."³⁵ As we proceed further in this direction it should not, however, be overlooked that the NRSV, in contrast to the RSV, has now, in light of the broader historical context of 1 Thessalonians, translated the several instances of θλῖψις and θλίβω in 1 Thessalonians (1,6; 3,3.4.7) as "persecution" or to "suffer persecution." Still, in light of our discussion and Harrison's appropriate counsel, a number of related texts need to reexamined. Given the parameters of this paper, our remarks will be brief and selective.

a. With regard to 1 Thess 1,7-8, in what way, might it be asked, have the believers in Thessalonica become a τύπος to "all the believers in Macedonia and in Achaia"? Their persecution and martyrdom for the sake of their faith in Christ might provide a reasonable indicator. Other options that one finds in commentaries old and new, including their "exemplary preaching of the Gospel,"³⁶ do appear, in contrast, to be remarkably abstract and vague.

b. Contrary to the position of Birger Pearson there is insufficient evidence to claim that 1 Thess 2,13-16 is a later interpolation.³⁷ Further,

---

33. C. F. D. MOULE, *An Idiom-Book of New Testament Greek*, Cambridge, 1960, 57, argues that this preposition with the genitive presents an attendant circumstance (cf. Acts 15,32; 2 Cor 2,4; Eph 6,18; Heb 13,22 and 2 Tim 2,2).

34. Cited in FRAME, *Epistles of St. Paul to the Thessalonians* (n. 32),170. See also Charles J. ELLICOTT, *St. Paul's epistles to the Thessalonians with a critical and grammatical commentary, and a revised translation* (4th ed), London, Longman-Green, 1880.

35. HARRISON, *Paul and the Imperial Authorities at Thessalonica and Rome* (n. 22), 50.

36. Abraham J. MALHERBE, *The Letters to the Thessalonians* (AB, 32B), New York, 2000, 116.

37. Birger A. PEARSON, *1 Thessalonians 2:13-16: A Deutero-Pauline Interpolation*, in *HTR* 64 (1971) 79-94. For a rebuttal to this position see Josef COPPENS, *Une diatribe antijuive dans I Thess. II, 13-16*, in *ETL* 51 (1975) 90-95.

1 Thess 2,16b should be appropriately translated not as "God's wrath 'has overtaken [ἔφθασεν] them at last" but rather as "God's wrath 'has drawn near' [ἔφθασεν] at last."[38] In light of such perspectives, especially that these verses are authentic, can it be convincingly argued that one finds here a distinctive piece of anti-Jewish rhetoric quite different from the rhetoric employed in Romans with regard to Judaism? The suggestion of Abraham Smith, viz., that these verses contain a sharp yet camouflaged critique of the "dominating pro-Roman elite in Thessalonica through an analogy with the pro-Roman priestly aristocracy in Judea"[39] should be given careful thought; in addition, his suggestion coheres with the translation of ἔφθασεν just given, viz., that "Paul anticipates the imminent beginning of a new *era* for his assemblies, in pointed contrast to the official Thessalonians declarations that new *eras* had begun with the victories of the Roman warlords Anthony and Octavian."[40]

In considering such an interpretative possibility for 1 Thess 2,13-16 in light of the entire context of 1 Thessalonians, the issue emerges whether or not the three authors of this letter are using "hidden transcripts" or "coded language" as they attempt to comfort believers in Christ in the midst of the threats employed by the imperial power. In this regard 1 Thess 1,4, with its reference to ἐκλογή and its possible relationship to the election of the Emperor,[41] 1 Thess 4,13-5,11 and 2 Thess 2,1-12, would all require similar and significant analysis. Let us turn to the second of these texts, 1 Thess 4,13-5,11, and then also share some brief comments on the third text when we turn to a consideration of 2 Thessalonians in its own right.

In 1 Thess 4,13-5,11 we note that that authors of this letter place their sharp criticism of the imperial "peace and security" propaganda in a concurrent framework of apocalyptic battle imagery. For some of the texts found at Qumran the eschatological battle is expected to be against the "Kittim," i.e., the Romans, and in 1QpHab there are some ten references[42] to the Kittim, frequently with a description of the horror

---

38. With regard to 1 Thess 2,15 MALHERBE, *The Letters to the Thessalonians* (n. 36), 169, makes an important observation: "The comma that is printed between vv 14 and 15 in Greek editions of the text and in modern translations is wrong, for it would set off a nonrestrictive clause that does not limit the action described to particular Jews, but would generalize it.... Paul uses a tradition about the killing of the prophets... but adapts it by relating it to the execution of Jesus and opposition to his own ministry."
39. SMITH, *"Unmasking the Powers"* (n. 21), 50.
40. SMITH, *"Unmasking the Powers"* (n. 21), 61.
41. See note 17 above.
42. 1QpHab 2,12.14.16; 3,4.9; 4,5.10: 6,1.10; 9,7.

associated with their actions. For example, 1QpHab 2,12-13 makes reference to those "who are quick and valiant at war, causing many to perish." In the War Scroll we have some sixteen similar references.⁴³ These highly negative portrayals of the Kittim would suggest that such apocalyptic documents are the products of specific historical situations that deal with constant and volatile crises between the Judeans as a people and the dominant Roman empire to which they are subject. And yet at the end, the hope of these texts is that the "rams' horns shall blow [a battle signal], a loud noise. As the sound goes forth, the infantry shall begin to bring down the slain of the Kittim, and all the people shall cease the signal, [but the priest]s shall continue *blowing on the trumpets* of the slain and the battle shall prevail against the Kittim" (1QM16,8-9).⁴⁴ The reference to "trumpets" in 1QM are numerous and have much to do with battle in its multiple dimensions as well as the gathering of the assembly as in 1QM 3,2, "On the trumpets for the assembly of the congregation they shall write, 'The called of God.'" A similar text is found in CD 11,22: "When the trumpets for assembly (הקהל) are blown...."⁴⁵ This is not an uninteresting text, given the reference to "trumpets" in 1 Thess 4,16. The authors of 1 Thessalonians use similar language in their description of the arrival of the "Day of the Lord" (1 Thess 5,2) when the "Lord Jesus Christ" (1 Thess 5,23) will consummate God's intervention in the world and the imperial order will no longer rule.

A not insignificant question that needs to be considered is why the authors of both 1 and 2 Thessalonians frequently employ explicit Jewish apocalyptic imagery in situations where the majority of believers addressed are predominantly Gentile. What is it in the actual historical situation being addressed that necessitates such pronounced eschatological and apocalyptic responses? Indeed, as the texts from Qumran cited suggest, the eschatological language that appears in 1 Thessalonians has political implications, especially when the authors of this letter make explicit reference to the weaponry needed for the eschatological battle immediately following their blatant attack on the "peace and security" propaganda circulating throughout the Empire. J. R. Harrison urges that "in 1 Thessalonians 4,13-5,11 Paul confronts the eschatology of the

---

43. 1QM 1,2,4,6,9,12; 11,11; 15,2; 16,3.6.8; 17,12.14; 18,2.4; 19,10.13.
44. Italics mine.
45. These three texts from the Dead Sea Scrolls follow the translation of Michael WISE, Martin ABEGG, Jr. and Edward COOK, *Dead Sea Scrolls: A New Translation*, San Francisco, Harper, 1966.

imperial gospel with his apostolic gospel, challenging its apotheosis traditions, and undermining its terminology and providential world-view."[46] Further, when a quarter of the references to παρουσία in the entire New Testament are employed in the Thessalonian correspondence, one may ask with Crossan whether terms like these, used for the visitation (παρουσία) and reception (ἀπάντησις) of Christ, are not indeed specifically calculated to be an anti-imperial *parousia* and that such a choice of metaphor is deliberately intended to be "both consolation and confrontaton?"[47] The declaration, for example, that God calls believers into "his own kingdom and glory" (1 Thess 2,11) is not only a word of encouragement but also simultaneously communicates imperial criticism.

It is precisely such "consolation and confrontation" that can be observed in the reference to the eschatological weaponry in 1 Thess 5,8-11: hope, certainly, but also the necessity to do battle with the ideology of the Empire and its imperial representatives in Thessalonica. This confrontation is escalated considerably in 2 Thess 2,6-10 ("For it is indeed just of God to repay with affliction those who afflict you, and to give relief to the afflicted as well as to us, when the Lord Jesus is revealed from heaven with his mighty angels in flaming fire, inflicting vengeance on those who do not know God and on those who do not obey the gospel of our Lord Jesus. These will suffer the punishment of eternal destruction, separated from the presence of the Lord and from the glory of his might, when he comes to be glorified by his saints and to be marveled at on that day among all who have believed, because our testimony to you was believed") in language and forcefulness that is in close proximity to 1QM: "All these shall pursue in order to destroy the enemy in the God's battle; a total annihilation" (9,4). Earlier in 1QM the identity of the protagonists and of the enemy is made known: "The Sons of Light and the forces of Darkness shall fight together to show the strength of God with the roar of a great multitude and the shout of gods and men; a day of disaster. It is a time of distress fo[r al]l the people who are redeemed by God. In all their afflictions none exists that is like it, hastening to its completion as an eternal redemption. On the day of their battle against the Kittim..." (1,11-12).[48] Not only is the darkness vs.

---

46. HARRISON, *Paul and the Imperial Authorities at Thessalonica and Rome* (n. 22), 72.
47. CROSSAN and REED, *In Search of Paul* (n. 28), 171.
48. All translations from the Dead Sea Scrolls in this paragraph are by WISE, ABEGG and COOK, *Dead Sea Scrolls*.

light contrast made in 1 Thess 5,4-5 but the explicit terminology "sons of light" (υἱοὶ φωτός) as used in Qumran (בני אור) is also used here by Paul, Silvanus and Timothy.[49]

3. *Patronage and Work in 1 Thessalonians*

In reminding the believers in Thessalonica "to work (ἐργάζεσθαι) with your hands" (1 Thess 4,11), the authors of this letter are also causing them to remember "our labor and toil, brothers and sisters; we worked night and day, so that we might not burden any of you while we proclaimed to you the gospel of God" (1 Thess 2,9). These exhortations suggest a mimetic ethos that both challenges the traditional structures of the imperial benefaction system and the social dominance of the benefactor in Thessalonica. In Roman Thessalonica and elsewhere in the empire, patronage[50] involved the exchange of benefits between those of status where the lower-status individual is indebted to a higher-status individual because of a variety of benefits that have been granted.[51] Cities themselves were dependent upon private generosity to provide many basic amenities and leading citizens were expected to provide free food and public entertainment. The members of Paul's new ecclesia were likewise expected – but for quite different reasons – to assume the role of benefactor and to perform acts of beneficence for those in need through the new network of their house churches and their own resources that were emerging. "Believers," suggests Harrison, "were to abandon reliance upon the provincial networks of imperial beneficence and assume the role of benefactors by working themselves and caring for the weak (1 Thess 2,5b.9; 4,11-12; 5,14; 2 Thess 3,6-13). This meant that the members of the house churches ought no longer to have to rely on and be obligated to the wealthy pro-imperial aristocratic elites of the provinces because of their benefits."[52] The pro-imperial aristocratic

---

49. The other three texts referring to the "sons of light" are Lk 16,8; Jn 12,36 and Eph 5,8.

50. On the theme of patronage in the Roman Empire see the summary of Holland Hendrix's work in DONFRIED, *The Cults of Thessalonica and the Thessalonian Correpondence* (n. 1), 36, and Holland HENDRIX, *Benefactor/Patron Networks in the Urban Environment: Evidence from Thessalonica*, in *Semeia* 56 (1992) 39-58.

51. Efrain AGOSTO, *Patronage and Commendation, Imperial and Anti-Imperial*, in HORSLEY (ed.), *Roman Imperial Order* (n. 21), 103-124. See further Andrew WALLACE-HADRILL (ed.), *Patronage in Ancient Society*, London, Routledge, 1989, and Richard SALLER, *Personal Patronage under the Early Empire*, Cambridge, 2002.

52. HARRISON, *Paul and the Imperial Authorities at Thessalonica and Rome* (n. 22), 330.

elites were loyal to a different gospel (εὐαγγέλιον), one that advocated the unsurpassed benefactions of Augustus and therefore fundamentally contradicted the confession that Jesus, and not Augustus, is κύριος. Faith in Christ as κύριος and participation in the new community of believers, involves earning one's one living and recognizes as well that the propagation of the faith and the encouragement of the community include both τοῦ ἔργου τῆς πίστεως and τοῦ κόπου τῆς ἀγάπης. The first of these phrases with its unique emphasis on ἔργον appears in the entire New Testament only here in 1 and 2 Thessalonians (1 Thess 1,3; 2 Thess 1,11) and the second, with its emphasis on κόπος, only in 1 Thessalonians (1,3).

The writers of 1 Thessalonians wished to break with such a pattern of imperial benefaction at several levels. This included the advocacy of an alternative ecclesia of mutual love and support that had at its core a significantly different pattern of leadership, one that did not derive its security from the dominant positions held by the Thessalonian elite who placed their confidence in the advantage of the imperial order. As a result the ecclesia of believers who were in Christ encouraged its members to work with their hands (1Thess 4,11) because their faith in Jesus as κύριος placed them "at the very opposite end of the imperial social structure from the aristocrats and magnates involved in the imperial and provincial patronage network."[53] The leadership characteristics of *this* ecclesia are outlined succinctly in 1 Thess 5,12-13: "But we appeal to you, brothers and sisters, to respect those who labor (κοπιῶντας) among you, and have charge of you in the Lord and admonish you; esteem them very highly in love because of their work. Be at peace among yourselves." The verb κοπιάω, involving a physical labor that is tiring and troublesome, surely would not be attractive to the ruling elite. As we have noted, Paul and his associates accent the themes of work and labor in relationship to faith and love (τοῦ ἔργου τῆς πίστεως καὶ τοῦ κόπου τῆς ἀγάπης); these are dimensions of the life of holiness in which members of the new ecclesia were to be actively engaged. Here, as well, we have identity markers that imply both laborious effort as they proclaim the Gospel in the midst of staggering opposition and work toward a new social order with all of troublesome dimensions that such efforts entail.[54] Faith in God the Father and in the Lord Jesus Christ in the midst of such

---

53. AGOSTO, *Patronage and Commendation, Imperial and Anti-Imperial* (n. 51), 111.
54. For a discussion of κοπιάω see further Horst BALZ and Gerhard SCHNEIDER (eds.), *Exegetical Dictionary of the New Testament*, Grand Rapids, Michigan, II.307.

an adversarial imperial context involves a participatory κόπος, an "exacting, 'shattering' *work*... [and] *hardship*,"⁵⁵ as well as a significant share in the type of toil (μόχθος) that was modeled through the night and day work of the three leaders (1 Thess 2,9). Not unimportant is the fact that this reference to κόπος is located in the midst of Paul, Silvanus and Timothy's response not, I would suggest, to the profile of peripatetic philosophers of the day nor of potential theological opponents but rather to the silhouette of the imperial representatives, those who had led to their maltreatment and persecution in Philippi and in Thessalonica, and who indeed hover in the background as this letter of encouragement is sent to the believers in Thessalonica.

These references to work and toil in 1 Thessalonians inevitably raise the question as to how one is to translate the adjective ἄτακτος in 1 Thess 5,14, and, what, if any, connection it might reveal with regard to patronage in Roman Thessalonica. The phrase, νουθετεῖτε τοὺς ἀτάκτους, is rendered by the NRSV as: "[And we urge you, beloved,] to admonish the idlers...." The vast majority of commentaries understand the ἄτακτοι as "idlers" or "loafers."⁵⁶ Malherbe observes quite correctly that had "Paul merely been concerned about the idleness of such people... he would have used more common words for idleness, such as *argoi* or *apraktoi* to describe them."⁵⁷ The translation "idlers" or "loafers" is so ambiguous that one is hard pressed to understand whom Paul is addressing and for what purpose. When Milligan suggests that "the special reference would seem to be to the idleness and neglect of duty which characterized certain members of the Thessalonian Church in view of the shortly-expected Parousia" he simply goes beyond the evidence of the text.⁵⁸ Is it possible to determine a meaning for ἄτακτος

---

55. For a discussion of κόπος see further *Exegetical Dictionary of the New Testament*, 307-308.
56. For example, D. Michael MARTIN, *1,2 Thessalonians* (NAC, 33), Nashville TN, Broadman & Holman, 1995, 176: "warn those who are idle;" Charles A. WANAMAKER, *The Epistle to the Thessalonians: A Commentary on the Greek Text* (NIGTC), Grand Rapids: Eerdmans, 1990, 197: "idle or lazy"; F. F. BRUCE, *1 & 2 Thessalonians* (WBC, 45), Waco, Word, 1982, 122: "loafers"; Ernest BEST, *A Commentary on the First and Second Epistles to the Thessalonians* (BNTC), London, A&C Black, 1979, 222: "admonish loafers"; FRAME, *Epistles of St.Paul to the Thessalonians* (n. 32), 197: "idlers".
57. MALHERBE, *The Letters to the Thessalonians* (n. 36), 317.
58. George MILLIGAN, *St Paul's Epistles to the Thessalonians*, London, Macmillan, 1908, 73. Robert Jewett, *The Thessalonian Correspondence*, Philadelphia, Fortress, 1986, 104, moves in a similar direction and cites approvingly the position of Willi MARXSEN, *Der erste Brief des Paulus an die Thessalonicher* (ZBK.NT,11.1), Zürich,Theologischer Verlag, 1979, 71]: "Judging from the details in 1 Thessalonians alone, Marxsen concludes that this group

that coheres more closely to the social, historical and theological intention of 1 Thessalonians?[59] Might ἄτακτος in 1 Thessalonians 5, within the context of Roman patronage, refer to lower-status individuals who continue to stand in debt to those of higher-status? While this would not be incorrect the question remains whether this suggestion conveys the full impact of the term as it is being used in 1 Thessalonians 5? It order to determine this a greater degree of clarity will need to be reached with regard to the meaning not only of the term ἄτακτος in 1 Thess 5,14 but also to ἀτακτέω in 2 Thess 3,7 and ἀτάκτως in 2 Thess 3,6 and 2 Thess 3,11, terms that only occur in the New Testament in these four verses.

In 1908 R. H. Charles suggested that the Aramaic and Greek fragments of the Testament of Levi are versions of a common Hebrew text and that neither is the translation of the other. בסרך and ἐν τάξει are twice used equivalently in both fragments. Stone[60] suggests that סרך, a term without parallel in the Hebrew Bible, may possibly have entered the vocabulary of the Qumran community as a result of the influence of the *The Aramaic Levi Document*.[61] A number of texts related to this community have close kinship with the Apostle Paul and the actual term, ἄτακτος, used in 1 Thess 5,14, is found in the *Greek Testament of Naphtali*.[62] The text of *T. Naph*. 2,9 reads: οὕτως οὖν, τέκνα μου, ἐν τάξει ἐστὲ εἰς ἀγαθά, ἐν φόβῳς Θεοῦ, καὶ μηδὲν **ἄτακτον** ποιεῖτε ἐν καταφρονήσει, μηδὲ ἔξω καιροῦ αὐτοῦ.[63] Hollander and de Jonge translate 2,9-10 in this way: "So then, my children, be in order unto good, in the fear of God and do nothing disorderly in scorn or out of its due season. For if you tell the eye to hear, it cannot; so neither will you be able to do works of light while in darkness."[64] The context of these

---

were 'enthusiasts who because of the nearness of the parousia are no longer taking seriously the things of everyday life.'"

59. See further Donfried in Karl P. DONFRIED and I. Howard MARSHALL, *The Theology of the Shorter Pauline Letters,* Cambridge, 1993, especially pp. 1-7.

60. Michael E. STONE and Jonas C. GREENFIELD, *The Third and Fourth Manuscripts of Aramaic Levi Document From Qumran (4QLevi^c aram and 4QLevi^d aram)*, in Le Muséon 109 (1996) 246-59.

61. DONFRIED, *Paul And Qumran: The Possible Influence of* סרך *on 1 Thessalonians,* in *Paul, Thessalonica and Early Christianity,* 221-32, here p. 223.

62. ἄτακτος is also found in HArt 9,23 (Artapanus) and ἀτακτέω in Prop (*Prophetarum vitae fabulosae*) 22,7; in the LXX only in 3 Macc 1,19.

63. M. DE JONGE, *The Testaments of the Twelve Patriarchs: A Critical Edition of the Greek Text* (PVTG), Leiden, Brill, 1978, 116.

64. H. W. HOLLANDER and M. DE JONGE, *The Testaments of the Twelve Patriarchs: A Commentary* (SVTP), Leiden, Brill, 1985, 301.

verses unmistakably recommends the translation "disorder" or "disorderly" for the term ἄτακτον.

The exhortation that the author of *T. Naph.* gives is straightforward: do not change the law of God by the disorderliness of your life and actions, because those who do so are like the Gentiles (see *T. Naph.* 4,1 and 1 Thess 4,5). An examination of the Hebrew and Aramaic equivalents to the terms ἐν τάξει and ἄτακτος in the Napthali and, especially, in the Levi materials, indeed suggests a nearness to the linguistic world of Qumran. Further, the proximity of 1 Thessalonians to this particular sector of Second Temple Judaism is most noteworthy given both the similar use of theological concepts (eg., election, holiness, apocalyptic eschatology)[65] and the utilization of identical terminology (eg. בני אור; קהל אל).[66] Some examples of contexts in which סרך appears includes the very title of 1QS [סרך] as used, for example, in 1QS 5,1: "This is the rule (הסרך) for the men of the Community who freely volunteer to convert from all evil and to keep themselves steadfast in all he prescribes in compliance with his will. They should...."[67] Also fundamental to understanding this term, especially in 1 Thessalonians, is that הסרך/τάξις are closely related to a broad range of military matters including battle formation. Typical of this usage is 1QM 5,3-4, "When their army is complete, to fill a front line, the line will be formed of one thousand men, with seven forward formations per line, each formation in its own order (בסרך), each man being behind the other."[68] As would be expected in a document like 1QM, many of the specific rules refer to military concerns in the context of eschatological warfare.

As one probes the function of ἄτακτος in 1 Thessalonians in greater detail, one notes that 1 Thess 5,12-15 refers back to 1 Thess 4,1-12 which contains a small collection of rules, παραγγελία, given by the Lord Jesus through Paul and his associates. The Apostle sternly warns that "whoever rejects (ἀθετῶν) this rejects (ἀθετεῖ) not human authority but God, who also gives his Holy Spirit to you" (4,8). It is also evident

---

65. See here David FLUSSER, *The Dead Sea Sect and Pre-Pauline Christianity*, in FLUSSER, *Judaism and the Origins of Christianity*, Jerusalem, Magnes, 1988, 23-74.

66. For a further discussion of the use of the *nomen gentilicum*, "of the Thessalonians," especially in 1 Thessalonians and its relationship to the texts found in Qumran, see Karl P. DONFRIED, *The Assembly of the Thessalonians*, in Rainer KAMPLING and Thomas SÖDING (eds), *Ekklesiologie des Neuen Testaments: Für Karl Kertelge*, Freiburg, Herder, 1996, 390-408.

67. Florentino GARCÍA MARTÍNEZ, *The Dead Sea Scrolls Translated*, Leiden. Brill, 1994, 8; see also, for example, 1QS 6,8; 1QSa1,1.6.21.

68. GARCÍA MARTÍNEZ, *The Dead Sea Scrolls* (n. 67), 98. See also 1QM15,5 and 1QSa1,23.

in 1 Thessalonians that the ἐκκλησία (1,1) to which Paul writes is organized around a certain principle, "holiness" (ἐν ἁγιασμῷ 4,7), which is a fundamental consequence of what it means to be ἐν Χριστῷ (4,16). As in *T. Naph.*, the ἄτακτοι of 1 Thessalonians are out-of-order/disorderly with regard to the commandments of God, standing on the side of darkness rather than light, and their lack of ethical behavior indicates that they are more like the Gentiles, who because of their idolatry, do not worship the one true God. Texts such as 1 Thess 1,9, 4,5, 4,13 and 5,5 show striking similarities with this line of reasoning. There is also, as we observed, a connection with the military use of סרך in Qumran. The ἄτακτοι of 1 Thessalonians, because of their being out-of-order with the commandments and the community of God, are also out-of-order with another dimension of Pauline advice, viz., adequate preparation for spiritual warfare: "But, since we belong to the day, let us be sober, and put on the breastplate of faith and love, and for a helmet the hope of salvation" (1 Thess 5,8). 1QM opens in this way: "For the In[structor, the Rule of] the War [ה]ספר סרך] המלחמה]. The first attack of the Sons of Light shall be undertaken against the forces of the Sons of Darkness, the army of Belial...." (1,1)[69] As the יחד of Qumran, so must the Thessalonian congregation be prepared for the struggle between light and darkness (1 Thess 5,5).

Briefly, then, the ἄτακτοι, the disorderly, must be instructed by the leaders of the Thessalonian congregation, in several areas, including (1) the παραγγελία given by the Lord, (2) the way of holiness that is central to the life of the ἐκκλησία, (3) preparation for the spiritual warfare against the forces of darkness, and. to this we would also add a fourth, (4) to understand the proper order of events at the parousia, particularly "concerning those have fallen asleep" (4,13-5,11, but especially 4,15-17). So important is this correct ordering that a "word from the Lord" gives it authority: οἱ ζῶντες οἱ περιλειπόμενοι εἰς τὴν παρουσίαν τοῦ κυρίου οὐ μὴ φθάσωμεν τοὺς κοιμηθέντας. All four areas of instruction cannot be neglected if the Thessalonian believers are to understand why the "Peace and Security" propaganda circulating in Roman Thessalonica is dangerous and why the existing patronage system in the city is morally and theologically bankrupt; without such exhortation they will not be adequately prepared for the eschatological battle in which they are and will be continue to be engaged by virtue of their

---

69. Translation from WISE, ABEGG and COOK (n. 45), *Dead Sea Scrolls*.

confession that Jesus, and not the Emperor, is Lord. At the conclusion of the letter, both as consolation and confrontation, Paul, Silvanus and Timothy remind their readers that God is a God of peace whose rulership is not characterized by corrupt power or marked by threats of arbitrary violence (1 Thess 5,23). God's intention, rather, is not that they be destined for wrath "but for obtaining salvation through our Lord Jesus Christ" (1 Thess 5,10)

III. 2 Thessalonians: Exegetical Probings

1. *The Escalating Conflict in Thessalonica*

The problem that must be confronted and responded to in 2 Thessalonians is stated in 2 Thess 2,2: "not to be quickly shaken [σαλευθῆναι] in mind or alarmed [θροεῖσθαι], either by spirit or by word or by letter, as though from us, to the effect that the day of the Lord is already here [ὡς ὅτι ἐνέστηκεν[70] ἡ ἡμέρα τοῦ κυρίου]." This false assertion, viz., that the parousia has *already* arrived, is further countered with these words: "Let no one deceive you in any way; for that day will not come unless the rebellion comes first and the lawless one is revealed, the one destined for destruction" (2 Thess 2,3). Without question powerful dynamics have altered the situation in Thessalonica since the writing of 1 Thessalonians. Paul especially (note the "I" language in 1 Thess 3,5) is sufficiently concerned about the "persecutions" [θλίψεσιν] that they are suffering that he sends Timothy to them "so that no one would be shaken by these persecutions. Indeed, you yourselves know that this is what we are destined for. In fact, when we were with you, we told you beforehand that we were to suffer persecution; so it turned out, as you know" (1 Thess 3,3-4). Paul, speaking on behalf of his co-authors as well, explains to these believers that such persecution is exactly what they were destined for and that this reality was announced to them when all three were previously present in the city.

The situation confronted by the writers of 2 Thessalonians had advanced considerably in terms of its negative consequences, provoked undoubtedly by more intense and systematic persecution, and, as a result, a far more uncompromising and forceful language was required. Replacing the verb "shaken" [σαίνεσθαι] in 1 Thess 3,3, for example, two

---

70. Third singular perfect active indicative.

verbs with greater potency are employed in 2 Thess 2,2 [σαλευθῆναι and θροεῖσθαι], both implying a degree of alarm and violence not found in the text of 1 Thessalonians.[71] Note also how the terms used in 1 Thessalonians (θλῖψις and θλίβω) (1,6; 3,4.7) are now sharpened by the use of διωγμοῖς in 2 Thess 1,4: "Therefore we ourselves boast of you among the churches of God for your steadfastness and faith during all your persecutions and the afflictions that you are enduring."[72] It is not difficult to comprehend how the heightened effect of persecution upon the believers in Thessalonica would allow the themes found in 1 Thess 5,2-4 ("For you yourselves know very well that the day of the Lord will come like a thief in the night. When they say, 'There is peace and security,' then sudden destruction will come upon them, as labor pains come upon a pregnant woman, and there will be no escape! But you, beloved, are not in darkness, for that day to surprise you like a thief") to be fundamentally misinterpreted in the way indicated by 2 Thess 2,2. Despite an underlying continuity, two significantly different social and historical contexts allow the same term, "Day of the Lord" [ἡμέρα κυρίου], to be accented and articulated in quite dissimilar ways within these two letters (1 Thess 5,2 and 2 Thess 2,2).

2. *The Use of Apocalyptic Language*

One immediately observes an escalation of apocalyptic motifs and language in 2 Thessalonians. Already in 1 Thessalonians Paul and his associates polemically countered the parallelism between the gospel of Jesus and the gospel of the Empire by employing such apocalyptic concepts and it is little wonder that the more intense ideological collision reflected in 2 Thessalonians is marked by the enhanced utilization of dramatic and hostile apocalyptic language and concepts. Its harshness is already apparent in 1 Thess 2,14-16 and in the use of eschatological war imagery in 1 Thess 5,8. And the fact that the first letter makes use of terminology significant for certain communities represented by the Dead Sea Scrolls (υἱοὶ φωτός; ἄτακτοι) should not surprise us. We observed earlier that a number of the concerns found in 2 Thessalonians are echoed in the War Scroll (1QM) where the struggle between the forces of Light and Darkness is portrayed in the context of a battle the contours

---

71. All three of these verbs are only used here within the Pauline corpus.
72. See also the use of διωγμός in Acts 8,1; 13,50; Rom 8,35; 2 Cor 12,10 and 2 Tim 3,11.

of which have been determined in advance. In 1QM one learns that for the "sons of darkness" there will be no escape when the "dominion of the Kittim shall come to an end and iniquity shall be vanquished" (1:5). The struggle with the Kittim will indeed be a time of "great tribulation for the people which God shall redeem."[73] As for the authors of 2 Thessalonians, the powers of Satan[74] and lawlessness will remain unconquered until the end and only then will they encounter decisive defeat at the hands of God. Those who "will suffer the punishment of eternal destruction, separated from the presence of the Lord and from the glory of his might" (2 Thess 1,9) are culpable precisely because they have rejected God by not believing His truth (2 Thess 2,12). Although the death and resurrection of Jesus unmask the working of Satan, the rulers of this age have not been overcome and still await the final triumph of God. Considerable echoes of this final defeat in 2 Thess 2,1-12 are apparent in 1QM 15,2: "There shall be eternal deliverance for the company of God, but destruction for all the nations of wickedness."[75] There is also a striking resemblance to 2 Thess 1,6-8 in 1QM 15,14-15, "The hosts of warrior 'gods' gird themselves for the battle, the Day of Revenge...;"[76] 16,1, "For the God of Israel has called out the sword against all nations, and He will do mighty deeds by the saints of His people;"[77] and, 18,2, "The Kittim should be crushed without remnant, and no man shall be saved from among them."[78]

In utilizing such forceful apocalyptic themes and language, the authors of 2 Thessalonians are heavily dependent on the apocalyptic framework of 1 Thess 4,13-5,11 in their attempt to expose both the danger and the demonic potential of Roman rule. Not only would ἐπιφάνεια ('appearance') in 2 Thess 2,8 "have recalled elements of imperial propaganda..." but the adjectival cognate of ἐπιφάνεια (ἐπιφανής) "is regularly applied to the Julio-Claudians."[79] Glenn Holland is correct to note that the phrase λεγόμενον θεὸν ἢ σέβασμα in 2 Thess 2,4 "captures the 'blasphemous claims of pagan rulers', with its pun on the 'Roman emperor's honorific

---

73. Translation from Geza VERMES, *The Complete Dead Sea Scrolls in English*, New York, Penguin, 1977, 164.
74. The common Jewish name for Satan is Belial and is frequently used in the Dead Sea Scrolls.
75. Translation from VERMES, *The Complete Dead Sea Scrolls in English* (n. 73), 179.
76. Translation from VERMES, *The Complete Dead Sea Scrolls in English* (n. 73), 179.
77. Translation from VERMES, *The Complete Dead Sea Scrolls in English* (n. 73), 180.
78. Translation from VERMES, *The Complete Dead Sea Scrolls in English*, (n. 73), 182.
79. HARRISON, *Paul and the Imperial Authorities at Thessalonica and Rome* (n. 22), 58.

title of Σεβαστός, 'Augustus.'"[80] Perhaps one should add at this point that any attempt to identify these and other enigmatic terms in 2 Thess 2,1-12, such as ὁ κατέχων, is an exercise in futility since these "participles describe actions and are not intended to identify persons."[81] The purpose of 2,1-12 is, however, unambiguous: to assert unequivocally that any "talk of the imminent eschatological demise of the imperial rulers and the world more generally was premature."[82]

Another intention of the apocalyptic language in 2 Thessalonians is, much like that of 1 Thessalonians, to offer comfort and encouragement to the struggling and harassed Thessalonian believers. The justice of God and his plan for execution, although locked in the mystery of God, is the foundation of consolation for those who find themselves in the midst of violent persecution. Instructive is a text found in 1QpHab 7,5-14 which makes reference to the Last Days as extended but also reminds its readers in 7,13 that "all the times fixed by God will come about in due course as He ordained."[83] As in the first letter, so in 2 Thessalonians we have a letter of consolation that is simultaneously hortatory and pastoral; the suffering of the Thessalonian believers is never ignored. One does observe, however, a major variation particularly with regard to the theme of the parousia in the two letters. In 1 Thess 4,13-18 "the coming of the Lord" serves positively as a comfort to the ones who are upset that some have been killed by the Romans prior to the arrival of the parousia of Christ; in 2 Thess 2,8 the theme of the parousia has primarily a negative function, viz., to correct erroneous teaching and to assure the new ecclesia that their great opponent, the lawless one, *will* be destroyed at "the manifestation of his coming" (τῇ ἐπιφανείᾳ τῆς παρουσίας αὐτοῦ). Once again we observe a forceful and hostile escalation of language not unlike that found in 1QM.

3. *Patronage and the Disorderly*

Much that has been said with regard to the issue of patronage in the discussion of 1 Thessalonians can be applied to 2 Thessalonians as well, especially with regard to translating ἀτάκτως in 2 Thess 3,6 and in

---

80. Glenn HOLLAND, *The Tradition that You Received from Us: 2 Thessalonians in the Pauline Tradition* (HUT), Tübingen, Mohr Siebeck, 1988, 93.
81. MALHERBE, *The Letters to the Thessalonians* (n. 36), 420.
82. HARRISON, *Paul and the Imperial Authorities at Thessalonica and Rome* (n. 22), 92.
83. Translation by Wise, ABEGG and COOK, *Dead Sea Scrolls: A New Translation* (n. 45), 119.

ἀτακτέω 3,7 as "disorderly" or "out of order." In 2 Thess 3,8 Paul and his co-workers refer back to their work ethic as they described it in 1 Thess 2,9, although here in 2 Thess 3,8 the following is added: "and we did not eat anyone's bread without paying for it [οὐδὲ δωρεὰν ἄρτον ἐφάγομεν παρά τινος]." In 2 Thess 3,10-13 this theme is picked up and expanded rather sharply: "For even when we were with you, we gave you this command: Anyone unwilling to work should not eat [εἴ τι οὐ θέλει ἐργάζεσθαι μηδὲ ἐσθιέτω]. For we hear that some of you are living in a disorderly manner [περιπατοῦντας ἐν ὑμῖν ἀτάκτως], mere busybodies [περιεργαζομένους], not doing any work [μηδὲν ἐργαζομένους]. Now such persons we command and exhort in the Lord Jesus Christ to do their work quietly [μετὰ ἡσυχίας ἐργαζόμενοι] and to earn their own living [τὸν ἑαυτῶν ἄρτον ἐσθίωσιν]." Some of these themes are indeed anticipated in 1 Thess 4,10-12: "But we urge you ... to aspire to live quietly [ἡσυχάζειν], to mind your own affairs [πράσσειν τὰ ἴδια], and to work with your hands [ἐργάζεσθαι ταῖς (ἰδίαις) χερσὶν ὑμῶν], as we directed you, so that you may behave properly toward outsiders and be dependent on no one [ἵνα περιπατῆτε εὐσχημόνως πρὸς τοὺς ἔξω καὶ μηδενὸς χρείαν ἔχητε]." Although expressed differently, the overall similarity between these texts is striking. These include: the references to the disorderly; the theme of physical work in 1 Thess 2,9 and 4,11, emphasized especially in 2 Thess 3,8.10.11 and 12; and, the mention of working quietly in 1 Thess 4,11 and 2 Thess 3,12. New or more highly nuanced terminology related to this theme in 2 Thessalonians include: ἄρτος in 3,8.12 as well as the theme of eating [ἐσθιέτω] in 3,10 that implies food [ἄρτος]; and, the theme of being a "περίεργος" in 2 Thess 3,11 [περιεργάζομαι].

Are there circumstances in Roman Thessalonica that would make intelligible the command in 2 Thess 3,10 that "Anyone unwilling to work [ἐργάζεσθαι] should not eat," especially in relationship to the accusation in 3,11 about being "disorderly" [ἀτάκτως], "not working" [μηδὲν ἐργαζομένους] and being "intrusively busy" [περιεργαζομένους]? Malherbe is correct when he urges that the "emphatic position and sharpness of *periergazesthai* demonstrates the importance that this offensive behavior has for Paul."[84] What makes it offensive, we would suggest, is precisely its intimate connection with Roman patronage and, along with it, the tendency to pay attention and to become involved in

---

84. MALHERBE, *The Letters to the Thessalonians* (n. 36), 453.

matters that are not of proper concern. The danger is that the different moral and ultimate concerns of the political/cultic ecclesiae of the Thessalonians and the ecclesia of Jesus as Lord become entangled and confused. The theme referred to in 1 Thess 4,12 ["so that you may behave properly toward outsiders and be dependent on no one"; ἵνα περιπατῆτε εὐσχημόνως πρὸς τοὺς ἔξω καὶ μηδενὸς χρείαν ἔχητε] is now sharpened considerably. To be dependent on others outside the believing community is precisely an indication of an improper involvement in that which should not be of concern and, as a result, such a person is "out-of-order/disorderly."

Both in their references to ἄρτος and with regard to the issue of acting with a misdirected curiosity [περιεργάζομαι], the writers of 2 Thessalonians are referring to the complex system of interdependency associated with Roman patronage. In this arrangement a wealthy patron would give his clients a variety of gifts often following their morning visit (*salutatio*) to his home, including a basket of food (*sportula*),[85] and the clients, in turn, would assist their patron in his private life as well as supporting and promoting him in a variety of public activities. Jones puts the matter succinctly when he writes that in first century Rome "there were many who preferred to be client to one or more patrons rather than to earn a precarious living by hard work. One of these was Martial. Coming to Rome from Spain, probably in the year 64 A.D., he successively flattered the emperor and paid court to wealthy patrons in the hope of gaining a livelihood."[86] In this way clientage became the most important social relationship not only in Rome itself but in the provinces as well.[87]

This centrality of patronage in the Empire creates social conflict between the position that Paul and his associates maintained, viz., that the interactions of believers at all levels must be marked by equality and horizontal symmetry and not inequality and vertical aspirations. Since patrons also shared legal counsel and legal aid with their clients, 1 Cor 6,1-6 may provide an example of the confusion existing between these

---

85. This supply of daily food was often converted into a cash dole (*centum quadrantes*). Martial writes in his satirical style that after having received such a handout at one house some would run off to the next hoping to receive a similar dole there as well (Martial, *Epigrams* 10.74). See further D. R. Schackleton BAILEY (ed. and trans.), *Martial Epigrams* vol 1-3 (LCL), Cambridge MA, Harvard, 1993 and Francis L. JONES, *Martial, the Client*, in *CJ* 30 (1935) 355-361.
86. JONES, *Martial, the Client* (n. 85), 355.
87. See further the discussion in SALLER, *Personal Patronage Under the Early Empire* (n. 51), 1-78.

conflicting social realms. Given the clear competition between the clients of different patrons, especially involving election to civic offices, some clients would vigorously lobby for their patron while publicly criticizing others with harshness, a process negating exhortations given in both 1 and 2 Thessalonians and calling forth the criticism of being "disorderly." Since such social interaction was determined by the conventions practiced by the other ecclesiae of the city and not the ecclesia of the Lord Jesus Christ, Paul, Silvanus and Timothy are critical of these practitioners, the *disorderly*, i.e., those who do not work for their bread because they were being "ordered" by patterns of behavior that are incompatible, in error and, therefore, *out-of-order*. Patronage as carried out by the Romans was in fundamental conflict with the new ecclesia "of the Thessalonians in God the Father and the Lord Jesus Christ" (2 Thess 1,2).

4. *2 Thessalonians and the Issue of Authorship*

The issue of authorship with regard to 2 Thessalonians is a hugely controversial one. In our discussion of 1 and 2 Thessalonians we found no compelling evidence against the fact that the three persons mentioned in each are involved as co-senders of each letter. I would go a step further and suggest that Paul, Silvanus and Timothy are indeed co-authors of each letter. Undoubtedly Paul, as the leader of the missionary team, has ultimate responsibility for the correspondence but the other two did indeed participate in a variety of ways, including discussion of the issues and problems that arose in Thessalonica and beyond, as well as making contributions of substance with regard to appropriate and effective responses to emerging challenges.

What necessitated the writing of 2 Thessalonians shortly after the initial letter was, as we have observed, the need to correct a significant number of misinterpretations. Among the factors that account for the similarities between the two letters was the need to clarify in 2 Thessalonians eschatological and apocalyptic statements that had been misinterpreted following the public reading/s of 1 Thessalonians to the community of believers. Such misinterpretation may have resulted from inattentive listening, deliberate intent or as a result of the increased pressure produced by intensified persecution. Major attention needed to be given to critical issues including the arrival of "the day of the Lord" and the challenge of "disorderliness." These challenges had to be responded to with a degree of exactitude so that it would become unmistakable that the second letter was, in fact, clarifying the first against those who had carelessly or blatantly misinterpreted it. In order to do this a copy of 1 Thessalonians in parchment notebook/proto-codex form was carefully reviewed and discussed prior to the writing and sending of 2 Thessalonians to its intended recipients.[88]

Often the argument for non-authenticity of 2 Thessalonians is based on such factors as its literary dependence on 1 Thessalonians, use of a different vocabulary and theological positions, especially with regard to eschatology, as well as its harsh personal tone. An extreme example of such a position is represented by Steven Friesen in his essay "Second Thessalonians, the Ideology of Epistles, and the Construction of Authority: Our Debt to the Forger" where he argues that 2 Thessalonians is a forgery.[89] He defines the term in this way: as "a work that misleads the audience about the identity of the real author because the deception is fundamental to the rhetorical aims of the text."[90] The eschatology of 2 Thessalonians as represented, for example, in 2,5 fundamentally contradicts the Pauline eschatology of 1 Thessalonians by asserting that the day of Lord will not come until there is a great apostasy and the man of lawlessness is revealed. "This new written command is supported by the fiction that it was first delivered orally. In other words, the author creates an oral tradition to support this new written tradition."[91] More problematic still is the elevation of 2 Thessalonians to the status of an actual forgery and the assertion that "this process was a shift in the ideology of letters from a mainstream view of letters as communication to a sectarian view of letters as authoritative statements of divine truth."[92] The indistinctness of the term "divine truth" is an indication of both the ambiguity and the ideological tendency implied by Friesen's entire approach.

---

88. See further Karl Paul DONFRIED, *Paul as σκηνοποιός and the Use of the Codex in Early Christianity*, in *Paul, Thessalonica and Early Christianity* (n. 1), 293-304. This article reaches the conclusion that "Paul used the (proto)-codex as a vehicle for his own correspondence" (p. 303).

89. Steven J. FRIESEN, *Second Thessalonians, the Ideology of Epistles, and the Construction of Authority: Our Debt to the Forger*, in Laura NASRALLAH, Charalambos BAKIRTZIS and Steven J. FRIESEN (eds), *From Roman to Early Christian Thessalonike*, Cambridge MA, Harvard, 2010, 189-210.

90. FRIESEN, *Second Thessalonians, the Ideology of Epistles, and the Construction of Authority: Our Debt to the Forger* (n. 89), 232.

91. FRIESEN, *Second Thessalonians, the Ideology of Epistles, and the Construction of Authority: Our Debt to the Forger* (n. 89), 204

92. FRIESEN, *Second Thessalonians, the Ideology of Epistles, and the Construction of Authority: Our Debt to the Forger* (n. 89), 207.

Those scholars who argue for the pseudepigraphic[93] nature of 2 Thessalonians, or that it is a forgery, often give considerable weight to 2 Thess 3,17 where the author makes a remark about Paul writing in his own hand (Ὁ ἀσπασμὸς τῇ ἐμῇ χειρὶ Παύλου, ὅ ἐστιν σημεῖον ἐν πάσῃ ἐπιστολῇ· οὕτως γράφω). For some interpreters these words have given force to the argument that this letter is a forgery, especially since Paul does not add a similar greeting at the conclusion of 1 Thessalonians. But is this really a cogent argument? By using the phrase οὕτως γράφω is not Paul simply suggesting that he wrote *something*, whether or not it involved his signature? Why could this custom not simply refer to his recognizable handwriting, i.e., he simply borrowed the pen from the amanuensis so that he might conclude the letter with a personal word or note? It is important, however, especially given our understanding of the relationship of 1 and 2 Thessalonians, to probe a bit further.

In which letters do we find some possible indication of Paul's handwriting at the conclusion? In addition to 2 Thess 3,17, we should also note 1 Cor 16,21; Col 4,18, Gal 6,11; Phlm 19 and Rom 16,22. Some brief comments with regard to the last two texts cited may be useful for our further reflection. With regard to Philemon where we read in verse 19, "I, Paul, am writing this with my own hand: I will repay it (ἐγὼ ἀποτίσω)," it is necessary to observe that ἀποτίνω is "a technical juridical term for the payment of a fine or the cost of damages"[94] and that these words are included here in Paul's handwriting as a legal assurance that Paul guarantees the reimbursement of funds discussed in v. 18. In other words, not a general but a specific situation calls for this handwritten addition in his own hand. With regard to Rom 16,22 and the reference to Tertius as the writer of this letter, Wilckens[95] states that normally this would have concluded the letter and that the greetings in the following verses were added by Paul himself. In ways not dissimilar to handwritten additions made in Philemon and possibly Romans, it may

---

93. It is not my intention in this paper to review the complex issue of pseudonymity in antiquity or early Christianity. For those interested in a summary review of the issues involved might wish to consult Frank W. HUGHES, *Pseudonymity as Rhetoric: A Prolegomenon to the Study of Pauline Pseudepigrapha,* in James D. HESTER and J. David HESTER (eds), *Rhetorics in the New Millennium* (Studies in Antiquity & Christianity), London, T&T Clark, 2010, 216-234.

94. Joseph A. FITZMYER, *The Letter of Philemon* (AB, 34C), New York, Doubleday, 2000, 118.

95. Ulrich WILCKENS, *Der Brief an die Römer (Röm 12-16)* (EKK, VI/3), Zürich, Benziger, 1982, 146.

not be far of the mark to consider the possibility that, at a minimum, 1 Thess 5,27 was added by Paul himself to make an explicit directive: "I solemnly command you by the Lord that this letter be read to all of them," especially given the reemergence of the "I" form only found in 1 Thessalonians here and in 2,18 and 3,5. Since, however, we do not possess the original, autograph copy there is no way for us to substantiate the change in handwriting. Also, one should hasten to add that changes in handwriting between that of the amanuensis and Paul would also not be observable in copies sent to the various groups of believers in the broader ecclesia of the believers, especially if the original letter to the Thessalonians would have remained with the first recipients.

IV. CONCLUSIONS AND SUGGESTIOINS RELATIVE TO THE RELATIONSHIP BETWEEN 1 AND 2 THESSALONIANS

1. *The role and function of co-senders* in the Pauline letters needs further exploration and consideration. With regard to 1 and 2 Thessalonians it is likely that Paul, Silvanus and Timothy did indeed play significant roles in the discussion and composition of these letters. The communal character of the letters (i.e., the "I-we" distinctions), as a whole, support their function as co-authors.

2. *The Roman imperial context* is critical for understanding both letters.

With regard to *1 Thessalonians* it can be said:

1. The purpose of this letter cannot be grasped unless one realizes that the Gospel proclaimed in Thessalonica was sharply critical of the religious perspectives propagated by the various cults of the city and that political conflict was unavoidable when Jesus and not the Emperor is proclaimed as Lord. As the result of such confrontation, ideological collision was inevitable.
2. At the heart of Paul's gospel was the death and resurrection of Jesus Christ; its framework is thoroughly Jewish with strong ties of language and imagery with that found in the Dead Sea Scrolls, particularly with regard to eschatology.
3. The exhortations expressed in 1 Thess 5,2-3 might have been misunderstood as referring to the imminent demise of the Emperor.
4. The political conflict in Thessalonica led to the limited persecution and martyrdom of some believers in Christ. These circumstances become an interpretative key for the entire letter and might allow a

more precise exegesis of texts that include 1 Thess 1,7-8; 2,13-16 and 4,13-5,11

5. This last text, 4,13-5,11, Paul's rebuttal of the "peace and security" propaganda of Imperial Rome, is linked to the Dead Sea Scrolls through its frequent use of apocalyptic concepts and language. Not unimportant for such a comparison is the identical contrast between darkness and light, the battle against the "Kittim" (i.e., the Romans) and the powerful military imagery involving the "Sons of Light," a phrase that is explicitly cited in 1 Thessalonians itself (5,5).

3. *The negative implications of Roman patronage* is also crucial for interpreting key passages in both letters. With regard to *1 Thessalonians* it can be said:

1. The strong emphasis on the work of the three associates, Paul, Silvanus and Timothy (also referred to as apostles in 2,7), is a strong challenge to the imperial benefaction system and the social dominance of the benefactor in Thessalonica. Loyalty to different gospels was at stake as well as different social structures within the competing ecclesiae. The Thessalonian believers need to be made cognizant of the fact that the "peace and security" propaganda circulating in Roman Thessalonica is dangerous and that the existing patronage system in the city is morally and theologically bankrupt from the perspective of the new ecclesia, the one that is "in God the Father and the Lord Jesus Christ." We rejected the translation of 5,14, ἄτακτος, as "idle" as well as any linkage between this term and the expectation of an imminent parousia.

2. With regard to term ἀτακτέω in 2 Thess 3,7, but also ἄτακτος in 1 Thess 5,14 and ἀτάκτως in 2 Thess 3,6 and 3,11, we observed again a close proximity to certain texts from the Dead Sea Scrolls both in terms of derivation and meaning. It was determined that the ἄτακτοι, the disorderly, must be instructed by the leaders of the Thessalonian congregation, in several areas, including 1) the παραγγελία given by the Lord (4,2), (2) the way of holiness that is central to the life of the ἐκκλησία (4,3), (3) preparation for the spiritual warfare against the forces of darkness (5,8), and to this we would also add a fourth, (4) the understanding of the proper order of events at the parousia, particularly "concerning those have fallen asleep" (4,13-5,11, but especially 4,15-17).

4. *2 Thessalonians* stands in close chronological proximity to 1 Thessalonians and the second letter suggests a sharp *increase in persecutions*

and, perhaps due to this situation a misreading of 1 Thess 5,4 takes place within the ecclesia of believers; we now learn that some are arguing that the parousia had *already* arrived. Paul, Silvanus and Timothy counter this distortion unambiguously: "Let no one deceive you in any way; for that day will not come unless the rebellion comes first and the lawless one is revealed, the one destined for destruction" (2 Thess 2,3).

1. We also observed that the theme of the *parousia* has a different function in the two letters. In 1 Thess 4,13-18 "the coming of the Lord" serves positively as a comfort to the ones who are upset that some have been killed by the Romans prior to the arrival of the parousia of Christ; in 2 Thess 2,8 the theme of the parousia has primarily a negative function, viz., to correct erroneous teaching and to assure the new ecclesia that their great opponent, the lawless one, *will* be destroyed at "the manifestation of his coming" (τῇ ἐπιφανείᾳ τῆς παρουσίας αὐτοῦ).
2. The *intense ideological collision* reflected in 2 Thessalonians between the ecclesia in Christ and those faithful to the Empire is illustrated by the enhanced utilization of dramatic and hostile apocalyptic language and concepts, again with very strong ties to the Dead Sea Scrolls. This phenomenon was already observed in 1 Thessalonians. Elsewhere I have argued for a strong linkage between Paul and the *yahad* of Qumran; one should also not overlook that Paul's co-authors themselves come from very Jewish backgrounds: Silvanus/Silas, a prophet from Jerusalem (Acts 15,22.32) and Timothy, a son of a Jewish woman, from Derbe/Lystra (Acts 16,1).

5. *Concerning patronage and the question of the disorderly in 2 Thessalonians,* many dimensions of the discussion in 1 Thessalonians are directly relevant to the second letter as well. More emphatic is 2 Thess 3,10-13 with its apodictic phrase that "Anyone unwilling to work should not eat" and the theme of the *periergazesthai*. Through an analysis of these complex texts and their implications, we suggested that Roman patronage was in fundamental conflict with the new ecclesia "of the Thessalonians in God the Father and the Lord Jesus Christ" (2 Thess 1,2) and therefore required a refutation.

6. *With regard to the authorship of 2 Thessalonians* we found a striking coherence – although with sharply different levels of intensity – between 1 and 2 Thessalonians in their attempt to encourage and support the continued existence of the Church of Jesus Christ in the midst of Roman harassment and persecution as well as to confront the threat of

the Roman patronage system and its attempt to subvert loyalty to the claim that Jesus is Lord. It became apparent as this study proceeded that how one understands the relationship of the two letters to one another is an important factor in determining and deciding the complex issues of authorship. In light of our analysis, we found nothing inconsistent with urging that the missionary team of Paul, Silvanus and Timothy, as co-authors, were responsible for the preparatory conversations and dialogs that led to the composition and dictation of these two letters. Further, our analysis of the two letters *could not uphold the claim that 2 Thessalonians was a forgery written decades after the composition of 1 Thessalonians* nor could we find credibility in the claim that 2 Thess 3,17 was an obstacle to maintaining that Paul, together with his two co-workers, were the writers of 2 Thessalonians.

7. If any of these recommendations have merit, inherited paradigms may need to be rethought, including the method of letter writing within the Pauline missionary domain, a domain that involved major regional centers, close to one hundred co-workers and a leader who not only traveled significantly for well over a quarter century but also found himself frequently imprisoned.

1 THESS 5,1-11 IM KONTEXT DER ESCHATOLOGIE DES 1. THESSALONICHERBRIEFES

RUDOLF HOPPE

EINLEITUNG

Für die übergeordnete Thematik „Der Zweite Thessalonicherbrief und die paulinische Eschatologie" ist der 1 Thess mit seinem eschatologischen Grundmuster von zentraler Bedeutung. Wenn der Autor des 2 Thess[1] die Parusie Christi und die Zusammenführung der Glaubenden zum Thema macht (2 Thess 2,1) und vor möglichen Behauptungen warnt, der „Tag des Herrn" sei bereits da (2,2), stehen zweifellos die Parusieaussagen aus 1 Thess, das σὺν κυρίῳ εἶναι aus 1 Thess 4,17 und die Rede vom ἡμέρα κυρίου (1 Thess 5,1) im Hintergrund. Meine Aufgabe sehe ich darin, 1 Thess 5,1-11 in den Mittelpunkt zu stellen, aber auch seine Funktion in der Korrespondenz zu den eschatologischen Aussagen in 1,9f und 4,13-18 zu beschreiben sowie den Gedankengang des Abschnittes auch unter ekklesialem Aspekt zu skizzieren.

I. DER ESCHATOLOGISCHE „BAUPLAN" DES 1 THESS[2]

1. *Konturen der Gründungsbotschaft des Paulus*

Ausgangspunkt der folgenden Überlegungen ist sowohl die Annahme der Authentizität des 1 Thess[3] und seiner Abfassung im Jahre 50/51 in

---

1. Hinsichtlich der Authentizität des 2 Thess stellt sich die Forschungslage divergierend dar; während die angloamerikanische Exegese eher für eine Zuweisung des Briefes an Paulus selbst plädiert (vgl. C. A. WANAMAKER, *The Epistles of the Thessalonians* [NIGTC], Grand Rapids MI, Eerdmans, 1990, pp. 37-45, der allerdings 2 Thess dem 1 Thess vorausgehen lässt; G. D. FEE, *The First and Second Letters to the Thessalonians* [NICNT], Grand Rapids MI – Cambridge, Eerdmans, 1990, pp. 237-241; A. J. MALHERBE, *The Letters to the Thessalonians* (AB, 32B), New York/London, Doubleday, 2000, pp. 349-374), wird in der deutschsprachigen Forschung der Brief stark überwiegend als pseudepigraphes Schreiben angesehen, teilweise sogar die Annahme vertreten, der Verfasser des 2 Thess wolle den 1 Thess verdrängen (vgl. W. MARXSEN, *Der zweite Thessalonicherbrief* [ZBK, 11/2], Zürich, Theologischer Verlag, 1982, pp. 110f).
2. Zur Eschatologie des 1 Thess vgl. die umfassende Studie von D. LUCKENSMEYER, *The Eschatology of First Thessalonians* (NTOA, 71), Göttingen/Fribourg, Vandenhoeck & Ruprecht, 2009.
3. Unlängst hat M. CRÜSEMANN, *Die pseudepigraphen Briefe an die Gemeinde von Thessaloniki* (BWANT, 191), Stuttgart, Kohlhammer, 2010, zwar die Echtheitsdebatte um den

Korinth nach der Rückkehr des Timotheus zu Paulus als auch die literarische Einheitlichkeit des 1 Thess.[4] Mit seinem Schreiben erinnert Paulus an „sein" Evangelium (vgl. 1 Thess 1,5),[5] das er zu seinem Gründungsaufenthalt nach Thessalonich gebracht hat, und geht zur Festigung seiner Beziehung zur Gemeinde auf Fragen ein, die aus seiner Sicht für die Adressaten relevant oder die in Thessalonich während seiner Abwesenheit zum Problem geworden sind und ihm von Timotheus unterbreitet wurden. Eine Differenzierung zwischen seiner „Erstverkündigung" und einer brieflichen Klärung neu aufgekommener Fragen lässt sich anhand seines Schreibens relativ gut vornehmen, da Paulus seine Gründungsverkündigung durch Wendungen wie „Ihr selbst wisst" (2,1), „Ihr erinnert euch" (2,9), „Ihr seid Zeugen" 2,10), „wie wir euch schon früher gesagt haben" (4,6), „wir euch aufgetragen haben (4,11)" oder durch die Aufnahme von urchristlichen Glaubenssätzen wie „Wenn wir glauben, dass ..." (4,14) noch gut erkennen lässt. Wenn man also zwischen der Botschaft beim Gründungsaufenthalt und darauf aufbauenden Reflexionen im 1 Thess differenzieren kann, fällt um so mehr ins Auge, dass Fragen der *Eschatologie* das Zentrum der paulinischen Botschaft beim Missionsaufenthalt ausmachten und auf dem Hintergrund der Timotheus-Informationen zur beherrschenden Thematik wurden. Sie ist auch der Bezugspunkt der im engeren Sinne theologischen (vgl. 1,4; 2,12; 5,9), christologischen (1,10; 3,13) und ekklesialen (1,4; 5,12-24) sowie ethischen (2,11f; 4,3-8; 5,4-6) Aussagen. Dem entspricht, dass sich der Begriff παρουσία oder die Vorstellung vom in naher Zukunft erwarteten Kommen Jesu wie ein roten Faden durch den Gesamtbrief hindurchziehen (1,9f; 2,19; 3,13; 4,15-17; 5,2.4; 5,23).

Dieser Befund bestätigt sich bei den Dispositionsmöglichkeiten des Schreibens: Ob man den Brief nach dem Muster der antiken Rhetorik

---

1 Thess aus dem 19. Jh. wieder aufgegriffen und vertritt die These einer erst nachpaulinischen Verfasserschaft; aber diese Studie ist zu sehr vom Versuch geleitet, Paulus von dem schwierigen Passus 1 Thess 2,15f zu entbinden als dass sie mit sprachlichen oder theologischen Argumenten überzeugen könnte.

4. In der Frage der literarischen Einheitlichkeit hat sich inzwischen ein weitgehender Konsens gebildet, der von der Hypothese einer Teilung des 1 Thess, wie sie u.a. noch H.-M. SCHENKE/K.M. FISCHER, *Einleitung in die Schriften des Neuen Testaments I. Die Briefe des Paulus und Schriften des Paulinismus*, Gütersloh, Gerd Mohn, 1978, pp. 65-74, und R. PESCH, *Die Entdeckung des ältesten Paulus-Briefes. Paulus – neu gesehen*, Freiburg/Br., Herder, 1984, pp. 39-111, vorgenommen haben, abgekommen ist.

5. Die Frage des „Wir" im 1 Thess soll hier nicht diskutiert werden; ich neige eher zu der Annahme, dass es sich um einen schriftstellerischen Plural handelt. Vgl. zum Problem bereits K. DICK, *Der schriftstellerische Plural bei Paulus*, Halle, Niemeyer, 1900.

oder eher nach den Ordnungsprizipien der Epistolographie gliedert,[6] die wesentlichen Schnittstellen sind immer die Fragen der Eschatologie, primär in Verbindung mit der Erwählungstheologie.

2. *Erwählungstheologie und Eschatologie (1 Thess 1,2-10)*

Im Proömium 1,2-10 bzw. – der Disposition des Schreibens nach dem Muster der antiken Rhetorik entsprechend – im exordium[7] werden die wesentlichen Themen des Briefes angesprochen: ἐκλογή durch Gott (1,4), δύναμις des Evangeliums und dessen pneumatischer Charakter (1,5), Hinkehr zum lebendigen und wahrhaftigen Gott in der Abkehr von den εἴδωλα (1,9), Auferweckung Jesu durch Gott und die Erwartung seines rettenden Kommens (1,10). Mit der Verbindung von Erwählung und Rettung hat Paulus bereits hier die maßgeblichen Koordinaten für das gesamte Schreiben gesetzt.

Die eschatologische „Ouvertüre" in Kap. 1 lässt sich gleichwohl inhaltlich noch weiter präzisieren: Paulus greift in V.9f sicher auf traditionsgebundene Elemente zurück;[8] sie bestehen vor allem in der Bekehrungsaussage ἐπεστρέψατε πρὸς τὸν θεὸν ἀπὸ τῶν εἰδώλων (V.9), in dem Motiv des Dienstes an Gott (δουλεύειν θεῷ)[9] sowie den Epitheta „lebendig" und „wahrhaftig" (ζῶντι καὶ ἀληθινῷ)[10] besonders aber in der Auferweckungsformel ὃν ἤγειρεν ἐκ [τῶν] νεκρῶν[11] (1,10). Diese

---

6. Vgl. exemplarisch die Übersicht bei H. J. KLAUCK, *Die antike Briefliteratur und das NT* (UTB, 2022), Paderborn, Schöningh, 1998, pp. 269-281, 284-291; R. HOPPE, *Der erste Thessalonicherbrief und die antike Rhetorik – Eine Problemskizze*, in R. HOPPE, *Apostel – Gemeinde – Kirche. Beiträge zu Paulus und den Spuren seiner Verkündigung* (SBAB, 47), Stuttgart, Verlag Katholisches Bibelwerk, 2010, 15-25; K. P. DONFRIED/J. BEUTLER (ed.), *The Thessalonians Debate. Methodological Discord or Methodological Synthesis?*, Grand Rapids MI – Cambridge, Eerdmans, 2000.

7. Vgl. F. W. HUGHES, *The Rhetoric of 1 Thessalonian*, in R. F. COLLINS (ed.), *The Thessalonian Correspondence* (BEThL, 87), Leuven, Peeters, 1990, pp. 94-116, der das exordium allerdings schon mit der Zuschrift 1,1 beginnen lässt.

8. Vgl. dazu T. HOLTZ, *Der erste Brief an die Thessalonicher* (EKK, XIII), Zürich/Neukirchen-Vluyn, Benziger/Neukirchener, 1986, p. 55; M. ZUGMANN, *Missionspredigt in nuce. Studien zu 1 Thess 1,9b-10*, Linz/Oö, Wagner, 2012, pp. 11-42.

9. Vgl. das universalistische δουλεύειν κυρίῳ in Ps 101,23 (LXX); Jes 56,6; Zef 3,9 (vgl. auch Jes 19,21-23 [wohl aus hellenistischer Zeit]; vgl. dazu H. IRSIGLER, *Zefanja* (HThKAT), Freiburg, Herder 2002, p. 375. Die Vorstellung des „Gott Dienens" ist breit bezeugt bei Josephus und Philo; vgl. insbesondere auch Ps-Kall 24,38.

10. Vgl. Dan 6,27; Esr 8,86; Jes 65,16; 2 Chr 15,3; Test Hi 37,2; Test Abr 17,11 (A); 3 Makk 6,18; Sib fr I,20; fr III, 46; Philo, spec 1,332; JosAs 11,10.

11. Vgl. zur eingliedrigen Auferweckungsformel P. HOFFMANN, *Der Glaube an die Auferweckung Jesu in der neutestamentlichen Überlieferung*, in P. HOFFMANN, *Studien zur*

Traditionselemente hat er zu seinem eschatologischen Konzept miteinander verbunden.[12]

Den Zusammenhang der Erwählung durch Gott und der Rettung durch „seinen Sohn" hebt er dadurch besonders hervor, dass er mit τὸν ῥυόμενον ἡμᾶς einen Objektwechsel vornimmt, der die Gemeinsamkeit zwischen ihm und den Konvertiten in der Rettungserwartung betont. Damit impliziert Paulus ein eschatologisches Vernichtungsgericht, von dem allein die Glaubenden durch das rettende Handeln des vom Himmel kommenden Sohnes ausgenommen werden.[13] Die bei Paulus singuläre Denkfigur des aus den Himmeln kommenden Sohnes ist strukturell zwar vergleichbar mit der aus vormarkinischer Tradition[14] stammenden Vorstellung vom Kommen des Menschensohnes, sie dürfte hier aber kaum im Hintergrund stehen; vielmehr ist die Aussage an der Qualifizierung Jesu zum Sohn kraft seiner Auferweckung und zum Vollzug des göttlichen Rettungshandelns interessiert.[15] Weitergehende Konkretionen nimmt Paulus hier nicht vor. Die eschatologische Vorstellung einer Sammlung der Glaubenden begegnet dann erst in 1 Thess 3,13;[16] dort liegt der Akzent allerdings auf der durch Gott selbst bewirkten ethischen Disposition der Glaubenden bei der Parusie Christi, aber wie in 1,10 liegt in diesem Gebetswunsch des Paulus der Akzent allein auf der Heilsperspektive für die Gemeinde.

Resümierend lässt sich sagen: 1 Thess 1,2-10 stellt sich mit der Themenreihe Erwählung – Evangelium – Hinkehr zu Gott – Rettung der

---

Frühgeschichte der Jesusbewegung (SBAB, 17), Stuttgart, Verlag Katholisches Bibelwerk, 1994, 188-256, hier pp. 191f.

12. Zum hinter 1 Thess 1,9f stehenden Gottesbild des Paulus vgl. W. SCHRAGE, *Unterwegs zur Einheit und Einzigkeit Gottes. Zum „Monotheismus" des Paulus und seiner alttestamentlich-frühjüdischen Tradition* (BThS, 48), Neukirchen-Vluyn, Neukirchener, 2002, 43-52.

13. Über den Rettungs*vorgang* hat sich Paulus bei seinem Gründungsaufenthalt offenbar noch nicht detailliert geäußert; Diese „Lücke" füllt er wohl aufgrund der Informationen des Timotheus in 4,16f (s. unten I.3.).

14. Vgl. E. BRANDENBURGER, *Markus 13 und die Apokalyptik* (FRLANT, 134), Göttingen, Vandenhoeck & Ruprecht, 1984, pp. 54-65, 166f; vgl. auch Q 17,24.

15. Vgl. G. HAUFE, *Der erste Brief des Paulus an die Thessalonicher* (THKNT, 12/I), Leipzig, Evangelische Verlagsanstalt, 1999, p. 29, der allerdings die Verwendung des Sohnestitels in jenen urchristlichen Kreisen verortet, die die Auferweckung Jesu als seine Einsetzung in die messianische Würdestellung verstanden haben. Der Unterschied besteht freilich darin, dass hinter Röm 1,3 die Denkfigur der messianischen Inthronisierung steht, also eine dezidierte Erhöhungsaussage (vgl. Eph 1,20), die den Blick gerade nicht auf die Wiederkunft Jesu richtet.

16. Dazu ist Mk 8,38 am ehesten vergleichbar: ... ὅταν ἔλθῃ (ὁ υἱὸς τοῦ ἀνθρώπου) ἐν τῇ δόξῃ τοῦ πατρὸς αὐτοῦ μετὰ τῶν ἀγγέλων τῶν ἁγίων. Vgl. dazu M. REICHARDT, *Endgericht durch den Menschensohn? Zur eschatologischen Funktion des Menschensohnes im Markusevangelium* (SBB, 62), Stuttgart, Verlag Katholisches Bibelwerk, 2009, pp. 120-129.

Glaubenden als ein in sich geschlossener Zusammenhang dar, der die Missionsbotschaft des Paulus bei seinem Gründungsaufenthalt in den Grundzügen erkennen lässt und die Konvertiten zur eschatologischen Heilsgemeinde qualifiziert.[17]

3. Eschatologische Krise in Thessalonich (1 Thess 4,13-18)

Von 1 Thess 1,9f spannt sich der Bogen des eschatologischen Konzeptes über 1 Thess 3,13 zunächst bis 1 Thess 4,13-18. Der Anlass für die lehrhafte Darlegung der endzeitlichen Ereignisse ist offenbar der Tod von einigen Gemeindemitgliedern vor der erwarteten Parusie Christi; Timotheus dürfte Paulus nach seiner Rückkehr zu ihm (vgl. 3,6.10) davon berichtet haben. Weil sich die Jesusgläubigen in Thessalonich deshalb vor Probleme gestellt sahen, die zur Zeit des Erstaufenthaltes des Paulus noch nicht virulent waren, muss er seine Grundbotschaft vorantreiben und damit der eingetretenen Situation Rechnung tragen. Hier geht Paulus in zwei Schritten vor:

In einem *ersten* Schritt spricht er in einem Bekenntnissatz[18] von Tod und Auferstehung Jesu sowie der Zusammenführung der Verstorbenen durch (den auferstandenen) Jesus mit ihm (Jesus), die Gott herbeiführen wird:[19] Ἰησοῦς ἀπέθανεν καὶ ἀνέστη – ὁ θεὸς τοὺς κοιμηθέντας διὰ τοῦ Ἰησοῦ ἄξει σὺν αὐτῷ. Die Aussage von Tod und Auferstehung Jesu, die offenbar bereits zum Inhalt seines Evangeliums bei seinem Missionsaufenthalt gehörte und auf fruchtbaren Boden stieß,[20] verbindet er nun angesichts des Todes einiger Gemeindemitglieder mit seiner festen Überzeugung, dass Gott die Verstorbenen durch Tod und

---

17. Vgl. J. BECKER, *Paulus. Der Apostel der Völker*, Tübingen, Mohr, 1989, pp. 138-148; J. BECKER, *Die Erwählung der Völker durch das Evangelium*, in J. BECKER, *Annäherungen* (BZNW, 76), Berlin/New-York, De Gruyter, 1995, 79-98.
18. Vgl. HOFFMANN, *Auferweckung* (n. 11), pp. 190.198.
19. διὰ τοῦ Ἰησοῦ ist auf Gott als Handlungsträger zu beziehen, nicht auf τοὺς κοιμηθέντας, so dass die „wegen", „in" oder „mit" Jesus Verstorbenen gemeint wären; zu den verschiedenen Positionen vgl. LUCKENSMEYER, *Eschatology* (n. 2), pp. 221-224. Der Vorschlag von S. SCHNEIDER, *Vollendung des Auferstehens. Eine exegetische Untersuchung von 1 Kor 15,51-52 und 1 Thess 4,13-18* (FzB, 97), Würzburg, Echter, 2000, p. 261, in V. 14b statt σὺν αὐτῷ am Schluss des Verses σὺν αὐτῷ zu lesen, scheitert an der Textbezeugung, aber auch am Gesamtduktus von V.13-18, da es um das Zusammensein mit dem Kyrios Christus geht (vgl. 4,16). Paulus spricht nicht von den „durch Jesus (im Sinne von „mit Jesus") Verstorbenen", sondern davon, dass Gott durch Jesus die Verstorbenen mit ihm führen (oder bringen) wird.
20. Darauf deutet εἰ γὰρ πιστεύομεν (V.14a) hin. Das εἰ drückt keine Bedingung aus, sondern ist eine Bekräftigung der Wirklichkeit im Sinne von „wenn demnach" (vgl. BDR §372,1).

Auferstehung Jesu in die Gemeinschaft mit Jesus führen wird. Die komplexe Konstruktion διὰ τοῦ Ἰησοῦ ἄξει σὺν αὐτῷ, die für 1 Thess nicht ungewöhnlich ist,[21] erklärt sich daraus, dass Paulus angesichts der Todesfälle in Thessalonich nicht mehr nur von der Auferstehung Jesu und seines rettenden Kommens für die Glaubenden sprechen konnte, sondern nun ihre Auswirkung besonders für die bereits Verstorbenen in den Blick nehmen musste. Sie stellt sich in der Zusammenführung der Verstorbenen zur Gemeinschaft mit dem Auferstandenen dar.

In einem *zweiten* Schritt lässt Paulus zur Vergewisserung seiner Adressaten in apokalyptischer Vorstellungsweise die „Ordnung" der eschatologischen Heilsereignisse in einem prophetischen Spruch[22] folgen: zuerst kommt der Kyrios vom Himmel, dann folgt die Auferstehung der Toten „in Christus", dann werden die Lebenden zur Begegnung mit dem Kyrios „entrückt".[23] Die Akzentuierung „in Christus" macht deutlich, dass Paulus von einer Begegnung mit Christus nur für die Glaubenden ausgeht. Schwer zu entscheiden ist die Frage, ob der vom Himmel kommende Kyrios auf die Erde kommt oder wo die Begegnung mit dem Kyrios stattfindet. Seit den einflussreichen Arbeiten von Peterson[24] hat sich überwiegend die Annahme durchgesetzt, die ἀπάντησις sei auf dem Hintergrund des antiken Brauches der Einholung einer hochgestellten Persönlichkeit durch die Bürgerschaft einer hellenistischen Stadt zu verstehen.[25] Dann wäre davon auszugehen, dass die Entrückung der Gemeinde das Ziel hat, den Kyrios feierlich einzuholen und mit ihm auf die Erde zurückzukehren. Das wäre innerhalb der griechisch-hellenistischen und atl.-jüdischen Entrückungsvorstellungen durchaus möglich, aber ein im Hintergrund stehendes Bild von einer Einholung des Kyrios

---

21. Vgl. die Konstruktion in 1,5.
22. Zur Diskussion um 1 Thess 4,15a vgl. U. B. MÜLLER, *Prophetie und Predigt im Neuen Testament* (StNT, 10), Gütersloh, Mohn, 1975, p. 223; LUCKENSMEYER, *Eschatology* (n. 2), pp. 186-190. Es handelt sich nicht um einen geprägten, rekonstruierbaren Prophetenspruch, den Paulus zitiert hätte, sondern um ein in der Autorität des Kyrios von Paulus unter Rückgriff auf Motive der jüdisch-apokalyptischen Tradition und der hellenistischen Umwelt gebildetes Wort, das er mit prophetischem Anspruch der Gemeinde unterbreitet. Vgl. auch H. MERKLEIN, *Der Theologe als Prophet*, in H. MERKLEIN, *Studien zu Paulus und Jesus II* (WUNT, 105), Tübingen, Mohr, 1998, 377-404, hier p. 388; allerdings spricht Merklein dann doch von einem „Zitat" und sieht es in V.15b (p. 385).
23. Zu ἁρπάζειν als Entrückungsterminus vgl. W. TRILLING, Art. ἁρπάζω, in *EWNT* I, pp. 377f.
24. E. PETERSON, *Die Einholung des Kyrios*, in *ZST* 7 (1930) 682-702; E. PETERSON, Art. ἀπάντησις, in *TWNT* 1, p. 380.
25. Vgl. die eingehende Darstellung des Forschungsstandes bei LUCKENSMEYER, *Eschatology* (n. 2), pp. 260-268.

durch die Seinen wird dadurch erschwert, dass die Gemeinde keinerlei aktive Rolle spielt, sondern Gott als der Handlungsträger agiert, der die Auferstandenen und die Lebenden entrückt.[26] In erster Linie kommt es Paulus auf die Begegnung von Lebenden und Verstorbenen mit Christus bei dessen Parusie und der damit verbundenen Entrückung sowie der bleibenden Gemeinschaft mit dem Kyrios an.[27] Das ist seine Trostbotschaft an seine Adressaten.

Über eine Frist bis zur Parusie äußert sich Paulus nicht; aus der Erwartung, dass die noch Lebenden mit den dann auferstandenen Verstorbenen zur Gemeinschaft mit dem Kyrios entrückt werden, lässt sich nur folgern, dass Paulus nicht an eine sich allzu weit ausdehnende Zeit denkt. Angesichts der Funktion der von ihm erteilten Unterweisung hinsichtlich der die Verstorbenen betreffenden Zukunftsfrage liefert der paulinische Gedankengang keinerlei Begründungsmöglichkeit für eine „enthusiastische" Parusieerwartung. Paulus will vielmehr mit seiner in V.15-17 entfalteten gemeinsamen Perspektive für die Verstorbenen und Lebenden die Adressaten in die Lage versetzen, die Gegenwart auszuhalten und sich in der Gemeinde gegenseitig zu bestärken (V.18).[28]

II. CHRISTLICHES EXISTENZVERSTÄNDNIS IN DER ERWARTUNG DES ἡμέρα κυρίου (1 THESS 5,1-11)

Die Frage der Verhaltensethik im eschatologischen Kontext hatte Paulus in seinem Schreiben bislang nur in seiner Mahnung in 2,12 thematisiert;[29] dieser Zusammenhang rückt jetzt aber deutlicher ins Blickfeld. Nach der in 1 Thess 4,13-18 vorgenommenen Klärung des Schicksals der vor der Parusie Verstorbenen wird die Lebenspraxis der Gemeindemitglieder in der Zeit vor dem Ende angesichts der ihnen

---

26. Für eine Entrückung in die himmlische Welt vor dem mit der Parusie einsetzenden Gericht plädiert M. KONRADT, *Gericht und Gemeinde. Eine Studie zur Bedeutung und Funktion von Gerichtsaussagen im Rahmen der paulinischen Ekklesiologie und Ethik im 1 Thess und 1 Kor* (BZNW, 117), Berlin/New York, De Gruyter, 2003, pp. 68f.

27. Die Nähe von 1 Thess 4,15-17 zu 1 Kor 15,51-53, aber auch der Unterschied in der Fragestellung ist unverkennbar. Vgl. den instruktiven Exkurs zum Thema „Kontinuität und Variabilität in der paulinischen Eschatologie" von HAUFE, *1 Thess* (n. 15), pp. 87f.

28. Eine Zuweisung des 1 Thess zur Gattung der Konsolationsliteratur anhand von 1 Thess 4,13-18 ist meines Erachtens mehr als fraglich. Vgl. aber J. BICKMANN, *Kommunikation gegen den Tod. Studien zur paulinischen Briefpragmatik am Beispiel des ersten Thessalonicherbriefes* (FzB, 86), Würzburg, Echter, 1998.

29. 1 Thess 4,1-12 steht nicht in explizit eschatologischem Kontext, sondern ist ein Aufruf zur von der früheren Lebensweise unterscheidenden Verhaltensethik, ohne dass diese eschatologisch begründet würde.

zugesprochenen Heilszukunft zum Thema; dem stellt Paulus die Aussichtslosigkeit der Außenstehenden als negative Kontrastfolie gegenüber.

1. *Thematischer Aufbau und formale Anlage*

Bei aller Komplexität des Abschnittes im Einzelnen ist die gedankliche Linienführung transparent: Der Erinnerung an das gemeinsame Wissen um die Plötzlichkeit des Hereinbrechens des Herrentages und dem daraus folgenden Urteil über die „anderen", welche sich Illusionen über die tatsächliche Wirklichkeit machen *(V.1-3)*, folgt ein grundlegender in die Metaphorik von „Licht" und „Tag" gekleideter Zuspruch an die Adressaten, der sie ihrer Zugehörigkeit zum *Heilsbereich* vergewissern will *(V.4f)*. Es schließt sich die ethische Konkretion eines der eschatologischen Wirklichkeit entsprechenden und von den Außenstehenden unterscheidenden Lebensverständnisses an *(V.6-8)*. Paulus führt schließlich dieses Lebensmodell dem Ziel eines dauerhaft von den Kriterien Gottes bestimmten und durch den Tod Christi erwirkten „Lebens mit Christus" zu *(V. 9f)*. Der Abschnitt schließt mit einem Aufruf zur gegenseitigen Bestärkung der gemeinsamen Überzeugung (V.11).

Nach der einführenden rhetorischen Figur der praeteritio[30] hat der Appell an das gemeinsame Wissen (οἴδατε ὅτι) um den „Tag des Herrn" den Charakter einer Proklamation, die auf die Dringlichkeit des folgenden Geschehens aufmerksam macht: „Der Tag des Herrn kommt wie ein Dieb in der Nacht".[31] Damit wird nicht nur das Kommen als solches angesagt, sondern auch, dass die mit dem „Tag" verbundene eschatologische Wirklichkeit bereits in die Gegenwart hineinragt[32] und die Gegenwart neu qualifiziert. Die Zukunft wird bereits im Jetzt antizipiert.[33]

---

30. Vgl. J. MARTIN, *Antike Rhetorik* (HAW, II/3), München, Beck, 1974, p. 289; vgl. auch R. VOLKMANN, *Die Rhetorik der Griechen und Römer*, Leipzig, Teubner, 1885, p. 262; KLAUCK, Briefliteratur (n. 6), pp. 278f.

31. Vgl. MÜLLER, *Prophetie* (n. 22), p. 149. Ähnliche Proklamationen finden sich Röm 13,11f (ebenfalls mit der Metapher „Schlaf-Wachsein" [vgl. 1 Thess 5,6f]); Mk 1,15 (Proklamation der Nähe der βασιλεία); Lk 21,8 (Verweis auf ein Wort möglicher Falschpropheten: ὁ καιρὸς ἤγγικεν [= LkR]); Lk 10,9 (Ausruf der ausgesendeten Jünger: ἤγγικεν ἐφ' ὑμᾶς ἡ βασιλεία τοῦ θεοῦ [im Zusammenhang mit Heilungen]).

32. Vgl. F. FROITZHEIM, *Christologie und Eschatologie bei Paulus* (FzB, 35), Würzburg, Echter ²1982, p. 12: „gegenwärtige Heilsdimension christlicher Existenz".

33. Vgl. ähnliche Proklamationen in Offb 3,3; 16,15; 2 Petr 3,10. Müller, *Prophetie* (n. 22), p. 149, versteht den Spruch als „nominalen Ausruf": „Der Tag des Herrn – wie der Dieb in der Nacht".

V.3 hat die Form der prophetischen Gerichtsrede. Als Beispiel aus der Prophetie des AT sei nur das Gerichtswort des Elija gegen König Ahab nach dem Mord an Nabot genannt: „Weil du dich hergabst, das zu tun, was dem Herrn missfällt, werde ich Unheil über dich bringen. Ich werde dein Geschlecht hinwegfegen ..." (1 Kön 21,20f).[34] Die Glieder dieses prophetischen Schelt- und Drohwortes entsprechen in der Struktur denen von 1 Thess 5,3: „Wenn sie sagen: ‚Friede und Sicherheit', dann kommt plötzlich das Verderben und keiner kann entrinnen".[35]

V.4f tragen den Charakter einer *Vergewisserung* in sich, gleichwohl haben die Indikative „Ihr seid nicht" (V.4) und „Ihr seid" (V.5) auch appellativen Charakter; allerdings überwiegt durch den Personenwechsel von „Ihr" zu „Wir" in V.5b der Vergewisserungscharakter des Seins.[36] V.6f gehen zur *Paränese* über, die durch die „Wir"-Formulierung aber eher indirekten Charakter trägt. Wenn Paulus sich mit der Willensäußerung „wir wollen nicht schlafen wie die übrigen" in die Adressatengemeinde einbindet, kommt das einer indirekten Ermahnung gleich. V.9f tragen in theologischer Begründung wieder den Charakter einer Vergewisserung und Abgrenzung gegenüber den Außenstehenden.

1 Thess 5,1-8 basiert demnach auf vier Schwerpunkten, die auf ihre theologische Begründung unter Rückgriff auf die im vorpaulinischen Urchristentum gebildete Deutung des Todes Jesu (V.9f) als eines heilsmittlerischen „Sterbens für" zum Leben „mit ihm" (Christus) zulaufen. Das Gerüst des Abschnittes besteht

(1) aus einer prophetischen Proklamation, welche die Aufmerksamkeit für die Plötzlichkeit des Tages schärfen will (5,2);
(2) einem prophetischen Gerichtswort gegen die Außenstehenden (5,3);
(3) einer appellativen Erinnerung an den Heilsstand (V.4f);
(4) einer indirekten Paränese (V.6.8) mit einer eingeschalteten Abgrenzung gegen „die übrigen" (V.7).

Semantisch sind 1 Thess 5,1-11 charakterisiert durch überwiegend in Metaphern gekleidete Oppositionen, die alle das Thema Unheil – Heil chiffrieren. Im Einzelnen sind es „Nacht – Tag", Friede/Sicherheit – Verderben", „Finsternis – Licht", Schlafen – Wachen". Metaphorische

---

34. Vgl. auch Jes 8,5-8; Ez 13,10, im NT die bedingte Gerichtsankündigung Offb 3,3.
35. Dabei ist nicht so entscheidend, ob der Ausruf εἰρήνη καὶ ἀσφάλεια auf die Prophetie zurückgreift oder eine woanders beheimatete Parole ist, entscheidend ist die Struktur der prophetischen Redeform.
36. Vergleichbar ist Offb 2,1-6, wo dem Wissen des Propheten um die Entschiedenheit der Adressaten der Appell zur Rückkehr zum ursprünglichen Verhalten folgt. Vgl. auch den in rhetorische Frageform gekleideten Indikativ 1 Kor 3,16 oder die Zusage Röm 8,9.

Gestaltung findet sich auch außerhalb der Oppositionen: „Dieb" (V.2.4), „Wehe über die Schwangere" (V.3), „Panzer" (V.8), „Helm" (V.8).

2. Der Text 1 Thess 5,1-11

a) Erinnerung an den Gründungsaufenthalt (1 Thess 5,1f)

Die ausdrückliche Hervorhebung des Paulus, den Adressaten angesichts ihres genauen Wissens hinsichtlich Zeiten und Fristen nichts schreiben zu müssen (V.1), lässt den Schluss zu, dass bereits bei seinem Gründungsaufenthalt die Frage nach einem möglichen Zeitraum bis zu den Endereignissen zwar thematisiert, aber doch im Allgemeinen gehalten wurde.[37] Die Diebmetapher soll für die notwendige Aufmerksamkeit sensibilisieren, dass der „Tag" unvermittelt kommt, ist aber kein Hinweis auf ein Zeitmaß. Paulus geht also nicht auf eine Terminfrage[38] ein und gibt sich anders als manche Apokalyptiker[39] nicht den Anschein, Kenntnisse über den Weltenverlauf erhalten zu haben, sondern hat bei seinem Gründungsaufenthalt offenbar nur davon gesprochen, *dass* das gerichtliche Ende in aller Plötzlichkeit kommt.[40] Paulus erweckt hier den Eindruck, sich diesbezüglich mit den Adressaten im Konsens zu befinden, und setzt für die Thessalonicher ein „genaues" Wissen voraus (ἀκριβῶς), das auf seine Unterweisung bei seinem Erstaufenthalt zurückgeht.

Die Frage der Zeiträume bis zum Ende verlässt er konsequenterweise, um an den in seiner Sicht ebenfalls bestehenden Konsens in der Frage, „wie" der Tag sich einstellt, zu erinnern. Der Zusammenhang mit 4,15.17 legt nahe, dass in seiner Erwartungshaltung und der der Gemeinde der „Tag des Herrn" (ἡμέρα κυρίου) mit der Parusie des Kyrios

---

37. Deshalb ist es auch unwahrscheinlich, dass Paulus hier auf eine Anfrage reagiert. Mit περὶ δέ-Satzeinleitungen (1 Kor 7,1.25; 8,1.4; 12,1; 16,1.12; 2 Kor 9,1; 1 Thess 4,9; 5,1) bezieht Paulus sich nur in 1 Kor 7,1 deutlich erkennbar auf eine Anfrage.

38. Die „Zeiten und Fristen" (περὶ δὲ τῶν χρόνων καὶ τῶν καιρῶν) sind nicht weiter zu differenzieren, sondern eine fest geprägte Formel, die sowohl griechisch-hellenistisch (vgl. Dem or 3,32,16: τίνα γὰρ χρόνον ἢ τίνα καιρὸν ὦ ἄνδρες ...; ep 2,3) als auch in LXX belegt ist (vgl. Dan 2,21; 4,37; 7,12; Weish 8,8; vgl. die eschatologische Bedeutung in Apg 1,7); vgl. E. BEST, *The First and Second Letters to the Thessalonians* (BNTC), London, Black, 1972, pp. 203f; MALHERBE, *Thess* (n. 1), p. 288; KONRADT, *Gericht* (n. 26), p. 135 mit nn. 619, 620).

39. Vgl. 4 Esr 7,44; 12,9; Apk Bar (syr) 14,1; 56,2; 1 Hen 93,1 u.ö.

40. Wie die Apokalyptik ist auch Paulus davon überzeugt, dass das vernichtende Gericht nur die Gottlosen trifft (Apk Bar [syr] 13,1-5; 25,1-4; 85,14f; 4 Esr 7,112f).

unmittelbar verbunden ist. Wenn Paulus diese Verbindung herstellt, ist dieser Tag für die Glaubenden ein *Tag des Heils* und die Realisierung dessen, was unmittelbar vorher mit dem Kommen des Kyrios zum Ausdruck gebracht wurde (4,17). Das entspricht dem, was bereits die Tradition Israels mit der Rede vom Tag JHWHs verband, die Heilszusage in der Erwartung des Eingreifens Gottes in die Geschichte zugunsten seines Volkes.[41] Die Begriffsbildung selbst geht denn auch auf die alttestamentliche Tradition und die jüdische Apokalyptik zurück und ist Paulus bereits vorgegeben.[42]

Allerdings wohnt der Deutung des Tages des Herrn schon von seiner ambivalenten Ausprägung im AT her,[43] besonders aber im Zusammenhang der Dieb-Metaphorik, auch ein retardierend-mahnendes Element inne, das eine einseitige „Heilseuphorie" nicht aufkommen lässt; denn das Dieb-Motiv ist durchaus negativ und drohend zu verstehen. Es hat eine synoptische Parallele in Q 12,39,[44] findet sich aber auch Offb 3,3;[45] 16,15 (im Zusammenhang mit γρηγορεῖν), ebenso in 2 Petr 3,10, das aber möglicherweise von 1 Thess 5,2 literarisch abgängig ist. Da sich das Dieb-Motiv weder alttestamentlich-jüdisch noch außerbiblisch herleiten lässt[46] und nicht anzunehmen ist, dass Paulus das Bild unbeeinflusst von seiner Tradition gebildet hat, ist ein Rückgriff auf ihm zugeflossene Jesustradition wahrscheinlich, ohne dass man eine literarische

---

41. Hinter Am 5,18-20 dürfte ursprünglich die Erwartung des Eingreifens JHWH's zugunsten des Volkes gestanden haben, die der Prophet dann radikal ins Gegenteil umkehrt. In der späten Prophetie wird dann besonders die mit dem Tag JHWHs gegebene Heilsperspektive für das Gottesvolk betont (Joel 3,1-5; 4,14). Zum Tag JHWHs vgl. H.-P. MÜLLER, *Jahwetag*, in *NBL* 2, 266-268, p. 266; vgl. auch den gründlichen Überblick über die prophetische Tag-JHWH-Tradition bei IRSIGLER, *Zephanja* (n. 9), pp. 127-130; M. BECK, *Der „Tag YHWHs" im Dodekapropheton. Studien im Spannungsfeld von Traditions- und Redaktionsgeschichte* (BZAW, 356), Berlin/New York, De Gruyter, 2005; vgl. M. BECK, *Der Tag JHWHs. Ein Schlüsselbild für das Zwölfprophetenbuch*, in *BiKi* 68 (2013) 25-31.

42. Vgl. FROITZHEIM, *Christologie* (n. 32), pp. 3-9; J. PLEVNIK, *Paul and the Parousia. An exegetical and theological investigation*, Peabody, Hendrickson, 1995, pp. 11-44; MALHERBE, *Thess* (n. 1), pp. 290f; W. RADL, *Ankunft des Herrn. Zur Bedeutung und Funktion der Parusieaussagen bei Paulus* (BET, 15), Frankfurt, Lang, 1981, pp. 158f.

43. Vgl. die vorige Anmerkung.

44. Vgl. C.-P. MÄRZ, *Das Gleichnis vom Dieb. Überlegungen zur Verbindung von Lk 12,39 par Mt 24,43 und 1 Thess 5,2.4*, in F. VAN SEGBROECK ET AL. (ed.), *The Four Gospels* (BETL, 100), Leuven, Peeters, 1992, 635-648; KONRADT, *Gericht* (n. 26), pp. 139-143. Skeptisch gegenüber einer Rezeption von Jesustradition in 1 Thess äußert sich C.M. TUCKETT, *Synoptic Tradition in 1 Thessalonians?*, in R. F. COLLINS, *The Thessalonian Correspondence* (BETL, 87), Leuven, Peeters, 1990, 160-182.

45. Hier steht das Wort im Kontext einer Drohung: Der Erhöhte lässt den prophetischen Seher sein Kommen zu einer ungewissen Stunde ankündigen.

46. Jer 30,3(LXX); Ob 5 kommen als Parallelen nicht in Frage.

Beziehung zur Spruchquelle Q annehmen müsste. Der Vergleich mit dem Dieb diente Paulus bei seiner Gründungsverkündigung dazu, die Erwartungshaltung zu begründen und für den Ruf Gottes in seine βασιλεία bereit zu sein (vgl. 2,12).

b) *Das Gerichtswort über die Nicht-Christen (1 Thess 5,3)*

Lässt sich V.2 als eine bedingte Heilszusage verstehen, so werden mit V.3 die nicht näher konkretisierten Kreise, die nur mit „ὅταν λέγωσιν" in die Unterweisung polarisierend einbezogen werden, negativ von der Gemeinde abgesetzt. Hier wird nicht anonym davon gesprochen, dass „man" sich Friede und Sicherheit einredet.[47] Mit αὐτοὶ ἀκριβῶς οἴδατε („ihr wisst selbst genau") in V.2 und der Anrede ἀδελφοί in V.1 wird nämlich zunächst die Gemeinde als Adressatin des Heils angesprochen, mit dem akzentuierten ὑμεῖς δέ in V.4 will Paulus dann die zum Christusglauben gekommenen Thessalonicher in ihrer Entscheidung ausdrücklich unterstützen. Vor allem das abgrenzende ὑμεῖς δέ erfordert dann aber ein konkretes, von der Gemeinde negativ abgegrenztes Gegenüber. Wenn man schließlich das ὅταν λέγωσιν mit den „übrigen, die keine Hoffnung haben" (4,13) verbinden kann, sind die der Ekklesia gegenüberstehenden Vertreter in der paganen Gesellschaft gemeint.[48] Es sind diejenigen, die das Evangelium abgelehnt und sich nicht dem lebendigen Gott zugewandt haben und im Urteil des Paulus deshalb den Zorn Gottes auf sich ziehen. Dabei ist freilich nicht an „Gegner" der Gemeinde zu denken,[49] vielmehr steht der jesusgläubigen Minorität die gesellschaftliche Majorität gegenüber, welche in ihren Repräsentanten Konkurrenzkonzepte vertreten, die in der Sicht des Paulus die Wirklichkeit vernebeln.

Das überkommene, im gesellschaftlichen Umfeld sich äußernde Selbstverständnis stellt sich punktuell in Slogans wie εἰρήνη und ἀσφάλεια dar. Allerdings ist es fraglich, ob Paulus hier eine geprägte Parole „zitiert", um deren Vertretern mit dem Verdikt des ὄλεθρος zu begegnen. Diese Auffassung wird von denen vertreten, die εἰρήνη καὶ

---

47. HOLTZ, *1 Thess* (n. 8), p. 215, spricht von einem „unbestimmte(n) λέγωσιν", das kaum an die Nichtchristen denken lasse.

48. Vgl. auch KONRADT, *Gericht* (n. 26), pp. 144f. C. VOM BROCKE, *Thessaloniki – Stadt des Kassander und Gemeinde des Paulus* (WUNT, 2.125), Tübingen, Mohr, 2001, pp. 169f, weist darauf hin, dass in 1 Thess 1,9; 2,16, wo Paulus sonst noch in der 3. Person Plural spricht, Kreise außerhalb der Gemeinde gemeint sind.

49. So aber CRÜSEMANN, *Briefe* (n. 2), p. 221. Schon gar nicht kann von einer „zu vernichtenden Gruppe" (ebd.) die Rede sein.

ἀσφάλεια von der Ideologie einer vermeintlichen römischen pax et securitas-Propagandaformel ableiten.[50] Doch ist hier Vorsicht angebracht, denn eine fest formulierte Formel εἰρήνη καὶ ἀσφάλεια bzw. pax et securitas ist nicht als zusammenhängende „Parole" belegt.[51] Zudem muss Paulus schon deshalb „Friede und Sicherheit" hier nicht als „Parole" rezipieren und damit „zitieren", weil die beiden Begriffe, wie die zahlreichen Belege zeigen, auch einzeln für sich verstanden werden können, zumal sie auch weitgehend so in Umlauf waren. Es ist deshalb eher unwahrscheinlich, dass sie ein zusammenhängender, geprägter Slogan sind.

Das spricht gleichwohl nicht dagegen, dass Paulus in Aufnahme der Signale „Friede" und „Sicherheit" das religiös-politische Selbstverständnis der hellenistischen Umwelt in der mazedonischen Hauptstadt chiffriert, um diesem (seiner Gemeinde gegenüber) den Untergang anzusagen und damit seine Adressaten vor Irrwegen zu schützen. Die zahlreichen Belege für den schon in voraugusteischer Zeit erhobenen Anspruch der Pax Romana sind in der Literatur umfassend verzeichnet;[52] sie machen den Anspruch Roms und seiner Institutionen, Stabilität zu gewährleisten, unabweisbar. Das im hellenistisch-römischen Selbstverständnis dominierende Kontinuitätsdenken, das seine Basis in der Revitalisierung des überlieferten Götterglaubens hat, ist es, das Paulus für hoffnungslos hält.

---

50. So verstehen im Anschluss an E. BAMMEL, *Ein Beitrag zur paulinischen Staatsanschauung*, in *TLZ* 85 (1960) 837-840; VOM BROCKE, *Thessaloniki* (n. 48), pp. 70-178; vgl. auch K. WENGST, *Pax Romana. Anspruch und Wirklichkeit*, München, Kaiser, 1986, p. 99 („eine strukturkonservative Parole, die die bestehende Ordnung bejaht und sie bewahrt sehen will. Paulus nimmt sie in 1 Thess 5,3 auf.") mit pp. 216f Anm. 50; CRÜSEMANN, *Briefe* (n. 2), pp. 221-224. Vgl. auch J.A.D. WEIMA, *‚Peace and Security' (1 Thess 5,3): Prophetic Warning or Political Propaganda?*, in *NTS* 58 (2012) 331-359, pp. 358f; E. FAUST, *Pax Christi et Pax Caesaris, Redaktionsgeschichtliche, traditionsgeschichtliche und sozialgeschichtliche Studien zum Epheserbrief* (NTOA, 24), Freiburg (Schw.)/Göttingen, Universitätsverlag Freiburg/Vandenhoeck & Ruprecht, 1993, p. 444.

51. Vgl. KONRADT, *Gericht* (n. 26), p. 145 n. 676 mit Berufung auf H. L. HENDRIX, *Archaeology and Eschatology at Thessalonica*, in B. A. PEARSON (ed.), *The Future of Early Christianity. Essays in Honour of Helmut Koester*, Fortress, Minneapolis 1991, p. 114 n. 20. Plut Ant 40,7 (τοῦ δὲ Πάρθου ταῦτα μὲν ἐᾶν κελεύοντος, ἀπιόντι δ' εὐθὺς εἰρήνην καὶ ἀσφάλειαν εἶναι φήσαντος ...) ist keine „Parole", ebenso wenig wie die von WEIMA, *Peace* (n. 50), p. 341 n. 32 angeführte Inschrift (SEG XLVI) ἀποκαθεστακότα δὲ [τὴν εἰρ]ήνην καὶ τὴν ἀσφάλειαν καὶ κατὰ γῆν καὶ κατὰ Θάλασσαν. Dasselbe gilt für PsSal 8,18. Vielmehr hat man zu bedenken, dass „Friede und Sicherheit" für eine tiefere Wirklichkeit eines Selbstverständnisses stehen, das Paulus attackiert, weil es die Endzeit nicht ernst nimmt.

52. Vgl. KONRADT *Gericht* (n. 26), pp. 144-146 mit nn. 667-679; VOM BROCKE, *Thessaloniki* (n. 48), pp. 170-178; HENDRIX, *Archaeology* (n. 51), pp. 113f; WEIMA, *Peace* (n. 50), pp. 333-355, besonders die numismatischen Belege pp. 333-341.

Doch wäre es zu vordergründig, die Äußerung des Paulus als Widerspruch gegen politische Ansprüche zu verstehen; denn es bleibt zu beachten, um was es Paulus letztlich geht, nämlich um die Entscheidung in der Gottesfrage, die sich gerade in der Bindung an die Alternative Εἰρήνη/Pax[53] oder den „wahrhaftigen Gott" aus 1,9 entscheidet: Es geht ihm mit seinem prophetischen Spruch weniger um einen direkten Widerspruch gegen die Politik Roms als vielmehr um die Festigung jener Abkehr von den εἴδωλα und ihrer Hinwendung zum „wahrhaftigen Gott" einschließlich der damit verbundenen Ausrichtung auf den kommenden Sohn, die er in 1,9f positiv in Erinnerung gerufen und in 4,16f mit Nachdruck untermauert hatte. Es geht ihm also um das identitätsstiftende religiöse System des christlichen Gottesglaubens, für das die Thessalonicher sich entschieden hatten, es geht um ihre Erwartungshaltung gegen alle Illusion des propagierten Stabilitätsdenkens. Den Anspruch auf Friedensstiftung und Sicherheitsgewährleistung kennen seine Adressaten aus ihrem gesellschaftlichen Umfeld, diesem sollen die Konvertiten der Gemeinde mit ihrem Lebensmodell dauerhaft widerstehen können.

Das Problem des falschen Sicherheitswahns kennt Paulus freilich bereits aus seiner prophetischen Tradition. Jer 6,14 kritisiert Falschpropheten, die „schalom, schalom" (LXX: εἰρήνη) rufen und damit oberflächlichen Optimismus in politisch labiler Situation verbreiten (vgl. auch Ez 13,10). Jeremia kritisiert in seiner Zeit – kurz vor der Zerstörung Jerusalems durch die babylonische Großmacht – nicht nur die trügerische Sicherheit, die aktuelle Krise werde vorüberziehen, sondern tiefgreifender das verbreitete Sicherheitsgefühl, das mit einem Eingreifen JHWHs nicht mehr rechnete.[54] Ob Paulus hier auf Jer 6,14 zurückgegriffen hat, ist kaum mit Sicherheit zu entscheiden, sogar eher unwahrscheinlich;[55] das Problem der Scheinsicherheit ist aber in jedem Falle ein Thema der exilisch-nachexilischen Prophetie (vgl. Jes 47,8 [Spruch gegen den Größenwahn Babels]; Zeph 2,15 [Gerichtsspruch über die Nachbarvölker]). So wie die Prophetie das Sicherheitsgefühl der Bedränger Israels ironisiert, so fällt Paulus über die politisch-religiösen Strukturen, denen ihre Scheinüberlegenheit nur noch befristet belassen wird, das vernichtende Urteil.

---

53. Vgl. E. SIMON, *Eirene und Pax. Friedensgöttinnen in der Antike,* Stuttgart, Steiner, 1988.
54. Vgl. G. FISCHER, *Jeremia 1-25* (HThKAT), Freiburg, Herder, 2005, 270f; W. HARNISCH, *Eschatologische Existenz. Ein exegetischer Beitrag zum Sachanliegen von 1 Thessalonicher 4,13-5,11,* (FRLANT, 110), Göttingen, Vandenhoeck & Ruprecht, p. 79.
55. Nachdrücklich bestreitet das VOM BROCKE, *Thessaloniki* (n. 48), p. 171 im Anschluss an WENGST, *Pax* (n. 50), pp. 216f n. 50.

Damit erübrigt sich die (Schein-)Alternative „politischer" vs. „prophetischer" Kontext. Die prophetische Kritik Israels bietet Paulus das gedankliche Rüstzeug, das Festhalten am „lebendigen Gott" in den schwierigen Rahmenbedingungen der mazedonischen Hauptstadt einsichtig zu machen.

Dem Überraschungsmoment des Einbrechens des Tages entspricht die besondere Betonung des plötzlichen Verderbens (αἰφνίδιος[56] ὄλεθρος[57]). Gedacht ist natürlich an das Verderben, das Gott herbeiführt. ὄλεθρος verwendet Paulus sonst nur noch in 1 Kor 5,5 gegen ein Gemeindemitglied, das sich der Unzucht schuldig gemacht hat;[58] hier aber geht es anders als in 1 Kor 5,5 um das unabänderliche Verderben derer, die die Zeit nicht als Endzeit wahrnehmen. Eine 1 Thess 5,3 vergleichbare prophetische Ansage des ὄλεθρος für die Heiden findet sich bereits in Ob 12-16,[59] wo den Völkern am „Tag des Herrn" die Vernichtung, dem Haus Jakob aber die Rettung angesagt wird (V.17).[60] Das Präsens ἐφίσταται ist nicht im Sinne eines *Drohens* des Unheils zu verstehen, sondern drückt das unweigerliche und *tatsächliche* Hereinbrechen des Verderbens aus.

Paulus verbindet das mit dem Bild von der „Wehe" (ὠδίν) über die Schwangere, das in der prophetisch-apokalyptischen Tradition breit bezeugt ist und dort den unausweichlichen Gerichtsvollzug JHWHs zum Ausdruck bringen kann (vgl. Jes 13,8 [in Verbindung mit dem „Tag des Herrn" 13,6]; 21,3; 26,17f; Jer 6,24;[61] Hos 13,12f; 6 Esr 16,36-39).[62]

---

56. Vgl. Weish 17,14 (αἰφνίδιος καὶ ἀπροσδόκητος φόβος); Thuk II, 61,3 (τὸ αἰφνίδιον καὶ ἀπροσδόκητον συμβαῖνον); vgl. zur Bezeichnung der Plötzlichkeit und des Überraschungsmomentes Jos ant 6,79; 7,73; 8,377; 9,199; vgl. bes. 12,413 (Tod des Hohenpriesters Alkimos durch einen plötzlichen Schlag durch die Hand Gottes).

57. Im Sinne des tödlichen Endes findet sich das Wort seit Homer, besonders bei den Tragikern; vgl. auch Plat Phaed 91D.

58. Die Perspektive für das ausgeschlossene Gemeindemitglied ist aber am „Tag des Herrn" die Rettung seines Geistes. Vgl. zum Verständnis von 1 Kor 5,5 W. SCHRAGE, *Der erste Brief an die Korinther. 1. Teilband 1 Kor 1,1-6,11* (EKK VII/1), Zürich/Neukirchen-Vluyn, Benziger/Neukirchener, 1991, pp. 373-378.

59. Vgl. bes. V.13 (LXX: ἐν ἡμέρᾳ ὀλέθρου) und V.15 (LXX: ἐγγὺς ἡμέρα κυρίου ἐπὶ πάντα τὰ ἔθνη).

60. 4 Makk 10,15 stellt den „seligen Tod" (μακάριος θάνατος) des zweiten Bruders dem „ewigen Verderben" (αἰώνιον ὄλεθρον) des Tyrannen gegenüber; Philo legt in der Exegese von Ex 12,23 das Verderben auf die Veränderung der Seele aus, die zu ihrem völligen Vergehen führt (all II,34); somn I,86 stehen σωτηρία und ὄλεθρος gegenüber: Der Logos Gottes steht den Tugendhaften zur Rettung bei, den Entgegengesetzten schickt er ὄλεθρος καὶ φθορὰν ἀνίατρον.

61. Die „schalom-Parole" und die das Gericht signalisierende Wehe stehen bei Jeremia zumindest in einem gedanklichen Zusammenhang (Jer 6,14.24).

62. Vgl. auch die bei HARNISCH, *Existenz* (n. 54), pp. 62-72 zusammengestellten Belege; HOLTZ, *1 Thess* (n. 8), p. 216.

In der prophetischen Verwendung des Motivs wird allerdings die Brücke auch zum Heil geschlagen, das dem Bild eigentlich innewohnt (vgl. Mi 4,9f). Dieser Aspekt kommt in 1 Thess 5,3 nicht zum Tragen, vielmehr ist hier der Skopus die ausschließliche Ansage des ὄλεθρος über diejenigen, die sich mit dem hinter „Frieden" und „Sicherheit" stehenden Existenzverständnis identifizieren.[63]

Das proklamiert Paulus mit prophetischer Gewissheit[64] in der die Unausweichlichkeit der vernichtenden Zukunft ansagenden οὐ μή-Form.[65] Der entscheidende Aspekt liegt aber in der Heilsfunktion seines Verdiktes für diejenigen, die sich von der Selbstgewissheit der Umwelt nicht beeinflussen lassen und an ihrer Erwartungshaltung festhalten; sie stehen im Blickpunkt des Interesses.

c) *Licht und Tag – Metaphern für die Zugehörigkeit zum Heilsbereich (1 Thess 5,4f)*

Deshalb hat der Indikativ οὐκ ἐστέ zwar primär vergewissernden, aber auch appellativen Charakter. Er will die Adressaten einerseits darin bestätigen, dass sie zum Heilsbereich gehören, andererseits aber auch auf den Anspruch des Heils verpflichten. In der Seinszusage liegt aus der Sicht des Paulus auch ein kohortatives Element.[66] ἵνα ist deshalb nicht rein konsekutiv zu verstehen,[67] sondern in ihm ist das Motiv einer Warnung mitenthalten. Paulus will seine Adressaten darin bestärken, dass ihr Wissen um die Plötzlichkeit des Herrentages verhindern möge, dass dieser sie „wie ein Dieb" überrascht.[68]

Der Gedanke schließt sich damit an V.2 an, nimmt das bedrohliche Potential, das in der Dieb-Metapher enthalten ist, wieder auf und richtet es appellativ auf die Adressaten aus. Mit ἡ ἡμέρα ist dann der

---

63. Ob zwischen 1 Thess 5,3 und Lk 21,34-36 eine traditionsgeschichtliche Beziehung steht, muss hier offen bleiben, ist auch für die vorliegende Fragestellung nicht von substantieller Bedeutung. Vgl. dazu Konradt, *Gericht* (n. 26), pp. 154f. mit n. 702.

64. Vgl. oben II.1.

65. Vgl. BDR §365.

66. U. B. Müller sicht im Hintergrund die Erinnerung an die Taufe und weist die Aussage der Predigt zu, „die mit ihrem Wort das Heilsgeschehen immer wieder Wirklichkeit werden lässt" (*Prophetie* [n. 22], p. 154). In der Sache ist ihm zuzustimmen, nur sollte man das Gegenüber von Finsternis und Licht genauer in der Bekehrung verorten.

67. Anders Konradt, *Gericht* (n. 26), p. 157; vgl. aber W. Bornemann, *Die Thessalonicherbriefe* (KEK, 10), Göttingen, Vandenhoeck & Ruprecht 1894, p. 219; J. Eadie, *A Commentary on the Greek Text of the Epistles of Paul to the Thessalonians*, London, Macmillan 1877, p. 181.

68. Zum Verhältnis zu Q 12,39f vgl. oben zu V.2.

eschatologische Tag gemeint, der zur Scheidung zwischen den Glaubenden und den Außenstehenden führt.

Das Bild der Finsternis (V.4) ist die Negativfolie für den Zuspruch an die Adressaten in der mit ihr korrespondierenden Licht-Metapher. Diese Gegenüberstellung weckt die Assoziation an die vollzogene Hinwendung zu Gott (vgl. 1,9f) und die damit gewonnene neue Lebensauffassung. Für die paulinische Rezeption der dualisierenden Metapher „Finsternis" – „Licht" von besonderem Gewicht ist diese Opposition in der jüdisch-hellenistischen Bekehrungstheologie. JosAs 8,9 (vgl. 15,12) ist der Wechsel von der Finsternis zum Licht gleichbedeutend mit dem Übergang vom Tod zum Leben, was nichts anderes bedeutet als den Übertritt vom Heidentum zum Judentum.[69] Durch die Ergänzung „Söhne des Tages" in V.5a hebt Paulus eine potentielle Gleichgewichtigkeit der Bereiche „Finsternis" und „Licht" auf und unterstreicht damit den Heilsbereich, in dem die Adressaten sich befinden. Er unterlegt dem Begriff ἡμέρα damit einen Bedeutungswandel, indem er den „Tag" nun wie das „Licht" zur Chiffre für den Heilsstatus der Gemeinde macht.[70] Der „Tag" in V.5a ist also nicht im Sinne von V.2.4 zu verstehen, sondern ist eine Zugehörigkeitsbestimmung, die auf die Selbstwahrnehmung der Gemeinde als Heilsgemeinde hinwirken will. Präsentische Heilserfahrung und eschatologische Orientierung kommen hier zusammen.

In V. 5b bezieht Paulus sich unmittelbar in die Zugehörigkeitsaussage mit ein,[71] die er wie V.4a mit der Negation οὐκ ἐσμέν wiederum thetisch formuliert. Durch die Disponierung von V.5b schafft er einen Chiasmus und profiliert damit den Kontrast zwischen Vergangenheit und Gegenwart: „Ihr alle nämlich seid Söhne des *Lichtes* und Söhne des *Tages* – wir sind nicht des *Nachts* und nicht der *Finsternis*".[72] Inhaltlich wird mit υἱοί die Herkunft oder Abstammung, mit dem Genitivus

---

69. Vgl. auch die von KONRADT, *Gericht* (n. 26), pp. 160f + nn. 731-741 angeführten Belege.
70. Vgl. RADL, *Ankunft* (n. 42), pp. 163f; LUCKENSMEYER, *Eschatology* (n. 2), pp. 298f; KONRADT, *Gericht* (n. 26), pp. 161f. Andere Autoren beziehen die Wendung υἱοὶ ἡμέρας auf den eschatologischen Tag; vgl. HAUFE, *1 Thess* (n. 15), p. 94: Die Wendung „bezeichnet die Leser als solche, insofern sie intensiv auf diesen Tag warten und schon in seinem Licht leben". Vgl. auch HOLTZ, *1 Thess* (n. 8), p. 221; PLEVNIK, *Parousia* (n. 42), p. 110.
71. Vgl. zum kommunikativen Plural H. THYEN, *Der Stil der jüdisch-hellenistischen Homilie* (FRLANT, 47), Göttingen, Vandenhoeck & Ruprecht, 1955, pp. 90ff.
72. Die chiastische Anlage des Satzes spricht zusätzlich dafür, dass mit dem „Tag" nicht der eschatologische Tag, sondern der gegenwärtige Heilsbereich gemeint ist. Dass die Zugehörigkeit zum „Tag" auch vor der Überraschung durch das Eintreten des eschatologischen Tages bewahrt, ist damit selbstverständlich impliziert.

pertinentiae⁷³ νυκτός/σκότους primär der Herrschaftsbereich angegeben (vgl. 1 Kor 1,12; 3,23; Röm 14,8; Gal 3,29).

d) *Das von den λοιποί unterscheidende Leben (1 Thess 5,6-8)*

V.6-8 ziehen die paränetische Konsequenz aus dem Status der Gemeinde als Heilsgemeinde und grenzen sie – auf ihre Lebenspraxis bezogen – noch einmal von denen ab, die in V.3 mit dem prophetischen Verdikt des Verderbens bedacht worden sind.⁷⁴ Hatten die Indikative in V.4f bereits den appellativen Charakter zumindest impliziert, so geht Paulus nun zur Paränese über, in die er sich in Kontinuität zum οὐκ ἐσμέν in V.5b wieder selbst mit einbezieht. Die Konjunktive μὴ καθεύδωμεν und γρηγορῶμεν καὶ νήφωμεν haben dabei die adressatenorientierte Funktion, die Statusbestimmungen von V.4f mit οὐκ ἐν σκότει und υἱοὶ φωτός/ἡμέρας im praktischen Gemeindeleben zur Lebensrealität werden zu lassen. Der paränetische Grundduktus legt es deshalb nahe, die Gegensätze von „Nacht" und „Tag", von „Finsternis" und „Licht" im Sinne eines Entscheidungsdualismus mit seinen ethischen Alternativen zu verstehen, die ihren letzten Grund in der Ausrichtung auf den Herrentag auf der einen und das illusionäre Sicherheitsdenken auf der anderen Seite haben.⁷⁵ Paulus ordnet das καθεύδειν, wie der distanzierende Vergleich mit den λοιποί in V.6 und V.7 verdeutlicht, konsequent dem Bild der Nacht zu und erweitert in V.7 die negative Bedeutung des „Schlafens"⁷⁶ noch mit der die Wirklichkeit vernebelnden Praxis des „Sich-Betrinkens".⁷⁷ „Nicht schlafen" bedeutet also

---

73. Vgl. E. BORNEMANN, *Griechische Grammatik*, Frankfurt, Diesterweg, 1978, §176.
74. Das macht das einleitende ἄρα οὖν deutlich.
75. καθεύδειν findet sich bei Paulus nur im Zusammenhang 1 Thess 5,6-10 und kommt im Corpus Paulinum sonst nur noch in dem Zitat Eph 5,14b (wohl Fragment eines urchristlichen Taufliedes) vor. G. SELLIN, *Der Brief an die Epheser* (KEK, 8), Göttingen, Vandenhoeck & Ruprecht, ⁹2008, 1. Auflage dieser Neuauslegung, p. 410, sieht in 1 Thess 5,1-11 den „beste(n) Kommentar" zu Eph 5,14.
76. Vgl. zur negativen Bedeutung von καθεύδειν im übertragenen Sinne bereits in der Antike A. OEPKE, Art. καθεύδω, in *TWNT* 3, pp. 435f; sprichwörtlich ist auch die atl. Weisheitstradition (Spr 6,4-10; 10,5). Jes 51,20 wird die Ohnmacht der verbannten Israeliten auf den Zorn JHWHs zurückgeführt und mit dem Bild des Schlafes verbunden: οἱ υἱοί σου οἱ ἀπορούμενοι, οἱ καθεύδοντες ἐπ' ἄκρου πάσης ἐξόδου ὡς σευτλίον ἡμίεφθον, οἱ πλήρεις θυμοῦ κυρίου …. (LXX). Die positive Bedeutung des Schlafens für die religiöse Erfahrung, die gut belegt ist, kommt in 1 Thess 5 nicht zum Tragen.
77. Philo, cher 92 steht der „Schlaf (ὕπνος) am Tage, wenn die Zeit für das Wachen (ἐγρήγορσις) ist", in der Reihe eines Lasterkatalogs, der die griechischen Festfeiern charakterisiert.

positiv die Ausrichtung auf den eschatologischen Tag. Entsprechend nachdrücklich formuliert Paulus die positive Alternative zu καθεύδειν mit γρηγορῶμεν καὶ νήφωμεν.

Das „Wachen" findet sich in Verbindung mit der Dieb-Metaphorik im NT sonst noch in Offb 16,15, im Parusiekontext als paränetische Aussage in Mk 13,34-37, ebenso in ähnlicher Ausrichtung in Q 12,37.[78] Das ist ein deutlicher Hinweis darauf, dass das „Wachsam-Sein" ein Topos ist, der mit der Parusieerwartung verbunden ist.[79] Ein explizit theologischer Bezug der „Wachsamkeit" findet sich aber auch im zeitgenössischen Judentum.[80] νήφειν verwendet Paulus nur hier, aber bemerkenswert ist, dass er in der Auseinandersetzung mit den Auferstehungsleugnern in Korinth zum ἐκνήφειν aufruft und den Korinthern vorwirft, in ihren Reihen befänden sich solche, die von Gott nur ἀγνωσία hätten.[81] Den Aspekt der Klarheit im Gegensatz zu aller geistiger Trübung betont das νήφειν auch bei Philo und Plutarch.[82] Eigentliche und metaphorische Bedeutung können bei Philo ineinander übergehen: So verbietet es sich, den Vater des Alls in Trunkenheit zu verehren (*ebr* 131), was dann auf den nüchternen Geist übertragen wird, dem die freie, ungebundene und ungetrübte Vernunft zugrundeliegt (*ebr* 151f). Die Nüchternheit ist deshalb dazu geeignet, zur Anerkennung Gottes als des Schöpfers und Vaters des Alls zu führen (post 175), die sogar so weit gehen kann, dass die von Gott Begeisterten trunken erscheinen, aber dennoch nüchtern sind (ebr 147-149).[83] Eschatologische Ausrichtung und ethische Lebensführung kommen in 1 Thess 5,6f zusammen[84] und grenzen gegen die

---

78. Vgl. oben II.2.b.
79. Vgl. auch U. LUZ, *Das Evangelium nach Matthäus* (EKK, I/3), Zürich/Neukirchen-Vluyn, Benziger/Neukirchener 1997, pp. 455f.
80. Vgl. nur Ps Sal 3,1f. Bei Philo, wo nicht das Verb γρηγορέω, sondern das Substantiv ἐγρήγορσις belegt ist, begegnen unterschiedliche Ebenen: ebr 159; sobr 5 führen Wachsamsein und Nüchternheit des Geistes zur Erkenntnis (vgl. auch migr 222), her 257 bewirkt die Wachsamkeit des Geistes die Untätigkeit der (negativ gedeuteten) Sinne; Wachsamkeit und Schlaf können aber auch das Himmlische und das Irdische abbilden (Jos 147).
81. Es scheint also, dass bei Paulus die intellektuelle Ebene angesprochen wird. Das fügt sich gut in den Grundgedanken des mit dem eschatologischen Tag verbundenen Existenzverständnisses ein.
82. Vgl. O. BAUERNFEIND, Art. νήφω, in *TWNT* 4, pp. 936-938; vgl. die umfassenden Belege bei E. LÖVESTAM, *Über die neutestamentliche Aufforderung zur Nüchternheit*, in *ST* 12 (1958) 80-102; E. LÖVESTAM, *Spiritual wakefulness in the New Testament*, Lund, Gleerup, 1963, pp. 45-58.
83. Zur Dialektik von Trunkenheit und Rausch vgl. BAUERNFEIND, νήφω (n. 81), p. 938. Vgl. ebenda den Hinweis auf Plut II, 503.
84. Vgl. diesen Zusammenhang auch in 1 Petr 1,13 (νήφοντες τελείως ἐλπίσατε ... ἐν ἀποκαλύψει Ἰησοῦ Χριστοῦ); 5,8 (νήψατε, γρηγορήσατε).

heidnische Lebensweise ab, die sich in der Sicht des Paulus in Lastern wie des μεθύσκειν und μεθύειν zeigt.

Die Identitätsfindung in der Abgrenzung wird in V.8 unter zwei Aspekten zugespitzt: zunächst greift Paulus den Indikativ πάντες ... ἐστε καὶ υἱοὶ ἡμέρας (V.5a) mit ἡμεῖς δὲ ἡμέρας ὄντες wieder auf und verbindet den Heilsstand der Gemeinde dann kohortativ[85] mit der Trias Glaube – Liebe – Hoffnung, die in Rückgriff auf 1,3 an die Gründungsverkündigung erinnert. Mit der Panzer- und Helm-Metaphorik bringt Paulus seine Intention zur Geltung, die Adressaten in ihrem Heilsstatus zu sichern und in ihrer Heilshoffnung gegen andere auf sie eindringende Konzepte zu festigen.[86]

e) ... σὺν αὐτῷ ζήσωμεν *(1 Thess 5,9f)*

Die polarisierende Strukturierung der gesamten lehrhaften Unterweisung[87] steht nicht in sich, sondern hat ein theologisches Aussageziel, wenn Paulus das bisher schon in Metaphern wie „Nacht" und „Tag" oder „Schlafen" und „Wachen" zur Sprache gebrachte Gegenüber in die eschatologischen Begriffe ὀργή und σωτηρία überführt und damit die Thematik der „Ouvertüre" des Schreibens (1,2-10) wiederaufnimmt. Das einleitende ὅτι hat deshalb nicht nur begründende Funktion für die vorausgehende Trias in V.8, sondern bezieht die kohortativen Heilszusagen in V.4f und die Paränese in V.6-8 mit ein.[88] Die Gegensätze von Finsternis und Licht, von Nacht und Tag, Schlafen und Wachen haben in der Setzung Gottes, die nicht mit „Vorherbestimmung" zu verwechseln ist, ihren letzten Grund. Es ist möglich, dass Paulus mit der Wendung οὐκ ἔθετο ἡμᾶς ὁ θεὸς εἰς ὀργήν biblisch geprägte Sprachform aufnimmt,[89] er integriert sie aber sehr eigenständig in sein theologisches Konzept;

---

85. Das Partizip ἐνδυσάμενοι ist in Angleichung an den Konjunktiv νήφωμεν kohortativ zu verstehen; vgl. HAUFE, *1 Thess* (n. 15), pp. 95f; deshalb rekurriert Paulus hier auch nicht auf die Taufe selbst, sondern lenkt die Aufmerksamkeit auf die mit der Taufe gegebenen ethischen Implikationen.

86. Zwar unterscheidet sich die Verwendung der militärischen Metaphorik (Helm, Panzer) von der in Eph 6,11 dadurch, dass in 1 Thess 5,8 nicht von einer direkten „Kampfessituation" die Rede ist, aber Paulus sieht doch die Gefährdung der Gemeinde durch die paganen Einflüsse und will sie gegen diese immunisieren.

87. οὐκ ἐστέ ἐν σκότει (V.4) – ὑμεῖς υἱοὶ φωτός ἐστε καὶ υἱοὶ ἡμέρας (V.5); μὴ καθεύδωμεν – ἀλλὰ γρηγορῶμεν καὶ νήφωμεν (V.6).

88. Dafür spricht die antithetische Anordnung von V.9, die V.4-8 strukturell weiterführt. Vgl. auch HAUFE, *1 Thess* (n. 15), pp. 96f.

89. Vgl. HOLTZ, *1 Thess* (n. 8), p. 228 n. 461.

von einer vorgegebenen Tradition, die Paulus hier aufgenommen hätte,[90] kann jedenfalls keine Rede sein. Immerhin begegnet die Wendung τίθεσθαι τινα τι auch 1 Kor 12,28,[91] einer sicher paulinischen Schöpfung, die dem hier verwendeten ἔθετο τινα εἰς τι zumindest sehr nahe kommt. Unabhängig von einer Entscheidung über eine mögliche Rezeption von Tradition ist freilich entscheidend, dass mit der Aussage die freie Wahl Gottes eigens zum Ausdruck gebracht wird, so dass die Setzung[92] εἰς περιποίησιν dem Erwählungshandeln Gottes gleichkommt.

Die vorangestellte Negativformulierung οὐκ ἔθετο ἡμᾶς ὁ θεὸς εἰς ὀργήν entspricht in der Struktur der Satzfolge V.4-8,[93] wo jeweils einer Negation als erstem Satzglied die positive Heilsaussage folgt; auf ihr liegt fraglos der Hauptakzent. Das erste Satzglied bezieht sich auf das künftige Gericht, das über diejenigen, welche den Tag des Herrn in seiner Tragweite nicht erkennen, hereinbricht;[94] sie haben wie in V.4 die Funktion einer Negativfolie für die Heilswirklichkeit der Glaubenden. Im Blick ist also in erster Linie die Perspektive der σωτηρία für die Konvertiten, um sie in ihrem neuen Selbstverständnis aufzubauen.

Paulus spricht nicht von der Bestimmung zur Rettung, sondern von der Bestimmung zur *περιποίησις σωτηρίας*. Es geht nicht um eine Vorherbestimmung zur Rettung, sondern die Konversion der Adressaten im Lebensvollzug als Entscheidungsvorgang wird hier sehr ernst genommen. Der Begriff περιποίησις, der im Corpus Paulinum sonst nur noch Eph 1,14; 2 Thess 2,14[95] begegnet, ist mehrdeutig.[96] Er kann im Sinne von „Erwerb", „Besitz", auch „Bewahrung/Rettung" verstanden werden. Die letztgenannte Bedeutung „Bewahrung"[97] verliert angesichts des

---

90. So noch HARNISCH, *Existenz* (n. 54), pp. 122-125.
91. οὓς μὲν ἔθετο ὁ θεὸς ἐν τῇ ἐκκλησίᾳ πρῶτον ἀποστόλους.
92. Zum medialen ἔθετο vgl. BDR §316,1.
93. Vgl. Anm. 86.
94. Die positive Korrespondenzaussage findet sich in 1,10 (Errettung der Glaubenden vom kommenden Zorn). Das direkte Verwerfungsverdikt über die Nichtglaubenden drückt sich in 5,3 aus (vgl. auch 4,6).
95. Dort wohl in Rezeption von 1 Thess 5,9.
96. Vgl. HOLTZ, *1 Thess* (n. 8), p. 228 n. 464.
97. Für „Bewahrung" plädiert jüngst T. JANTSCH, *„Gott alles in allem" (1 Kor 15,28). Studien zum Gottesverständnis des Paulus im 1. Thessalonicherbrief und in der korinthischen Korrespondenz* (WMANT, 129), Neukirchen-Vluyn, Neukirchener, 2011, pp. 102-104. C. ESCHNER, *Gestorben und hingegeben „für" die Sünder. Die griechische Konzeption des Unheil abwendenden Sterbens und deren Aufnahme für die Deutung des Todes Jesu Christi. Band 1: Auslegung der paulinischen Formulierungen* (WMANT, 122), Neukirchen-Vluyn, Neukirchener, 2010, bringt eine Variante in die Diskussion und schlägt die Übersetzung „Überlebenverschaffen" vor: „Als Gott die vom Tod Christi Begünstigten, welche sich die bei diesem Tod bereitstehende Waffenrüstung tatsächlich angezogen haben, in der Taufe in

ethisch-paränetischen Kontextes von V.6-8 an Plausibilität, was auch für die Bedeutung „Besitz" gilt.[98] Da die σωτηρία aber noch aussteht und ein Hoffnungsgut ist, das die Wachsamkeit der Adressaten erfordert (V.8), kommt das Verständnis der „Erlangung" der Aussageintention am nächsten; gemeint ist dann die Bestimmung der Thessalonicher nicht zum Eigentum des im Vernichtungsgericht bestehenden Zorns, sondern der σωτηρία,[99] die sich aber erst noch – als Tat Gottes – erweisen wird durch den Kyrios Jesus Christus. Die Partizipialwendung τοῦ ἀποθανόντος ὑπὲρ ἡμῶν ist hier entscheidend. Nachdem Paulus vom Tod Jesu in 2,14f – situativ bedingt – in der Deutung des Prophetengeschicks gesprochen, ihm in 4,14 aber keine weitere Sinndeutung verliehen, sondern ihn unmittelbar mit der Auferstehung verbunden hatte, führt er hier nun die Sinndeutung des „Sterbens für" ein, um dem Tod Jesu die ihm zukommende Bedeutung für den eschatologischen Heilsempfang für die Glaubenden zu verleihen: Der Weg zur Rettung ist der Tod Jesu „für" die Glaubenden.[100] Die ausdrückliche soteriologische Bedeutung des Todes Jesu fehlte noch in 1,9f; sie kommt auch in 4,14 nur implizit darin zur Geltung, dass Paulus dort von der Zusammenführung der Verstorbenen mit Jesus „durch Jesus" spricht, und zwar durch sein Sterben und seine Auferstehung. Aber von der expliziten soteriologischen Deutung des Todes Jesu, die zu den bereits in vorpaulinischer Tradition vorgenommenen Reflexionen gehört, war bislang noch nicht die Rede. Was Paulus für die Verstorbenen impliziert hatte, wird nun für die Lebenden explizit ausgeführt: die Rettung am eschatologischen Tag mit der Folge des Lebens „mit Christus". Wenn die Priorität in der paulinischen Predigt beim Erstaufenthalt in Thessalonich auf der Erwählung und der eschatologischen Erwartungshaltung mit der Konsequenz einer dementsprechenden Lebensführung gelegen hat (vgl. 2,12), ist es gut möglich, dass die

---

ihrer Waffenrüstung auf den Wachposten aufgestellt hat (diese Interpretation wird vorher erläutert – R.H.), da war sein Blick dabei nicht auf den Zorn und die mit ihm verbundene Vernichtung gerichtet, sondern umgekehrt darauf, den mit ‚wir' Bezeichneten auf diese Weise ein Überleben bis zur bzw. für die Rettung durch ihren Herrn Jesus Christus zu verschaffen" (p. 183). Diese Erklärung läuft dann doch auf „Bewahrung" hinaus.

98. LXX 2 Chr 14,12; Hag 2,10 bedeutet περιποίησις „Bewahrung/Rettung", Mal 3,17 „Besitz".

99. σωτηρίας ist Genitivus subjectivus, der zum Ausdruck bringen will, dass die jungen Christen „Eigentum" des künftigen Heils sind.

100. τοῦ ἀποθανόντος ὑπὲρ ἡμῶν geht kaum auf eine fest geprägte vorpaulinische Formel zurück, wohl im Grundgedanken auf Bekenntnistradition. Vergleichbar ist Röm 5,8: Gott hat seine Liebe dadurch erwiesen, dass Christus für uns (ὑπὲρ ἡμῶν) starb. Vgl. MALHERBE, *Thess* (n. 1), p. 299.

Frage nach der heilstiftenden Bedeutung des Todes Jesu beim Gründungsaufenthalt des Paulus noch nicht hinreichend reflektiert worden war, sondern erst durch den Tod der verstorbenen Christen aufgeworfen wurde (4,13f). Daran lässt zumindest die Tatsache denken, dass Paulus mit εἴτε γρηγορῶμεν εἴτε καθεύδωμεν die Verbindung zur Frage nach dem Schicksal der Verstorbenen herstellt.[101] Von größerem Gewicht aber ist, dass das als Heilstod gedeutete Sterben Jesu der Schlüssel für das kommende Heil der Glaubenden ist und Basisfunktion auch für die vorher ergehende Paränese hat.[102] Der Tod Jesu ist es, der letztlich das Lebensmodell nach der Hinwendung zu Gott ermöglicht und die Perspektive des künftigen Lebens mit Christus erschließt. Nicht weniger bedeutsam ist, dass Paulus hier sein Theologumenon von der Erwählung durch Gott mit dem Heilstod Jesu verbindet.

f) *Eine abschließende Mahnung (1 Thess 5,11)*

Zum Abschluss greift Paulus seine Ermahnung zum gegenseitigen Zuspruch aus 4,18 noch einmal auf, intensiviert ihn aber noch durch die Aufforderung zur gegenseitigen individuellen Zuwendung in der Gemeinde, wie er sie selbst nach seinem Selbstzeugnis in 2,11 an den Tag gelegt hatte. Das entspricht ganz seinem bereits in 2,8 geäußerten Ansinnen, die Gemeinde selbst ihre Herausforderungen annehmen zu lassen. Da der Abschnitt deutlich kohortativen Charakter trägt, erhält der Imperativ παρακαλεῖτε auch eher die Bedeutung der Ermutigung als des Trostes. In diese Richtung weist ja auch das parallele οἰκοδομεῖτε.[103]

---

101. Die Wendung ist kaum auf die ethische Ebene von V.6 bezogen, denn damit würde Paulus die Mahnung von V.6f entschärfen. Die zweifellos bestehende Umprägung von „Wachen" und „Schlafen" wird einsichtig, wenn man sie mit den Lebenden und Verstorbenen von 4,13-18 verbindet. Vgl. auch HAUFE, *1 Thess* (n. 15), p. 97; MALHERBE, *Thess* (n. 1), p. 300. M. LAUTENSCHLAGER, *Εἴτε γρηγορῶμεν εἴτε καθεύδωμεν. Zum Verhältnis von Heiligung und Heil in 1 Thess 5,10*, in ZNW 81(1990) 39-59, versteht „Wachen" und „Schlafen" in V.10 dagegen ethisch analog zu V.6. Paulus wolle sagen, dass selbst die ethische Verfehlung die Heilsteilhabe nicht mehr in Frage stelle: „Die Wirklichkeit des neuen Seins im ‚Licht' wird selbst durch ein die Möglichkeiten dieses Seins verfehlendes Tun nicht aufgehoben" (p. 56). Eine solche Botschaft widerspricht allerdings diametral V.4b.

102. Vgl. M. WOLTER, *Der Heilstod Jesu als theologisches Argument*, in J. FREY/J. SCHRÖTER (ed.), *Deutungen des Todes Jesu im Neuen Testament* (WUNT, 181), Tübingen, Mohr, 2005, 297-313, p. 311: „daß vom Heilstod Jesu aus auf das noch ausstehende eschatische Geschehen geblickt wird".

103. Vgl. auch HOLTZ, *1 Thess* (n. 8), pp. 233f.

Schlussüberlegung

Die Ergebnisse des Durchgangs durch 1 Thess 5,1-11 im Kontext der Eschatologie des 1 Thess lassen sich zusammenfassen:

Die Eschatologie ist der Schlüssel zum Verständnis des 1 Thess. Es bestätigt sich, dass das Schreiben einen „eschatologischen Bauplan" hat. Erwählungs-Theologie, Christologie und Paränese finden ihre innere Einheit in der Überzeugung, dass Gott durch seinen vom Himmel kommenden Sohn aus dem für die übrige Welt unausweichlichen Verderben rettet und die von ihm Erwählten zu einer von denen, die Gott nicht kennen (vgl. 1 Thess 4,5), unterscheidenden Lebensauffassung qualifiziert.

Gott ist der „lebendige und wahrhaftige Gott", der sich in seinem Erwählungshandeln heilstiftend für die Ekklesia erwiesen hat und auch künftig erweisen wird. Dieser Erweis Gottes hat sich in seinem Auferweckungshandeln an seinem „für uns" gestorbenen Sohn bereits dargestellt und gewinnt seine endgültige Realisierung in dessen künftigem Kommen. Die Zukunft kann bereits jetzt antizipiert werden und führt zu einem Lebensverständnis, das sich auf den Zuspruch des Heils gründet und sich in der Zugehörigkeit zum „Licht" äußert.

Die Gerichtsaussagen des 1 Thess sind für die Adressaten kein eigenes Thema, sondern haben als Abgrenzungsaussagen gegen die Nichtglaubenden die Funktion, zum Festhalten an der einmal getroffenen Konversionsentscheidung angesichts der Perspektive eines Lebens „mit Christus" zu motivieren.

Für die Rezeption des 2 Thess liegt der Anknüpfungspunkt in der Gerichtsthematik, die beim Nachpauliner sehr viel eingehender zum Stabilisierungsinstrument für die Adressaten und zum beherrschenden Thema wird.

1 KOR 15,20-28:
WELTGESCHICHTE UND PERSÖNLICHE HOFFNUNG
IM LICHTE DES PAULINISCHEN EVANGELIUMS

PETR POKORNÝ

1. ZIELSETZUNG

Die Eschatologie des Paulus ist ein Thema, das eng mit dem Kern seiner Theologie zusammenhängt. Die Eschatologie hängt unmittelbar mit dem Evangelium zusammen – mit der Botschaft und dem Zeugnis von Jesus, der durch die Auferstehung von den Toten als Sohn Gottes eingesetzt ist (Röm 1,4). Wenn die nachösterlichen Nachfolger Jesu den Begriff „Auferstehung" (im Griechischen meistens mit Hilfe der Verben ἐγείρω oder ἀνίστημι ausgedrückt)[1] benutzt haben, verstanden sie die Auferstehung als den Anfang der allgemeinen oder mindestens kollektiven Auferstehung, die die jüdischen apokalyptischen Texte am Ende „dieses Äons" erwartet haben. Die Osterbotschaft war also nicht nur eine Rehabilitierung Jesu seitens Gott, sondern auch eine Hoffnungsgarantie für andere Menschen. Den Fachausdruck Apokalyptik begreife ich in dem im 20. Jahrhundert üblichen Sinne, als prophetische Darstellung und Periodisierung des Endes unseres Zeitalters (der Geschichte), die theologisch motiviert und paränetisch eingestellt ist,[2] wie wir ihr im Spätjudentum begegnen, wenn auch aus religionsgeschichtlicher Sicht das Motiv der Offenbarung der Geheimnisse die Apokalyptik vielleicht besser charakterisiert.[3]

Bei der Exegese des Abschnitts aus 1 Kor 15 dürfen und müssen wir die entsprechenden Stellen aus dem 1. Thessalonicherbrief (1,10; 4,13-18) berücksichtigen, die Paulus am Anfang der fünfziger Jahre des ersten christlichen Jahrhunderts schrieb. 2 Kor 5,1-10 – ein anderer Abschnitt

---

1. Beides war offensichtlich eine Übersetzung der von dem hebräischen Stamm ק-ו-ם abgeleiteten Ausdrücke.
2. E. KÄSEMANN, *Zum Thema der urchristlichen Apokalyptik* (1962), zuletzt in DERS., *Exegetische Versuche und Besinnungen II*, Göttingen, Vandenhoeck & Ruprecht, ²1965, 108-131, hier pp. 112-118 bes. Anm. 1.
3. M. WOLTER, *Apokalyptik als Redeform im Neuen Testament*, in NTS 51 (2005) 171-191.

aus der Korrespondenz des Apostels mit den korinthischen Christen – ist offensichtlich bald nach 1 Kor 15,20-28 entstanden und soll bei der Deutung dieses Abschnitts berücksichtigt werden. Angesichts des überwiegenden Zweifels an der Authentizität des 2. Thessalonicherbriefes, können wir nicht voraussetzen, dass Paulus die dort auftauchenden apokalyptischen Vorstellungen zur Zeit der Abfassung des 1. Korintherbriefes gekannt hat.

Bei der Exegese müssen wir andere ähnliche Texte aus der hellenistischen und frühkaiserzeitlichen Zeit berücksichtigen, um besser zu verstehen, wie der paulinische Text gewirkt hat und wie er heute aktuell sein könnte.

2. PAULINISCHE KONTEXTE

1. *1 Thess 4,13-18*

In 1 Thess 4,13 warnt Paulus die Thessalonicher Christen, damit sie unter Umständen nicht in eine fatale Verzweiflung geraten, wie diejenigen „die keine Hoffnung haben". Es musste sich um die „Ultraapokalyptiker"[4] handeln, die das nahe Kommen des auferstandenen Jesus als Weltherrn erwarteten. Die Gläubigen sollten dann ihrer Vorstellung nach in seine Nähe entrückt und verwandelt werden. Die Auferstehung der Menschen hat hier keinen Platz gehabt und das Sterben vor der Parusie – Paulus hat damals damit gerechnet, dass er die Parusie selbst „im Leibe" erlebt (4,17) – ist dadurch zum Problem geworden. Paulus hat in diesen Zeilen eine theologische Lösung dieses Problems mit weitreichenden kirchen- und kulturgeschichtlichen Konsequenzen gefunden. Diese muss rekonstruiert werden:

Die ersten nachösterlichen Anhänger Jesu begriffen ihre Erfahrung von der neuen Präsenz ihres Lehrers als Konsequenz seiner Neubelebung im Sinne der apokalyptischen Berufung aller Menschen zum Jüngsten Gericht. Danach sollte die Erde in der Endzeit die sterblichen Menschen („aus Erde vom Acker" – Gen 2,7), „welche in ihr gesammelt sind, zurückgeben" (*1 Hen* 51,1).[5] Die Auferstehung war demnach eine neue Schöpfertat Gottes, denn der Mensch wurde als ein zeitiges Wesen

---

4. So werden sie heute bezeichnet.
5. Vgl. „Die Erde gibt wieder, die darinnen ruhen, der Staub ‚lässt los', die darinnen schlafen, die Kammern erstatten die Seelen zurück, die ihnen anvertraut sind." (*4 Ezra* 7,32 [Übers. H. Gunkel] vgl. Gen 2,7: „Da machte Gott ...den Menschen aus Erde...und blies ihm den Odem des Lebens in seine Nase.").

geschaffen. Die nach Ostern gezogene Folgerung war der Anfang christlicher Theologie als Reflexion des Glaubens: Das apokalyptische Bild des Endgeschehens haben die nachösterlichen Anhänger Jesu ihrer Glaubenserfahrung (der „Wirklichkeit") angepasst. Sie haben Jesus für den ersten auferstandenen Toten erklärt. Diese von mehreren Forschern übernommene These von E. Käsemann[6] hat man oft kritisiert, weil sie von den apokalyptischen Bildern abgeleitet ist. In Wirklichkeit ist sie mit einer tiefen Umdeutung der apokalyptischen Erwartungen verbunden. Der auferstandene „Christus" ist nicht nur der Anfang, sondern auch die Garantie der Hoffnung anderer Menschen.[7] In 1 Thess 1,10 charakterisiert Paulus den auferstandenen Jesus als den Retter beim Jüngsten Gericht (dem „zukünftigen Zorn"). Es handelt sich offensichtlich um eine Zusammenfassung des Evangeliums (εὐαγγέλιον), das in 1,5 erwähnt wird. Jesus spielt da eine ähnliche Rolle wie in der (äthiopischen) Henochapokalypse der „Auserwählte" des Herrn (*1 Hen* 51,3).

In 1 Thess 4 wird das Problem der vor der Parusie verstorbenen Christen durch die Schlussfolgerung gelöst, wonach Jesus als der lebendige Christus, wie er durch den Glauben erkannt und anerkannt wird, als der Auferstandene nicht nur am Ende der Geschichte steht, sondern mit den Menschen auch über ihren Tod hinaus unsichtbar (im Geist) verbunden ist. Er ist nicht nur der Grund der Hoffnung, sondern als der gekreuzigte und auferstandene Herr auch ein Modell der endzeitlichen Verwandlung sterblicher Menschen (vgl. 1 Kor 6,14). Seine Wiederkunft (Offenbarung am Ende dieses Äons) wird gleichzeitig eine Auferstehung der Toten bedeuten, zu denen auch die gestorbenen Christen aus Thessalonich gehören. Die Auferstehung ist dadurch zum Ziel der Geschichte und zum Horizont des einzelnen menschlichen Leben geworden. Dies ist übrigens eine der Vorstufen der bekannten Aussage des Paulus von der Rechtfertigung des Sünders vor dem Jüngsten Gericht, die aus Gnade Gottes erfolgt (Gal 2,16; Röm 3,21-26).

2. *1 Kor 15,1-11*

Der unmittelbare Kontext von 1 Kor 15,20-28 im Rahmen des 1. Korintherbriefes ist die Polemik gegen die Leugner der Auferstehung

---

6. E. KÄSEMANN, *Zum Thema der urchristlichen Apokalyptik* (Anm. 2), pp. 108ff.
7. J. A. FITZMYER, *First Corinthians* (AB), New Haven – London, Yale University Press, 2008, p. 91.

(ἀνάστασις νεκρῶν οὐκ ἔστιν – V. 12). Die Ausgangsposition von Paulus ist, dass die Auferstehung der Kern des Evangeliums ist, das er selbst aus der Tradition übernommen und weitergegeben hat (παρέλαβον – παρέδωκα – παρελάβετε –1 Kor 15,1.3) und das offensichtlich auch die Leugner der Auferstehung anerkannt haben: „...durch das ihr auch selig werdet wenn ihr's festhaltet in der Gestalt, in der ich es euch verkündigt habe" (15,2a) und „Ist aber Christus nicht auferstanden, so ist unsere Predigt (κήρυγμα) vergeblich, so ist auch euer Glaube vergeblich" (V.14). Paulus geht von dem Evangelium in der Gestalt der sog. Pistis-Formel aus (1 Kor 15,3b-5), die zweigliedrig ist, d.h. von dem Tod und der Auferstehung Christi spricht, und für die Erscheinung (Offenbarung, „ist gesehen worden" – Gr. ὤφθη) des Auferstandenen auch die Zeugen anführt: Kephas (Petrus) und die Zwölf. Paulus hat die Liste der Zeugen der Auferstehung erweitert, nicht nur um die Auferstehung Jesu verlässlich zu bezeugen. Die erweiterte Liste der Zeugen stellt eine ökumenische Gruppierung dar, die den Kern der späteren Kirche darstellt. Am Ende der Liste nennt Paulus auch sich selbst: Er ist der letzte, die „Fehlgeburt" (1 Kor 15,8) und mit ihm endet die Reihe derjenigen, die Jesus als den Herrn unmittelbar bezeugen können. Es bedeutet praktisch, dass der apostolischen Autorität keine andere neue Eingebung entgegengesetzt werden kann. Die endgültige Offenbarung Gottes konzentriert sich in der Zeit Jesu und der ersten Zeugen.

3. *1 Kor 15,12-19*

Nach 1 Thess 4,13-18 ist 1 Kor 15 die nächste Stufe des paulinischen Theologisierens[8] über die letzten Dinge. Sie ist durch die Leugnung der Auferstehung hervorgerufen, die „einige" Korinther Christen (ἐν ὑμῖν τινες) geäußert haben. Nicht die Auferstehung der schon gestorbenen Christen wird hier in Frage gestellt, wie es der Fall in 1 Thess 4 war, sondern die Auferstehung der Menschen überhaupt.

Wie es die kritisierte Gruppe der Korinther gemeint hat, können wir nur mit Hilfe indirekter Hinweise aus anderen Teilen der Korinther Korrespondenz deduzieren. In 1 Kor 4 werden die Christen in Korinth vor einer vorzeitigen Proklamation des Gerichts über andere Menschen gewarnt. Erst Christus bei seiner Parusie, der auch das verborgene Trachten der Herzen kennt, wird dazu berechtigt sein (4,5). Die Gegner von

---

8. Es handelt sich um Theologie in unserem Sinne. Damals hat man das Denken des Glaubens (noch) nicht Theologie genannt.

Paulus unter den Adressaten werden als diejenigen ironisch dargestellt, die schon satt und reich sind und im Reich Gottes regieren, während der Apostel immer noch hungert und leidet und doch seine Gegner segnet (4,8-13). Es handelt sich um keinen paränetischen Abstecher, denn Paulus kritisiert eine solche Einstellung als Geringschätzung der Gnade Gottes. Es muss seine große Sorge gewesen sein. Das Mirror-Reading solcher Aussagen führt zu dem Schluss, dass es in Korinth eine einflussreiche Gruppe der Christen (offensichtlich ursprünglich Paulusschüler) gab, die auf sich schon die Verheißungen der Seligpreisungen aus der Logienquelle (Feldrede/Bergpredigt) bezogen hat (Luk 6,21-22; Matth 5,3-6). Sie haben die Auferstehung schon geistig erlebt (die Glossolalie, von der in Kap. 14 die Rede ist, passt zu dieser Art der Frömmigkeit) und sich für die Armen gehalten, die schon ins Reich Gottes versetzt worden sind, die reich sind und mit Christus regieren. Ihre Auferstehung ist schon in der enthusiastischen Erfahrung[9] passiert. Sie sind schon in das neue Leben übergegangen.[10]

Das, was Paulus als die extreme Konsequenz ihrer Einstellung anführt, nämlich „lasst uns essen und trinken; denn morgen sind wir tot" (15,32b), ist ein wörtliches Zitat aus Jes 22,13 (LXX). Es betraf die Einstellung des gottlosen Jerusalems, das vor dem Gericht Gottes nicht bestehen kann. In der neutestamentlichen Zeit entsprach es dem damaligen oberflächlichen Bild des Epikuräismus und hat Analogien in der

---

9. Zu dieser Charakteristik der korinthischen Leugner der Auferstehung s. W. SCHRAGE, *Der erste Brief an die Korinther (1 Kor 15,1-16,24)* (EKK, VII/4), Zürich/Düsseldorf, Benzinger, Neukirchen-Vluyn, Neukirchener, 2001, pp. 113-119; E. Brandenburger, *Adam und Christus* (WMANT, 7), Neukirchen, Neukirchener, 1962, pp. 70ff.; P. HOFFMANN, *Die Toten in Christus* (NTA NF, 2), Münster, Aschendorff, ²1969, pp. 246-247; David W. KUCK, *Judgment and Community Conflict: Paul's Use of Apocalyptic Judgment Language in 1 Corinthians 3:5-4:5* (NT.S, 66), Leiden, Brill 1992, pp. 25-37; T. W. GILLESPIE, *The First Theologians. A Study of Early Christian Prophecy*, Grand Rapids MI, Eerdmans 1994, pp. 205ff. (er benutzt das gnostische Modell). Ähnlich hat schon in 1930 den Charakter der korinthischen Häresie Hans von SODEN charakterisiert: *Sakrament und Ethik bei Paulus: Zur Frage der literarischen und theologischen Einheitlichkeit von 1 Kor. 8-10*, in H. FRICK (Hg.), *Marburger theologische Studien* (FS R. Otto), Gotha, L. Klotz, 1931.

10. Nach G. SELLIN, *Der Streit um die Auferstehung der Toten* (FRLANT, 138), Göttingen, Vandenhoeck & Ruprecht 1986, pp. 13, 37, handelt es sich hier um die Äußerung einer dualistischen Anthropologie und spiritualisierten Eschatologie. Das schließt jedoch nicht aus, dass es als Leugnung der Auferstehung bezeichnet werden kann. Die konkrete Folge der Auferstehung ist für Paulus die Begegnung mit Christus, den die ersten apostolische Zeugen mit Augen gesehen haben (1 Kor 15,5). Die durch Auferstehung entstandene Leiblichkeit, wenn auch neuer Art, ist Träger der Beziehungen, die durch ein geistiges Erlebnis nicht ersetzt werden kann.

Geschichte der griechischen Kultur und Religion[11] (z. B. Aischylos, *Agamemnon* 572ff. – die Toten stehen nicht auf und haben keine Kopfschmerzen), die auf den Grabmalen manchmal satirisch klingen: „Sei guten Mutes, keiner ist unsterblich!" (CIG 5200b), und zwar auch unter den Menschen, die sich sonst als fromm erklären.[12] Der Eindruck, dass wir es an dieser Stelle mit einer skeptischen Leugnung der Auferstehung zu tun haben, ist jedoch nicht richtig. Der Apostel sagt den Leugnern der Auferstehung: „Gibt es keine Auferstehung der Toten, so ist auch Christus nicht auferstanden" (15,13). Die kritisierten Adressaten („einige unter euch" – 15,12) haben also mit der Auferstehung Jesu gerechnet (vgl. 15,29ff.) und verbanden mit ihr offensichtlich ihre Hoffnung. Wenn es nicht die Hoffnung der Auferstehung im Tode war,[13] muss es eine Hoffnung gewesen sein, die schon während des Lebens verwirklicht werden kann. Sonst hätten sie keinen Grund, Christen zu werden. Es musste die Hoffnung einer geistigen Auferstehung gewesen sein, die mit der Gabe des Geistes verbunden war. Dass es sich nicht um denselben Fall handelt, den Paulus in 1 Thess 4 lösen musste, verrät schon der Unterschied in der Argumentation. Das, was er in 1 Thess 4 sagte, wird in 1 Kor 15,51-52 nur kurz erwähnt und der Nachdruck verschiebt sich auf die Behauptung, dass die Überwindung der Mächte, die mit der Sünde zusammenhängen, hier, auf der Erde und in diesem Leben beginnt. Nach 2 Kor 5,1-10, wo von dem Endgericht (wie in 1 Kor 3,9-12) die Rede ist, gefällt das zu Lebzeiten geleistete Gute dem Herrn. Das epikuräisch klingende Zitat kritisiert also vor allem die mangelnde soziale Verantwortung der Menschen, die die Hoffnung des Glaubens so verstanden. Es ist keine Ermahnung zur Werkgerechtigkeit, denn die Garantie der Hoffnung ist jedenfalls durch Christus als dem auferstandenen Herrn gegeben (2 Kor 5,19ff.).[14] Paulus war überzeugt, dass auch die

---

11. A. A. T. EHRHARDT, *Unsterblichkeitsglaube und Politik im Römerreich*, TZ 2 (1946) 418-437; P. POKORNÝ, *Die Zukunft des Glaubens* (AzTh, 72), Stuttgart, Calwer, 1992, pp. 33f.

12. Z.B. die von R. Herzog herausgegebene Grabinschrift, die bei A. DEISSMANN, *Licht vom Osten*, Tübingen, Mohr-Siebeck, ⁴1923, pp. 250-251, reproduziert ist. Ein Verehrer der Nymphen ermahnt dort den Passanten zum frohen Trinken.

13. Im Lichte dieser Schlussfolgerung bietet die Hypothese, wonach die Leugner der Auferstehung ihre Hoffnung in der Unsterblichkeit der Seele sahen, nur eine ungenaue Antwort. Eine solche Hypothese vertrat P. BACHMANN, *Der erste Brief des Paulus an die Korinther* (KNT, 7), Leipzig, ⁴1936, ad loc.; so auch J. H. ULRICHSEN, *Die Auferstehungsleugner in Korinth*, in T. FORNBERG – D. HELLHOLM (Hg.), Texts and Contexts (FS L. Hartman), Oslo etc., Scandinavian University Press, 1995, 781-799, hier p. 797, und andere.

14. F. LANG, *Die Briefe an die Korinther* (NTD, 7), Göttingen, Vandenhoeck & Ruprecht, 1986, p. 290.

Gewissheit des Mit-Christus-Seins nach dem Tode (2 Kor 5,8)[15] nicht zur Todessucht führen kann und wenn er auch in Phil 1,23 die Flucht in den Tod ernst erwägt, hat er sich doch entschieden, sich um die Genesung und um Entlassung aus dem Gefängnis zu bemühen, was ihm noch weitere Gelegenheit zur Arbeit bieten konnte, und zwar gerade aus der Solidarität mit den Adressaten.[16]

Eine Analogie zu der Einstellung der Korinther Gegner des Paulus ist im Johannesevangelium bezeugt und der Kontext verrät deutlich, dass es sich um eine geistige Vorwegnahme der apokalyptischen Auferstehung gehandelt hat: „Amen, Amen, ich sage euch: Es kommt die Stunde und ist schon jetzt, dass die Toten hören werden die Stimme des Sohnes Gottes, und die sie hören werden leben" (Joh 5,25). Es kann sein, dass die Korinther die Auferstehung bei der Taufe als Begabung des Geistes erlebt haben[17] und dass Paulus selbst durch einige seiner Aussagen dazu Anlass gegeben hat. Er hat allerdings mit einem Zwischenzustand zwischen dem Tod einzelner Christen und der Ankunft des neuen Äons gerechnet, wie er es in 1 Thess 4 ausgedrückt hat. Durch ihren Glauben bilden nach 1 Kor 12,13.27 die Christen mit Christus einen vom Heiligen Geist beherrschten Leib. Eine gegen eine doketische Deutung nicht geschützte These lesen wir in 2 Kor 3,17f.: „Der Herr ist der Geist" und „...wir werden verklärt in sein Bild". Der Sinn solcher Aussagen ist, dass der neue Mensch im Inneren des gläubigen Menschen wächst, sonst wäre der Glaube des Gläubigen nicht der wirkliche Glaube: 2 Kor 4,16; Gal 2,20; 4,19. Das ist allerdings nur der Keim der neuen Kreatur,[18] kein voller Übergang der apostolischen Autorität in das ewige Leben während des irdischen Lebens. Allerdings, ohne nähere Deutung können solche Parolen leicht missverstanden werden. In Röm 6 hat Paulus geschrieben, dass der Christ durch die Taufe mit Christus in seinem Tode verbunden und von der Versklavung durch die Sünde befreit ist (6,3-7). Dies

---

15. Das „wir" in 1 Kor 15,52 (vgl.V. 51) kann dieselbe Erwartung wie 1 Thess 4,17 bezeugen, aber inzwischen hat sich Paulus mit dem Tode einiger Christen vor der Parusie grundsätzlich auseinandergesetzt. Die Abschätzung seiner persönlichen Hoffnung muss er allerdings erst zwischen 1 Kor 15 und 2 Kor 5 / Phil 1 geändert haben; siehe W.WIEFEL, *Die Hauptrichtung des Wandels im eschatologischen Denken das Paulus*, in TZ 30 (1974) 65-81.

16. Zu diesem Problem s. U. LUZ, *Das Geschichtsverständnis des Paulus* (BET, 49), München, Kaiser Verlag, 1968, pp. 355-358; N. WALTER, *Der Brief an die Philipper* (NTD, 8/2), Göttingen, Vandenhoeck & Ruprecht, 1998, pp. 43f.

17. Nach Irenäus *Adv. haer.* 1,23,5 war für den Gnostiker Kerinth die Taufe das Tor zur Unsterblichkeit.

18. H. LIETZMANN, *An die Korinther I/II* (HNT, 9), Tübingen. Mohr Siebeck, ⁴1949, p. 117. Siehe auch hier den das von M. HOOKER geschriebene Kapitel.

bedeutet nicht, dass er automatisch heilig ist (6,3.15; 7,7), sondern dass er mit der Sünde nicht schicksalhaft verbunden ist und kann ihr Widerstand leisten. Die wiederholten Warnungen vor Missbrauch verraten, dass einige theologische Aussagen von Paulus oft falsch verstanden wurden.[19]

Das Problem, das entstanden ist, kann also als ein inneres Problem paulinischer Theologie betrachtet werden. Von einem direkten gnostischen Einfluss können wir die Einstellung der Gegner in Korinth nicht ableiten.[20] Die gnostische Terminologie und die gnostischen mythischen Systeme sind in der korinthischen Korrespondenz des Paulus nicht spürbar und historisch wäre es ein Anachronismus. Das, was wir heute unter dem Stichwort Gnosis verstehen, ist erst am Anfang des 2. Jhdts nachweisbar. Die gnostischen Texte sind jedoch wegen des mit dem korinthischen Enthusiasmus gemeinsamen Spiritualismus, Akosmismus und Heilsperfektionismus als phänomenologische Analogie hilfreich. Im 1. Logion des Thomasevangeliums lesen wir, dass derjenige, „der die (wahre) Deutung (ἑρμηνεία) der Worte des Herrn findet, wird den Tod nicht schmecken". Das ekstatische Staunen (kopt. *štorter*) über die Teilnahme am Göttlichen in der geistigen Theophanie (Log. 2) gleicht dem ewigen Leben.[21] Justin Martyr berichtete um das Jahr 160 n. Chr. über einige Christen (Gnostiker), die am Anfang des 2. Jh. behaupteten, dass sie schon mit Gott verbunden seien (*Dial.* 80).

In solchen Texten wird der Begriff Auferstehung nur ausnahmsweise für die Hoffnung der Menschen benutzt. Nur z. B. im Polykarpbrief aus der ersten Hälfte des 2. Jh. wird gegen diejenigen gewarnt, „die die Auferstehung und Gericht bestreiten" (*Polyc.* 7,1). In Grunde handelt es sich jedoch um einen Dualismus, der den Leib unterschätzt. Es ist keine einfache Leugnung christlicher Hoffnung, sondern ihre andere Erfüllung als in der leiblichen Auferstehung. Erst als die Auferstehung der Toten zum festen Ausdruck der christlichen Hoffnung in der Hauptströmung der Kirche geworden ist, haben diejenigen, die die paulinische Lösung nicht aufgenommen haben, selbst von der schon geschehenen

---

19. Dass paulinische Theologie gegen solche Interpretationen nicht ganz immun war, zeigt E. H. PAGELS, *The Gnostic Paul*, Philadelphia, Fortress Press, 1975, pp. 53-94; sie konzentriert sich allerdings vor allem auf die gnostische Deutung von 1 Kor 15, nicht so sehr auf die inneren Voraussetzungen solcher Deutung in der Theologie des Paulus.

20. Mit Gnostikern hat W. SCHMITHALS die Leugner der Auferstehung identifiziert: *Die Gnosis in Korinth* (FRLANT, 66), Göttingen, Vandenhoeck & Ruprecht, ³1969, pp. 137-146, 191f.

21. P. POKORNÝ, *Die Eschatologie des Thomasevangeliums*, in ZAC 13 (2009) 48-53.

Auferstehung gesprochen. In dem gnostischen Philippusevangelium (NHC II.3 56,15b-20) aus dem 2. Jh. werden diejenigen kritisiert, die behaupten, dass der Herr zunächst gestorben ist und erst dann wurde er erweckt, wobei die wahre Reihenfolge ist: auferweckt – gestorben. Der Tod schadet nicht dem geistig auferstandenen Menschen.[22]

Im Kol 2,12 lesen wir eine im Namen von Paulus formulierte Beteuerung: „Mit ihm (Jesus Christus) seid ihr begraben worden durch die Taufe; mit ihm seid ihr auch auferstanden durch den Glauben." Im Epheserbrief, der an den Kolosserbrief anknüpft, ist das noch profilierter gesagt, offensichtlich in Verteidigung vor einem verbreiteten religiösen Enthusiasmus seiner Zeit, der mit Visionen und jenseitigen Spekulationen verbunden war (Proto-Gnosis) und in einigen Bereichen der Kirche Fuß gefasst hat: „…und er (Gott) hat uns mit auferweckt und mit eingesetzt im Himmel in Christus Jesus" (Eph 2,6). Dass dies keine unproblematische Behauptung war, bestätigt das Wort aus dem 2 Tim 2,18, wo mit Hilfe paulinischer Terminologie vor Hymenäus und Philetus gewarnt wird, „die von der Wahrheit abgeirrt sind und sagen, die Auferstehung sei schon geschehen." In der paulinischen Schule ist die Gestalt der Hoffnung schon im Rahmen des Neuen Testaments zu einer Streitfrage geworden.

[Albert Schweitzer hat die Leugnung der Auferstehung als eine konsequent apokalyptische Einstellung verstanden.[23] Die Ultraapokalyptiker haben die Parusie Jesu Christi und das Kommen des Reiches Gottes erwartet, die Auferstehung hat in ihrer Erwartung keinen Platz gehabt. Seine Meinung hat mit unterschiedlichem Schwerpunkt (die Korinther konnten sich nicht die Wiederbelebung der Toten vorstellen) 1971 B. Spörlein übernommen.[24] Aber Paulus setzt in seiner Argumentation voraus, dass die Leugner gemeinsam mit ihm mit einem geistigen Leib des Menschen rechnen (1 Kor 15,45); der Unterschied („aber" im V. 46) besteht darin, dass die Leugner über die Reihenfolge der Leiber nicht im Klaren sind, dass nämlich der geistige Leib erst nach dem „natürlichen" (ψυχικόν, ψυχὴ ζῶσα – VV. 44-46) kommt. Das bedeutet, das der Tod die Grenze bildet und die Auferstehung im sterblichen Leben eine feste Hoffnung, nicht aber die Realität (vgl. Röm 6,2-8) ist. Eine solche Argumentation, wie in 1 Kor 15 hätte gegen die Ultraapokalyptiker keinen Sinn.]

---

22. Vgl. mit der Deutung der korinthischen Häresie, s. oben Anm. 14.
23. *Die Mystik des Apostels Paulus*, Tübingen, Mohr Siebeck, 1930, pp. 93f.
24. *Die Leugnung der Auferstehung*, München, Pustet, 1971, pp. 195f.

3. 1 KOR 15,20-28

In 1 Kor 15 und besonders in 1 Kor 15,20-28 geht es Paulus um die Bewahrung der spezifischen Spannung zwischen den zwei Polen der nachösterlichen eschatologischen Hoffnung: Die Geschichte Jesu samt der Kreuzigung und Auferstehung, die die Erfüllung garantiert, ist mit der Auferstehung der Menschen zum Jüngsten Gericht als dem anderen Pol durch den Glauben verbunden. Wenn die Auferstehung mit der geistigen Erleuchtung und dem Gläubig-Werden identisch ist, verliert der Glaube sowohl seine Rückkopplung in Jesus von Nazareth, der beim Jüngsten Gericht die entscheidende Rolle spielt, als auch seine soziale und geschichtliche Perspektive. Das ist nicht nur eine Sache des Weltbildes. In 15,19 desavuiert Paulus einseitig den Glauben der Leugner der Auferstehung, indem er sagt, dass sich ihre Hoffnung nur auf diese Welt bezieht. Das würden sie bestreiten, denn sie haben in ihrem Glauben Ewigkeit erlebt. Wenn Paulus sagt, dass ihre Hoffnung auf dieses Leben begrenzt ist,[25] meint er, dass ihre Hoffnung mit dem Erlebnis in diesem Leben verbunden ist. Sie ist nicht mit dem Geschehen verbunden, das mehr als ihr Erlebnis ist und das ihr Gegenüber ist – dass den Menschen in der Auferstehung Jesu als Tat Gottes begegnet und sie aus dem fatalen Druck der Sünde (Entfremdung) befreit. Das ist in 1 Kor 15,17-19 angedeutet und wir erkennen, dass es eng mit dem paulinischen Hauptthema der Rechtfertigung aus Gnade Gottes zusammenhängt.

Wir haben eben erwähnt, dass die eschatologische Erwartung mit dem Kommen einer messianischen Figur, dem Jüngsten Gericht, der Auferstehung der Toten, und den neuen Äon (bzw. Reich Gottes) wie wir sie in den apokalyptischen Texten, bei den Pharisäern, bei den Essenern und im späteren Rabbinat, aber im Grunde auch schon bei Jesus finden, bei Paulus in zwei Pole gespalten ist.[26] Das kann als ein Defizit betrachtet werden: Der Messias ist ohne das messianische Reich gekommen.[27] Es drückt allerdings die reale Erfahrung der ersten Christen aus, die nach der Passion Jesu und nach Ostern, den schon im Geiste präsenten Jesus als den ersten Auferstandenen sahen. Zwischen den zwei Polen, der

---

25. Das „allein" ist auf „dies Leben" zu beziehen, nicht auf das Hoffen. Siehe SCHRAGE, *Der erste Brief an die Korinther* (Anm. 9), ad loc.

26. Das ist die These von J. B SOUČEK, die er in seinen tschechisch publizierten Studien geprägt hat. Zusammenfassend berichtet darüber P. Pokorný, *In Honor of Josef Souček*, in DERS. und J. B. SOUČEK, *Bibelauslegung als Theologie* (WUNT, 100), Tübingen, Mohr Siebeck 1997, pp. 13-23; hier pp. 134f.

27. In anderem Zusammenhang von A. SCHWEITZER, *Das Messianitäts- und Leidensgeheimnis* (*Das Abendmahl*, 2), Tübingen, Mohr Siebeck, 1929, p. 77, formuliert.

Auferstehung Jesu als des Messias (νυνὶ δὲ Χριστὸς ἐγήγερται – V. 20) und der allgemeinen Auferstehung – der Überwindung des Todes als des letzten Feindes (ἔσχατος ἐχθρός - V. 26), entfaltet sich nach Paulus die Endzeit, die sich erweitern wird sodass später, in den lukanischen Schriften, das Kreuz und die Auferstehung Jesu als die Mitte der Zeit betrachtet werden. In gewisser Hinsicht ist es gerade Paulus, dem wir die später formulierte und heute wieder kritisierte Idee der Heilsgeschichte verdanken. Allerdings dient sie bei ihm vor allem als Hintergrund der Paränese, die vor den Folgen eines Lebens warnt (rhetorisch eine *refutatio*)[28], das mit der endzeitlichen Auferstehung und Überwindung der bösen Mächte nicht rechnet (VV. 25-26).

1. *V. 20.*

Die positive Deutung des Problems der Zeit nach der Auferstehung Jesu (νυνί) und der Vollendung des Heils (rhetorisch *probatio*) beginnt mit einer theologischen Charakteristik der Auferstehung Jesu: Grundsätzlich bedeutet Vers 20, dass die Auferstehung (Erweckung: ἐγήγερται – *perf. passivi, passivum divinum*) Jesu kein Mirakel im Sinne eines Eingriffs in die Ordnung der Welt (der Schöpfung) ist, sondern eine Äußerung ihrer bisher verborgenen grundlegenden Dimension: Die Auferstehung betrifft grundsätzlich alle Menschen. Man kann sagen, dass es sich hier um eine Offenbarung im späteren dogmatischen Sinne der Selbstoffenbarung Gottes in Jesus Christus handelt. Im Unterschied zu der älteren Selbstoffenbarung Gottes in Israel, wonach Gott derjenige ist, der sein Volk aus Ägyptenland, aus der Knechtschaft geführt hat (Ex 20,2), hat im Neuen Testament die Erfahrung mit dem neu präsenten (auferstandenen) Jesus zur neuen Charakteristik Gottes geführt, nämlich als denjenigen, „der die Toten lebendig macht, und ruft, was nicht ist, daß es sei" (Röm 4,17; vgl. Apg 26,8). Nicht zufällig wird dies mit der Verheißung für „viele Völker" verbunden, die schon Abraham zuteil geworden ist (Gen 17,5).

Als „Erstling" (ἀπαρχή) ist Jesus nicht nur der erste in der Reihe der Auferstandenen, sondern, weil er zum Messias, Christus, dem Gesalbten geworden ist, ist er auch Garant der künftigen (ἔπειτα – V.23) Hoffnung der anderen Menschen. In V. 23 werden „die Anderen" als diejenigen charakterisiert, die „Christus angehören" (οἱ τοῦ Χριστοῦ). Hat Paulus an die Christen gedacht? Kaum auf die Christen in heutiger Bedeutung.

---

28. SCHRAGE, *Der erste Brief an die Korinther* (Anm. 9), p. 154.

Zwischen dem νυνί und ἔπειτα hat er ohne Zweifel eine Menge von neuen, dem Christus gehörenden Juden, Griechen und Barbaren erwartet. Und aus dem weiter Gesagten folgt, dass er darüber hinaus grundsätzlich auch an Menschen gedacht hat, die vor Christus gelebt haben. Der „Erstling" ist also der Anfang und Grund einer universalen Verheißung.

2. VV. 21-22.

In den zwei nächsten Versen werden Adam und (Jesus der) Christus als zwei parallele Gestalten gesehen. Durch die eine ist (in die Welt) der Tod (V. 22 „alle sterben"), durch die andere die Auferstehung (V. 22 „alle werden lebendig gemacht") gekommen. Einen Vorgänger hat diese Sicht der zwei Menschen bei Philo von Alexandrien, bei dem beide Gestalten in der Schöpfungsgeschichte auftauchen, der himmlische Mensch in Gen 1 und der irdische in Gen 2, also in umgekehrter Reihenfolge (de opif. mundi 134). Oft spricht man von Archetypen (s. τύπος in Röm 5,14), denn es handelt sich um keine erbliche Weitergabe der Sünde. Der Tod herrschte „von Adam bis Mose" auch über die Menschen, die nicht durch die gleiche Übertretung gesündigt hatten, wie Adam (Röm 5,14). Wie wir gesagt haben, schreibt Paulus für die christliche Gemeinde und in V. 23 werden bei der Parusie Christi diejenigen „lebendig gemacht, die Christus angehören" (οἱ τοῦ Χριστοῦ) . Am Ende wird jedoch Gott „alles in allem" sein (V. 28). Wenn in V. 22 gesagt wird, dass in Christus alle (πάντες) lebendig gemacht werden, bedeutet es, dass sich die negative Analogie zwischen Adam und Christus als grundlegende Bestimmung grundsätzlich auf alle Menschen bezieht (siehe das ὥσπερ – οὕτως). Wie gesagt, muss Paulus das Problem mindestens soweit reflektiert haben, dass die Perspektive der Auferstehung auch für die vor Christus Gestorbenen gilt. In dem parallelen Abschnitt aus Röm 5 wird auf „alle Menschen" die inhaltlich ähnliche Aussage als Rechtfertigung durch die Gerechtigkeit des Einen gedeutet. „Jedenfalls bleibt πάντες ohne jede Beschränkung und Bedingung, ja läßt gerade so die den ganzen Kosmos betreffende Dimension des Auferstehungsgeschehens sichtbar werden".[29] Das später formulierte Problem der ἀποκατάστασις πάντων wird hier nicht gelöst.[30] Doch müssen

---

29. SCHRAGE, *Der erste Brief an die Korinther* (Anm. 9), pp. 164f; dort auch zur Diskussion.

30. Paulus weiß von der Möglichkeit der Ablehnung des Heils: Die Sünde bezahlt ihren Dienern als Sold den Tod. Das ist die Absurdität des Bösen (Röm 6,23; vgl. 21). Allerdings, er erzählt das alles, um alle Leser (Hörer) vor dieser Gefahr zu retten.

wir zusammenfassend sagen, dass Paulus die Adressaten anredet und ihnen die Gefahr des Lebens ohne die gemeinsame (geschichtliche) Perspektive der Vollendung des Heils (τέλος – V. 24) in der allgemeinen Auferstehung zeigen will. Er möchte sie ermahnen, dass sie die Mitmenschen nicht richten (vgl. 1 Kor 4,5), sondern sie im Lichte der Hoffnung sehen, die in der Auferstehung Christi gegründet ist.

Der Apostel ist überzeugt, dass die christliche Gemeinde das Rückgrat der Menschheit bildet. Diese Überzeugung, die hinter den einzelnen Bildern steht, hat ihre Polysemie begründet, die sie auch für den säkularen Menschen gewissermaßen verständlich macht.[31] Das eindrückliche Bild des Reiches Gottes aus 1 Kor 15,28 ist die Perspektive der ganzen Menschheit.

[Einen weiteren Schritt in seinem theologischen Denken hat Paulus in Phil 2,9-10 gemacht. Dort bekennen die Christen Christus als den von Gott eingesetzten Herrn (vgl. Ps 110,1) im Namen der ganzen Schöpfung. Die Hoffnung, die in der Auferstehung Christi gegründet ist, führt auch dazu, dass die Christen in Christus den Sinn der ganzen Schöpfung sehen und in ihrem Gottesdienst und in dem ganzen Leben Christus auch im Namen der ganzen Schöpfung loben.]

Diese Tendenz zur Universalität des Heils ist in 2 Thess nicht zu finden. Wie in mehreren anderen Schriften der dritten christlichen Generation wird hier eher dem Heil der Christen das Unheil ihrer Gegner entgegengestellt (1,8-10; 2,9-12). Die beiden Tendenzen sind auch in den Bildern der menschlichen (sprachlichen) Welt zu finden, die zur späteren christlichen Kultur gehören. Eine bedeutende Dimension der Mission im europäischen und amerikanischen Kulturbereich wird die Neuinterpretation der Symbole, Bilder und Texte, die in unserer Kultur reich vorhanden sind und die nicht, oder nicht gut, verstanden werden. Die warnenden Bilder können wir nicht aus unserem Erbe ausschließen, aber in der Deutung des Evangeliums haben die mit dem universalen Heil verbundenen Bilder und theologische Aussagen Priorität. Die westliche Kultur wird ihre Identität durch eine radikale Neuinterpretation ihrer Grundlagen neu entdecken müssen, wenn sie sich in den gegenwärtigen Problemen orientieren will.

Adam und Christus haben ihre spezifischen Stellen in der Geschichte. Bei Jesus ist es klar, er ist der Gekreuzigte (1 Kor 1,23) und das Evangelium kennt die Zeugen, die die Identität des heute im Geist

---

31. M. E. BORING, *The Language of the Universal Salvation*, in *JBL* 105 (1986) 269-292.

wirkenden Christus mit Jesus von Nazareth bestätigen (1 Kor 15,5ff.). Die mit ihm verbundene Offenbarung Gottes ist geschichtsgebunden und die Aussage über Gott, der die Toten ins Leben ruft, ist eine Generalisierung der mit ihm gemachten Erfahrung. Mit Adam ist es anders: Er verkörpert den Menschen, der den Glauben verloren hat und von den überindividuellen Mächte der Natur und der Geschichte versklavt ist. Der Tod ist der stärkste von ihnen und wegen der menschlichen Entfernung von Gott ist er für ihn zur letzten Wirklichkeit geworden (Röm 5,14). Das Gesetz hat diese Entfremdung geoffenbart und benannt (Röm 5,13). Weil die Sünde als Entfremdung etwas unnatürliches und gottwidriges ist, hat man die Sage über Adam erst nach der Entstehung der Welt als der guten Schöpfung Gottes platziert. Das Versagen Adams ist ein Missbrauch der ihm vom Schöpfer gegebenen Freiheit und Verantwortlichkeit. Mit Adam fängt die Weltgeschichte an, in der sich die menschlichen Leben abspielen. In der Gegenwart begrenzt der Horizont des Todes die Hoffnung der Menschen („alle sterben"), die Auferstehung der Menschen, die einer Neuschöpfung gleicht, ist eine Sache des Glaubens, der Zuversicht und des Vertrauens dem apostolischen Zeugnis gegenüber („alle werden lebendig gemacht"). Dies ist der Kern des heilsgeschichtlichen Denkens von Paulus, das tiefer als nur in der Perspektive der Kirche oder der einzelnen Christen verankert ist.

3. *VV. 23-24*.

Mehrere Forscher (und Kommentare) halten 1 Kor 15,23-28 (24-28) für eine chiastisch gestaltete, diskursive Einheit mit den VV.25b-26 (-27) als ihrer Mitte.[32] Überzeugender ist allerdings die Gliederung, wonach der Verfasser zunächst eine These (VV. 23-24) formuliert, die in den Versen 25 und 28 erläutert wird (*explicatio*).[33] Dies ist für die Auslegung dieses Abschnitts von Bedeutung.

In der These knüpft Paulus auf die Tradition der apokalyptischen Bilder der erwarteten Ereignisse der Endzeit, wie wir sie schon aus einigen apokalyptischen Texten kennen: Messianisches Reich – Reich Gottes. Schon die These deutet an, dass das messianische Reich (anders als in

---

32. Siehe bes. A. LINDEMANN, *Parusie und Herrschaft Gottes*, in *Wort und Dienst* NF 19 (1987) 87-107.
33. J. LAMBRECHT, *Structure and Line of Thought in 1Cor 15:23-28*, in *NT* 32 (1990), 143-151, hier p. 148. Seine Auffassung der Struktur von 1 Kor 15,23-28 gilt, wenn wir auch die paulinische Argumentation anders verstehen.

der Apokalyptik) schon begonnen hat. Die Auferweckung Christi ist sein Anfang oder Angeld (ἀπαρχή) und es wird mit der allgemeinen Auferstehung enden (τέλος).

4. *Exkurs über die Mächte und Gewalten*

Schon im V. 24 lesen wir die These über die Vernichtung (Ausschaltung[34]) der verschiedenen überindividuellen „Mächte" (Herrschaften, Mächte, Gewalten). Man kann nicht eindeutig sagen, was unter solchen Bezeichnungen gemeint ist. Sie treten in den Vordergrund sowohl in den Deuteropaulinen, aber insbesondere im Epheserbrief. Mit Sicherheit können wir nur sagen, dass es sich um überindividuelle Wirklichkeiten handelt, die nach dem damaligen Weltbild zwischen Gott und den Menschen standen. In Röm 8,38 sind sie neben den Engeln genannt. Ihre Funktion wird nicht eindeutig definiert. Hier wird ihre Vernichtung erwartet und in Eph 6,12 sind sie als böse Geister „unter dem Himmel" charakterisiert, gegen die (nicht gegen „Fleisch und Blut", d. h. gegen Menschen) der Christ kämpfen soll. Auf der anderen Seite wird in Kol 1,16 Christus gelobt, dass durch ihn auch das Unsichtbare, d. h. die „Throne, Herrschaften, Mächte, und Gewalten" geschaffen sind. Dies ist offensichtlich eine spätere Entfaltung der paulinischen Erfahrung, die jedoch indirekt schon bei Paulus verankert ist. Es bedeutet, dass man als „Mächte" die durch menschliche Sünde missbrauchte Dimensionen der Schöpfung bezeichnet hat. Wenn es sich auch um eine Schöpfung Gottes handelt, wurden und werden die „Mächte" als Götter angesehen. Nach den Deuteropaulinen ist es der Teufel (hier διάβολος genannt: Eph 4,27; 6,11-17), der dabei mitwirkt. Paulus bezeichnet die Leugnung der Auferstehung als Sünde. Diesen Aussagen von Paulus und seinen Schülern können wir folgen, dass für den sündigen (entfremdeten) Menschen, der die Auferstehung und Erhöhung von Jesus Christus (vgl. Phil 2,9-11) leugnet, die „Mächte" als die letzte Wirklichkeit über und vor ihm sind. Die Sünde emanzipiert sich von dem Sünder und tritt als ein selbständiges Subjekt auf.

[Heute würden wir die „Mächte" vielleicht als personifizierte biologische Gesetze, geschichtliche Gesetzlichkeiten oder Ideologien identifizieren, die einen Druck auf den Menschen ausüben, der beharrlich ist. Z. B. die Verleumdung oder die Nachrede ist eine solche

---

34. So übersetzt das *katargō* in seinem Kommentar Ch. WOLFF, *Der erste Brief des Paulus an die Korinther II* (THKNT, 7/II), Berlin, EVA, 1982, ad loc.

übermenschliche Macht. Der Verleumder kann sich bei dem Beschädigten entschuldigen, aber die Nachrede hat schon ihr eigenes Leben, sie läuft weiter und muss als eine selbständige, Macht bekämpft werden. Die von Gott gewollte Funktion der Beharrlichket der Information, wurde durch die Sünde missbraucht.]

Der Kampf gegen eine solche sogenannte göttliche Macht hat eine gute Verheißung. Der Glaube, der durch die „Auferstehung" motiviert ist, enthüllt (offenbart) solche Mächte als die vorletzten Wirklichkeiten, die den Menschen zwar beeinflussen, aber nicht fatal bestimmen. Das ist der Anfang der Befreiung. Die „Vernichtung" der Mächte kann als deren Entmächtigung verstanden werden. So hat Paulus die verschiedenen vergöttlichten Mächte in 1 Kor 8,5-6 „entmächtigt": Er gab zu, dass es im Himmel (d. h. über den Menschen) Wirklichkeiten gibt, die die Menschen Götter nennen (λεγόμενοι θεοί; vgl. Gal 4,8), aber der Christ weiß in seinem Glauben, dass es nur einen Gott gibt (d. h. denjenigen, der den Herrn von den Toten erweckt hat – 1 Kor 6,14). Das bedeutet, dass die Mächte keinen göttlichen Charakter haben und der Mensch von ihnen nicht schicksalhaft beherrscht wird. Ihre böse Wirkung ist ihr Missbrauch.

5. *V. 25*

In dem Kommentar (VV. 25-28), der durch das γάρ im V. 25 eingeleitet ist, werden die Ereignisse der Endzeit wieder in derselben Reihenfolge kommentiert. Diese notwendige Ordnung (τάγμα) ist von Gott gegeben (V. 25).[35] Paulus argumentiert dadurch gegen diejenigen, die sich schon erlöst, auferweckt und unsterblich fühlen, und plädiert für das „noch nicht" der allgemeinen Auferstehung. Das Ziel und die Vollendung der Geschichte kommt erst nach der Überwindung aller „Mächte", wie es in den Versen 25-27 mit Hilfe des Zitats aus Ps 8,6 näher charakterisiert wird.

In den apokalyptischen Narrativen kommt etwa an dieser Stelle das Jüngste Gericht. Hier drückt Paulus dasselbe Geschehen „von außen

---

35. Das griechische Wort kann „Abteilung" oder „Gruppe" bedeuten, hier tritt allerdings die Bedeutung Ordnung oder das Festgesetzte in den Vordergrund; s. G. DELLING, *TWNT* 8, p. 31.

her", aus der Sicht Gottes, nämlich als Beseitigung der Mächte, die den Menschen beeinflussen und sogar versklaven aus. Ihre Wirkung wird durch die Kraft des Evangeliums neutralisiert. Im V. 51 wird darüber hinaus von der Verwandlung der Menschen gesprochen, was zu dem Bild des Gerichts passt, den Paulus in 1 Kor 3 entfaltete.

Der Satz von dem Herrschen Christi ist eine Entfaltung der Aussage von der Erhöhung Jesu Christi (Phil 2,9-11; Eph 1,21; 1 Petr 3,22 – ihm sind die Engel, Gewalten und Mächte untertan), als einer Deutung von Ostern. Jenes Bekenntnis wird unter dem Einfluss der apokalyptischen Vorstellung vom messianischen Zwischenreich entfaltet (4 Esra 7,26-28; Offb 20–21). Das messianische Reich kommt nach dem Ende dieser Geschichte als ihr Gipfel und als der Sieg Gottes guten Willens mit den Menschen.

Da sehen wir jedoch, dass das Modell der apokalyptischen Erwartung, in welche das messianische Reich als letzte Etappe der Geschichte eingebaut ist, in 1 Kor 15 wieder tief adaptiert, ja umgebogen ist.[36] Das messianische Reich hat schon angefangen: Der Anfang des Herrschens (βασιλεύω – V. 25) Christi war die Auferstehung und Erhöhung Jesu. Er ist der Erstling der Auferstandenen (V. 20). Das *interregnum Christi*, in manchen Apokalypsen das endzeitliche messianische (1000 oder 400 Jahre dauernde) Reich,[37] liegt zwischen seiner Auferweckung und der Parusie, nicht zwischen Parusie und dem τέλος.[38] Was in der Zukunft steht, ist die Unterwerfung *aller* Feinde unter die Füße Christi (V. 25 als Anspielung auf Ps 110 [LXX 109],1), wobei es nicht ganz klar ist, wer im V. 25 das Subjekt der Unterwerfung ist. Weil im V. 24 Christus das Subjekt ist, muss es auch im V. 25 Christus, der „Sohn" sein.[39] Das θῶ vom Ps 109,1 (LXX) wird in θῇ verwandelt.

---

36. L. HARTMAN, *The Function of Some Apocalyptic Timetables*, in NTS 22 (1975) 1-14, hat auf die Einzigartigkeit der paulinischen Theologie aufmerksam gemacht, die sich von den vorgegebenen Gattungen (hier Apokalyptik) nicht ableiten lässt.

37. Vgl. *1 Hen* 93,1-14; *VitAd* 42; *3 Sib* 652-660; *2 Bar* 73; Offb 20,1-6 u. a.; 400 Jahre nach *4 Esra* 7.

38. So H. CONZELMANN, *Der erste Brief an die Korinther* (KEK, 5/11), Göttingen, Vandenhoeck & Ruprecht, 1969, pp. 321f.; Ch. SENFT, *La première épître de Saint Paul aux Corinthiens* (CNT, 7), p. 199; LANG, *Die Briefe an die Korinther* (Anm. 14), p. 225; SCHRAGE, *Der erste Brief des Paulus an die Korinther* (Anm. 9), pp. 174f.; S. SCHNEIDER, *Auferstehen. Eine neue Deutung von 1 Kor 15* (FzB, 105), Würzburg, Echter, 2005, p. 197.

39. So in den oben erwähnten Kommentaren (an ältere Traditionen anknüpfend) z. B. CONZELMANN (pp. 323f.), LANG (p. 226), SCHRAGE (pp. 177f.)

6. V. 26

Unter die „Mächte und Gewalten" gehört als die gefährlichste von ihnen – der Tod. Wo das Heil eine soziale Größe ist, wie es im V. 28 angedeutet wird, dort ist der Tod ein Feind. In den dualistischen Strömungen kann der Tod als Befreiung der geistigen Substanz betrachtet werden. Wir haben schon das Philippusevangelium erwähnt, wo die Auferstehung in einer individuellen mystischen Erkenntnis vor dem Tod passiert und der Tod kann den geistigen Menschen, den Besitzer dieser Erkenntnis nicht bedrohen. Wo jedoch das Leib als Träger der individuellen Identität, des Personseins und vor allem der persönlichen Beziehungen für die Hoffnung bedeutend ist, dort wird der Tod zum Feind. Im Alten Testament ist die Möglichkeit der Unsterblichkeit des Menschen (Gen 3,22), von Gott nicht beabsichtigt (Gen 3,4.24). Der Mensch ist ein zeitiges, sterbliches Geschöpf (Jes 51,12). Er darf allerdings wissen, dass Gott an ihn denkt (Ps 8,5). Was das bedeutet, darüber wagte der Israelit angesichts der Heiligkeit Gottes nicht zu spekulieren.

Paulus hat in dem Evangelium eine grundlegende Stütze der Hoffnung gewonnen: Jesus, den Herrn (κύριος), der verlassen und in Todesangst starb, hat Gott erweckt (1 Kor 6,14). Und das Evangelium von seiner Erweckung von Gott bedeutet Hoffnung für alle. Wir wissen schon, dass er auch im Tode nicht allein war. Das ist die Grundbedeutung der Bekenntnisse über den Tod Jesu „für uns", die Paulus auf verschiedene Weisen interpretiert (Erlösung, Versöhnung, Rechtfertigung vor dem Gericht): Gott hat sich durch Christus als derjenige geoffenbart, der bei den sterbenden steht, wenn sie auch kein sichtbares Zeugnis seiner Gegenwart haben und sich verlassen fühlen. Gott erweckt die Toten (2 Kor 1,9; Hebr 11,19). Wir könnten weiter denken und sagen, dass wenn der von Gott aus dem Tod Erweckte die Sünden vergeben hat, ist seine Auferweckung auch eine Hoffnung für die Sünder. Aber so denkt Paulus nicht. Vom irdischen Jesus ist für ihn vor allem das DASS seiner freiwilligen Erniedrigung als des inkarnierten himmlischen Wesens bedeutend (2 Kor 8.9; Phil 2,6-8; Rom 6,10f.). Er war gehorsam (ὑπήκοος) bis zum Tode und „darum hat ihn Gott erhöht". Hier, wo es um die Überwindung des Todes handelt, ist also nicht Christus, sondern Gott selbst das Subjekt. Die Zweideutigkeit hängt von der spezifischen Art der Kampfes Jesu ab: Er kämpft durch seinen Gehorsam Gott gegenüber, der dadurch auch in den vorhergehenden Versen das indirekte Subjekt der Handlung war. Die Sterblichkeit des Menschen wird dadurch nicht aufgehoben. Die Begrenzung des menschlichen Lebens hängt mit seiner persönlichen Einzigartigkeit und Einmaligkeit zusammen. Die Einmaligkeit ist mit der Zeitlichkeit verbunden. Als solches, als einmaliges und zeitiges Leben mit Namen und Gesicht ist das menschliche Leben im Gedächtnis des Schöpfers aufbewahrt. Der Tod wird also nicht durch ein unendliches Leben ersetzt. Das wäre eine absolute Degradierung des Lebens, der in seiner Unendlichkeit seine Einmaligkeit verlieren würde.[40] Die Überwindung des Todes ist seine Überwindung als des letzten Feindes, des letzten Horizonts des menschlichen Lebens, und zwar durch die Auferstehung Jesu Christi. Der Tod ist der letzte Feind, solange die Sünde dem Menschen den Tod als die letzte Wirklichkeit suggeriert – 1 Kor 15,55-57. Paulus hat die von dem Auferstehungsglauben abgeleitete Hoffnung in folgender Logik ausgedrückt: Wenn Gott sich zu Christus bekannt hat, und die Menschen sich zu Christus bekennen, kann weder die Gegenwart noch die Zukunft, weder das Leben noch der Tod sie bedrohen. Das ist in 1 Kor 3,22-23 in umgekehrter Reihenfolge gesagt und in Röm 8,37-37 in der *catena aurea* verdeutlicht: Der Tod kann „uns" nicht von der Liebe Gottes trennen, die „uns" in Jesus erreicht hat. Das „wie" der Hoffnung für das zeitliche Leben, das im Gedächtnis Gottes aufbewahrt ist, bleibt grundsätzlich offen, wir werden nur einige Grundlinien der Hoffnung formulieren können (unten zu 1 Kor 15,51.57).

7. V. 27.

Es folgt, dass auch im V. 27 Gott selbst das Subjekt der Handlung ist. Das wird aus dem Zitat aus Ps 8,7 deutlich. Der Psalmist sagt es (in der LXX) zwar in der 2. Person als Lob Gottes (ὑπέταξας) und Paulus transformiert es in die 3. Person zu einer Aussage über die Handlung Gottes, es ist aber deutlich, dass nachdem über die Überwindung des Todes die Rede war, Gott als das wahre Subjekt der Handlung in den Vordergrund tritt (siehe V. 28b; siehe auch Hebr 2,8).[41] So wird Ps 8,7 auch in Eph 1,22 verstanden. Das ganze Geschehen steht unter dem „muss" (δεῖ – V.25a) der Absicht Gottes.

---

40. Das war übrigens das Anliegen Karl BARTHs in seiner *Kirchlichen Dogmatik* III/2, pp. 671ff. 683.
41. In Phil 3,21 ist es Christus, der sich alle Dinge untertan machen kann. In Phil 4,19 ist es aber Gott, in dessen Kraft Christus handelt.

Das ὅταν δὲ εἴπῃ ὅτι πάντα ὑποτέτακται im V. 27 konnte als eine zukünftige Aussage Gottes (nicht Christi)[42] übersetzt werden:[43] „Wenn er aber gesagt haben wird, dass Sämtliches unterworfen sei". Das entspräche der Aussage des Psalmisten im Ps 8,7. Da allerdings der Nachdruck auf dem Argument aus der Schrift liegt, ist das εἴπῃ als Hinweis auf die Schriftstelle („Wenn es aber heißt")[44] zu verstehen.

8. V. 28.

Über eine kurze Rezidive der satanischen Macht wird im Unterschied zu den Apokalypsen (*1 Hen* 93,9ff.; *3 Sib* 660ff.; Offb 20,7ff.; *4 Esra* 7,29ff.) nicht gesprochen, die Reihenfolge der Ereignisse deutet nur an, dass das Reich Christi noch nicht das τέλος ist. Eigentlich ist das Bild im Unterschied zu der Apokalyptik noch tiefer umgestaltet: Wenn Christus in der Kraft Gottes die feindlichen Mächte voll überwinden wird, dann wird er sich als der Sohn Gott (dem Vater) selbst unterordnen. D. h. das Unterordnen unter die Füße des Sohnes, das schon in der Schrift vorhergesagt und versprochen ist, und damit das ganze messianische Reich, ist in der Sicht des Apostels ein Prozess,[45] das mit der Auferstehung beginnt und bis zu (ἕως) seiner Vollendung dauert. In dem Moment (ὅταν im V. 24 und 28) als es vollendet ist, wird ein Umbruch kommen, der in der Zeit von Paulus – und das möchte er hervorheben – noch in der Zukunft liegt und in dem die Gottesherrschaft anfangen soll.

[Intensiv wurde in der Auslegungsgeschichte das Problem des Verhältnisses dieses Bildes zu dem Schluss des christologischen Artikels des Nicäno-Konstantinopolitanum, der die Ewigkeit des Reiches Christi proklamiert (τῆς βασιλείας [des Sohnes] οὐκ ἔσται τέλος *telos*).[46] Mehrere Exegeten versuchten, die Aussage von Paulus zu entschärfen. Die einzige Lösung ist jedoch, die Intentionen beider Aussagen zu bestimmen und sie zu vergleichen. Paulus hat beabsichtigt, die alte jesuanische Tradition über das Reich Gottes zu interpretieren, das der Horizont der Hoffnung ist. Jesus Christus, der die Menschen „von unten" zum Vater

---

42. WOLFF, *Kommentar* (Anm. 34), p. 183.
43. Die Übersetzung von C. F. G. HENRICI in Meyers Kommentar, näheres bei CONZELMANN, *Kommentar* (Anm. 34), pp. 326f.
44. So LANG, *Die Briefe an die Korinther* (Anm. 14), pp. 221, 227, SCHRAGE, *Der erste Brief des Paulus an die Korinther* (Anm. 9), pp. 213ff..
45. Vgl. WOLFF, *Kommentar* (Anm. 34), p. 182.
46. Eine Übersicht siehe in SCHRAGE, *Der erste Brief des Paulus an die Korinther* (Anm. 9), pp. 189ff.

führen sollte, wird durch die Unterordnung der ganzen Schöpfung unter den Schöpfer sein Werk vollenden. Ein Subordinatianismus ist es nicht, weil dadurch die Rolle Jesu Christi nicht entwürdigt wird. Das Werk des Sohnes wird dadurch nicht abgelehnt, sondern durch die Übergabe an den Vater verewigt. Übrigens in dem griechischen Original dem NC-Bekenntnis wird im ersten Artikel Gott Vater als κοσμοκράτωρ – Weltherrscher bezeichnet. Die Betonung der Ewigkeit des Reiches Christi im zweiten Artikel soll eher hervorheben, dass das, was Jesus repräsentiert, vor Gott ständig als das höchste Gesetz gilt.]

Das „wie" des Heils ist offen. Die Schilderung des Lebens in dem neuen Äon ist asketisch auf das „dass" seiner Gestaltung nach dem Willen Gottes begrenzt.[47] Man muss sich mit der feierlichen Zusage begnügen, wonach „was kein Auge gesehen hat und kein Ohr gehört hat und in keines Menschen Herz gekommen ist, was Gott bereitet hat denen, die ihn lieben" (1 Kor 2,9, Zitat von Jes 64,3).

Das wirkliche Ziel, die Gottesherrschaft, wird so geschildert, dass der heutige Leser den Eindruck einer pantheistischen Idee hat: „Wenn aber ihm das alles untergeordnet (ὑποταγή) sein wird, dann wird sich auch der Sohn selbst dem, der ihm alles Untergeordnete (τῷ ὑποτάξαντι) unterordnen(ὑποταγήσεται), damit Gott alles in allem (πάντα ἐν πᾶσι) sei." Die pantheistische Deutung schließt aber das dreifache Anwendung des Zeitworts ὑποτάσσομαι, das bei Paulus deutliche soziale Konnotationen hat, aus. So ist es z. B. in 1 Kor 16,16, wo es um die Unterordnung der verantwortlichen Christen oder in Röm 13,1 um die Unterordnung der „Obrigkeit" geht. Gegen die pantheistische Deutung spricht auch schon die Tatsache, dass hier Jesus als „der Sohn", ein geschichtliches Wesen, in das göttliche Ganze integriert wird, sodass es deutlich ist, dass die Geschichte in ihrer zeitlichen Dimension sowie die zeitlichen menschlichen Leben mit dem Endziel verbunden sind.[48] Auch die Stellung der Natur (κτίσις), die der Mensch nach Gen 1,28 beherrschen soll, wird in Röm 8,20 als Unterordnung charakterisiert, die wegen der Sünde des Menschen zur Unterwerfung der Vergänglichkeit geworden ist: ματαιότητι ἡ κτίσις ὑπετάγη. „Gott alles in allem" bedeutet, dass dann alle Beziehungen dem guten Willen Gottes entsprechen und gleichzeitig, dass die Schöpfung wieder den guten Willen Gottes gemäß

---

47. A. C. THISELTON, *The First Epistle to the Corinthians* (NIGTZC), Grand Rapids MI – Cambridge/Carlisle, Eerdmans – The Paternoster Press, 2000, p. 1201.
48. Vgl. G. THEISSEN, *Die Religion der ersten Christen*, Gütersloh, Kaiser/Gütersloher Verlagshaus, 2000, p. 371.

verwaltet wird. Die Enthusiasten, die den Tod ignorieren, überlassen dem Tod paradoxerweise die ganze Schöpfung.[49]

4. FORTSETZUNG IN 1 KOR 15,29-58 UND IN 2 KOR 5,1-10

In *15,29-34* zeigt Paulus, dass das Ertragen des Leids und der Widerwärtigkeit um des Glaubens Willen nur aus der Sicht der Hoffnung auf die Auferstehung sinnvoll ist und die Sorge um das Heil der Toten (Taufe für die Toten) nur im Zusammenhang mit der Auferstehung der Toten einen Grund hat. Mit Hilfe eines in griechischer Literatur mehrmals benutzten Sprichworts (V.33) warnt Paulus vor den sog. Leugnern der Auferstehung, als wären sie schon eine Gruppe, die sich außerhalb der Gemeinde befindet.

Der Abschnitt *1 Kor 15,35-50* ist der Beweisführung zugunsten der leiblichen Auferstehung gewidmet. Zunächst benutzt Paulus die Pflanzen als eine Analogie auf niederer Ebene. Der Same einer Pflanze „stirbt" in der Erde und dann gibt ihm Gott einen Leib, jeder Pflanzenart einen anderen. Das gilt auch für die himmlischen Körper. Der „erste Adam", das Urbild der jetzigen Menschen (und mit ihm „wir" alle), ist auch zu einer solchen Metamorphose bestimmt: der Träger seiner Identität (der Samen – σπέρμα), wird von Gott einen neuen, himmlischen Leib bekommen. Warum ist für Paulus der Leib so wichtig? Nicht wegen seiner Fleischlichkeit oder Materialität. Die Hoffnung verbindet Paulus mit einem geistigen Leib. Der Leib ist eigentlich als Mittler der Beziehungen von Bedeutung.[50] Das Gesicht, die Stimme, die gereichte Hand, die Tischgemeinschaft – das kann nicht ohne Leib zustanden kommen. Vorstellen können wir es uns nicht, aber Paulus stellt es sich als eine Analogie der irdischen Begegnung auf höheren Ebene vor: „Wir sehen jetzt (Gott als) durch einen Spiegel, ein dunkles Bild (durch Zeugnis vermittelt); dann aber von Angesicht zu Angesicht" (1 Kor 13,12). Das ist die persönliche Begegnung. Die verschiedenen, einmaligen Menschen werden also in ein neues, sozial gestaltetes Ganzes verbunden, in dem alle, ein jeder mit seinem unwiederholbaren Gesicht, dem Willen Gottes entsprechen werden. Das entspricht dem Bild der Herrschaft Gottes aus V.28. Es handelt sich um eine Annäherung an Gott durch das

---

49. SELLIN *Der Streit um die Auferstehung der Toten* (Anm. 10), p. 276.
50. POKORNÝ, *Zukunft* (Anm. 11), pp. 62ff.; F. VOUGA, *Körper und Realpräsenz bei Paulus*, in ZNT 14 (2011) Nr. 27, 36-44, hier p. 38.

Mit-Christus-Sein.⁵¹ Dass Fleisch (σάρξ) und Blut das Reich Gottes nicht ererben können (V. 50) ist eine Anspielung auf die Sündigkeit des sarkischen Leibes, der nicht vom Geist Gottes beherrscht wird (vgl. Röm 13,14),⁵² also keine Auflösung des Personseins. Das Wort vom Reich Gottes bestätigt, dass die Auseinandersetzung über die Sozialität der Hoffnung eine Neuinterpretation der Erwartung des Reiches Gottes ist, wie wir sie aus den Traditionen über Jesus kennen.⁵³

In *15,51-57* folgt ein apokalyptischens Bild der Umwandlung, das dem von 1 Thess 4 ähnlich ist (s. oben unter 2). Dahinter steckt eine ziemlich tiefe Reflexion der Beziehung der menschlichen Zeitlichkeit und der ewigen Hoffnung: „… das Sterbliche muss anziehen die Unsterblichkeit" (V. 53). Das Sterbliche, d. h. die Einmaligkeit der menschlichen Schicksale wird verewigt. In diesen Fall deutet das „anziehen" an, dass die Verwandlung doch die persönliche Identität bewahrt. Es handelt sich um keine Fortsetzung des Lebens. Das zeitliche Leben als Ganzes, das nur Gott von Geburt bis zu dem Tod sieht und im Gedächtnis hat, wird in den neuen Äon aufgenommen und mit anderen Leben konfrontiert. Dieser Bezug zwischen dem neuen Äon und den anderen Menschen die dazu gehören, gibt dem menschlichen Leben seinen tiefsten Sinn.⁵⁴

Die Sterblichkeit, die Begrenzung in Zeit, gehört, wie schon gesagt, zu der Einmaligkeit des Menschen, zu seinem Personsein.⁵⁵ Wenn alle Leben ewig wären, wäre es nur ein Leben ohne Gestalt und ohne Bedeutung. Der Leib gehört also zum guten Ziel des Lebens, weil die Grausamkeit des Todes in der absoluten Einsamkeit besteht, in der er „erlebt" wird. Die individuelle Erlösung, das individuelle Heil kann von dem sozialen Heil nicht getrennt werden. Ein individuelles Leben kann sein „ich" nur in den Beziehungen zu den anderen gewinnen, und eine Gemeinschaft, ein Organismus kann nur von unersetzlichen Bestandteilen gebaut werden. Deswegen ist schon in den apokalyptischen Bildern

---

51. G. HAUFE, *Individuelle Eschatologie des Neuen Testaments*, ZTK 83 (1986) 436-463, bes. p. 461.

52. Zur dichotomischen und trichotomischen Anthropologie des Paulus s. E. BRANDENBURGER, *Fleisch und Geist* (WMANT, 29), Neukirchen, Neukirchener Verlag 1968, bes. pp. 42ff.; SELLIN, *Der Streit um die Auferstehung der Toten* (Anm.15), pp. 181f.; R. J. SIDER, *The Pauline Conception of the Resurrection Body in I Corinthians xv.35-54*, in NTS 21 (1974-75) 428-439.

53. Vgl. K. P. DONFRIED, *The Kingdom of God in Paul*, in W. WILLIS (Hg.), *The Kingdom of God in 20th-Century Interpretation*, Peabody, Hendrickson, 1987, 175-190, bes. p. 183.

54. Zur antiken Anthropologie s. T. K. SEIM – J. ØKLUND (Hg.), *Metamorphoses* (Ekstasis, 1), Berlin/New York, de Gruyter, 2009.

55. Siehe oben zu Vers 26.

die Auferstehung der Menschen als ein Ereignis am Ende der Geschichte platziert, damit die einzelnen Menschen an dem Ziel der Geschichte und der Regierung Gottes teilnehmen können.

Zuletzt wird noch einmal das Thema der Auflösung des Todes aus V. 26 aufgenommen: Nach einem kombinierten Zitat von Jes 25,8 und Hos 13,14 (das Zeugnis zweier Zeugen ist glaubwürdiger) folgt ein Aufruf in der Gestalt einer rhetorischen Frage. Aus der Sicht der Performanzkritik können wir voraussetzen, dass der Vorleser hier nicht die versammelte christliche Gemeinde, sondern auch die Gestorbenen anreden [56] und erst nach einer Pause fortsetzen soll: „Der Stachel des Todes ist die Sünde, die Kraft aber der Sünde ist das Gesetz." Es handelt sich um eine Kette zweier verschachtelter Argumente, die die Art der Unterwerfung des Todes kommentieren. Das Gefährliche, das der hier personifizierten Tod benutzt, ist sein Stachel ($\kappa\acute{\epsilon}\nu\tau\rho\text{o}\nu$) – das, was die Menschen quält. Der Gedankengang ist etwa: Die Sünde führt die Menschen zur göttlichen Verehrung verschiedener Kräfte und Ideen, die zur Schöpfung gehören und das Gesetz, sobald es als der einzige Heilsweg betrachtet wird, gehört zu ihnen. Wenn Gott Jesus erweckt hat, der auf dem Holz starb, was dem Gesetz nach ein Tod des Verfluchten ist (Gal 3,13; Deut 21,23), dann ist die durch den Missbrauch des Gesetzes ausgeübte Macht der Sünde (der Stachel des Todes) gebrochen. Dies ist der Grund der abschließenden Ermahnung der Adressaten, wonach ihre Mühe im „Werk des Herrn" nicht vergeblich ist (V. 58). Das Werk des Herrn ist offensichtlich die Arbeit am Aufbau der Gemeinde im Unterschied zu der Bedrohung der Gemeinde durch diejenigen, die als Leugner der Auferstehung bezeichnet sind.

2 Kor 5,1-10 ist eine neue Behandlung des Themas als des eigentlichen Evangeliums (von der Auferstehung), und zwar angesichts des Gerichts Gottes. Der sterbliche menschliche Leib wird mit einer Hütte verglichen, die durch ein himmlisches Haus (in 1 Kor: geistigen Leib) ersetzt wird. Die Frage der Integration des Sterblichen im Ewigen (1 Kor 15,54) wird hier als Verschlingen des Sterblichen vom Leben begriffen, aber es steht da nicht im Vordergrund. Das Problem ist eher der Tod als Zwischenzustand der „Nacktheit", d. h. des beziehungslosen Zustandes der Einsamkeit. Dies ist für Paulus mit der Verzögerung der Parusie ein persönlich existentielles Problem geworden. Er setzt sich damit mit dem Hinweis auf die Gabe des Heiligen Geistes auseinander, den er im

---

56. SCHRAGE, *Der erste Brief des Paulus an die Korinther* (Anm. 9), pp. 380f.

Glauben als Garantie des Mit-Christus-Seins begreift. Er weiß auch, was für den Gläubigen der Weg des Heils ist: entsprechend dem aus Gottes Gnade geschenkten Heil zu handeln, denn jeder wird vor dem Richterstuhl Christi stehen, um seinen Lohn zu empfangen (V. 10; vgl. Eph 6,8). Christus taucht hier als der Repräsentant des Willen Gottes beim Endgericht auf, wobei unterstrichen wird, dass es sich um das Handeln im Leibe handelt. Der Grund des Heils bleibt offensichtlich die durch die Geschichte Jesu Christi geoffenbarte Gnade Gottes, aber beurteilt wird das, was auf diesem Grund gebaut worden ist. So müssen wir es uns in Bezug auf die nächste Analogie in 1 Kor 3,10-15 vorstellen. Dort erklärt Paulus angesichts der Streite unter den einzelnen Gruppen innerhalb der korinthischen Gemeinde, dass das Gericht Gottes quer durch die einzelnen Menschen verläuft. Jeder wird sehen, was von dem, was er/sie getan hat, vor Gott besteht und was das Feuer des Gerichts verzehrt. Der im Glauben aufgenommene Grund, nämlich das, was Jesus in seiner Geschichte repräsentiert, wird allerdings bleiben. Wenn jemandem sein Werk verbrennt, wird er Schaden haben, wird aber „wie durch Feuer hindurch" gerettet. Wessen Werk bleibt, wird Lohn ($\mu\iota\sigma\theta\acute{o}\varsigma$) empfangen (V. 14). So müssen wir uns den Lohn auch hier, in 2 Kor 5,10 vorstellen.[57]

5. FOLGERUNGEN

Wie in 1 Kor 15, so wird auch in 1 Thess 4 und 2 Kor 5 die Eschatologie in der individuellen und der sozialen (die Geschichte betreffenden) Dimension theologisch reflektiert. Paulus hat dadurch die zwei Seiten der einen menschlichen Hoffnung definiert, die zum wesentlichen Teil der Anthropologie christlicher Kultur geworden sind: Der Mensch braucht es für etwas zu leben, was ihn transzendiert (die Sinngebung), und gleichzeitig möchte er nicht nur als Material zur Erreichung eines höheren (d.h. aber nicht-menschlichen) Ziels benutzt werden. Deswegen war die Auferstehung der Menschen erst am Ende der Geschichte erwartet, damit die einzelnen Menschen das Leben im neuen Äon (Reich Gottes), das sie in ihren Leben aktiv gesucht haben, in seiner Vollkommenheit als Gemeinschaft aller Generationen der Menschen mit dem einen Gott genießen können. Das Noch-nicht des Heils hängt eng mit

---

57. Eine andere, dem geistigen Enthusiasmus entsprechende Vorstellung von den Gläubigen, die in das Gericht nicht kommen, vertritt das Johannesevangelium in 5,24.

seiner Sozialität zusammen.[58] Schon in 1 Thess 4,15-18 ist die Sozialität der christlichen Hoffnung in der Gestalt der Sprache deutlich sichtbar: „Wir, die wir leben ... werden den Entschlafenen nicht zuvorkommen. Der Herr wird ... herabkommen vom Himmel...Danach werden wir... entrückt werden... dem Herrn entgegen; und so werden wir bei dem Herrn sein. So tröstet euch mit diesen Worten untereinander." Kein individuelles Heil und keine Auflösung in der Gottheit,[59] sondern eine Gemeinschaft, die dem Willen Gottes nach gestaltet wird.

Dadurch ist schon der Anlass zur theologischen Entfaltung der paulinischen Eschatologie und Soteriologie in 1 Kor 15 angedeutet. Die soziale Gestalt der Hoffnung ist gleichzeitig ein Modell zur Stärkung der Gemeinde als eines sozialen Ganzen, das aus verschiedenen Menschen besteht.[60] Die Enthusiasten werden dadurch aufgefordert, die Mitverantwortung für die ganze Gemeinde zu übernehmen.

Einige Forscher[61] haben schon auf den theologischen Zusammenhang der Ausführungen aus 1 Kor 15 mit der Ermahnung aus 1 Kor 11,17-22 gegen die Missstände beim Herrenmahl in Korinth hingewiesen. Das individuelle Essen bei gemeinsamen Herrenmahl und die Unfähigkeit mindestens innerhalb des Gottesdienstes, die sozialen Unterschiede zu überbrücken, hat dort praktisch eine Spaltung der Gemeinde verursacht. Schon in Gal 2,15-16 formulierte Paulus die Lehre von der Rechtfertigung aus der Gnade Gottes als Reaktion auf die Spaltung der Gemeinde beim gemeinsamen Essen (offensichtlich auch beim Herrenmahl), wie es in Gal 2,11-14 dargestellt wird. Das war und ist bisher leider das Problem der Kirche auf ihrem Wege durch die Geschichte.[62]

(Wenn nicht anders angegeben, sind die Bibelzitate in deutscher Übersetzung der Lutherbibel, Revision 1984, entnommen.)

---

58. Vgl. BRANDENBURGER, *Adam und Christus* (Anm. 10), pp. 71f.
59. HOFFMANN, *Die Toten in Christus* (Anm. 10), pp. 223f.
60. W. A. MEEKS, *The Temporary Reign of the Son: 1 Cor 15:23-28*, in T. FORNBERG – D. HELLHOLM (Hsg.), *Texts and Contexts* (FS L. Hartman), Oslo etc., Scandinavian University Press, 1995, 801-811, hier p. 804.
61. G. THEISSEN, *Soziale Integration und sakramentales Handeln. Eine Analyse von 1 Cor xi,17-34*, NT 16 (1974) 179-206; DERS., *Die Religion der ersten Christen* (Anm. 48), pp.218f.; vgl. MEEKS, *The Temporary Reign of the Son* (Anm. 60), p. 805.
62. Diese Studie entstand im Rahmen des Forschungsvorhabens „Geschichte und Interpretation der Bibel" (GA ČR P401/12/G168), gefördert von der Forschungsagentur der Tschechischen Republik (Czech Science Foundation).

2 CORINTHIANS 5,1-10 IN CONTEXT

Morna D. Hooker

It is disheartening, to say the least, to discover that the passage assigned to one for interpretation is described by commentators as "notoriously difficult",[1] or even as "arguably the most difficult passage in the whole Pauline corpus".[2] In view of the difficulties encountered elsewhere in the Pauline literature, comments such as these mean that one inevitably approaches these verses with considerable trepidation. Nor can any consideration of their meaning be confined to these verses alone, for they form one part of a much longer argument, itself a notoriously difficult section, and looking at them in isolation, as is sometimes done, is bound to distort them.

Since monographs continue to be written on these verses,[3] and the authors of multi-volume commentaries find it impossible to deal with all the issues,[4] it would obviously be foolish to attempt to analyze the passage in detail, or to seek a new interpretation of Paul's words. My purpose in this paper will therefore be to explore the extent to which the hope expressed in this passage corresponds with what Paul writes elsewhere.

The main issue that has been endlessly debated by commentators can be summed up in the question "Has Paul changed his mind?" In 1 Corinthians 15 his future hope is centred on the Parousia, and it seems clear that he himself expects to be alive at the Lord's return. Although some Christians will have died before then, all alike will be "changed in a flash" at his coming. Paul uses two images to describe this transformation: the first is that of resurrection – "the dead will be raised

---

1. C. K. Barrett, *A Commentary on The Second Epistle to the Corinthians* (BNTC), London, A&C Black, 1973, p. 150. So also Fredrik Lindgård, *Paul's Line of Thought in 2 Corinthians 4,16–5,10* (WUNT 2.189), Tübingen, Mohr (Paul Siebeck), 2005, p. 1.

2. Nigel Watson, *The Second Epistle to the Corinthians*, London, Epworth 1973, p. 49.

3. E.g. Lingård, *Line of Thought* (n. 1). A survey of the interpretation of the passage from Calvin to 1973 was made by F. G. Lang, *2.Korinther 5,1-10 in der Neueren Forschung* (BGBE 16), Tübingen, Mohr (Paul Siebeck), 1973. The literature was already immense.

4. See the comment by Margaret E. Thrall (in a two-volume commentary!), *The Second Epistle to the Corinthians*, Vol. 1 (ICC), Edinburgh, T&T Clark, 1994, p. 397, regarding the difficulty of doing this.

imperishable" (v. 52), and the second that of being clothed – "for this perishable body must be clothed with the imperishable, and the mortal with the immortal" (vv. 53f.). Both metaphors depend on what is the crucial central truth for Paul – that *the believer shares the experience of Christ*. Christians will be raised to life because Christ was raised; they will be "made alive in him" (vv. 20-23); they will be clothed with imperishability because they are to "wear the likeness of the heavenly man" (v. 49).

Resurrection is said to take place "at his coming" (v. 23), when "we shall all be changed" (v. 51), dead and living alike. Since the focus in this discussion is on this future resurrection, nothing is said about the condition of the dead *between* their death and resurrection, but since "all" are changed "in a moment, in the twinkling of an eye" (v. 52), it is clear that Paul regards the dead – like the living – as "perishable" and "mortal", and so in need of drastic change; their situation appears to be no more favourable than that of the living – but this is not an issue with which Paul is here concerned.

In 2 Cor 5,1-10, however, the focus has shifted from the Parousia to what will take place to Paul himself after death. Facing up to the possibility that he is likely to die before the Lord's return, Paul apparently expects his mortal body to be swallowed up by life at his death (5,1-5). Moreover, he now regards it as a positive personal advantage to be one of those whom the world would classify as "dead". He would rather, he declares, be "away from the body and at home with the Lord" than "at home in the body and away from the Lord" (vv. 6-9). This is strange language from one who expressed so strongly his joy in living with Christ and in Christ, but is perhaps explained by the image he uses in Phil 3,20, where he describes Christians as those who have their citizenship in heaven. However joyful his present experience of living in Christ, it is only a foretaste of a future reality, and to be "at home" with Christ – "in heaven" – will be even better.

In 1 Corinthians 15, then, Paul describes a sudden change that takes place at the Parousia, whereas in 2 Cor 5, 1-10 he depicts the culmination of a process which begins in this life, and is seemingly completed at death. There is an obvious tension between these two pictures. Is the lapse of time between the two letters sufficient to account for the change in outlook? Have recent events, such as his near-experience of death in Asia (2 Cor 1,8f.), changed Paul's perspective? That may well be true, though it is clear from 1 Cor 15,30-32, as well as from the long list of dangers in 2 Cor 11,23-9, that Paul had long been aware that his mission might end in premature death. Could it be, then, that 2 Corinthians 5 reflects a significant change in belief? The change in eschatological perspective was described by C. H. Dodd as a "definite change of outlook", and as of far more significance than a mere "readjustment ... of the eschatological time-table".[5] Others explain the different approach in 2 Corinthians as due, neither to a change in belief nor a simple change in perspective, but rather to the fact that in this letter he is concerned with a different issue.

Turning back to 1 Corinthians 15, we note that the number of Christians who have died has already grown since Paul wrote 1 Thessalonians, as we would expect with the passing of time. Whereas in 1 Thessalonians the death of Christians was apparently exceptional, Paul now says that "we shall not *all* die" (v. 51) – but since many have, he needs to explain what future resurrection means for them: it takes place at the Parousia, and involves "putting on" a new kind of body. By the time that 2 Corinthians 5 is written, Paul is facing the probability of his own death before the Parousia, but though that letter may reflect an increased expectancy of death on Paul's part, the real issue with which he is concerned there, and which is in fact the dominant theme of the whole letter, is the defence of his ministry. Confronted by accusations concerning his understanding of ministry, Paul defends himself by insisting that his words and actions are a proclamation of the crucified and glorified Christ. If he always carries the death of Jesus in his body, it is so that the life of Jesus may be seen in his body. The life-through-death that he experiences already in this life cannot be broken by his own death.

Paul's hope of future resurrection, which is based on Christ's resurrection, is, of course found in all his letters. In Romans, he is concerned with the question which he had discussed earlier, in Galatians, of the role of Israel, and God's purpose concerning Jews and Gentiles. As in Galatians, discussion in Romans is centred very much on Christian experience in the present. There is no mention in either letter of the Parousia

---

5. C. H. DODD, *The Mind of Paul*, in *New Testament Studies*, Manchester, Manchester University Press, 1953 (reprinted from *BJRL* 18 [1934]), 83-128, at p. 112. Dodd argues that differences between the epistles "represent real development, and are not merely the result of the circumstances of the particular aim of the several epistles" (p. 84). Contrast the view of John LOWE, who took issue with Dodd (among others) in a paper delivered to the Oxford Society of Historical Theology in May 1940 (subsequently published as *An Examination of Attempts to detect Developments in St Paul's Theology*, in *JTS* 42 [1941] 129–42). He wrote "with one minor exception, the evidence available does not enable us to trace any development whatever in St Paul's thinking from beginning to end" (p. 129).

as such, though there are references in Romans to the day of judgement (2,1-16) and the day of salvation, which is drawing near (13,11f.). The great eschatological passage in Rom 8 looks for a future resurrection (v. 11) and for the revelation of glory (v. 18), which surprisingly involves, not the revelation of God's Son, but that of God's sons (*sic*) and the restoration of creation (vv. 19-21). The climax of the passage comes with the declaration that neither death nor life nor anything else will be able to separate us from the love of God in Christ. Although the emphasis throughout Romans is on present experience, we see now that this is to become more intense hereafter, for what we enjoy at the moment is merely "the first fruits" of the Spirit. Present suffering cannot be compared with future glory (v. 18); we have already been saved, but it is in hope of something greater (vv. 24f.). And once again that hope is nothing less than a becoming like Christ – being conformed to the image of God's Son (v. 29).

In the well-known "hymn" of Philippians 2, Paul speaks of the exaltation of Christ rather than his resurrection (2,9), and so not surprisingly goes on to refer to Christians' future transformation into the likeness of Christ's glorious body, rather than of their resurrection (3,20f.).[6] Written towards the end of Paul's life,[7] this letter undermines the notion that Paul changed his mind in any significant way between writing 1 Corinthians 15 and 2 Corinthians 5, for although in Philippians 3 we find Paul affirming his hope in the Parousia (3,20f.),[8] when (as in 1 Corinthians 15) his body will be changed into the likeness of Christ's, this process has apparently already begun, since he speaks also of knowing already the power of Christ's resurrection as he shares the sufferings of Christ, and of being conformed to his death, in hope of attaining the resurrection from the dead (3,10f.). Moreover, a couple of chapters earlier, when considering the likely outcome of his impending trial, he declares that he would prefer to die and "be with Christ", than remain alive (1,20-6). If his trial ends with execution, then that will be for him a gain, since he will be "with Christ" in an even closer sense than at present.

Side by side, then, we find Paul expressing the hope of being with Christ immediately after death, the idea of a growing conformity to

---

6. But see 3,10f., below.

7. It seems far more likely that the letter was sent from Rome than from Ephesus or Caesarea, and thus was written when Paul faced a capital charge there. See the summary of the various arguments in Markus BOCKMUEHL, *The Epistle to the Philippians* (BNTC), London, A&C Black, 1997, pp. 25-32.

8. Cf. also the references to "the day of Christ" in 1,10 and 2,16.

Christ through present suffering, and the expectation of Christ's arrival from heaven, when our bodies will be transformed into his likeness. If these ideas co-exist in the same letter, it is clearly inappropriate to speak (as Dodd did) of Paul "changing his mind".[9] Nevertheless, his thinking on the future life may well have developed, as he thought through the implications of his faith in the light of events. The hopes he expresses in both 2 Corinthians 5 and Philippians 1 are clearly linked to his experiences – in the first case, his constant exposure to danger and to "wear and tear", in the second, the possibility of imminent execution. The change from thinking of himself as among the living at the Parousia (as in 1 Thessalonians 4) to realizing that he is unlikely to survive would naturally lead him to think out what might await him. Instead of thinking of death as a "sleep" (as in 1 Thess 5,10; 1 Cor 15,20), he describes it in his later letters as being "at home with the Lord" (2 Cor 5,9), or as being "with Christ" (Phil 1,23). It has sometimes been suggested that in 2 Corinthians Paul has abandoned Jewish "apocalyptic" and adopted Hellenistic ideas.[10] But is there perhaps a link that holds his various pictures of the afterlife together? To answer this question we need to look in greater detail at 2 Cor 5,1-10.

SHARING THE EXPERIENCE OF CHRIST

Before we examine that passage, however, we must look at what Paul says in one or two earlier passages. We begin with *1 Thessalonians*, where in 1,10 Paul introduces one of the main themes of the letter[11] when he reminds his readers that their response to the gospel had been "to turn to the true and living God from idols, and to wait eagerly for his Son – whom he had raised from the dead – to appear from heaven". Paul's chief concern in this letter is to reassure the Thessalonians that Christians who have died have not been lost (4,13),[12] and in v. 14 he

---

9. It is sometimes argued that chapters 1–2 and 3–4 belong to different letters, but the language and argument of chapter 3 pick up those of 2, demonstrating the unity of the letter. Moreover, there are parallels to both 1 Cor 15 and 2 Cor 5 in Phil 3.

10. This idea was famously explored by W. F. KNOX, *St Paul and the Church of the Gentiles*, Cambridge, Cambridge University Press, 1961, pp. 125-45.

11. Cf. M. D. HOOKER, *1 Thessalonians 1.9-10: a Nutshell – but What Kind of Nut?* in H. LICHTENBERGER (ed.), *Geschichte – Tradition – Reflexion: Festschrift für Martin Hengel zum 70. Geburtstag, Volume III Frühes Christentum*, Tübingen, J. C. B. Mohr (Paul Siebeck), 1996, 435-48.

12. The grief of the Thessalonians is most probably due to a fear that Christians who have died have missed out on salvation, not simply that they will in some way be disadvantaged at the Parousia, as is argued among others by A. F. J. KLIJN, *1 Thessalonians 4,13–18 and its*

assures them that "God will bring *with Jesus* those who have fallen asleep". Paul's conviction depends on the fact that "Jesus died and rose" – a summary which may well be an early creed, since it refers to "Jesus" rather than "Christ" (as is more normal in Paul) and uses the verbs in the active, not passive. The link between belief in Christ's death and resurrection and the hope that God will bring with Christ those Christians who have died is expressed in the words οὕτως καὶ. Logically, we expect Paul to say "Christ died and rose; even so those who have died (with Christ) will be raised", but instead he speaks of God *bringing* "with Jesus those who have fallen asleep".

There is considerable debate as to whether the phrase διὰ τοῦ Ἰησοῦ in v. 14 should be taken with "fallen asleep" or with "bring"; the latter suggestion makes the phrase seem awkward and redundant, since σὺν αὐτῷ is already attached to that verb, but if it is correct, it stresses the role of Christ. Taking it with "fallen asleep" is often regarded as difficult,[13] but perhaps Paul uses it to stress the fact that those who have fallen asleep were *already united with Christ*: those who fall asleep through Jesus – or "in Jesus"[14] – will be *brought with him*. Although Best argues that "it seems rather late in the passage to identify the dead as the Christian dead",[15] it would surely have seemed important to make this identification, since Paul is distinguishing between pagans (v. 13), who had no hope for the dead, and the Thessalonians, who *did* have (or *should* have had!) hope for those fellow-Christians who had died. Whichever way we take the phrase, however, Paul affirms that Christians who have "fallen asleep" will be brought with Christ, and that *this depends on the fact that Christ died and rose*.

Background, in M. D. HOOKER and S. G. WILSON (ed.), *Paul and Paulinism: Essays in honour of C.K. Barrett*, London, SPCK, 1982, 67-73, and by J. DELOBEL, *The Fate of the Dead According to 1 Thes 4 and 1 Cor 15*, 340-47, in Raymond F. COLLINS (ed.), *The Thessalonian Correspondence*, Leuven, Leuven University Press, 1990, 340-347. Whichever interpretation is adopted, however, Paul is reassuring the Thessalonians about the fate of Christians who have died. See, on this verse, a paper contributed to an earlier meeting of the Pauline Colloquium: J.M.G. BARCLAY, *Death and Early Christian Identity*, in Morna D. HOOKER (ed.), *Not in the Word Alone: The First Epistle to the Thessalonians* (Monographic Series of *Benedictina* 15), St Paul's Abbey, Rome 2003, 131-53.

13. See, e.g., the discussion by E. BEST, *A Commentary on The First and Second Epistle to the Thessalonians* (BNTC), London, A&C Black 1972, pp. 188f.

14. Charles MASSON, *Les deux épîtres de Saint Paul aux Thessaloniciens* (CNT 11a), Neuchâtel/Paris, Delachaux & Niestlé, 1957, pp. 55f., insisted that διὰ τοῦ Ἰησοῦ should not be equated with ἐν Χριστῷ, but the meaning of the phrases is often similar: see 1 Thess 4,2, where we might have expected Paul to write ἐν Χριστῷ, and 1 Cor 1,10.

15. *1-2 Thessalonians* (n. 13), p. 189.

There has been considerably less debate as to what is meant by the statement that God will bring the Christian dead with Christ. It is generally assumed that this is a reference to the Parousia, and that Paul is thinking of Christ's return to earth. If Christ brings them to earth with him, does this mean that Paul is already thinking of the dead as in some sense enjoying being "with him" immediately after death, as in 2 Cor 5,8f. and Phil 1,23? But in fact Paul has not yet mentioned the Parousia, and we should beware of assuming that he is already thinking of Christ's return to earth. If that is what he meant, he would most naturally have written: "*Christ* will bring with him those who have died". In fact he stresses the action of *God*, and it therefore seems more probable that he is thinking of Christ's final exaltation into heaven, taking believers with him, rather than of the Parousia.[16] Otherwise, we have the strange notion that the dead-in-Christ are brought back to earth at the Parousia, simply in order to be raised! Paul is *not*, after all, describing a 3-stage programme for the events surrounding the Parousia, running:

1) God brings the dead-in-Christ to earth with him (vv. 13f.).
2) When Christ returns, the dead-in-Christ are then raised (v. 16).
3) Living Christians are then caught up into the clouds to meet the Lord, together with the dead-in-Christ (v. 17).

Rather, he is expressing his conviction about Christians who have died *in two different ways*. First, in vv. 13f., he contrasts the grief of pagans with the hope of Christians, and what this hope means, assuring the Thessalonians that God will "bring" these "sleeping" Christians with Christ (into God's presence?). Having affirmed this, Paul then quotes a "word of the Lord" to the effect that the living will have no precedence over the dead, and goes on to describe, with apocalyptic imagery, how this is so (vv. 15-17): "The Lord will descend from heaven, and the dead-in-Christ will be raised, following which we who are alive will be caught up *with them* to meet the Lord. And so we shall be with the Lord for ever."

It seems more probable, then, that when Paul says, in v. 14, that "God will bring with him those who have died", *he is thinking of Christ's final return to heaven, not of the Parousia*. The dead-in-Christ will be brought with Christ into God's presence by God himself, following the

---

16. So, e.g., E. von DOBSCHÜTZ, *Die Thessalonicher-Briefe* (MeyerK 10), Göttingen, Vandenhoeck & Ruprecht, 1909, p. 191f.; James Everett FRAME, *The Epistles of St. Paul to the Thessalonians* (ICC), Edinburgh, T&T Clark, 1912, pp. 170f.; B. RIGAUX, *Les épîtres aux Thessaloniciens* (EBib) Paris, Gabalda, 1956, p. 537.

resurrection. This, incidentally, makes more sense, not only of the fact that Paul uses both διὰ τοῦ Ἰησοῦ and σὺν αὐτῷ, but also of the οὕτως καί: just as Christ died and rose, *even so* will God exalt the dead-in-Christ (διὰ τοῦ Ἰησοῦ) *with* Christ (σὺν αὐτῷ) into his presence. Resurrection and exaltation belong together. The resurrection of Christ is truly a guarantee of what is still to come.

That this is the true meaning of ἄξει seems confirmed by a comparison with 2 Cor 4,14,[17] "for we know that he who raised the Lord Jesus will raise us also with Jesus, and bring us, with you, into his presence". As in 1 Thess 4,14, all is dependent on the death and resurrection of Jesus, and as there, God "brings" us – this time, specifically, into his presence (παραστήσει). The main difference is the fact that the two groups here are referred to, not as "the dead" and "the living", but as "us" and "you" – presumably because Paul has just been describing how he is being given up to death, "so that death is at work in us, but life in you"; he now realizes that he is likely to be among the dead, rather than the living. In 2 Cor 4,14, Paul compresses his earlier double explanation into one sentence:

1 Thess 4,14, we believe that Jesus died and rose again;
2 Cor 4,14, the one who raised the Lord Jesus
1 Thess 4,16, the dead in Christ will rise.
2 Cor 4,14, will raise us also with Jesus,
1 Thess 4,14, God will bring with him those who have fallen asleep;
2 Cor 4,14, and will bring us with you
1 Thess 4,17, we shall be with the Lord for ever.
2 Cor 4,14, into his presence.

1 Thess 4,14, then, is not a reference to the Parousia, but an assurance that the dead-in-Christ will be brought into God's presence, an assurance that is then repeated, though expressed differently, in "the word of the Lord" which follows. It is noticeable that, in his attempt to explain how it is that the dead will not be disadvantaged, Paul uses language in these verses which is picked up later in both 1 and 2 Corinthians.

In the following chapter, Paul warns the Thessalonians about the coming "Day of the Lord". Christians can expect it to be a day of salvation, not wrath, because "our Lord Jesus Christ died for us, so that whether we are awake or asleep we may live with him". Once again, he insists

---

17. The parallel is noted by Joseph PLEVNIK, *Paul and the Parousia*: *An Exegetical and Theological Investigation*, Peabody MA, Hendrickson, 1997, p. 74.

that there is no distinction between those who are alive and those who are dead, and once again he speaks of being "with Christ". The credal summary is expressed in the familiar format of the so-called "interchange" passages: "Christ died for us, *in order that* we might live with him".[18] But as in similar passages, this is *not an exchange*: Paul writes, *not* "Christ died, in order that we might live," but Christ died, in order that we might live *with him*". In other words, Christians share his resurrection: by sharing our human death, Christ enabled us to share his life. The credal statement has been curtailed, since what Paul clearly means (as in 4,14) is "Christ died and rose". In 4,14, the conclusion drawn from the credal summary was that since Jesus died and rose, God will bring the Christian dead *with him* (i.e. as sharers in his resurrection); here, it is that we may live *with him*. Does this refer to a life here and now – the dead "in heaven", the living on earth? It is more probable, in view of the context, that Paul is thinking of the life that follows the Day of the Lord. He is once again assuring the Thessalonians that the dead in Christ share "the hope of salvation" (5,8).

In 1 Thessalonians 4–5, then, Paul expresses the eschatological hope in three different ways: the dead-in-Christ will be brought into God's presence "with Christ"; they will be raised at his coming, and be caught up – with the living – in the clouds to meet the Lord; and they will live "with him".

2 Thessalonians, though largely concerned with eschatology, has nothing to say that is relevant to our purpose apart from 2,1, where the author (who may or may not have been Paul) discusses "the Parousia of our Lord Jesus Christ and our being gathered to him". This image is closest to 1 Thess 4,17, where believers are to be "caught up in the clouds ... to meet the Lord", but adds nothing to the picture found there.

We turn next to *1 Corinthians 15*, where we have Paul's fullest statement of what he understands by future resurrection. The problem Paul addresses appears to be very similar to that which caused the problem in Thessalonika – a failure to grasp Paul's teaching about future resurrection. In 1 Thess 4,13, he spoke of non-believers as those who had no hope. Here, he describes those whose hope in Christ is confined to this world as pitiable, since their faith is vain. His argument stresses the link between Christ's death and resurrection and our own – a link which we have already seen in 1 Thess 4,14 and 5,10:

---

18. See M.D. HOOKER, *From Adam to Christ: Essays on Paul*, Cambridge, Cambridge University Press, 1990. Cf. Irenaeus *Adv. Haer.* 5 praef.

If there is no resurrection of the dead, then Christ has not been raised.
That means that our gospel and your faith are empty.
If the dead are not raised, Christ has not been raised.
That means that your faith is futile,
and those who have fallen asleep in Christ have perished (vv. 12-19).

He goes on to insist that Christ *has* been raised, and that – as in 1 Thess 4,16 – those who belong to him will be raised at his coming (vv. 20-23). Paul's own hope of resurrection is demonstrated in his willingness to face constant danger (vv. 30-33).

But what does Paul mean by future resurrection? Paul spells out his answer to this question in vv. 35-58. At the heart of this description is his conviction that Christians will bear the image of Christ himself. Since their resurrection depends on his (vv. 12-19), it is hardly surprising that their resurrection body will be like his. The link is established in the use of Adam/ Christ imagery: as all die in Adam, so all will be made alive in Christ (v. 22); as we have borne the image of the man of dust (Adam) so we will bear the image of the man of heaven (Christ, vv. 45-9).

Paul's imagery stresses both the continuity between what dies and what is raised, and the differences between them, expressed in a series of opposites. In spelling out what he believes will happen, Paul uses two metaphors; the first is taken from horticulture, and speaks of sowing a bare grain, which then comes to life (v. 37). The metaphor is appropriate in speaking of the dead, who are "sown" and then "raised", and is spelt out in a series of contrasts between what is sown and what is raised. The naked seed is exchanged for a living plant, dishonour and weakness give way to glory and power, the physical body to a spiritual body. All this is necessary because flesh and blood cannot inherit the kingdom of God, and neither can the perishable inherit what is imperishable (v. 50). But this principle applies to the living, as well as to those who have "fallen asleep", which means that, although "we shall not all die, we will all be changed" (v. 51). Paul next describes what this means for those who are alive at the Parousia. We too (for Paul includes himself among their number) will be changed (v. 52); Paul now uses the metaphor of dressing – the perishable body will put on (ἐνδύω) imperishability, and the mortal body immortality (vv. 53-4). So death will be swallowed up in victory. It should be noted that whereas the metaphor of sowing entailed a dramatic exchange, that of clothing means a "putting" on of something over what presently exists. The former is appropriate when talking about the resurrection of the dead (the main question under discussion), the latter when describing what happens to those who are alive at the Parousia.

Nevertheless, both groups are going to be changed, and take on the image of Christ.

In this section (1 Cor 15,42-54), then, we have a series of contrasts:
Perishable/imperishable
Dishonour/glory
Weakness/power
Physical/spiritual
First Adam/last Adam
Living physical being/life-giving spirit
From earth/from heaven
Mortal/immortal.

If we are to bear the image of the man from heaven (glory, power, etc.), it is because he himself first bore the image of the man from earth (dishonour, weakness, etc.). In the familiar words of Irenaeus,[19] Christ became what we are, in order that we might become what he is. Paul will pick up much of the language used in this chapter in 2 Corinthians.

We have noted already that *Galatians* makes no reference to the Parousia. The emphasis throughout the letter is very much on believers' present experience. The Galatians have already been set free from the present evil age (1,3), have already been set free from slavery and been adopted as God's children (4,1-7). Paul's language in the second passage stresses the link between Christ and ourselves: God has sent his Son, in order that we might become his sons (*sic*, 4,4f.); it is in Christ Jesus that we are God's sons (*sic*, 3,26), for those who have been baptized into Christ have clothed themselves with Christ (3,27). The verb (ἐνδύω) reappears in 1 Cor 15,53f., but there, as we have seen, it is used of what takes place at the Parousia, whereas here it refers to what happened at baptism. *Already, then, we have in some sense taken on Christ's image.* In the case of the Galatians, however, this is far from complete, since Paul declares that he is once again "in labour" with them until Christ is formed in them. Of his own experience, he says that he has been crucified with Christ, and so lives no longer: rather, Christ lives in him.[20] Yet this is only one way of expressing it, since either side of this statement he declares that having died to the law he now lives to God, and that the life he now lives he lives by trust in the Son of God (2,19f.). Whether it

---

19. *Adv. Haer.* 5 praef.
20. A similar idea is expressed in 1,16 if we give ἐν its most natural meaning, and understand Paul to be saying that it pleased God to reveal his Son *in* him or through him – i.e. in his life and mission.

is Paul who lives to God, or Christ who lives in him, we have here words that will be echoed in 2 Cor 5,15, "He died for all, in order that the living might no longer live for themselves, but for him who died and was raised for their sake."

Life in Christ is therefore a present experience for Paul, as is life in the Spirit (3,1-5), under whose guidance the Galatians are urged to live (5,16-26). At the same time, however, the Spirit is a guarantee of what lies in the future. Through the Spirit, we are assured that we are God's sons (*sic*), and so heirs of God's promises (4,6). Those born of the Spirit are children of the inheritance (4,28-30). Through the Spirit we await the *hope* of righteousness (5,5), and that hope is to inherit the kingdom of God (5,21); in other words, if we live by the Spirit rather than the flesh, our reward will be eternal life (6,8).

Paul's concern in Galatians is not with the Parousia, but with the issue of circumcision and obedience to the Law. It is not surprising, then, that the emphasis is on the present. At the same time, however, we see the tension which characterizes all his letters, between present Christian experience on the one hand and hope for the future on the other.

In *Romans*, this tension pervades the whole argument, especially in chapters 5–8. Although Paul refers to the coming day of wrath (2,5), the day of judgement (2,16), and the day of salvation (13,11f.), he makes no attempt to describe what takes place when the Lord returns. At the end of chapters 1–4, which discuss God's dealings with Jews and Gentiles, he concludes with a credal summary which declares that "God raised Jesus our Lord from the dead" (4,25). This leads on to the conclusion, introduced in 5,1 with a triumphant "Therefore": Therefore, since we have already obtained access to grace, we boast *in hope of sharing the glory of God*. The tension between what we already have and what we still hope for is set out in vv. 9-10:

We *have been* "rightwised" by his blood,
we *will be* saved through him from the wrath of God.
We *were* reconciled to God through the death of his Son,
we *will be* saved by his life.

How this happens is then spelt out in terms of a contrast between Adam and Christ. Adam's sin led to death for all, but the grace of God, effective though Christ, means that the situation has been reversed. On the one hand, we have Adam's disobedience, on the other, Christ's obedience. Whereas Adam's sin led to condemnation and death for all, Christ's righteous act has led to acquittal and life for all. Sin is replaced by grace, which leads to eternal life. In this passage Paul picks up the contrast between Adam and Christ which he used in 1 Cor 15,20-22 and 42-9, and spells out the difference between them, not in terms of "physical" and "spiritual", but in terms of "obedience" and "disobedience", "sin" and "righteousness" – a contrast which was only hinted at in 1 Corinthians (15,17. 56), since Paul's concern there was to reassure his readers about the coming Resurrection.

What Christ's reversal of Adam's fall means for the Christian is explained in chapter 6. In being baptized into Christ, we have been baptized into his death – buried with him into death, so that, as Christ was raised, "we too might walk in newness of life. For if we have been united with the form of his death, we shall also be united with his resurrection" (vv. 3-5). These verses encapsulate the tension of the Christian life: already dead to sin, already buried with Christ, already sharing in his risen life, and yet not *fully* sharing his resurrected life, since conformity to his resurrection lies in the future.[21] But this future life is important for Paul's argument. "Eternal life" was the goal of 5,21, and in 6,8 we are reminded again of the eschatological goal: "if we have died with Christ, we believe that we shall also live with him". That is why, in this present life, "you must consider yourselves dead to sin and alive to God in Christ Jesus" (v. 11).

In chapter 8, Paul spells out at length his future hope. Once again, this is firmly rooted in what God has already done, and so we are aware of the eschatological tension between what characterizes Christians' lives here and now, and what awaits them in the future. God sent his Son in the likeness of our sinful flesh to deal with sin, and the result is that we, who live according to the Spirit, and not according to the flesh, are set free from the power of sin (vv. 3f.). Moreover, this Spirit is the guarantee that the one who raised Jesus from the dead will give life to our mortal bodies (v. 11). As in 6,5, it is possible to take this as referring to "the vivifying energy of the Spirit"[22] in the present life, but most commentators take it to refer to the future resurrection.[23] The Spirit is the spirit of

---

21. It is possible (so Franz J. LEENHARDT, *The Epistle to the Romans: A Commentary*, ET London, Lutterworth, 1961, in loc.) to take the future indicative ἐσόμεθα in v. 5 as logical – "we must be" – and so as a reference to the present, but most commentators agree that this does not fit the context. C. E.B. CRANFIELD, *The Epistle to the Romans* (ICC), Vol. 1, Edinburgh, T&T Clark, 1975, in loc., understands it to refer to the moral life (as v. 4 suggests), but v. 8 clearly has a future reference.

22. LEENHARDT, *Romans* (n. 21), p. 210.

23. E.g. E. KÄSEMANN, *An die Römer* (HNT 8a), Tübingen, Mohr (Paul Siebeck), 1980, ET *Commentary on Romans*, London, SCM 1980, in loc.; CRANFIELD, *Romans* (n. 21), in loc.

adoption (υἱοθεσία), so that we, too, are sons (*sic*) of God (vv. 15f.). And yet we still *await* adoption (v. 23)! This time the word υἱοθεσία refers to "the redemption of our bodies". Although we already know ourselves to be God's children, the whole of creation awaits "the revelation of the sons of God" (v. 19). This dual use of υἱοθεσία, together with the ambiguity of verses such as 6,5 and 8,11, demonstrates again the eschatological tension that pervades the whole section. Paul's admonitions are not merely "Be what you are", as Bultmann so famously expressed it, but "Be what you *will* be" – or rather, since the Christian life is a process, "Be what you are becoming". Paul himself neatly sums this tension up in v. 24, "you were saved in hope", and the hope is that Christians will be conformed to the image of his Son (v. 29). Yet clearly this hope, although defined in v. 24 as future, is in some sense already being realized, for the verbs he uses in v. 30 are all aorists. It is unsurprising to find Christians described as having been predestined, called, and "rightwised", but in what sense have they *already* been glorified? As recently as v. 17 glorification was set out as a future promise. Is this aorist used merely in order to express certainty? Or is it rather that there is a sense in which glory is not simply a future hope, but something already in the process of realization – as in 2 Cor 3,18? Christians are already "sons" of God, and so conformed (if not fully) to the image of his Son. But this glory remains hidden until the day when the sons of God are revealed (v. 19). This section of Romans ends with the confident declaration that nothing in all creation – including death itself – can separate us from the love of God in Christ Jesus our Lord. What this means in terms of post-mortem existence he is not here concerned to explain.

In another of Paul's late letters, *Philippians*, we find that he several times refers to "the Day of Christ", which is a day of judgement (1,6.10; 2,16). This day is apparently imminent, since in Phil 4,5 Paul writes that "the Lord is near". In 3,20f., he again expresses his hope for Christ's Parousia, declaring that we are expecting our Saviour, the Lord Jesus Christ, from heaven, and that he will transform our bodies of humiliation, conforming them to his own body of glory (v. 21).[24] As in 1 Corinthians 15, then, it is at the Parousia that believers are to be transformed into Christ's likeness. Christ will effect a change in our "body", but instead of speaking of perishable/imperishable and mortal/immortal, Paul

---

24. The language of v. 21 picks up that of 2,6-11: μετασχηματίσει, ταπεινώσεως, σύμμορφον, δόξης, πάντα.

uses the language of humiliation and glory – language picked up from the so-called "hymn" of 2,6-11. Paul's description of what he hopes for in 3:20f. needs to be read alongside this earlier passage, in which Christ is said to have taken the form of a slave and the likeness of men, and to have humbled himself to a shameful death on a cross. It is *because* (διό) he did this that God exalted him (vv. 9-11) – and it is because he has been exalted above all things that he is able to conform us to his likeness, through the power given to him at his exaltation. Here we have a powerful expression of what some of us have termed "interchange" – *not* an exchange, but an *inter*change of experience – whereby the fact that Christ identifies himself with humanity – becoming what we are – enables us to share in what he is.[25] This too, in different language, is the understanding of redemption expressed in terms of the First and Last Adams in 1 Corinthians.

When Paul writes in Phil. 3,20f. that "we are expecting a Saviour", who "will transform the body of our humiliation", he appears once again to number himself among those who will be alive at the Parousia, as he did in 1 Thess 4,15 and 1 Cor 15,52f.[26] Yet his survival is far from certain, as Phil 1,12-26 makes plain. The subject here is Paul's forthcoming trial. Philippians may well be Paul's last letter, in which case it was probably written from prison in Rome.[27] Certainly it is in Philippians 1, more clearly than anywhere else, that he confronts the possibility of his imminent death. He looks forward to his coming trial, in the confident expectation that he will be enabled to speak with boldness, and will not be put to shame (1,20). He is apparently facing a capital charge and wondering what the outcome will be – and what he should hope for. "To me," he writes, "to live is Christ and to die is gain (κέρδη)". The statement that "to live is Christ" recalls what he wrote in Gal 2,20, while his conviction that "to die is gain" is similar to the hope expressed in 2 Cor 5,8. His words are also reminiscent of his argument in 1 Thessalonians, where he assured his readers that Christians who had fallen asleep would not be at a disadvantage: now, however, he considers it a positive

---

25. Cf. Irenaeus, *Adv. Haer.* 5 praef.
26. Even if, as some suggest, vv. 20f. are a non-Pauline fragment (so John REUMANN, *Philippians 3,20-21 – a Hymnic Fragment*, in *NTS* 30 [1984] 593–609), Paul presumably includes himself when reciting an article of faith.
27. Philippians appears to be Paul's "final testimony". See Morna D. HOOKER, *Philippians: Phantom Opponents and the Real Source of Conflict*, in Ismo DUNDERBERG, Christopher TUCKETT, and Kari SYREENI, *Fair Play: Diversity and Conflicts in Early Christianity: Essays in Honour of Heikki Räisänen*, Leiden/Boston/Köln, Brill, 2002, 377-395.

advantage to die! "My own desire", he writes, "is to depart and be with Christ". Yet he thinks that the Churches need him, and that he should therefore "choose" to remain; it would seem that his actions are governed, not by what he himself wants, but by what will serve others. Is Paul here deliberately modelling himself on Christ's example, which he describes in 2,1-11? Certainly he portrays his own Christian life in Philippians 3 in terms that suggest he saw it as a conscious "imitation" of Christ[28] – and there, too, he rejects what might have seemed "gain" (κέρδη) for something better (v. 7).

In Philippians 1, then, the idea that he will be "with" Christ in a closer sense after death is dominant, as in 2 Cor 5,6-10, and it is in no sense dependent on the Parousia. But in chapter 3, Paul confidently awaits the Parousia! Yet the transformation that awaits believers when the Lord appears is not totally new, but the completion of a process described in 3,7-17. Paul's purpose is "to be found in Christ" (3,9), and "to know the power of his resurrection, by sharing his sufferings and becoming like him in death" (v. 10). "Our citizenship is in heaven", writes Paul in 3,20, using a noun (πολίτευμα) which picks up the verb used in 1,27 (πολιτεύεσθε). Those who live as citizens of heaven are *already* being conformed to the likeness of Christ, as Paul's argument in chapters 2 and 3 makes clear.

Philippians, we have suggested, may well be Paul's last letter. Although some may argue for an earlier date, that would not help the hypothesis that Paul abandoned expectation of an imminent Parousia after writing 1 Thessalonians and 1 Corinthians, and came to believe instead in a transformation which took place immediately after death, unless one assumed also that Philippians consists of more than one letter, and that chapters 1 and 2 were written considerably later than chapters 3-4.[29] As we have noted, however, chapters 1 and 2 themselves contain references to the "Day of the Lord"! Philippians alone, therefore, should persuade us that it is incorrect to suggest that Paul "changed his mind" in-between writing 1 Corinthians and 2 Corinthians.

---

28. Paul picks up the verb ἡγοῦμαι from 2,6, and uses it to refer to what, as a Christian, he considered to be worthless; whereas the result of Christ's decision was that he was found in the fashion of a man (εὑρεθῶ, 2,7), Paul is found in Christ (3,9). His aim is to be conformed to Christ's death (συμμορφιζόμενς τῷ θανάτῳ αὐτοῦ, 3,10), picking up language used in 2,6-8. The final goal is expressed in 3,21, in language which echoes the vocabulary of the whole hymn: see n. 24 above.

29. The suggested division of the letter at 3,2 is unconvincing, however, since there are close links between chapters 2 and 3.

This brief survey of Paul's letters (apart from 2 Corinthians) has demonstrated that it is impossible to trace a change in Paul's outlook, and that what appear to modern scholars to be incompatible images are used side by side. These are always relevant to the particular point that Paul is making, and are influenced both by his readers' circumstances and his own. Moreover, whether Paul is describing changes that occur at the Parousia or at death, his hopes are expressed in language that he uses elsewhere of his present experience as someone who now lives "in Christ".

2 CORINTHIANS 5

We come, finally, to 2 Cor 5,1-10 – but these verses are only a short section in a much longer passage in which Paul is defending his ministry, and cannot be rightly understood without seeing them in that context. It is misleading to treat them as a "digression", as do some commentators.[30] Although Paul is clearly already on the defensive in chapters 1 and 2, his argument really begins in 3,1 with the comparison between the ministry of the old covenant, entrusted to Moses, and the ministry of the new, entrusted to himself. With extraordinary boldness, he compares his own behaviour in openly proclaiming "the gospel of the glory of Christ" (4,4) with that of Moses, who concealed God's glory from the Israelites with a veil (3,13). The glory of the earlier ministry of condemnation, which led to death, is nothing in comparison with the glory of the ministry which leads to righteousness, and so to life (3,4-11). This glory is fully revealed in Christ, and those who turn to him not only see his glory but reflect it, while they are "transformed into the same image, from one degree of glory to another" (3,12-18). The glory glimpsed by Moses and now fully revealed is of course the glory of God himself, and if it is revealed in Christ, that is because he is the image of God (4,4). The light first seen at creation now shines in Christ, and has shone in the hearts of believers (4,1-6). Christians are therefore being recreated after God's own image – restored to what God intended them to be. Paul explains here how transformation into the likeness of Christ and

---

30. The term is, for example, used of these verses by BARRETT, *2 Corinthians* (n. 1), in loc. The vast majority of commentators treat them as a separate paragraph, but Furnish is surely right in refusing to regard 5,1 as marking a break in the argument; see Victor Paul FURNISH, *II Corinthians* (Anchor Bible), Garden City NY, Doubleday, 1986, in loc.

glorification are a *present* experience for Christians.[31] The creative light of Christ has *already* shone into them. He picks this up in 5,17, when he sums up his argument: "if anyone is in Christ, there is a new creation. Everything old has passed away; see! new things have come into being." In the verses in between, however, he spells out the paradoxical nature of that experience in his own life, which means that (in conformity to the pattern of Christ) he is handed over to death in order to bring life to others (4,10-12). Whatever happens to him is a means of spreading the gospel, and so glorifies God (4,13-15).

Paul's claim, then, is that he proclaims the glory of Christ, not only in his message, but in his life, since he himself reflects the message of the gospel.[32] To the Corinthians, however, Paul's claims do not seem to correspond with reality. No-one looking at him would regard him as glorious! This "treasure" is, he confesses, contained in "clay jars" (4,7). He admits that he is afflicted, perplexed, persecuted, struck down (4,8f.). How, then, can he claim to reflect Christ's glory? The answer is that he interprets all these experiences as "always carrying in his body the dying of Jesus – in order that, in his body, the life of Jesus may be revealed" – an idea so important that he spells it out again (4,10f.). By sharing in Christ's death – not only in baptism but in his ministry – Paul is enabled to share in his life, and so weakness and shame are turned into strength and glory. But this is not all, since this life overflows to others: "death is at work in us but life in you" (v. 12).

Some commentators suggest that this could mean that Paul expects to die before the Parousia, while the Corinthians will survive,[33] but there appears to be a direct causative link between Paul's sufferings and the "life" that is at work in them. It is an idea that has already been expressed in the opening lines of the epistle, where Paul speaks of the consolation given to him in his affliction – consolation which allows him to console others who are themselves being afflicted:

> For as the sufferings of Christ overflow to us, so, through Christ, our consolation overflows to you. For if we are afflicted, it is for your comfort and salvation; if we are comforted, it is for your comfort.

In much the same way, the author of Colossians (who may or may not be Paul himself) speaks of *suffering for the sake of Christ's body, the*

---

31. Cf. Rom 8,30.
32. Cf. the probable meaning of Gal 1,16, "It pleased God to reveal his Son *in* me".
33. DODD, *The Mind of Paul* (n. 5), pp. 110f.

Church, and describes this as "completing", in his flesh, "the sufferings of Christ" (Col 1,24).³⁴

Paul's defence of his ministry is clearly rooted in his understanding of the gospel, which was, quite simply, "Jesus Christ, and him crucified" (1 Cor 2,1). Yet this apparently foolish message was the power and wisdom of God (1 Cor 1,18-25), since he had raised Christ from the dead. Now Paul claims that his own life has taken on the pattern of the gospel, since he experiences life in the midst of death. Even more than this, *because he is in Christ, and shares his risen life, he becomes a mediator of Christ's risen life to the Corinthians.*³⁵

But now Paul turns to the future. He shares the faith of the Psalmist, who believed, and therefore spoke. Paul, too, proclaims what he believes – and what he believes is expressed in another credal formula: "he who raised the Lord Jesus will raise us also with Jesus, and make us stand, with you, before himself" (4,13f.). The reasoning corresponds with that in 1 Thessalonians 4 and 5 and 1 Corinthians 15, and Paul is surely referring to the final, future, resurrection. His words echo 1 Thess 4,16f., and suggest a distinction between what will happen to "us" and to "you", but this time Paul includes himself among those who will be raised. The Corinthians may well still be alive at the Parousia, even if he is not – but as in 1 Thess 4,17, they will *all* be in God's presence. He then reminds the Corinthians that his motive for all his actions is not simply his own vindication, but their salvation, and the glorification of God (4,15).

The "therefore" (διό) in v. 16 indicates that *the reason that Paul does not lose heart lies in his belief in the future resurrection.* Already, in the present, his "outer man" is wasting away, but his "inner man" is being renewed day by day. The word ἄνθρωπος picks up the word which Paul used in 1 Cor 15,21 and 42-49, in the contrast between Adam and Christ.³⁶ In other words, what he spoke of there as a future event is seen here as a process that has already begun. Already he is taking on "the

---

34. Cf. the essay by W. F. FLEMINGTON, *On the interpretation of Colossians 1:24*, in William HORBURY and Brian MCNEIL, *Suffering and Martyrdom in the New Testament: Studies presented to G. M. Styler by the Cambridge New Testament Seminar*, Cambridge, Cambridge University Press, 1981, 84-90.

35. For further discussion of this theme see Morna D. HOOKER, *A Partner in the Gospel: Paul's Understanding of his Ministry*, in Eugene H. LOVERING, Jr. & Jerry L. SUMNEY (ed.), *Theology and Ethics in Paul and His Interpreters: Essays in Honor of Victor Paul Furnish*, Nashville TN, Abingdon, 1996, 83–100.

36. He uses it again in Rom 5,12-19, again with reference to the contrast between Adam and Christ. The phrase κατὰ τὸν ἔσω ἄνθροπος is also used in Rom 7,22, but in a very different context and contrast.

image of the heavenly" (1 Cor 15,49), for he has seen the glory of the Lord in Christ, and "is being transformed into the same image" (2 Cor 3,18). Yet Paul's present experience is only a foretaste of the future reality. The eternal weight of glory that is prepared for Christians is overwhelmingly greater than their present affliction. What can be seen is temporary, while the unseen is eternal (vv. 17f.).

The link to 5,1 is made with the word γάρ, since what follows is a continuation of the argument, though the image of "earthenware pots", used in 4,7, has given way to that of a temporary dwelling. "What is seen" is now described as an "earthly house – a tent", while "what is unseen" is "a building from God, a dwelling not made with hands, eternal, in the heavens". It is impossible within the constraints of this paper to debate the extent to which Paul might have adopted "Greek" ideas.[37] The suggestion that he is thinking in Hellenistic terms of the body as the dwelling-place of the soul, which is released from it on death, seems unlikely, however, since the hope he expresses here is not for the release of the soul, but rather for the exchange of his present dwelling for a better one[38] – the hope, that is, which is expressed in different language, in 1 Corinthians 15.

The use of the term σκῆνος and the idea of a house not made with hands reminds us of the saying about the temple attributed to Jesus in Mark 14,58 (cf. John 2,19-22), and there are possible echoes also of Paul's image of believers as "God's temple" in 1 Cor 3,16f. and 6,19. Whatever the origin of his terms, he here affirms his belief that, even if he dies, he will "have" (ἔχομεν) an eternal building from God in heaven.[39] What is not yet clear is whether he now expects to inhabit this building immediately after death, or whether he will have to wait for the Parousia. The significance of the verb ἔχομεν has been the subject of intense debate: does Paul's use of the present tense mean that he is now thinking of an immediate transformation, taking place at the moment of death,[40] or is it to be understood as an indication of his certainty about

---

37. For discussion of this point, see the commentaries.
38. Jan LAMBRECHT, *Understanding What One Reads II: Essays on the Gospels and Paul*, Leuven/Paris/Walpole MA, Peeters, 2011, p. 248, suggests that though Paul's use here of language from Wisd 9,15 indicates Hellenistic influence, one should not assume "a radically Hellenized content". Paul's thought is not strictly dualistic, since he does not envisage "existence without a body".
39. Cf. John 14,2.
40. So THRALL, *2 Corinthians* (n. 4), in loc.

what *will* take place at the Parousia – as described in 1 Corinthians 15?[41] Or is this perhaps the wrong question? Many commentators have pointed out that the idea that the Age to Come exists already in heaven is a common feature in Jewish apocalyptic: [42] what exists already in heaven represents what *will* be on earth,[43] and so depicts what the righteous will finally enjoy. In *1 Enoch* 39,4, for example, we find Enoch describing how he saw "the dwelling-places of the holy, and the resting places of the righteous".[44] It is in this tradition, perhaps, that Paul declares in Phil 3,20 that "our citizenship is in heaven". Does his use of the present tense and the phrase "eternal in the heavens" in 2 Cor 5,1 indicate that Paul is thinking of the future as a present reality in heaven, as in some apocalyptic writings? If so, his image is not intended to answer the question "When?" but to affirm the certainty that his hope will be fulfilled.

Other commentators have suggested that the echo of Mark 14,58 is significant.[45] Whether or not Paul is familiar with a tradition going back to Jesus, the idea of a heavenly temple – the pattern for what will be set up when the Age to Come is finally realized – is widespread in biblical and pseudepigraphal writings.[46] Paul's use of Temple imagery in 1 Cor 3,16 (an image he picks up in 2 Cor 6,16) suggests that he is perhaps thinking in 2 Cor 5,1, not of individual resurrection "bodies", but of corporate existence in the body of Christ.[47] This may well be true, but since this verse comes at the end of his discussion in 4,7-18, we may expect it to affirm his belief that he himself will not be "crushed ...

---

41. Cf. Hans LIETZMANN, *An Die Korinther I/II* (HNT), Tübingen, Mohr (Siebeck), 1969, in loc.; BARRETT, *2 Corinthians* (n. 1), in loc.; Andrew T. LINCOLN, *Paradise Now and Not Yet*, Cambridge, Cambridge University Press, 1981, pp. 63-5.

42. See e.g. W.D. DAVIES, *Paul and Rabbinic Judaism*, London, SPCK, 1955, 314-9; FURNISH, *II Corinthians* (n. 30), in loc.

43. This is rooted in the idea that God's purposes go back to creation, and so are "pre-existent".

44. See also *4 Ezra* 10,25-57; *2 Bar.* 4. Paul is perhaps influenced by this idea in Gal 4,21-31.

45. A. FEUILLET, *La Demeure Céleste et la Destinée des Chrétiens*, in *RSR* 46 (1956) 161-92, 360-402; for Feuillet, the heavenly dwelling is the resurrection body of Christ (pp. 377f.). Similarly J-F. COLLANGE, *Énigmes de la deuxième épître aux Corinthiens: Étude exégétique de 2 Cor. 2:14–7:4* (SNTSMS 18), Cambridge, Cambridge University Press, 1972, pp. 179-98. On the significance of the temple saying, see also R. F. HETTLINGER, *2 Corinthians 5.1-10*, in *SJT* 10 (1957) 174-94; E. Earle ELLIS, *II Corinthians V.1-10 in Pauline Eschatology*, in *NTS* 6 (1960) 211-24.

46. In Exod 25,9.40; 26,30; 27,8, we find the idea that the earthly sanctuary is a copy of the heavenly pattern. See also Wisd 9,8, *T. Levi* 3,4-6, and Heb 8,2.

47. J. A. T. ROBINSON, *The Body: A Study in Pauline Theology*, London, SCM, 1952, pp. 73-80; ELLIS, *II Corinthians V.1-10* (n. 45).

forsaken ... [or] destroyed". As long as he continues "in this tent" he groans, but is nevertheless sure of the final outcome, of which God's Spirit is the guarantee (5,2-5).

In v. 2, he picks up the idiom of dressing which he used in 1 Cor 15,53f., where he described the change that is to take place to the living at the Parousia as a putting on of imperishability and of immortality. In a typically Pauline mixed metaphor, he speaks of his hope, not to be "unclothed", but to be "further clothed" with his heavenly dwelling, so that mortality may be swallowed up by life (vv. 2,4). Like the image of the heavenly dwelling-place, the idea of heavenly garments for the righteous can be found in Jewish tradition,[48] and this suggests again that Paul is more concerned with the certainty of his hope, than with the question "When?" Some commentators, however, believe that – notwithstanding 2 Cor 4,14 – Paul is still hoping, as in 1 Corinthians 15, that he will be alive at the Parousia. If so, then what he expresses in vv. 2-4 is a deep desire to be "clothed upon" with the heavenly body *before he dies*. He groans (vv. 2,4), longing for the time when he will be clothed, because he does not wish to have the old body stripped off, and longs rather to be covered by the new body, superimposed upon it (as in 1 Cor 15,53f.) – in other words, he longs for the mortal to be swallowed up (v. 4, καταποθῇ, another echo of 1 Cor 15,54) by life.

The problem with this interpretation is that it seems to be out of step, not only with 2 Cor 4,14, but with what follows, in 5,6-8, where Paul is apparently eager for death because this means that he will be "at home with the Lord". This does not in itself rule it out, since it is of course possible for Paul to put what appear to be contradictory ideas side by side: the frequent examples of "eschatological tension" between present experience and future hope are a good example! But it is possible that his thought here is more consistent than this. Is he perhaps now hoping that he will "put on" the resurrection body *immediately upon death*? Realizing now, in 5,1-5, that he is likely to die before the Lord's return, is he perhaps expecting his mortal body to be swallowed up by life at his death? If so, this would not mean that he has radically changed his views since writing 1 Corinthians, but rather that increasing sufferings have changed his perspective. Death may be "the last enemy to be destroyed" (1 Cor 15,26), but by the time he writes Romans he is confident that not even death can separate him from the love of God in

---

48. Cf. *1 Enoch* 62, 15f.; 1QS 4,7f. Cf. *4 Ezra* 2,45; Rev 6,11; 9,9.

Christ Jesus (Rom 8,38f.), and perhaps that confidence lies behind his words here. Realistically, he knows that he is unlikely to be alive at the Parousia, but he still longs to experience the transformation which he described in 1 Cor 15,51-57. So is he now perhaps hoping that this will take place *when he dies*? The mixed metaphor of a building with which one is clothed may, indeed, be due to a conscious desire to use the imagery he employed earlier. The compound verb, ἐπενδύομαι, corresponds to what he wrote in 1 Cor 15,53f. about the mortal putting on immortality, and the imperishable putting on immortality. There it described what happened to those who were alive at the Parousia, and Paul apparently still hopes that this "putting on" will be his lot, even if his death precedes the Lord's return.

But how confident is Paul that he will be *immediately* "clothed upon" at death? What is the significance of his aside in v. 3? – and what is the correct reading of that verse? The Nestle-Aland text follows the Western text in reading ἐκδυσάμενοι, suggesting that Paul is here raising the possibility – and rejecting it – that he may have to "put off" the earthly habitation before being clothed with the heavenly, and so be found "naked" (presumably at the Parousia). Many commentators prefer the reading ἐνδυσάμενοι, however,[49] and this has better manuscript support.[50] If we accept this reading, the meaning is very similar, though expressed with more confidence – especially if, with P[46] B D et al., we read εἴπερ for εἴ γε. Paul hopes that he will be able to "put on" immortality and imperishability, as he described in 1 Cor 15,53-4.[51] In other words, he hopes that he will be clothed with the heavenly habitation over his present body, and so not be found "naked" on that day (v. 3). The adjective "naked", which picks up the term γυμνός used of the seed sown in the earth in 1 Cor 15,37, might be seen to support the view that Paul means that he hopes not to be among the dead.[52] The word γυμνός, however, refers not simply to the state of being dead, but rather to being without a habitation – disembodied – a suggestion that Paul immediately

---

49. E.g. BARRETT, *2 Corinthians* (n. 1), in loc; THRALL, *2 Corinthians* (n. 4), in loc.
50. P[46] ℵ B C D² Ψ 0243 maj lat sy co; Cl.
51. See C. F. D. MOULE, *St Paul and Dualism: The Pauline Conception of Resurrection*, in *NTS* 12 (1966) 106-23, p. 122: "death, even in [2 Corinthians 5], marks, not so much the escape of the soul from the prison of the body as the completion of the transformation of the σῶμα ψυχικόν into the σῶμα πνευματικόν".
52. Cf. J. N. SEVENSTER *Some Remarks on the ΓΥΜΝΟΣ in II Cor. V. 3*, in J. N. SEVENSTER and W. C. VAN UNNIK (ed.), *Studia Paulina in honorem Johannis De Zwaan*, Haarlem, Bohn, 1953, 202-214.

rejects, since he is confident that God has a heavenly habitation in store.[53] But *why* might one be found naked? Since we have assumed that the background here is not Hellenistic dualism, there is no reason to think that Paul is thinking of a "soul" that has been stripped of its body, though he could, of course, be briefly dismissing the views of those who did think in those terms.[54]

An alternative interpretation is suggested by the fact that γυμνός is sometimes used in the LXX of those who are guilty and ashamed when judgement takes place.[55] Some commentators therefore suggest that Paul uses the word here in this sense, and that he has the last judgement in mind (as at v.10).[56] He immediately dismisses the idea that he might be found naked as imposssible, since he has *already* been clothed, ἐνδυσάμενοι, and what he now longs for is to be *further* clothed, ἐπενδύομαι. If this is his meaning, then the most likely explanation of his language is that Paul is referring to the fact that he has already been clothed with Christ, at baptism (as in Gal 3,27), and that what he is now longing for is a further stage in this process.

Verse 4, however, seems to tell against this interpretation, since there Paul uses the image of "taking off" clothes, which must refer back to the idea of the "earthly tent" of v. 1 being destroyed. He picks up the verb στενάζω, "to groan", from v. 2. He longs to be "further clothed", rather than "unclothed", and that means that mortality will be "swallowed up" by life. The verb καταπίνω was used, as we have noted, in the same sense in 1 Cor 15,54, together with the image of "putting on". Here, certainly, the imagery refers to mortality, and not to the fact that he has "put on" Christ.

We have to remember, however, that when Paul speaks of his "earthly tent" in 5,1 this is an alternative way of describing the "outer man" of 4,16, and that he has claimed that though this is being destroyed, the

---

53. Cf. THRALL, *2 Corinthians*, in loc.

54. It is possible, of course, that Paul is using the language of Corinthian "Gnostics", only to dismiss it, but why should he do so here?

55. Isa 47,3; Ezek 16,37; 23,29; Hos 2,3; Amos 2,16. Cf. also the parable of the wedding garments, Matt 22,11-14. According to Gen 3,7.10f., Adam and Eve *became aware* that they were naked as soon as they sinned; but in 2,25 they were *already* naked. Nakedness, then, can hardly be interpreted here as an indication of guilt. Later Jewish texts, however, understand Adam to have been naked because he had been stripped of his glory: *3 Bar.* (Gk) 4,16; *Apoc. Mos.* 20,1f.

56. See ELLIS, *II Corinthians V.1-10* (n. 45), pp. 219-21; LANG, *2.Korinther 5,1-10* (n. 3), p. 188; FURNISH, *II Corinthians* (n. 30), in loc.; A. OEPKE, γυμνός, *TWNT* I, 773-5 (*TDNT* I, 773-5).

"inner man" is being renewed. The basis of this claim is that he carries in his body the death of Jesus, in order that the life of Jesus may also be seen in his body (4,10). When he changes metaphors in chapter 5 to that of a tent versus a heavenly house, we might have expected him to declare that he will not be left homeless. Instead, he switches metaphors once again, and speaks about a change of garments. This, however, makes perfect (if somewhat confusing!) sense if we remember that he believes that *the process of taking on the image of Christ* (to revert to his original metaphor of 3,18!) *has already begun*. As long as he remains in his "tent", he groans, longing for something better – namely to be "clothed upon" (v. 2). The introduction of this new image leads Paul to make an aside:[57] since his "inner man" is being renewed daily, he is of course presupposing[58] that he will not be left naked when he dies, since he has already "put on" (ἐνδυσάμενοι[59]) Christ.[60] In v. 4 he repeats what he told us in v. 2: as long as he remains in the tent, he groans. He does not wish to be "unclothed" (i.e. to die), but to be "clothed upon". He is confident that – to put it another way – the mortal will be "swallowed up" by immortality, since this is God's plan (v. 5).

Whatever happens, then (and however we interpret these four verses!), Paul is confident that a heavenly building awaits Christians, and that this hope is guaranteed by the presence of the Spirit, who is the ἀρραβῶν of what awaits us (vv. 5f.). But this reference to the Spirit as an ἀρραβῶν of what is to come reminds us that *already* we see the glory of the Lord, and are being transformed into the likeness of Christ, through the power of the Lord, who is the Spirit (3,18).

---

57. Jerome MURPHY-O'CONNOR, *The Theology of the Second Letter to the Corinthians*, Cambridge University Press, 1991, p. 52, regards v. 3 as a parenthesis, in which Paul "uses the symbol of "clothed" in a new sense".

58. Commentators agree that both εἴ γε and εἴπερ, found in P[46] B D, convey assurance.

59. This paraphrase assumes that the correct reading here is ἐνδυσάμενοι. As we have noted, however (n. 49), some mss read ἐκδυσάμενοι. If the reading ἐνδυσάμενοι is correct, we should note that Paul does *not* use here the verb ἐπενδύομαι of vv. 2.4, a verb which implies putting on an additional garment. BARRETT, 2 *Corinthians* (n. 1), says that the word is simply "repeating the sense of the compound verb of the preceding verse", but we suggest that the change is deliberate. If we read ἐκδυσάμενοι, then Paul is affirming that even if his "outer man" is completely destroyed, he will not be left naked, but the reason is the same – he has already "put on" Christ.

60. R. F. HETTLINGER, 2 *Corinthians 5.1-10* (n. 45), believes that the idea that "the Christian is already clothed with Christ" is significant, and that Paul could not "have regarded death as an interruption of ... incorporation [into Christ] – as nakedness" (p. 188f.). He nevertheless translates v. 3 as "on the assumption *of course* that when we shall have put on this clothing *at death* we shall not be found naked *before God*" (p. 190).

In v. 6, however, Paul introduces a new idea. We have already seen that what he says in 4,14 is reminiscent of the picture painted in 1 Thess 4,15, where dead believers are raised to life and are joined by "those of us who are still alive", caught up in clouds to "meet the Lord". We have noted that one crucial difference is that Paul no longer expects to be among the survivors at the Lord's return. More radically, however, he now regards it as *a positive personal advantage* to be one of those whom the world would classify as "dead". Whereas, in writing to the Thessalonians, he had assured them that the living would "have no advantage" at the Parousia over those who had died (1 Thess 4,15), he now suggests that it may be better to be dead (in the Lord) than alive, since he believes that those who have died are "at home with the Lord", while the living are in a sense in exile 5,6-8. This is strange language from one who expressed so strongly his joy in living with Christ and in Christ, but it corresponds to the belief he expresses in Phil 1,23, that "to depart" is to "be with Christ". It is perhaps explained by the image he uses in Phil 3,20, where he describes Christians as those who have their citizenship in heaven. However joyful his present experience of living in Christ, it is only a foretaste of future joy, and to be "at home" with Christ – "in heaven" – will be even better. But "whether at home or away", he declares in 2 Cor 5,9, "our aim is to please the Lord". This serves to introduce the theme of judgement (v. 10) – and so reminds us of Paul's original concern, which was a defence of his ministry; not, of course, that he was answerable to the Corinthians, for he – like them – must appear before the judgement seat of Christ.

In 2 Cor 5,11, then, Paul points out the relevance of his arguments for his main theme – the defence of his ministry – with the linking "therefore". What he has written is not intended to be a way of commending himself (v. 12) – for, as he wrote in 4,5, he proclaims not himself, but "Jesus Christ as Lord". In everything he is constrained by the love of Christ. The gospel he proclaims is that he "died for all, and the consequence of this (ἄρα) is that all have died" (v. 14). Moreover, "he died for all, in order that (ἵνα) those who live might live no longer for themselves, but for him who died and was raised for them" (v. 15). The repetition of the first clause emphasizes the importance of what is being said:

> *One* died for *all*, and the consequence of this (ἄρα) is that *all* have died.
> He *died* for all, in order that (ἵνα) those who live might *live*
> – no longer for themselves, but for him who died and was raised for them.

The reciprocal nature of the gospel – he died for all, *in order tha*t they might live for him – spells out a little more fully what Paul expressed in earlier letters. It is, for example, very similar to the early summary of belief in 1 Thess 5,10: "Our Lord Jesus Christ died for us, so that whether we are awake or asleep we may live with him", while Gal 2,19 expressed Paul's own experience: "I died to the Law, in order that I might live to God".

Since all have died, and those who live no longer live for themselves, but for Christ, there is now "a new creation" (v. 17). Paul's claim is equivalent to saying that the Age to Come is already here: "the old has passed away, and the new has arrived". The promises of Old Testament prophets such as Isaiah are fulfilled. Paul's claims emphasize the present reality of what had hitherto been only a future hope. This dramatic change is the result of God's action in reconciling us to himself through Christ. Now he has entrusted this ministry to Paul and others, who are ambassadors for Christ. Their message is that all should be reconciled to God, and if one wonders how this reconciliation is possible, it is because God made Christ, "who knew no sin, to be sin, in order that in him we might become the righteousness of God" (5,21).[61]

Paul continues his appeal to the Corinthians in the following chapter, where he once again insists that his ministry has meant enduring both suffering (6,4f.) and demonstrating Christian spiritual gifts (6,6f.).[62] In the eyes of the world he has been as good as dead, and yet he is alive; he has been poor, yet has made many rich (and so shared the ministry of Christ, 8,9); has had nothing, yet possessed all things (6,8-10). So the Corinthians in turn, believers in Christ, must live as the people of God, called to holiness (6,14–7,1).

Conclusion

The different hopes expressed in Paul's letters appear to reflect changes in Paul's circumstances rather than a radical change of view, but far more importantly *they reflect the different subjects under discussion and the different problems addresse*d.

It is in 1 Thessalonians and 1 Corinthians that we find Paul spelling out what he believes will happen at the Parousia, and in both cases, this is

---

61. On the possible significance of this verse, see Morna D. HOOKER, *On Becoming the Righteousness of God: Another Look at 2 Cor 5,21*, in *NT* 50 (2008) 358-75.
62. Cf. FURNISH, *II Corinthians* (n. 30), in loc.

because a particular problem about the future resurrection has arisen in the church that he is addressing. His hopes about what might happen to him personally after death are found in 2 Corinthians and Philippians – in each case, *because of the particular situation in which he finds himself*. In Galatians and Romans there is no extended discussion of either question, since his main concern is to spell out what God has done and is doing for those who trust in Christ; nevertheless, the ultimate goal is always in sight, and in Romans especially we are aware of the eschatological tension between what has already been done and what lies in the future.

How, then, are we to make sense of 2 Cor 5,1-10? In 4,14, Paul has stated his faith that the one who raised the Lord Jesus will bring him into his presence. He is confident that the pattern of death/life already at work in him will continue after death: affliction is the preparation for glory (4,16-18). That means that if his "earthly tent" is finally destroyed, there is an eternal house awaiting him in heaven. As long as he is alive, he groans, waiting for what is better, hoping for the day when he will be clothed with his heavenly dwelling, trusting that he will not be found naked. Although Paul does not refer directly to the Parousia, he is using the language associated with the Parousia in 1 Cor 15,51-5, and appears to be referring to that event. What he is describing is his present situation – confident of the future, and wishing that what is promised were already here, but meanwhile enduring the afflictions of the present. This is the burden he must bear, as long as his ministry continues. That is what it means to be "at home in the body but away from the Lord" (5,6). That is what it means to walk by faith – the faith expressed in 4,14. In other words, what he is describing in 5,1-5 is a continuation of what he writes in 4,7-18, i.e. *a description of his present situation, as he awaits the Lord's return, rather than what he expects to happen to him if he dies before that occurs*. It sums up his confident hope that his present affliction is preparing "an eternal weight of glory" (4,17). As long as he continues in this life, he groans, longing for the glory that awaits him. Of course he would *prefer* to be "away from the body and at home with the Lord" (v. 8)! Whether that will take place immediately after his death or only after the Parousia he does not specify. His concern is only to express his confidence in the final outcome (vv. 6 and 8).

If this interpretation is correct, then 2 Cor 5,1-10 is in no way opposed to the picture which Paul draws in 1 Corinthians – rather, it draws on it. As there, so here (4,14), what he says is founded on his belief in future resurrection. Those who live in Christ are eager for the Parousia, when – as in 1 Cor 15,53f. – "the mortal will be swallowed up by life" (5,4).

Certainly Paul introduces a new idea – the thought that he himself may die before the Parousia – but if that happens the heavenly habitation will still be his. Whichever happens, he is confident that what God has planned will be fulfilled (v. 5).[63]

In 5,8 Paul expresses the hope that it will be better to be "away from the body, and at home with the Lord", a hope that reappears later in a bolder form in Phil 1,21, where he says that for him, "to live is Christ, to die is gain", and goes on to declare that "to be with Christ is far better" (v. 23). Bolder, too, is his declaration there that he is sure that Christ will be magnified in his body, whether by life or death (Phil 1,20). In 2 Corinthians, Paul already expressed that same idea, though somewhat more tentatively: his aim, he says, is to please the Lord, whether he is "at home or away" (2 Cor 5,9), since (whether we live until the Parousia or not), "we must all appear before the judgement seat of Christ". As we have noted, the nucleus of this idea is found already in the early summary of belief in 1 Thess 5,10: "Our Lord Jesus Christ died for us, so that whether we are awake or asleep we may live with him", and in Gal 2,19, where Paul says that he died to the Law, in order that he "might live to God".

The fact that in two letters – 2 Corinthians and Philippians – Paul uses language about the future which seems to us to juxtapose incompatible ideas suggests that we are asking the wrong questions if we wonder whether his views changed radically with time.[64] The language of resurrection (found in 1 Corinthians, 2 Corinthians and Philippians) is a way of affirming confidence in the future, a confidence based on what God has done in Christ, and carrying with it all the ideas associated with new creation and new life. The hope of the Parousia (referred to in 1 Corinthians and Philippians) expresses the conviction that all things will finally be put under the rule of Christ. When that takes place, death itself will be defeated (1 Cor 15,54). The conviction that those who die will be "with Christ" (2 Corinthians and Philippians) arises from the belief that, in view of this final victory, death itself cannot separate those who have died and been raised with Christ from God's love in Christ (Rom

---

63. In view of Paul's changed circumstances, the development between 1 Corinthians 15 and 2 Corinthians 5 is a natural one. Cf. MOULE, *Dualism* (n. 51), p. 123: "the essential distinction between his positions in I Cor. xv and II Cor. v is only that, in the former, he too lightly looked for addition, whereas, by II Cor. v, he was more realistically reckoning with exchange".

64. Cf. C. F. D. MOULE, *The Influence of Circumstances on the Use of Eschatological Terms*, JTS ns 15 (1964) 1-16.

8,38f.). Paul does not bother to explain how this hope relates to the hope of the Parousia – and had he been asked, he might well have dismissed the question as foolish, as in 1 Cor 15,36! The tension between the two is part of the eschatological tension that pervades *all* of Paul's writing – the tension between the now and not yet.[65] It is perhaps significant that in 1 Thessalonians, Paul already spoke both of the Parousia *and* of future resurrection. Moreover, he spoke of living "with Christ" as something experienced both by the living and by those who have died "in Christ" (1 Thess 4,16; 5,10).

Finally we should note that we find this same tension between the now and the not yet in other New Testament writings, most notably in the Gospel of John. Although John does not refer to the Parousia,[66] there is a tension between present and future experience. Jesus is said to have described himself as "the resurrection and the life" (John 11,25). But what does this mean? It means that "those who believe in me, even though they die, will live"; it also means that "everyone who believes in me will never die". These two statements are placed side by side. Elsewhere, he is said to claim that anyone who believes through hearing his word "has eternal life and does not come under judgement, but has passed already from death to life" (John 5,24). Immediately after this, however, he speaks of a future resurrection to judgement (v. 28). Is he perhaps referring to a different group – i.e. non-believers? Not in 6,40, where we read that God's purpose is "that all who see the Son and believe in him may have eternal life; and I will raise them up on the last day". Although eternal life is continually spoken of as a present experience, resurrection remains in the future. The Fourth Evangelist apparently sees no problem in combining a belief in future resurrection with that of eternal life enjoyed here and now. The tension is well summed up in his phrase "The time is coming and now is".

It seems that Paul and John shared the problem of expressing the idea of the life given to believers except by using images which – logically – seem to us to be contradictory. The reason is perhaps that they are both attempting to describe a relationship with God, who is outside time, and for whom past, present, and future are all one.

---

65. Cf. LOWE, *Developments*, (n. 5), p. 136, commenting on the sudden transformation in 1 Corinthians and the gradual change in 2 Corinthians, writes: "this is precisely that alternation between present process and final result which is characteristic of Paul's thinking from start to finish".

66. The references to Jesus coming again in John 17 are explained in terms of the coming of the Paraclete, and so applied to a *present* experience of the Gospel's readers.

SUMMARY

1. The passage must be read in context, *not* taken as a digression. It is part of Paul's defence of his ministry. Following his description of what it means for him to experience sharing the sufferings and resurrection of Christ in his everyday life, he insists that this pattern of "life through death" will continue even when his mortal body is destroyed. He is confident of the outcome of the final judgement (in contrast to the spurious judgements of the Corinthians).
2. There is no reason to suppose that Paul has changed his mind in any significant way since writing 1 Corinthians. There are many overlaps with what he says about his present experience of Christ and his future hope to suppose that this is so. Although Paul may be less confident than he was then that he will survive until the Parousia, differences are mainly accounted for by the fact that the issue he is addressing in 2 Corinthians is his own situation, not the doubts of the Corinthians about the future resurrection.
3. In all these passages, Paul describes the Christian's future life in terms of life *with* Christ, *in* Christ, and *for* Christ. He understands this future life as the fulfilment of present experience, which he sees in terms of a growing conformity to Christ. This theme unites 1 Corinthians 15 and 2 Corinthians 5, and is far more important than any differences in imagery and perspective.

LIBERATION OF ENSLAVED BODIES:
CHRISTIAN EXPECTANCY ACCORDING TO ROM 8,18-30

CILLIERS BREYTENBACH

Dedicated to Jan Lambrecht, S.J.[1]

The text that has been entrusted to me was treated at the *Colloquium Oecumenicum Paulinum* at the 1974 meeting, but not exegetically. D. E. H. Whiteley read a "hermeneutical" paper on Rom 8,18-39.[2] There were two exegetical papers on Rom 8; one by Eduard Lohse on Rom 8,1-17 and another one by the late Ignace de la Potterie on Rom 8,14.[3] Verses 18-30 do deserve exegetical treatment, and I will attempt to fill some gaps in the Colloquium's exegetical treatment of the passage.[4]

From the very outset, the meaning of the word "expectancy" in the subtitle needs to be clarified. Paul uses the word δέχομαι in the sense of "to receive something",[5] and notably expresses the meaning "to wait for someone/-thing" by ἐκδέχομαι.[6] He also uses the verb ἀπεκδέχομαι.[7] Does this verb express a sense which is distinguishable from δέχομαι and ἐκδέχομαι?[8] The word does not have a high frequency, but its

---

1. Jan Lambrecht presided over the first meeting of the *Colloquium Oecumenicum Paulinum* to which I was invited in 1992 (cf. J. LAMBRECHT [ed.], *The Truth of the Gospel [Galatians 1:1–4:11]* [SMBen, 12], Rome, St. Paul's Abbey, 1993). He is no longer travelling to Rome to amicably apply his philological yardstick in person, but his meticulous and accurate exegesis should remain our benchmark. Cf. J. LAMBRECHT, *The Groaning Creation: A Study of Rom 8:18-30*, in *LS* 15 (1990) 3-38.
2. Cf. D. E. H. WHITELEY, *Rom. 8,18-39: A Hermeneutical Approach*, in L. DE LORENZI (ed.), *The Law of the Spirit in Romans 7 and 8* (SMBen, 1), Rome, St. Paul's Abbey, 1976, 167-178.
3. Cf. E. LOHSE, *Zur Analyse und Interpretation von Röm 8,1-17*, and I. DE LA POTTERIE, *Le chrétien conduit par l'Esprit dans son cheminement eschatologique (Rom 8,14)*, both in DE LORENZI, *Law of the Spirit* (n. 2).
4. Within the scope of this paper, it is not possible to give due attention to the source domains of all the metaphors Paul used in this passage.
5. E.g. 1 Cor 2,14; 2 Cor 6,1; 8,17; 11,4. Cf. LSJ, *s.v.*; BDAG, *s.v.*
6. E.g. 1 Cor 11,33; 16,11. Cf. LSJ, *s.v.*; BDAG, *s.v.*
7. Paul uses the verb in Rom 8,19.23.25; 1 Cor 1,7; Gal 5,5 and Phil 3,20.
8. Ἀπεκδέχεται could either have been formed from ἀπό + ἐκδέχομαι or from ἀπέκ + δέχομαι. Its translation with "to expect" probably goes back to Jerome's Vulgata. The entry under ἀπεκδέχομαι in LSJ glosses "to expect anxiously, to look for, await".

use,⁹ also in the NT,¹⁰ suggests a slightly different focus. The compound preposition ἀπεκ- means "away, out of", adding the notion of still being separated from the action expressed by δέχομαι "to receive or to accept".¹¹ In Pauline usage, the word ἀπεκδέχομαι thus seems to express to expect to receive something or someone, the state in which one is still separated from that what one expects to receive,¹² rather than the emotion of expectation.¹³

In constructing Paul's expectancy, I shall concentrate on his letter to the Romans, focusing on 8,18-30.¹⁴ During the discussion of Whiteley's paper at the 1974 meeting, Sabbas Agourides repeatedly stressed that chapters 5–8 form a unit.¹⁵ Since difficult issues of interpretation can only be decided by taking into account the entire letter, the wider context of Rom 8,18-30, viz. Rom 5,1–8,39, is initially discussed. In the second part of the paper, a summary of the argument of Rom 7,7–8,17 as presupposition for the understanding of 8,18-30 is given. In the third part, a close reading of Rom 8,18-30 is given, followed by concluding remarks in part four. Finally, as an addendum, a brief comparison with 2 Thess 1,3-12 is provided.

1. Introduction: Rom 8,5-30 within Rom 5,1–8,39

In the second main part of his letter to the Romans (5,1–8,39), Paul explains what the justification of the sinners implies. The whole argument is framed by 5,1-11 and 8,31-39 and the recurrence of several topics has been noted by various scholars since Dahl's seminal essay.¹⁶ One

---

9. Cf. Alciphron, *Epistulae* 3,4,6; Aristonicus, *De signis Iliadis* 16,41 schol. 4; Attalus, *Fragmenta Aratea* 11,10; 15,14; 16,9; Heliodorus, *Aeth.* 2,35,3; 7,23,5; Sextus Empiricus, *Math.* 2,73; *Acta et Martyrium Apollonii* 42,5.
10. Cf. note 6. Also Heb 9,28 (cf. 10,13) and 1 Pet 3,20.
11. Cf. LSJ, *s.v.*
12. Cf. *T. Ab.* A 16,3; *Acts Paul* 3,3.
13. I thus do not follow Meißner's suggestion to translate Paul's use of ἀπεκδέχεσθαι with "empfangen, aufnehmen". Cf. J. Meissner, *Das Kommen der Herrlichkeit: Eine Neuinterpretation von Röm 8:14-30* (FzB, 100), Würzburg, Echter, 2003. The sense "aufnehmen" seems to fit Apollonius Dyscolus, *De coniunctionibus* 226,20 and Hipparchus, *In Arati III* 1,7,7 and 18.
14. For a wider perspective see C. Breytenbach, *"For in Hope we were Saved:" Discerning Time in Paul's Letter to the Romans*, in Id., *Grace, Reconciliation, Concord* (NovTSup, 135), Leiden, Brill, 2010, 239-256.
15. Cf. his contributions in the documentation of the "Discussion" in de Lorenzi, *Law of the Spirit* (n. 2), pp. 184-187, 205-206.
16. Cf. N.A. Dahl, *Two Notes on Romans 5*, in *ST* 5 (1951) 37-48. For the discussion since Dahl and additional aspects, cf. C. Eschner, *Die Hingabe des Sohnes "für" uns alle:*

vital intention is to assure the addressees that their justification as formerly impious sinners, or to put it alternatively, their changing from being God's enemies into his friends (= reconciliation),[17] will end in their rescue from the wrath of God (5,6-10). The current state of being justified or reconciled was brought about by trust in the effect of the death of Christ as proclaimed in the gospel.[18] Ending the section in 8,31-39, Paul repeats this assurance. Since God has delivered his own Son for the sake of "all of us", those who are trusting in God's gospel about the death and resurrection of Jesus Christ need not fear final judgement. Their hope to be acquitted is not in vain. But Paul has a second intention. His focus is not on future salvation only. In 5,1-5 he focuses on the present. He and his addressees already stand firm in the favour[19] of God and take pride on the basis of their hope which anticipates the "δόξα of God". They express their confidence loudly in contrast to their current circumstances, a topic Paul reintroduces in 8,17. In 5,3 he states that in tribulation they are proud, knowing that affliction also gives the opportunity to endure oppression and that perseverance enables one to stand the test. This validation in its turn promotes hope, and this anticipation will not be disappointed. Why will the hope not be in vain? In Rom 5,5b Paul gives a reason: ὅτι ἡ ἀγάπη τοῦ θεοῦ ἐκκέχυται ἐν ταῖς καρδίαις ἡμῶν διὰ πνεύματος ἁγίου τοῦ δοθέντος ἡμῖν. In Rom 8,9-11.12-17 he takes up this topic and elaborates on it.

After the introductory passage in chapter 5 (5,1-11), Paul compares in the first section of his argument the favour of God in which the believers now stand firmly with the power of sin (5,12-21). Since the grace of God that leads to justification exceeds sin, he poses the question whether this would allow those who believe in Christ to continue sinning. By explaining the consequences of being baptised into Christ's death, he sharply refutes such behaviour in the second section of his elaborations (6,1–7,6).[20] Within his argument he returns to the δόξα τοῦ θεοῦ of 5,2 by calling it δόξα τοῦ πατρός (6,4). The believers take pride on the basis

---

Zur Wiederaufnahme des Sterben-"für"-Motivs aus Röm 5:6-8 in Röm 8:32, in U. SCHNELLE (ed.), *The Letter to the Romans* (BETL, 226), Leuven, Peeters, 2009, 659-678, pp. 659-662.

17. For this interpretation of καταλλάσσω, cf. BREYTENBACH, *Grace* (n. 14).
18. On this cf. ESCHNER, *Hingabe* (n. 16).
19. For the reasons why I translate with "favour", cf. BREYTENBACH, *Grace* (n. 14).
20. Some exegetes take 6,1-23 and 7,1-25 as units; cf. E. KÄSEMANN, *An die Römer* (HNT, 8a), Tübingen, Mohr Siebeck, 1974; C. E. B. CRANFIELD, *The Epistle to the Romans. Vol. I* (ICC), Edinburgh, T&T Clark, 1975; E. LOHSE, *Der Brief an die Römer* (KEK, 4), Göttingen, Vandenhoeck & Ruprecht, 2003.

of hope to experience the δόξα of God, the same δόξα through which Christ was resurrected from the dead. Those believing in the gospel were baptised into Christ's death in order that, in analogy to the resurrected Christ, they can live a new life (6,4b). In baptism, they already shared the experience of his death; in future they will share the experience of his resurrection (6,5). From 8,9–11 onwards, Paul will develop his idea of the interconnectedness of the believers with the Spirit of God who resurrected Christ in more detail.

2. ROM 7,7–8,17 AS PRESUPPOSITION FOR THE INTERPRETATION OF ROM 8,18-30

At the beginning of the third section of the argument (7,7–8,17), Paul first clarifies the relation between sin and the Torah. The latter is good and holy and leads to the recognition of sin, but the power of sin is so overwhelming that the commandment which is good incites the sinful deed leading to death. In this way sin becomes known. In 7,14–8,4 Paul returns to his main argument. How are humans freed from captivity by sin? Man is sold to sin and thus like a slave. He or she is not free, but under command of the owner, sin. Verses 7,21-23 are of particular interest, since Paul specifies the slave imagery as being taken as prisoner of war. Even though man delightfully agrees with the law (Torah) of God, he is held as prisoner of war (αἰχμαλωτίζω) by the law affected by sin. In his bodily parts this affected law wages war (ἀντιστρατεύομαι) with (the real intention of) the law of God on which man has set his mind. Human beings are not free to do as they wish, they are captives of sin. In verse 24 Paul laments: "Wretched man that I am! Who will rescue me from this body of death?" The liberation (ῥύομαι) he longs for is the freedom of the body which is subjected to death (ἐκ τοῦ σώματος τοῦ θανάτου τούτου), which is been held as prisoner of war by the sin affected law.

In Rom 8,1-4 Paul brings the argument of 7,7-25 to a close. In 8,3 he explains how God convicted sin in the weak human flesh of Christ. This is why he can claim that there is no condemnation for those who are in Christ (8,1). The law of the Spirit which brings life in Jesus Christ freed them from the Torah which was under the power of sin and thus led to death. But we have to wait until 8,23 to learn how the bodies of those who live according to the Spirit (8,4) will be freed. This is the main line of argumentation developed in 8,18-30: the liberation of the enslaved body.

The fourth section (8,5-17) formulates several presuppositions important for the understanding of 8,18-30. In verses 5-9 Paul develops the opposition between σάρξ and πνεῦμα he introduced in verse 4. The intention, mindset (φρόνημα), of the weak human flesh is against God and leads to death. Those who are ἐν σαρκί cannot win God's favour. However, since the Spirit of God lives in the addressees, they are not "in the flesh". Of course, he does not deny bodily existence (Gal 2,20), but they are no longer ruled by the flesh. The next step Paul takes presupposes that the Romans have the Spirit, since they belong to Christ. Paul develops the ethical aspect of being in the Spirit.[21] In the current context it is crucial to understand verses 10-11. Even under the condition of having the Spirit and thus having Christ in them, the human body stays dead because of sin.[22] In contrast to the dead body, the human spirit of those having Christ in them is life, since they have been justified. This is the current situation. In 8,11 Paul calls the bodies of those having the Spirit not dead (νεκρά) but mortal (θνητά).[23] This difference between dead and mortal refers back to Rom 6. Paul has argued that those who have been baptised into Christ's death died with him (6,8a.11). The body was crucified with Christ in baptism in order to be released from the obligation (καταργέω) of sin.[24] Sin does not rule over the body any more (6,6b). The baptised are dead to sin (νεκροὺς ... τῇ ἁμαρτίᾳ – 6,11) and instructed that they are not to let sin rule in their mortal bodies (ἐν τῷ θνητῷ ὑμῶν σώματι – 6,12a). The theme of the mortal body is now reintroduced in 8,11. Paul still argues on the basis that the addressees have the Spirit in them, but he shifts his focus to the future as one can see from the tense of the verb ζῳοποιήσει (8,11). The πνεύματα of the Romans are already a means of life, because the Spirit of God lives in them (vv. 9-10), but God will also make their mortal bodies alive through the same Spirit by which he resurrected Christ from the dead. This situation of the believers, their πνεῦμα "alive" and their bodies mortal but due to be vivified, has important implications for their current lifestyle. Paul develops this in verses 12-17.

---

21. Cf. also D. ZELLER, *Der Brief an die Römer* (RNT), Regensburg, Pustet, 1985, p. 150.
22. The causal interpretation of both διά and accusative phrases is to be preferred, as most commentators do.
23. According to 6,6 the body qualified by sin was destroyed in baptism, but man still lives in the mortal body (6,12).
24. For the interpretation in the sense of καταργεῖν τι ἀπό τινος (cf. LSJ and BDAG, *s.v.*), cf. the ἀπό in 6,7 and 7,2b.

Those who are of Christ are not obliged to live according to the σάρξ; if they do, they will die. By implication they are under obligation to live according to the Spirit. Through the Spirit they have to kill the deeds of the body. Paul reassures the addressees that the Spirit of God, which they have already received, guarantees that they are already adopted by God as his children. As in the case of the confession that Christ is Lord (1 Cor 12,3), it is through the Spirit that they can call God "Father" and expect to be his heirs together with God's own Son. Together with the resurrected Son, they will be glorified. What Paul means when he says that the children of God will be glorified with Christ remains to be clarified within the passage 8,18-30, to which we now turn. Paul argues that since sin has been condemned in the Son and the believers have been given the Spirit, they will become like the risen Son (8,29).

3. ANALYSIS OF ROM 8,18-30

The rest of Paul's argument can be subdivided into three more subsections.[25] In the first part (8,18-21), Paul comments on his statement in 8,17c. There he concludes that if he and his addressees are children of God, then they are also heirs, heirs of God and joint heirs with Christ. If, in fact, they currently suffer with Christ they may also be "glorified" with him in future. I put the word "glorified" in inverted commas, because it is crucial to clarify what συνδοξάζω and δόξα mean and to what Paul refers when using these words in Rom 8.

In *verse 18*, Paul gives his opinion on the present suffering with Christ. He is assured (λογίζομαι) that the sufferings (τὰ παθήματα) of this present time are not worthy of comparison with[26] the δόξα, that is "about to be" (μέλλουσα)[27] revealed by God. The δόξα is – albeit currently still undisclosed – with God, it will be revealed to[28] "us". Two questions immediately arise: In the first instance, to what do τὰ παθήματα τοῦ νῦν καιροῦ refer? Second, what is meant by "the δόξα about to be revealed to us"? Both questions can be answered by referring to what

---

25. LAMBRECHT, *Groaning Creation* (n. 1), p. 6, underlined the argumentative character of the passage by referring to the repetitive use of γάρ and οἴδαμεν and of λογίζομαι.

26. For this use of πρός cf. F. BLASS, A. DEBRUNNER, and F. REHKOPF, *Grammatik des neutestamentlichen Griechisch*, 18th ed., Göttingen, Vandenhoeck & Ruprecht, 2001 (BDR), §239 n. 8.

27. Cf. BDR (n. 26) §356 n. 4.

28. For this use of ἀποκαλυφθῆναι τι with εἴς τινα instead of the dative, cf. BDR (n. 26) §207 n. 2.

Paul has said up to this point. In 5,2 he already remarked that he and his hearers boast on the basis of the hope for the δόξα τοῦ θεοῦ. He immediately qualifies the circumstances in which pride is taken as καυχώμεθα ἐν ταῖς θλίψεσιν (5,3), θλῖψις being distress that is brought about by outward circumstances.[29] There is no indication that Paul refers to specific circumstances of the Roman believers.[30] What is meant by δόξα? Before we simply translate the Greek word with "glory", it might help us to remember what we have read up till now. In 5,2-3 Paul took up an opposition he had already introduced in 2,9-10 between θλῖψις and στενοχωρία on the one hand and δόξα on the other. The contrast between current suffering and future δόξα is repeated in 8,17-18. As he and the Romans listening to the reading of his letter are suffering with Christ, they will also be approved together[31] with him (8,17).

> The word δόξα is not only used in contrast to suffering (θλῖψις, στενοχωρία and πάθημα): it also belongs to the semantic opposition "honour" and "shame", as can be seen from 1 Cor 4,10: ὑμεῖς ἔνδοξοι, ἡμεῖς δὲ ἄτιμοι ("you are honoured but we are in disrepute"). Its opposite can be κενοδοξία, "empty honour" (Phil 2,3). Paul warned the Galatians (Gal 5,26): μὴ γινώμεθα κενόδοξοι ("we should not become falsely proud"). But which components of meaning does the word δόξα entail positively? It combines with χαρά, "joy" (1 Thess 2,20), ἔπαινος, "praise" (Phil 1,11), τιμή, "esteem", ζωὴ αἰώνιος, "eternal life" (Rom 2,7), and εἰρήνη, "peace" (Rom 2,10).

In Romans δόξα refers to a specific quality attributed to God as imperishable in contrast with his creatures that are subject to decay (1,23). This is why Paul says in Rom 6,4 that Christ has been raised from the dead by the δόξα of the Father (ἠγέρθη Χριστὸς ἐκ νεκρῶν διὰ τῆς δόξης τοῦ πατρός).

In *8,19* Paul gives the reason for his statement in verse 18.[32] The subject of the sentence, ἡ ἀποκαραδοκία, is used in Christian texts only.[33]

---

29. Cf. BDAG, *s.v.*
30. But see R. JEWETT, *Romans: A Commentary* (Hermeneia), Minneapolis, Fortress, 2007, p. 509.
31. For this meaning of συνδοξάζεσθαι, cf. LSJ, *s.v.*
32. Verses 19-23 are part of the Pauline argument and cannot for ecotheological reasons be isolated and treated as a narrative; *pace* C. HUNT, D. HORRELL, and C. SOUTHGATE, *An Environmental Mantra? Ecological Interest in Romans 8:19-23 and a Modest Proposal for Its Narrative Interpretation*, in *JTS* 59 (2008) 546-579.
33. Cf. Origen, *Cels.* 7,65; 8,15; *Comm. Jo.* 1,26,170.

The verb ἀποκαραδοκέω³⁴ is used widely.³⁵ Aquila,³⁶ Josephus³⁷ and Polybius³⁸ used it to express the state of waiting to see what is going to happen and it is probably an intense form of the more usual verb καραδοκέω, meaning to wait with an outstretched head.³⁹ The meaning of the noun is less clear. The Suda and Hesychius interpret it with προσδοκία, thus deriving from (προσ)δοκάω, "expect", instead of δοκέω. As iterative of δέχομαι, δοκέω can also have the meaning "to expect", but the focus is more on "think, suppose, imagine".⁴⁰

In Rom 8,19 the noun ἀπο + καραδοκία is determined by τῆς κτίσεως and the expression should be explained as a unit. The somewhat metaphorical phrase ἀποκαραδοκία τῆς κτίσεως expresses something like "the forward leaning expectancy of the creation".⁴¹ Paul is using language which personifies creation. Here he refers to the whole of creation, juxtaposing it to the children of God.⁴² The creation expects the revealing of the sons of God as eagerly as a person protruding his/her head in expectancy to see what will happen.⁴³ But the children of God are still concealed. Ἀποκάλυψις τῶν υἱῶν τοῦ θεοῦ rephrases δόξαν ἀποκαλυφθῆναι εἰς ἡμᾶς of verse 18 since the noun ἀποκάλυψις takes

---

34. According to BDR (n. 26) §119 n. 2 from κάρα, "head", and δοκέω, but rather δέχομαι. H. LIETZMANN, *An die Römer* (HNT, 8), Tübingen, Mohr Siebeck, 1928, p. 84, translated aptly with "ausspähen nach etwas".

35. Cf. BDAG, *s.v.*

36. Cf. Ps^α' 36,7.

37. Cf. Josephus, *B.J.* 3,264.

38. Cf. Polybius, *Historiae* 16,2,8; 18,48,4; 21,36,3 and A. MAUERSBERGER, *Polybios-Lexikon: Band I*, Berlin, Akademie Verlag, 1956, *s.v.*

39. Cf. LSJ, *s.v.*

40. Cf. LSJ, *s.v.*

41. It expresses a concept different from ἀπὸ καταβολῆς in the phrase ἀπὸ καταβολῆς κόσμου ("from the foundation of the world" – Matt 13,35; 25,34; John 17,24; Heb 4,3; 9,26; Rev 13,8; 17,8), or ἀπ' ἀρχῆς in the phrase ἀπ' ἀρχῆς κτίσεως ("from the beginning of creation" – Mark 10,5; 13,19; 2 Pet 3,4).

42. Early patristic evidence (cf. O. KUSS, *Der Römerbrief*, Regensburg, Pustet, 1963, pp. 622-623) included humankind under the reference of κτίσις. See also KÄSEMANN, *Römer* (n. 20), pp. 224-225. For Paul κτίσις can refer to humans (2 Cor 5,17; Gal 6,15), include humans (Rom 8,19-20.39) or the creation of humans (1,20: ἀπὸ κτίσεως κόσμου). But he can also use the word distinguishing between creation and the children of God (8,21-22) or even the unjust and godless (1,25: καὶ ἐσεβάσθησαν καὶ ἐλάτρευσαν τῇ κτίσει παρὰ τὸν κτίσαντα). CRANFIELD, *Romans* (n. 20), *in loco*, discusses various proposals, and wants to isolate the children of God from creation and confine the reference to the sub-human world. This is not necessary, since presently the children of God are also subjected to decay (cf. Rom 8,10; 1 Cor 15,50-51). Here and in Rom 8,22 κτίσις focuses on non-human creation, but this does not mean that for Paul humanity is not also subjected to decay. For a review of early interpretations of κτίσις cf. HUNT, HORRELL, and SOUTHGATE, *Mantra* (n. 32), pp. 547-549.

43. Cf. G. BERTRAM, *Ἀποκαραδοκία*, in *ZNW* 49 (1958) 264-270, p. 265.

up the verb ἀποκαλυφθῆναι and the expression "sons of God" refers to the same group as the pronoun "us". Consequently the unveiling of the sons of God also entails that they will receive δόξα. What does this mean?

Verse 20 explains the statement of verse 19. The forward stretching expectancy of the creation awaits the revelation of the sons of God, because the creation was subjected to purposelessness (ματαιότης). The Greek word expresses the state of being without use or value[44] (like idle talk)[45] and might have come to Paul via Israelite-Jewish wisdom.

> Ps[LXX] 38,6 expresses the idea that human life is purposeless,[46] Ps[LXX] 77,33 that the lives of those punished by God end ἐν ματαιότητι.[47] It might have been the refrain from Qohelet, τὰ πάντα ματαιότης,[48] that has lead Paul to the idea that creation is subjected to ματαιότης.

After foregrounding the subjection of the creation to futility, Paul qualifies ὑπετάγη with an οὐκ ... ἀλλά construction, negatively (οὐχ ἑκοῦσα) and positively (ἀλλά ... ἐφ᾽ ἐλπίδι),[49] and explains that the creation is subjected not willingly, but God[50] subjected it in hope, in anticipation. The phrase οὐχ ἑκοῦσα implies a contrast between Adam and the creation and confirms the interpretation that κτίσις refers specifically to the non-human part of creation. Paul adds διὰ τὸν ὑποτάξαντα into the positive phrase. Taking up the line of argumentation from Rom 5,12-21, he explains that creation is subjected (perfect passive), because of him[51] (= God) who subjected it (aorist). Normally it is said that Paul alludes to Gen 3,17 (ἐπικατάρατος ἡ γῆ ἐν τοῖς ἔργοις σου ἐν λύπαις φάγῃ αὐτὴν πάσας τὰς ἡμέρας τῆς ζωῆς σου) and 5,29. According to *4 Ezra* 7,12-13, another text often used to explain Rom 8,20, Adam's sin made the ways of this world narrow and

---

44. Cf. Eph 4,17; *Jos. Asen.* 21,19.
45. Cf. Ps[LXX] 143,11; *Jos. Asen.* 21,19.
46. Πλὴν τὰ σύμπαντα ματαιότης πᾶς ἄνθρωπος ζῶν ("Surely, every person alive is the sum total of vanity"; trans. A. PIETERSMA, and B. G. WRIGHT [eds.], *A New Translation of the Septuagint and the Other Greek Translations Traditionally Included under That Title*, New York, Oxford University Press, 2007). Cf. Ps[LXX] 143,4; 2 Pet 2,18; also Qoh 1,2; 12,8 in *T. Sol.* B 8,2.
47. Cf. also Prov 22,8a.
48. Cf. Qoh 1,2.14; 2,11.17; 3,19; 11,8.
49. Cf. O. MICHEL, *Der Brief an die Römer* (KEK, 4), Göttingen, Vandenhoeck & Ruprecht, 1966, p. 267.
50. God is the logical subject of ὑπετάγη and the subject of διὰ τὸν ὑποτάξαντα. ZELLER, *Römer* (n. 21), p. 162, takes Adam as subject of the participle.
51. Or "by him"; cf. BDAG, *s.v.* B d β.

sorrowful and painful and full of perils coupled with great toils.[52] Recently scholars have drawn attention to parallels between Rom 8,20 and Isa^{LXX} 24,1-6.[53] E.g. "the earth shall be ruined by decay" (φθορᾷ φθαρήσεται ἡ γῆ – Isa^{LXX} 24,3a) as a consequence of God's response to human sin, or "the earth behaved lawlessly by reason of her inhabitants; because they have transgressed the law, and changed the ordinances – an everlasting covenant. Therefore a curse shall consume the earth, because those who inhabited it sinned ..." (Isa^{LXX} 20,5-6). These parallels are striking, especially if one recalls that Paul quoted Isa^{LXX} 25,8 in 1 Cor 15,54 and alluded to it in 2 Cor 5,4.

The ὅτι clause in *Rom 8,21* explains the content of the ἐλπίς. Since the creation is not meant to be subjected to purposelessness, what is anticipated? By introducing ἐλευθερόω as the counterpart to ὑποτάσσω and φθορά as the contrast to δόξα, it is clear that subjection will be turned into freedom, decay into δόξα. In both cases Paul used a divine passive, but with a difference in time. With Adam's fall God subjected the creation to futility in the hope that in future he will free creation itself from the enslavement to decay. Taking up the language of Rom 6,16-22, Paul depicts creation in terms of the metaphor of slavery. The use of the term φθορά sheds light on ματαιότης.[54] The futility of creation lies in the fact that it is subjected to decay. In the end it leads nowhere. So severe are the deadly consequences of sin (5,12). The future liberation is not only liberation from purposelessness and decay, but also freedom with a purpose. Keeping to the strategy to personifying creation, Paul states that, like a slave, creation will be liberated into the freedom that comes with the δόξα of the children of God. The δόξα of the children who belong to God entails their freedom and this freedom liberates them from the slavery caused by the breakdown of organic matter (φθορά). Paul draws a parallel between the subjection of the creation under purposelessness (ματαιότης) and the slavery caused by decay (δουλεία τῆς φθορᾶς).[55] The movement is from the enslavement to decay to the liberation marked by δόξα of the children of God, which entails their and

---

52. (12) ... *et facti sunt introitus huius saeculi angusti et dolentes et laboriosi, paucae autem et malae et periculorum plenae et laborum magnorum fultae.* (13) *nam maioris saeculi introitus spatiosi et securi et facientes inmortalitatis fructum* (Vulgate).

53. Cf. L. J. BRAATEN, *All Creation Groans: Romans 8:22 in the Light of Biblical Sources*, in *HBT* 28 (2006) 131-159, pp. 145-147. Braaten's observations are complemented by those of J. Moo, *Romans 8.19-22 and Isaiah's Cosmic Covenant*, in *NTS* 54 (2008) 74-89, pp. 83-85.

54. See also LIETZMANN, *Römer* (n. 34), p. 85.

55. Cf. also J. A. FITZMYER, *Romans* (AB, 33), New York, Doubleday, 1993, p. 505.

creation's liberation from decay. Again Paul distinguishes between creation and the sons of God, narrowing the reference of the first to the non-human world. The question of what will happen to those people who are not part of the children of God is not posed. In Rom 1,18–3,21 Paul has argued extensively that they will face the wrath of God. Although Paul expects the liberation of creation, focusing its reference on the non-human part, its return to a pre-Adamic state of no decay, this change is subject to the revelation of the sonship of the children of God, their δόξα. The question remains however, to what does δόξα refer?

Paul starts the next section (8,22-27) with two metaphors, childbirth and the adoption of children (cf. 8,15). He also expands on the topic under discussion in 8,18-21, comparing the current state of the creation with that of the hidden children of God. Introducing his sentence in *verse 22* with οἴδαμεν, he states something that is common knowledge to him and his addressees. The choice of the word συνωδίνω suggests that Paul takes up the metaphor of childbirth. Paul speaks of πᾶσα ἡ κτίσις, but in the next sentence he will distinguish it from those who have the first fruit of the Spirit. Presently the whole creation groans and suffers severe pain as if in travail. The use of the composite verbs with συν, συστενάζει and συνωδίνει, is significant. The whole creation groans and suffers pain together with ... whom?

Presupposing what Paul has said in 8,9-11 and 14-16, *verses 22b-23* give the answer. The children of God are included in the expectancy of creation.[56] Creation groans and suffers together with those who, like Paul and the Romans, have a part of the ἀπαρχή of the Spirit. The analogy lies in the parallel between childbirth and adoption.[57] The creation is depicted as a mother groaning in birth pangs, those who have the first portion of the Spirit as children expecting the fulfilment of their adoption. They also groan in the state of expectancy, expecting their adoption to come into effect. The last line of verse 23 explains what is meant by adoption as children: it implies the liberation of their bodies (τὴν ἀπολύτρωσιν τοῦ σώματος ἡμῶν). What the body will be liberated from can be inferred from the context. Those who are in Christ have already been liberated from sin (6,18), from being prisoners of war under sin (7,24 and 8,2), and the Spirit already lives in their bodies (8,5-11). The phrase θνητὸν σῶμα which is used in 8,11 occurs also in 6,12.[58]

---

56. Cf. LOHSE, *Römer* (n. 20), p. 248.
57. On the parallelisms in vv. 21-23, cf. JEWETT, *Romans* (n. 30), p. 506.
58. Cf. above under 2.

What is meant by this? The body of those baptised into Christ's death is no longer under the power of sin (6,6). They will become like the resurrected one (6,5) and will live with him (6,8); but until then, the body is still mortal (θνητόν). Paul urges his addressees that they should not allow sin to reign over their mortal bodies (6,12), nor place their body parts like weapons in battle at the disposal of sin (6,13). With the help of the Spirit, they should rather kill the acts of the body (8,13b). The liberation of the mortal body means that it will be made alive in such a way that its actions will no longer lead to death, its members no longer serving sin. It will no longer be subjected to corruption.[59] It is the liberation of the body from the possibility of leaving the realm of grace and reverting to sin, to be ruled by sin. For those who do not have τὴν ἀπαρχὴν τοῦ πνεύματος, who are not in Christ, the wages of sin are death (6,23), their situation stays unaltered.

As a short intermezzo, the *verses 24-25* elaborate on ἐλπίς. First, Paul makes two statements: "for in hope we were saved", and "hope that is seen is no hope". The situation, in which those who are saved live, is characterised by hope.[60] Rephrasing the statement as a rhetorical question, he implies that nobody hopes for something that can be seen. By choosing the present indicative for the following conditional sentence, Paul implies that the condition is fulfilled: under the condition that what "we" hope for cannot be seen, "we" wait "in patience", or to express it literally, "through perseverance". The διά with genitive ὑπομονῆς thus expresses the manner or way in which "we" wait.[61] The important question is: to what does the object of the hope, ὃ οὐ βλέπομεν, refer? It is something that cannot be seen presently and it must be the implied object of ἀπεκδεχόμεθα. If we trace this verb, its objects are τὴν ἀποκάλυψιν τῶν υἱῶν τοῦ θεοῦ (v. 19) and υἱοθεσίαν (v. 23b). The revelation of the still concealed sons of God, their υἱοθεσία, their "placing" (θέσις) as sons, is still invisible. The reason for this is that the revelation of the sons of God and their adoption as sons coincides with the liberation of their bodies (v. 23 *fin.*).[62] Hope thus designates the believers' current attitude of anticipating the full status they will have as children of God. Then their mortal bodies will have been made alive in such a way that sin has no effect on the body.

---

59. Cf. MICHEL, *Römer* (n. 49), p. 270; LAMBRECHT, *Groaning Creation* (n. 1), p. 9; JEWETT, *Romans* (n. 30), p. 519.
60. Cf. KÄSEMANN, *Römer* (n. 20), p. 220.
61. On this use of διά with a genitive, cf. LSJ, *s.v.* III 2.
62. LIETZMANN, *Römer* (n. 34), pp. 84 and 85, opts for "die Erlösung von unserem Leib".

Starting with "likewise" (ὡσαύτως) Paul recaps in *verses 26-27* on verses 22-23 and reintroduces the topic πνεῦμα from verse 23b. The recurrence of the root of the verb στενάζω (v. 23) in the noun στεναγμός in verse 26 confirms that Paul takes up the theme of verse 23. He develops it further, though, presupposing what he has already said in verses 9-11, 15-16 and expanding the topic.[63] Creation groans, those who belong to Christ groan, but they have the πνεῦμα θεοῦ living in them. Those who did not receive the Spirit, those who were not baptised into Christ's death, those who did not trust God's gospel, are excluded. Paul comforts his addressees. They are not alone in suffering. The Spirit groans too. Paul explains it in the following manner: they are sons of God; they have received a Spirit of adoption. During their present sufferings (v. 18), while they wait in patience (v. 25) for the revelation of their sonship (v. 23), the Spirit comes to aid their weakness. Paul's wording is reminiscent of the Jesus tradition,[64] but the role of the Spirit is somewhat different here in Romans. The Spirit assists the children of God during prayers directed to God with inexpressible, wordless groans. Interceding and thus mediating between the supplicant and God, it comes to the aid of their incapacity to express themselves as they ought, i.e. according to God's will.[65] This weakness is due to the fact that they are still in their mortal bodies and suffering, they do not know which words to say in prayer. But God, who searches the hearts,[66] recognises that the Spirit intercedes according to his will on behalf of the holy ones, the children of God.

The final section (*8,28-30*) starts with Paul's statement in *verse 28* that he has recognised that all things work together[67] for the good. He qualifies those who benefit in a double sense: from the human side it is those who love God, from a theo-logical perspective those who are called according to God's purpose.

With ὅτι in *verse 29* Paul introduces the reason for the claim that all things work together for their good. God knew them beforehand. But exactly for those he knew before, he decided (προορίζω) to have a form identical to the appearance[68] of his Son. The consequence of God's

---

63. Cf. LOHSE, *Römer* (n. 20), p. 248.
64. Cf. Luke^Q 12,11-12//Matt^Q 10,17-19/Mark 13,11.
65. Cf. also LAMBRECHT, *Groaning Creation* (n. 1), p. 10.
66. On this topos, cf. the references of ZELLER, *Römer* (n. 21), p. 163.
67. Πάντα is taken as subject, the reading πάντα ὁ θεὸς συνεργεῖ (P⁴⁶ A B 81 sa) is secondary.
68. LOHSE, *Römer* (n. 20), p. 253, understands εἰκών as "Wesen". The word rather expresses correspondence between the object and the form it resembles; cf. BDAG, *s.v.* The

decision to predetermine those whom he called to have a form identical to the appearance of his Son, is that the resurrected one will be the firstborn within a large family. The phrase τὸ εἶναι αὐτὸν πρωτότοκον ἐν πολλοῖς ἀδελφοῖς takes up the notion of the υἱοὶ θεοῦ (Rom 8,14.19), υἱοθεσία (Rom 8,15.23), τέκνα θεοῦ (8,16-17.21), and (συν)κληρονόμοι θεοῦ (Rom 8,17). Those whose adoption as children of God will be revealed are predetermined to become συμμόρφους τῆς εἰκόνος τοῦ υἱοῦ αὐτοῦ (8,29). Their bodies will be liberated (8,23c) when the Spirit that is living in them will make their mortal bodies alive (8,11). This means that their bodies as part of the creation will finally not be subjected to decay (φθορά). Their bodies will then no longer be mortal (θνητόν – 8,11). The resurrection can, as in Rom 8,11, be expressed in terms of causing to live, making alive (ζωοποιέω – cf. 1 Cor 15,22.45b).[69] Paul hereby draws his argument to a close: the liberation of the prisoners of war, kept by sin in their body parts (7,24), comes to its full effect when the mortal body is made alive (8,11), when the captured body is set free (8,23b), when it gets the form of the appearance of the resurrected Son who is the firstborn of the whole family of God's children. This is their future δόξα to be revealed (8,18), this is how they will be glorified with Christ (8,17c). The liberation of the body from decay caused by sin has its positive correlation in the revelation of the δόξα of those already adopted as God's other children, when it is made known that in appearance they are like God's own Son.

The first lines of *verse 30* merely take up οἱ κλητοί (v. 28) and προώρισεν (v. 29). When Paul says καὶ οὓς ἐκάλεσεν, τούτους καὶ ἐδικαίωσεν, he recaps the line of thought since 3,24-30 and prepares to return in 8,31-39 to the justifying effect of the death of Christ already expressed in 5,1 and 9. The statement οὓς δὲ ἐδικαίωσεν, τούτους καὶ ἐδόξασεν goes a step further, the ingressive aorist expressing that the process to give honour to those who are justified but still live as mortal bodies, to increase their splendour, has begun.[70] In baptism they already

---

interpretation with "Gestalt" (cf. ZELLER, *Römer* [n. 21], p. 165) or "image" (FITZMYER, *Romans* [n. 55], p. 525) is more accurate.

69. If one reads Rom 8,29 in the light of verses 11 and 23c, it is likely that the idea of transformation so explicitly expressed in 1 Cor 15,51-52 (cf. *2 Bar.* 51) is to be presupposed, as suggested by ZELLER, *Römer* (n. 21), p. 163.

70. Recently Harrison commented on the Roman ideal of glory and Paul's letter to the Romans. What could his understanding of eschatological glory have meant to the Christians in Rome? Cf. J. HARRISON, *Paul and the Roman Ideal of Glory*, in SCHNELLE, *Romans* (n. 16), 329-369, p. 330. Harrison argues that the Pauline concept of glory given through divine grace inverted the Roman ideals of glory achieved by the ruling class.

received the sonship, it is already a present reality with God and will be revealed when their mortal bodies will be made alive. They will be conformed to the image which the Son himself is.[71] Then they will be incorruptible as the image of the resurrected Son,[72] regaining the δόξα lost through sin (3,23). It is in this state that they will be able to inherit the imperishable (ἀφθαρσία) kingdom of God (cf. 1 Cor 15,50), which is closely associated with his δόξα (1 Thess 2,12).

4. Rom 8,18-30 and Paul's expectancy

In Romans, Paul's line of argument is somewhat different from that in the other letters. Whilst he has a different strategy with specific aims in every single case, some of the assumptions underlying his previous arguments are reused in Romans.

Paul had his focus on the present when writing to the Thessalonians. There he consoled those believers whose loved ones had died. On the basis of the common belief in the resurrection of Christ (1 Thess 4,14), he assured those who are left behind (περιλειπόμενοι) that they will not precede the deceased believers at Christ's parousia, calling on them to be vigilant until then. The aim was to console those who had lost relatives and friends and to warn his addressees to be on their guard, lest the coming of Christ surprise them.[73] In Rom 8 the resurrection of Christ by God is presupposed (6,4; 8,11), but the focus is on how the Spirit of him who resurrected Christ from the dead comes to the aid of the believers living in the body and guarantees the liberation and vivification of their mortal bodies.

In 1 Cor 15 Paul argues against those who reject bodily resurrection.[74] On the basis of the common tradition that Christ has been raised from

---

71. In the phrase καὶ προώρισεν συμμόρφους τῆς εἰκόνος τοῦ υἱοῦ αὐτοῦ (8,29) the first genitive is connected to an adjective (σύμμορφος), thus "having the same form of the image" (cf. BDR [n. 26] §182 n. 1). The second genitive is dependent on the preceding genitive and adnominal in function (cf. BDR [n. 26] §162,7): "the image belonging to the Son". Lambrecht, *Groaning Creation* (n. 1), p. 11, opts for a *genitivus appositivus* (cf. BDR [n. 26] §167,2): "the image which the Son is".

72. This was almost exactly Whiteley's point almost forty years ago: "I suggest that Paul meant that the physical created order would share man's glory, and would be transformed in the last day like our own bodies" (Whiteley, *Approach* [n. 2], p. 169; cf. also p. 182).

73. For a more detailed analysis, cf. C. Eschner, *Gestorben und hingegeben "für" die Sünder: Die griechische Konzeption des Unheil abwendenden Sterbens und deren paulinische Aufnahme für die Deutung des Todes Jesu Christi* (WMANT, 122), Neukirchen, Neukirchener Verlag, 2010, Vol. 1, pp. 131-187.

74. In this I follow D. Zeller, *Der erste Brief an die Korinther* (KEK, 5), Göttingen, Vandenhoeck, 2010, pp. 454-459.

the dead after three days (1 Cor 15,3-4), he argues that God resurrected Christ and as Creator he will change all believers. Like the body of the resurrected Christ, their perishable bodies will be changed into imperishable spiritual bodies and they will bear his heavenly image (cf. 1 Cor 15,42-51). In Romans Paul does not express explicitly that the bodies of those in Christ will be changed (ἀλλάσσεθαι) from perishable to imperishable, but common terms like ζῳοποιέω, κληρονομέω, φθορά, δόξα, ἀσθένεια and εἰκών refer to assumptions similar to those underpinning the argument in 1 Cor 15.

As in Rom 8,18-30 Paul sets the tone for 2 Cor 5,1-10 in 2 Cor 4,16-18 with the contrast between current suffering and future δόξα (4,17), between what is transient and what is eternal (4,18). In 2 Cor this contrast is exemplified with reference to Paul's own bodily existence.[75] The οἰκοδομήν he expects is an οἰκίαν ἀχειροποίητον αἰώνιον ἐν τοῖς οὐρανοῖς, an οἰκητήριον ... τὸ ἐξ οὐρανοῦ. Using another metaphor, Paul explains that to live in the permanent building or house means "to be at home with the Lord" (5,8b). His future is put in contrast to the temporary tent existence, which will be demolished (καταλύσθαι). Being at home in the body is "to be away from the Lord" (5,6). In 5,1-4 Paul expresses the transition between the tent and the house with the metaphor of clothing. The eternal building should be put on over (ἐπενδύσασθαι) the temporary tent to avoid nakedness.[76] Using a term to be reused in Rom 8,23 (στενάζω), Paul longingly groans that the mortal may be swallowed up by life (ἵνα καταποθῇ τὸ θνητὸν ὑπὸ τῆς ζωῆς – 2 Cor 5,4). As in Rom 8,13 it is still possible to do evil through the body (5,10), but God already prepared for his transition by having given him the first instalment of the Spirit (5,5).

The judgement scene ending in Rom 8 might be more encouraging and less of a warning than in 2 Cor 5,10, but Paul had struck a positive chord before Romans. His saying in 1 Cor 15,56 that the sting of death is sin and the power of sin the law encapsulates the argument of Rom 5–8 where he explains how God's good news about Jesus Chris saves all who believe from the all-encompassing effects of sin. Paul expects nothing

---

75. Following Thrall and Schmeller, I read the 1st person plural in 5,1-10 (as in 4,7-15 and 5,11–7,2) as a plural as a *pluralis sociativus*. Cf. M. E. THRALL, *The Second Epistle to the Corinthians. Vol. I* (ICC), Edinburgh, T&T Clark, 1994, p. 359; T. SCHMELLER, *Der zweite Brief an die Korinther: Teilband I (2Kor 1,1–7,4)* (EKK, 8/1), Neukirchen, Neukirchener Verlag, 2010, p. 293.

76. In verse 3 the reading ἐνδυσάμενοι should be preferred. Cf. THRALL, *Corinthians* (n. 75), pp. 373-374; SCHMELLER, *Korinther* (n. 75), p. 286.

less than the end of the mortality and decay of the human body which was caused by sin. Those who have the Spirit of God will be made alive like God's own Son already is. And when their true form as God's adopted children is revealed, creation will be free from decay. Creation will be liberated from the bondage to decay when the sonship of God's children comes to its fulfilment. This implies that Paul does not expect the end of the material world. As God's creation it is good. It will be freed from the effect of sin. For Paul decay and mortality is a result of the sin which came with Adam's action (5,18). Christ's act of righteousness will take this away.

Paul's expectancy is rooted in his trust in the power of the gospel which saves those who believe from death caused by sin. If one wants to use modern words: in Romans Paul's eschatology is approached through his anthropology. Through the death and resurrection of Christ God created those who trust in his gospel anew.

5. A brief comparison with 2 Thess 1,3-10.12

The comparison with this text from 2 Thessalonians is easy to make, because the author, whom we shall call "Paul", used words identical or similar to those used in Rom 8: ὑπομονή (1,4; cf. Rom 8,25), πάσχω (1,5; cf. συμπάσχω in Rom 8,17 and πάθος in 8,18), ἀποκάλυψις (1,7; cf. Rom 8,18-19), δόξα (1,9; cf. Rom 8,18.21) and ἐνδοξάζομαι (1,10.12 cf. [συν]δοξάζω in Rom 8,17.30). But the differences are considerable.[77] There is no word about the Spirit in connection with the expectancy of the believers. Regarding the future, Rom 8 expresses a reassuring message of hope, focussing on the addressees. 2 Thess 1 has a threatening tone of warning, focusing on the unbelievers who cause suffering to the addressees. The addressees are comforted: enduring tribulation pays in the end, for God's judgement will be righteous.

According to 2 Thess 1,6-7 it is surely just for God to render affliction (ἀνταποδοῦναι ... θλῖψιν) to those who oppressed the addressees and to provide relief (ἀνταποδοῦναι ... ἄνεσιν) to those who are being oppressed and to Paul. According to verse 8 this retribution will take place during the revelation of the Lord Jesus from heaven. He will execute God's judgement. With the angels of his power, in fiery flames, he gives punishment to those not acknowledging God and to those not

---

77. Cf. also W. Marxsen, *Der zweite Thessalonicherbrief* (ZBK, 11/2), Zürich, TVZ, 1982, pp. 61-62, 65-67.

obeying the gospel of "our" Lord Jesus Christ. Verse 9 clearly focuses on the punishment of these people: "they will pay the penalty of eternal destruction". The Lord Jesus will take vengeance; the destruction comes "from his face and the radiance of his might".[78]

The glorification of the Lord Jesus' name and the glorification of the believers "in him" through their present conduct is something "Paul" always prays for (1,12). No longer is the revelation of the hidden δόξα of the believers yearned for. The tables are turned. When the Lord comes, on that day, *he* will be honoured (ἐνδοξασθῆναι) by his saints and be marvelled at (θαυμασθῆναι) by all who came to believe (1,10). The focus has shifted from the believers' liberation from their bodily enslavement under sin to the condemnation of the non-believers and acknowledgement of the Lord Jesus as judge.

If one adds the cause of the dispute, the claim that "the day of the Lord has already come" and the "man of lawlessness" from 2 Thess 2,1-12 to this picture, the exegetical ἀποκαραδοκία is provoked to see whether 2 Thess 1–2 can be explained as the work of Paul.[79]

---

78. For this spatial understanding of ἀπὸ προσώπου and ἀπὸ τῆς δόξης see A. J. MALHERBE, *The Letters to the Thessalonians* (AB, 32B), New York, Doubleday, 2000, p. 403.

79. I thank Natalie Altnöder and Matthias Müller for their assistance in preparing the manuscript for publication.

CONTRIBUTORS

CILIERS BREYTENBACH, Professor for New Testament and Ancient Studies, Humboldt-Universität zu Berlin (Germany) and Stellenbosch University (South Africa)

KARL PAUL DONFRIED, Elizabeth A. Woodson Professor of Religion and Biblical Literature Emeritus, Smith College, Northampton, Massachusetts (USA)

DANIEL GERBER, Professeur de Nouveau Testament, Faculté de Théologie Protestante, Université de Strasbourg (France)

MORNA HOOKER, Lady Margaret's Professor of Divinity Emerita, University of Cambridge, and Life Fellow, Robinson College, Cambridge (UK)

RUDOLF HOPPE, Emeritus Professor of New Testament Studies, University of Bonn (Germany)

VASILY MIHOC, Professor of New Testament Studies, Orthodox Theological Faculty, the University of Sibiu (Romania)

PETR POKORNÝ, Professor Emeritus, and Senior Research Fellow of the Centre for Biblical Studies of the Academy of Sciences and Charles University, Prague (Czech Republic)

BENOIT STANDAERT, Benedictine monk at the Sint-Andriesabdij, Bruges (Belgium)

CHRISTOPHER TUCKETT, Professor of New Testament Studies, University of Oxford (UK)